# NEGRO EDUCATION IN ALABAMA

# Negro Education in Alabama

## A *Study in Cotton and Steel*

*The Susan Colver Rosenberger Prize Essay, 1937*
*The University of Chicago*

## HORACE MANN BOND

STUDIES IN AMERICAN NEGRO LIFE
*August Meier, General Editor*

**ATHENEUM**

NEW YORK

1969

PUBLISHED BY ATHENEUM
COPYRIGHT 1939 BY THE ASSOCIATED PUBLISHERS, INC.
ALL RIGHTS RESERVED
MANUFACTURED IN THE UNITED STATES OF AMERICA BY
KINGSPORT PRESS, INC., KINGSPORT, TENNESSEE
PUBLISHED IN CANADA BY MCCLELLAND & STEWART LTD.
FIRST ATHENEUM EDITION

TO MY WIFE

# CONTENTS

# LIST OF TABLES

# LIST OF ILLUSTRATIONS

# PREFACE

Many persons have been generous with advice and assistance in the preparation of this work. This has been true since the Summer of 1930, when I began work in the Alabama Archives. Their help has continued through the preparation of the thesis, "Social and Economic Influences on the Public Education of Negroes in Alabama, 1865-1930," which was accepted in 1936 by the Department of Education of the University of Chicago in partial fulfillment of the requirements for the degree of Doctor of Philosophy, and in the preparation of that thesis for publication under the present title.

I wish to acknowledge particularly the painstaking counsel of Dr. Newton Edwards, of the Department of Education of the University of Chicago. Dr. Edwards has given much time to the manuscript while it was being prepared. His lectures, with those of Dr. Charles Hubbard Judd, first called to my attention the importance of social and economic analysis of educational institutions. In my life it has been my good fortune to know many good teachers. It is pleasant for me to be able to think of Dr. Edwards and Dr. Judd, not only as good teachers, but as very good men.

My wife, Mrs. Julia Washington Bond, spent many hours of cheerful toil in the compilation of statistical materials, and in the copying of endless notes from the materials in the Alabama Archives. I am grateful for her patience and helpful intelligence, and for her utter dependability for exact detail.

I received, among others, two kinds of financial assistance that were indispensable to the final completion of this work. Over a period of years Mr. William Mather, of the Business Office of the University of Chicago, gave me help from time to time in securing employment in various capacities in connection with the culinary establishments maintained by the University. The spiritual and physical encouragement provided by these opportunities leaves me eternally in debt to Mr. Mather.

The Julius Rosenwald Fund provided a fellowship grant under the provisions of which I studied at the University of Chicago during the year 1931-1932. The Fund has also provided a grant to make the publication of this essay possible.

The officials of various libraries have been altogether gracious. I feel a special obligation to Mrs. Marie Bankhead-Owens, of the Alabama State Department of Archives at Montgomery, and to her associates; to Dr. W. D. Weatherford, who assembled a Southern and Negro collection at the Y.M.C.A. Graduate School in Nashville that is incomparable; to Mr. Edward A. Parsons, formerly of the New Orleans Public Library; to Mr. R. G. Usher, of the Howard Memorial Library of New Orleans; and to Miss Wilhelmina E. Carothers, of the Dillard University Library of New Orleans. These persons added to the formalities of library administration a warmth in facilitating access to the sources which remains as one of the more pleasant memories of this research.

As a matter of pure sentiment, I should like to conclude these acknowledgments by referring to a Negro trusty known to me only as Amos, who was in 1930-1932 attached to the Alabama State Department of Archives at Montgomery. By now I understand that Amos has paid his debt to society, and presumably is somewhere working out his destiny as a free member of the social order. By his thorough knowledge of the materials in the Alabama Archives, and his unvarying solicitude for the comfort of my wife and of myself, Amos remains as more than a pleasant memory. He has been a constant source of inspiration in the pursuit of this study.

HORACE MANN BOND

Fisk University
January, 1939

# NEGRO EDUCATION IN ALABAMA

CHAPTER I

# SOCIAL AND ECONOMIC FORCES IN THE MAKING OF ALABAMA

The public school in Alabama is a social institution. It is the product of a variety of forces, set in motion by human beings equipped with a social heritage, and reacting to a particular kind of natural and physical environment. An understanding of the consequences of these forces requires a knowledge, comprehensive and detailed, of the forces themselves, and of their interactions.

Early settlers brought to the State diverse sets of beliefs and social habits, embodied in institutions quickly transplanted to the wilderness. The first task of this study is to appraise the kind of wilderness to which these migrants brought themselves and their social baggage. The elemental natural endowment of the land had power to direct, first, the course of settlement, and, later, the process of acculturation.

## GEOGRAPHICAL FEATURES

According to geological surveys the political unit we now know as Alabama consists of three major regions. The first, beginning in the North, is comprised of old formations, with the Valley of the Tennessee river merging into the uplands of the Appalachian foothills. This includes the Mineral Region and the Cahaba Coal Measures. The Southern rim of the first division is the Metamorphic Region; in common parlance, "the hill country." There are two principal subdivisions to the remaining section of the State; the first is the Black Belt, or Canebrake, entering at the Eastern Georgia boundary and running across Alabama in a widening fan to the Mississippi line. The Coastal Plain begins where the rich soil of the Canebrake area ends.[1]

The State has a narrow access to the Gulf. Mobile Bay afforded a port for Spanish and French settlement long before the American colonization came from the hinterland. The rivers in

the State provided arteries for transportation and trade, and fertile valleys for cultivation.

The American culture that penetrated the State early in the
nineteenth century was predominantly agricultural. Pioneers
came in search of land to farm; the territory was a frontier that
tempted because of the promise of great agricultural productivity.[2]
"Common-sense" classifications recognized the fact in the division
of the State into discrete sections. Miller speaks of "the Cereal
Belt, the Mineral Belt, the Cotton or Black Belt, and the Timber
Belt"—all indices to the natural products of the land.[3]  Boyd
identifies five sections: (1) the Northern, or the Tennessee Valley,
(2) the Mineral Belt, (3) the Hill Country, (4) the Black Belt,
and (5) the Piney Woods.[4]  This easy progression from North to
South had social as well as geographical significance.

We need, perhaps, no nicer divisions; but we cannot neglect
a recent and admirable study that adds greatly to an understanding of the State and of its people. Pope[5] divides the State re-
gionally into ten sub-divisions, each of which is distinguished by
soil and climatic conditions. The necessity, for the purposes of
statistical comparison, of limiting these sub-regional boundaries
to county lines, does only a minor violence to geographical pre-
cision. A brief description of these areas follows:

I. *The Tennessee Valley,* including seven counties in North
Alabama traversed by the Tennessee River. The fertile valley
was a center for cotton culture from the period of the first settlement. Present counties included are Lauderdale, Colbert, Limestone, Madison, Jackson, Morgan, and Lawrence.

II. *The Upper Coastal Plain,* including thirteen counties in
a belt stretching from Northwest Alabama diagonally across the
State, almost to Southeast Alabama. This area skirts the hill
country formed by the southwestward extension of the Appala-
chians into Alabama. Soil and climate were responsible for establishing this area as one of small farms, in which the cotton
culture predominated. Successive developments have made the
area a major one for cotton cultivation at the present time. Present counties included are Franklin, Marion, Lamar, Fayette,
Pickens, Tuscaloosa, Bibb, Chilton, Autauga, Elmore, Macon, Lee,
and Russell.

III. *The Mineral District,* including three counties in North
Central Alabama. Still heavily forested, this area is notable for
rich mineral deposits and for a terrain unsuited to extensive
agricultural operations, except in restricted valley regions. Present counties included are Winston, Walker, and Jefferson.

IV. *The Sand Mountain Area,* including four counties through which run the ranges of the Appalachian foothills. This area was suitable for plantation culture only in the valleys. Present counties included are Cullman, Marshall, DeKalb, and Blount.

V. *The Limestone Valleys,* including six counties in Northeast Alabama. The Coosa River Valley became an extensive plantation area. Present counties included are Shelby, St. Clair, Etowah, Cherokee, Talladega, and Calhoun.

VI. *The Piedmont,* including six counties in Eastern Alabama following the general contour of an extension of the Georgia Piedmont. The Piedmont area in Alabama, as in other states, is distinguished by great potential water power. Relatively unimportant in the period of first settlement, this natural resource assumed increasing consequence with the industrialization of the State. Present counties included are Coosa, Clay, Cleburne, Randolph, Tallapoosa, and Chambers.

VII. *The Black Belt,* including ten counties in Central Alabama. Now applied loosely as a demographic descriptive, the name was originally given to the area because of the black waxy soils, particularly suited to cotton culture. Present counties included are Sumter, Greene, Hale, Marengo, Perry, Dallas, Wilcox, Lowndes, Montgomery, and Bullock.

VIII. *Southwest Alabama,* including six counties in an area sometimes called the "Piney Woods." Still heavily timbered, the area was outside of the principal plantation zone in ante-bellum times. Present counties included are Choctaw, Washington, Clarke, Monroe, Escambia, and Conecuh.

IX. *The Wiregrass,* including ten counties in Southeast Alabama. All of the counties in this area are not equally true to the type. A portion of the lower coastal plain, the sandy soil early set limits to the extension of the slave economy and cotton culture on the plantation scale. Present counties included are Butler, Crenshaw, Pike, Barbour, Covington, Coffee, Dale, Henry, Geneva, and Houston.

X. *The Gulf Region,* including the two counties of the coastal plain bordering on the Gulf of Mexico. These two counties were never notable for any considerable production of cotton, and were not developed, agriculturally, until comparatively recent times. Present counties in the Gulf Region are Mobile and Baldwin.

The varying adaptability to crops and systems of land tenure within these sections set a mark upon the people and the institutions introduced into Alabama during the first period of settlement; for future institutional structure and development was to be moulded within the limits set by the geographical features characterizing different portions of the State.

However heedless the early pioneers were of the mineral wealth that makes Alabama unique among Southern states, a recognition of its importance was soon forthcoming in certain circles. In 1850 Michael Tuomey, State Geologist, discussed at length the almost providential conjuncture of coal and iron in Alabama, in a report that was widely circulated.[6] The mining of coal began in 1853.[7] It was a prophetic instance that chose the Committee on Education of the legislature to make a favorable report in 1850 on a bill to authorize a geological survey of the State.[8] When Alabama politicians, in the decade 1850-1860, began to think in terms of internal improvements, they knew that the Northern portion of the State concealed immense coal measures interspersed with rich iron ores. They knew further, for Michael Tuomey had told the world, that there were few such instances of close proximity of the two basic raw materials of industry in the entire world.[9] Figure 2 shows how providentially these rich potentials for an industrial civilization were joined in Alabama.

## THE PEOPLE AND THEIR SOCIAL HERITAGE

The first external cultural influences in Alabama resulted from French and Spanish colonial efforts. By now almost entirely submerged by the process of a more vigorous American penetration, this Latin influence at one time formed a pattern unique to social institutions elsewhere in the State. The Latin culture tolerated, where it did not fully accept, the intermarriage of colonials with Negroes. The offspring of such unions, legitimate or illicit, were given partial recognition and acceptance by the dominant culture.[10] A colony of persons of part Negro extraction resulted from this practise.[11] The same colony furnished a notable exception to the general pattern of the education of Negroes in the State.

The population of the Alabama "frontier" increased with rapidity following statehood in 1819. In 1820 there were 85,451 white persons, and 42,450 Negro slaves. In 1830 the white population had doubled, with 190,406 enumerated, while the number of slaves had increased almost three hundred per cent to 117,549. By 1860 there were in Alabama 526,271 whites and 437,770 Negro slaves.[12]

Thirty-three per cent of the white population of 1860 had

been born in five slave states: Georgia, South Carolina, North Carolina, Tennessee, and Virginia.[13]  One-sixth—83,517—had been born in Georgia.  It is certain that the migrants from these slave states brought with them the attitudes which their institutions had engendered as a part of their social and individual personalities.

We are interested here in an institution for Negroes made possible only by the toleration or active support of the dominant white majority.  It may be granted that many of the attitudes current in the white population were derived from the relations they sustained to varying social and economic structures.  It therefore becomes necessary to examine here the economic systems —prime sources of attitudes—which were spread over the state.

## THE PLANTATION SYSTEM

In one passage Fleming states that there was little differentiation among the white population in 1860: . . . . "the state was too young.  In the wilderness classes had fused and the successful men were often those never heard of in the older states."[14]  But Fleming himself contradicts this opinion throughout his work.[15]  The settlers were agriculturists, and that meant cotton culture.[16]  Newcomers with capital, current in the form of Negro slaves, preempted most of the land suitable for the plantation culture of cotton; and the "poorer, less prosperous white people settled on the cheaper and less fertile lands of the Northern, the Eastern, and the Southeastern sections."[17]  The Great Bend of the Tennessee River in North Alabama was good cotton country.  The black waxy soil of the central section seemed almost miraculously adapted to its culture.[18]  The plantation system soon became entrenched as the predominant economic and social factor, with Negro slavery as an essential feature.[19]

## SECTIONALISM AND SOCIAL CLASSES

The plantation system dispersed itself geographically over the areas suitable for its extension, and as early as 1819 ". . . . when the territory was admitted as a State, the lines separating the slave-holding class from the non-slaveholders were tending to become distinct and were early quite noticeable."[20]  Slave-holding tended to concentrate in two sections; the fertile valley of the

Tennessee in North Alabama, and the Black Belt of the South Central section. Outside of the plantation regions, the land was "given over largely to the small farmer—a small proprietor or a tenant farmer."[21]

Economic class distinction easily passed over into political antagonism. The Whigs predominated in the Black Belt, the Democrats in the other sections of the State.[22] Every campaign showed a conflict between the economic interests of the large planter and slaveholder of the Black Belt, and those of the small farmer, who generally held no slaves; "political philosophy was constantly flavored with sectional animosity."[23] This sectional antipathy was strikingly in evidence in relation to the public educational system in the ante-bellum period. An educational bill passed in the session of 1853-1854 provided that schools should be established with support from two principal sources; a school fund, payment of which was based on the fictitious United States Surplus which had already been dissipated through the failure of the State Bank in 1837, and the revenue from the 16th section lands.[24] A controversy arose in the legislature regarding the equable per capita apportionment of funds. The Black Belt representatives wanted the money, to be derived from sixteenth section sales or leases, to be kept in the township from which it was derived; these lands in a wealthy plantation section were of much more value than they would be in the "hill" country. Their proposal was lost by the narrow margin of 40-41 votes.[25] The final vote on the educational bill of 1853-1854 showed 71 affirmative to 12 negative votes, and all of the dissenting members were from the Black Belt counties.[26] Only by compromise could the system be established, and sectionalism played a part in the amendment of the educational bill by the General Assembly of 1855-1856.[27]

In 1842 the "white" counties won a fight to base representation in the State legislature on the enumeration of the white population alone, as opposed to the "federal" basis which would have made every slave count for 3/5 of a white man.[28] Sectional antipathies, which were also class antipathies, continued through the Civil War with increased bitterness. In the Constitutional Convention of 1861 twenty-four members refused to sign the Ordinance of Secession; these men were from the "white" counties.[29] North Alabama contributed a considerable number of native whites to the Federal armies, and desertions from the Confederate

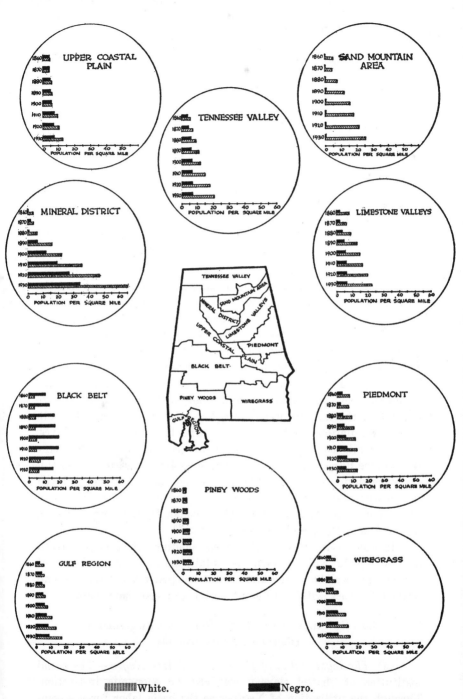

FIGURE 1.  WHITE AND NEGRO POPULATION PER SQUARE MILE IN ALABAMA AREAS, 1860, 1870, 1880, 1890, 1900, 1910, 1920, 1930.

Army by Alabamians were on a sectional basis.[30]  The slogan of
the deserters was that "it was a rich man's war and a poor
man's fight."[31]

In one passage Fleming, himself a lowlander, reveals the
typical class attitude of his own section toward the "hill billy."

The Alabama tory was, as a rule, of the lowest class of the
population, chiefly the "mountain whites" and the "sand mountain"[32] people who were shut off from the world, a century behind
the times, and who knew hardly anything of the Union or of the
questions involved.  There was a certain social antipathy felt by
them toward the lowland and valley people, whether in North
or South Alabama and a blind antagonism to the "nigger lord"
as they called the slaveholders.[33]

Yet Feming is certainly correct when he says that the "tories,"
"deserters," "the peace society men," the "conscripts," and the
"exempts," were of the class that became "scalawags" later.[34]

Thus the plantation system developed marked social antago-
nisms between white persons.  The extent of these cleavages is de-
batable.  The classic view has been that the white people in the
South were sharply divided into "aristocrats" and "poor whites."
But Hollender calls this view a historical and literary stereotype.
"Indeed, some such planters and some such 'poor whites' were
present in the ante-bellum South, but neither made up the bulk
of the population.  White farmers, who held only a few slaves,
if any at all, made up an independent yeoman group of primary
importance numerically."[35]  According to Hollender the slaveholders were divided into (a) the gentry, i.e., big planters, and (b)
the smaller planters and farmers.  The non-slaveholders were sub-
divided into (a) mountaineers, (b) yeoman farmers, present even
in the Black Belt, and (c) poor whites.[36]

It is necessary to remember these shadings of economic stratification among white persons to obtain an adequate estimate of
the relative weight of the attitudes developed toward slavery and
toward Negroes within different social and economic classes.

### The Social and Economic Rôle of the Negro as Defined by the System

(a) *The legal status of the slave and free Negro.*—The social
institution of chattel slavery was also an economic institution.
Through the utilization of Negroes as the basic labor force a com-

plication was introduced into the "natural" alignment of economic classes in Alabama. The ownership of slaves became the crucial index by which white people were separated, by themselves and by others, into gross social and economic classes. The slaves formed a social and economic class which was outside the stratification of the white population. The status of Negroes is important to a definition of their own rôle; more, it is necessary to an understanding of relationships between various classes of white persons.

In ante-bellum Alabama the term "negro" included "mulatto," according to the Code. The latter was a person of mixed blood descended from Negro ancestors "to the third generation inclusive," though one ancestor of each generation may have been a white person.[37] The statutes included numerous provisions defining the separate status of persons of Negro extraction, even when such persons were not slaves. Only white persons were accepted as qualified voters.[38] Only "free white male persons" were eligible to public office.[39] Negroes were barred from testifying in any civil or criminal case involving white persons.[40] The marriage of white with Negro persons was prohibited.[41]

Free Negroes were given attention in a special section of the Code. No free colored person was, after 1832, allowed to enter the State and remain for a period exceeding thirty days.[42] Free Negroes were forbidden to attend "unlawful assemblies" of slaves; [43] to retail liquors;[44] to furnish slaves with passes;[45] to trade with slaves;[46] to visit, or receive visits from slaves;[47] or to preach to slaves without a license.[48] Much of this legislation dates to 1832, and followed the Nat Turner insurrection in Virginia of the year previous.[49] More than a hundred white persons had been massacred in this uprising, inspired by a free Negro; and it was realized that the institution of slavery was in jeopardy if a considerable number of free persons of the same race as that of the slaves were permitted to remain in their midst.[50]

Slavery was qualified by the condition of "African heritage," and its legal recognition conferred on the master "property in and the right to the time, labor, and services of the slave."[51] Free Negroes were not barred from owning slaves. Many, particularly in Mobile County, were returned as slave owners by the census of 1830.[52] Stringent laws against free Negroes explain why there were only 2,790 in the entire State in 1860 out of a total population of 964,201.[53]

There were instances in which legal economic restrictions were added to social discriminations against free Negroes. Slaves or free Negroes were prohibited from engaging in the occupation of cotton sampling.[54] To prevent the surreptitious entry of Negroes into the State, a section of the Code was devoted to regulations restricting the freedom of entry of "free colored mariners."[55]

In and near the city of Mobile, the group of persons of part-Negro extraction known as "creoles" enjoyed a distinction peculiar only to their group. They were accorded status as citizens which, in the popular mind, removed them from classification as Negroes. In the treaty with France, by which rights to West Florida were adjudicated, a guarantee was given that all persons then resident there should continue to enjoy the rights and immunities of citizens of the United States.[56] These special immunities forced a modification of the Alabama law of 1832 prohibiting the education of persons of Negro descent.[57] During the Civil War the Mobile county Creole community was eager to contribute a regiment to the services of the Confederacy. "They have," said Major-General Maury in support of their request, "Negro blood in the degree which disqualifies other persons of Negro race from the rights of citizens, but they do not stand here on the footing of Negroes."[58] Another sponsor for their use as soldiers referred to them as "property-holders, owning slaves, and a peaceable, orderly class, and capable of doing good service."[59] By an Act approved November 20, 1862, the Alabama legislature authorized the "enrollment of the creoles of Mobile," but confined the scope of their operations to Mobile.[60] The Confederate Secretary of War, James A. Seddon, later approved the request of General Maury that the Creoles be freed from this restriction on their military activity. Seddon added a qualification of his approval that is an illuminating commentary on the status of this population: "Our position with the North and before the world will not allow the employment as armed soldiers of Negroes. If these creoles can be naturally and properly discriminated from Negroes, the authority may be considered as conferred."[61]

(b) *Concepts of the Negro implicit in slavery.*—The institution of chattel slavery produced social and psychological attitudes—forces—of immense vitality, in the minds of those surrounded by it. Only an appreciation of the all-pervasive, omnipresent, almost omnipotent strength of this fundamental institution will serve to explain this vitality. "Chattel slavery" was "Negro slavery";

and the basis of social and economic life in an entire section was a particular conception of race differences necessary to the legal recognition of slavery by the State.

Speaking in Congress shortly after the termination of the Civil War, Congressman Garfield of Ohio said: ''I do not expect seven million men to change their hearts—to love what they hated and hate what they loved—on the issue of battle. Nor are we set up as a judge over their beliefs, their loves, or their hatreds.''[62]

One of the most fundamental errors in the interpretation of Reconstruction has been the assumption by historians that ''seven million men'' could, or should have, changed their hearts—their *mores*—on the issue of the battle. There have been ''defenses'' of the Conservative viewpoint which have argued that these *mores* were changed but that Reconstruction excesses caused reversion to type. There have been ''attacks'' on the Conservatives because of their variation from the Humanitarian ethics of racial behaviour. Forgetting the issue of moral evaluation, clarity of understanding is aided by a realization that in studying Reconstruction we are face to face with the deep-seated *mores* of a folk, relatively undisturbed even by the catastrophe of a long and bitter war.

Paramount among the attitudes which the passing of the institution of slavery still left secure in most of its relicts was the deep conviction that the Negro race was inferior. The moral, mental, and physical inferiority of the Negro was, indeed, an article of faith with those for whom the institution had been, for all of their lives, a natural portion of the social and economic landscape. The belief found expression in the literature, and in the legal status of slave and free Negroes.[63] It was almost universally held, that ''. . . . the relation of master and servant harmonizes strictly with the best interests of the inferior or African race in particular, in securing to him that protection and support which his native imbecility of intellect disqualifies him from securing for himself.''[64] The institution thus became one vast, benevolent mission enterprise, in which slaveholders thought of themselves as the agents of a Divine Providence engaged in rescuing the heathen African from his savage state, and introducing him to the blessings of Christianity.[65]

The persistence of these attitudes after the legal abolition of slavery may be taken for granted. They were shared by most white persons involved in the slave economy; but the economic stratification of the white population resulted in a variation. All white persons might regard Negroes as inferior, but it was a part of the tradition for the members of the upper classes to insist upon their deep affection for the Negro "in his place."[66] The literature is replete with reminiscences of the deep affection existing between whites and black under the old regime; and it became, in later years, a mark of status to follow this traditional pattern. To do so identified the possessor of the attitude with the upper classes.[67]

A definite spirit of antipathy toward Negroes among the lower economic classes of whites has been mentioned by students of the ante-bellum and post-war periods. One of the few articulate "poor whites" was Hinton Rowan Helper, who claimed to be the "voice of the non-slave-holding South . . . . one identified with them by interest, by feeling, by position."[68] Helper's little known second book, published two years after the end of the Civil War, was prefaced with the statement that "God's simple truth would be told" if he declared the "primary object of this work" was to "write the Negro out of America." "The secondary object," continued Helper, was "to write him . . . . out of existence."[69]

It would appear from available testimony that Helper's feeling was typical of his class in Alabama. Attorney William H. Forney, a democratic lawyer called before the Ku Klux investigating committee in 1871, testified that ". . . . the class of people who reside in the South and have never owned Negroes are more bitterly opposed to social equality than slaveholders. They hate the Negroes worse, and the Negro hates them worse; the Negro calls them poor white trash."[70] Judge John A. Minnis, a "scalawag," said that "There is, no doubt, a very violent prejudice that exists against Negroes with white men generally, and especially against their exercising any of the priveleges that they consider belonging to white men, and among that class of men who never held any Negroes that prejudice is very violent."[71] General Crawford, commander of Federal troops in the State during Reconstruction, believed that "the greatest hostility to the Negro was in the mountain region."[72] The planter, he continued, did not have that kind of prejudice; the Negro "was still valuable to him, and he does not want to kill him, or drive him away." The antipathy of the mountain whites to the Negro, he concluded, came from the fact that Negroes were looked upon by the lower classes as their economic rivals.

Why the non-slaveholding white disliked both planter and slave is apparent from a letter written by Robert C. Tharin, who endeavored to set up a newspaper, the *Non-Slaveholder,* shortly before the outbreak of the war. The newspaper proposed to represent the economic interests of the ''poor white''; but Tharin was expelled from the State.

He had seen the rich man's Negro ''come in contact'' with the poor white blacksmith, the poor white bricklayer, wheelwright and agriculturist. He had seen the preference invariably given to the rich man's Negro in all such pursuits and trades; like me, he had heard the complaints of the poor white mechanic of the South against the very Negro equality the rich planters were rapidly bringing about. These things he had heard and seen in Charleston, New Orleans, Mobile, Montgomery and Wetumpka.
Have not the planters for years condemned every mechanic in the South to Negro equality? . . . . My dislike to them arose from . . . . their daily usurpations of power and privileges at variance with my rights and the rights of my class.[73]

Meanwhile, the Negroes, ''secure on the plantations,'' ''accustomed to observing, and, in a way, identifying themselves with 'quality','' harbored a deep ''contempt for white people of small property and no social distinction.''[74]  The blacks, no less than the whites, exhibited in their personalities the result of the impress of a powerful social institution, in turn affected by the elemental configuration of the land upon which they lived and labored.

CHAPTER II

## THE EDUCATION OF NEGROES UNDER "THE PECULIAR INSTITUTION"

Southern legislators, said Bishop H. N. M'Tyeire in 1859, seem to have taken the view "that slavery is an older institution than schools—that it was before reading and writing or the art of printing."[1]   The distinguished churchman recognized the limitations imposed upon those Christian masters who had a deep interest in the intellectual and spiritual condition of their slaves: "Circumstances have imposed a prohibition to the formal education of slaves, as a luxury beyond their condition, or an acquirement incompatible with domestic quiet."[2]

The domestic quietude of the South had been rudely disturbed in the early Autumn of 1831.  A bloody massacre of men, women, and children had been engineered by Virginia slaves, and the leader was a Negro preacher, Nat Turner.  Turner had been taught to read by his parents, and further instruction had been given to him by the young white man who owned him in his youth. A visionary, it was said that he had been led to revolt through reading the Bible and identifying himself with the "Moses" chosen to lead his people out of bondage.[3]

In Virginia the revolt was suppressed with the utmost rigor; but the news quickly spread throughout all parts of the South, with rumors multiplying as to the imminence of the long-feared rising of the blacks against their masters.  The Governor of Virginia believed that Nat Turner had been incited by "incendiary publications" disseminated by Northern agents of abolition societies; his fears were shared widely in the South.[4]  Accordingly, Southern states hastened to adopt laws whch would prevent the acquirement, by the slaves, of the accomplishments so "incompatible with domestic quiet."  Where such laws already existed, they were reinforced.

14

Admitted to the Union in 1819, Alabama immediately adopted a slave code based upon that of Georgia. Not until 1832, the year following Turner's insurrection, was any effort made to prohibit the education of Negroes. In that year a statute was enacted making it a crime to instruct any Negro, free or slave, in the arts of reading and writing; a fine of from $250 to $500 was imposed upon persons found guilty of this offense.[5] Assemblages of Negroes gathered together for any purpose, including religious exercises, were prohibited unless "five respectable slaveholders" were present, or the preacher in charge held a license from the mother church of which the slaves were members.[6]

The law of 1832 was immediately challenged by the "Creoles" of Mobile and Baldwin County, who had been guaranteed rights as American citizens by codicils attached to the treaties ratifying the Louisiana Purchase.[7] As a result of a petition addressed to the Legislature of the State in 1833, a special grant permitted the Mayor and Alderman of the city to issue licenses to "persons deemed suitable" for the instruction of the direct descendants of the original Creole population of the city and county.[8] It appears that one or more schools for these "Creole" children were maintained in Mobile County as a part of the regular school system. Expenditures of $4,440 for Mobile, listed in 1852, were allocated to "Methodist, Catholic, and Trinity Schools."[9] One sum of $1,350 was allocated "for various other schools."[10] It is probable that the "Creole" schools were among this latter number, although current oral tradition in Mobile has it that "Negro Creoles" attended Catholic schools with white children until comparatively recent years. The Census of 1860, in spite of existing statutory prohibitions of the education of Negroes, showed 114 "free colored" children in the city of Mobile attending school.[11] The editor of a Reconstruction newspaper, the *Mobile Nationalist*, was described as of "the creole class," "educated at a public school before the war, at the expense of the people of Mobile, and all the education he has is at their expense."[12]

With this possible exception, there is no record of a school for Negro children in the State of Alabama prior to 1860. Indeed, the same legislature which enacted the School Law of 1856 passed another statute entitled "To Prohibit the Teaching of Slaves to Read and Write." This law, which remained in force until the end of the Civil War, provided that

. . . . if any person or persons shall teach or be engaged in teaching, in this State, any slave or slaves to read or write, he, she, or they shall be liable to indictment therefor, and on conviction, shall be fined not less than one hundred dollars and be imprisoned in the county jail not less than three months, one or both, at the discretion of the jury trying the case.[13]

The Negroes were "thralls, wanted only for their brawn";[14] and, says Gaines, "the denial of educational opportunity to the blacks" is a fact that is indubitable.[15] The historian of the African Methodist Episcopal Zion Church commented on the fact that the ministers in the Alabama Conference of the denomination lacked leaders who were as "well equipped as those who were nearer to the northern border."[16] By contrast,

There were private schools for colored children in New Berne, Wilmington, Fayetteville, and some other points in North Carolina long after they ceased to be tolerated in any other part of the South, and the effect thereof is seen upon North Carolinians wherever dispersed. In Alabama and other more Southern states, the flame of intelligence in the mind of the slave was more effectually quenched; hence when emancipation came there were fewer in that section who had the intellectual capacity for the work of the ministry. The men were there . . . . they had the piety and the zeal, but the opportunity for culture had been wholly denied them.[17]

A collection of one hundred and seventy-eight biographical sketches of eminent American Negroes, published in 1887, listed but one person born in Alabama, and only two resident there.[18] One of the Alabama residents was Booker T. Washington, born and educated in Virginia, who had come to the State of Alabama but six years prior to the appearance of the biographical account.[19] The other was William H. Councill, President of the State Normal School at Huntsville, who was born in North Carolina in 1849 in slavery and sold, with his mother, into Alabama, in 1857. Councill's first schooling came in 1864. After leaving the plantation of his master in North Alabama in the wake of an invading Federal army, he entered a school for Freedmen established in the environs of Chattanooga by a Federal Army Chaplain.[20] The sole native representative of Alabama in the volume was W. Q. Atwood, listed as "Lumber merchant and Capitalist—Orator."[21] The son of an Alabama white planter and a Negro woman, Atwood was born in Wilcox County, Alabama, in 1839. His mother was illiterate, although his father "traced his line of descent back to . . . . a surgeon in Oliver Cromwell's army."[22] As a child, he boasted, "he did not feel the curse of slavery, except in the want of a school training."[23] He received no formal education until, at the death of his father in 1853, the family with seventeen other slaves was manumitted and transported to Ohio by the terms of their master's will.[24] The Negro Congressman, James T. Rapier, had a similar background. The mulatto son of a free Negro woman and a plantation owner near Huntsville, Rapier was sent to Canada by his father, and afterward to Scotland, where he was graduated with a bachelor's degree from the University of Glasgow.[25]

There are other instances to indicate that "there were many masters who were kinder than the slave code,"[26] and that enslaved Negroes were taught by their masters, or acquired the rudimentary tools of a formal education through their own efforts, in spite of prohibitory laws. Occasionally a rare exception to the rule of enforced illiteracy appeared among the great mass of slaves. Phillips[27] quotes a letter from the slave Harford to his master, Charles Tait, dated at Mobile, November 6, 1826, six years prior to the prohibition of Negro instruction in the State:

Mobile, Nov. 6, 1826

My dear Master

Your kind favor to me through Mr. Caulborne has been duly recd and I now hasten to answer the same and inform you how your affairs are going here. I left the plantation the 31st ultimo at which time they were coming on very well with the crop. Eighty bales had been picked, and they think they will have eighty more. I think the cotton is much cleaner than it was last year (ample room). The corn crop is very good, and I think they will have plenty for the next year . . . I am sorry to have to inform you that nine of the children have died at the plantation, mostly with the Hooping Cough . . . . There will be five births at the plantation, and among the number Nancy is to give birth to one, after a suspension of fourteen years . . . . Times have been so hard that I have made but little for myself, but I am now in hopes that I shall now do better . . . . I have another son named after myself . . . . the respects of your affec. Svt. unto D(eath) in hopes ever to merit your esteem

Your most dutiful servant,
HARFORD.

In 1827 a Georgia owner advertised in an Alabama newspaper for his "Negro girl, named Amanda," who was "a sensible girl, and speaks very correct and intelligent for a Negro."[28]   The subscriber believed that Amanda had either forged a "free pass" or obtained one from some "designing white person."   Evidently Amanda was a mulatto; ". . . . consequently she will attempt to pass herself off as a white person, or a free person of color."[29]

In 1850 the illiteracy of free Negroes in the State was but slightly higher than that reported for the white population, 20.7 per cent as compared to 18.9 per cent for the whites.[30]   The illiteracy rate for white persons in Arkansas, North Carolina, and Tennessee was higher than that for free Negroes in Alabama.   It is probable that the favorable showing of the free Negroes of Alabama was due to the high percentage resident in the Mobile community.   Yet, the 2,790 free Negroes resident in the State in 1860 represented only one-half of one per cent of the total of 437,770 members of the race enumerated in that year.

For the great majority of slaves the plantation was a school of sorts.   The historian of Alabama, Thomas McAdory Owens, testified to this fifty years after the abolition of slavery and in so doing furnished a significant document with respect to the attitude of Alabama whites toward later efforts to educate the Negro. "The ante-bellum plantation was the best school the Negro ever had.   Under wise and intelligent direction he developed the use of hand and muscle and strength that made him the best fixed labor in the world."[31] On this self-sustaining unit the slave artisan was an indispensable aid to the system, and owners purchased, where they could not train, skilled workers in all branches.   James P. Bryan of Marengo County advertised "100 valuable Negroes for sale, including several first-rate mechanics . . . . one No. 1 Brickmason and Plasterer, and two first-rate Carpenters . . . . The remainder are well trained plantation hands, having been raised in this country, and are valuable Negroes."[32] Also listed for sale were "from 30 to 40 valuable young work mules on the same terms."

"In a certain way," said Booker T. Washington,

every slave plantation in the South was an industrial school.   On these plantations young colored men and women were constantly being trained not only as farmers but as carpenters, blacksmiths, wheelwrights, brick masons, engineers, cooks, laundresses, sewing women and housekeepers.[33]

But he added, "This training was crude, and was given for selfish purposes."[34]

In addition to prohibiting slaves from learning how to read and write the institution required that justifications for this denial of learning, so harshly criticized at the North, be built up on the concept of racial inferiority; under no other theory of the Negro intellect could slavery find any rational excuse. In 1865 a Northern soldier quoted with approval the conviction of Southern planters regarding the educational possibilities of the Negro: ". . . . It is labor lost entirely; that it would be useless to undertake such a work; and others (object) on the ground that it would be a positive injury to labor . . . ."[35] Phillips stated that among the benefits the slaves received from their education were those "invaluable texts for homilies; 'Servants, obey your masters;' 'Render unto Caesar the things that are Caesar's,' and 'Well done, thou good and faithful servant'."[36]

In all instances the participation of Negroes in religious exercises was under the closest surveillance of white persons. As the years drew on toward the outbreak of the Civil War, it became customary to separate the Negroes from the whites, where formerly the two races had worshipped together (the Negroes seated in the gallery), and to establish branch churches for the Negro members. The First African Baptist Church of Montgomery had its own officers, and in 1865 had three hundred members who worshipped with the white congregation but who were nominal members of the Negro branch. Six hundred members occupied a building of their own.[37] The African Baptist Church of Mobile was established in 1839, the Negro members of the First Baptist Church (white) of that city withdrawing to form their own church under the supervision of the white congregation.[38]

According to Fleming, after the separation of the Northern and Southern branches of the various denominations, the planters were much more enthusiastic in the forwarding of mission work among Negro slaves.[39] Many planters paid the salaries of mission preachers among their "people," and erected chapels and churches at their own expense for the use of the missionaries.[40] The Alabama Conference of the Methodist Episcopal Church appropriated $340,166 for slave missions in the state between 1845 and 1864.[41] Gaines said: "It is likely that every master who was devoutly pious wanted his slaves to receive the benefit; and it is certain that many more worldly-minded masters offered religious training for its good effect on slave order.''[42]

The effect of the discipline of slavery upon the slaves was remarkable. Booker T. Washington frequently used the illustration of the Negro's loyalty to the South during the Civil War as an argument for better treatment of the race. ''Cast down your bucket where you are. Cast it down among the 8,000,000 Negroes whose habits you know, whose fidelity and love you have tested in days when to have proved treacherous meant the ruin of your firesides.''[43] The Southern planters had learned a valuable lesson from the bloody insurrections of Negro slaves in the West Indies, and from Nat Turner's in Virginia. It is, perhaps, not too cynical to believe that the qualities boasted of by Washington, and which have found their way into the pages of all of the romantic literature concerning the ante-bellum South, were less the result of a native, racial nobility of soul than of direct training. The ''fidelity and love'' of the Negroes ''was due in a large degree to the religious training given them by white and black preachers and by the families of slaveholders.''[44]

This ''education,'' however, had serious limitations as preparation for any life outside of the mould of the institution of chattel slavery. In the debate on the Blair Bill in the Senate in 1886, Senator Morgan, lawyer, Brigadier-General of the Confederacy, and citizen of Dallas County in the heart of the old Black Belt, stated that slavery taught and enforced family disorganization and general dependence on the part of the Negroes.[45] James L. Pugh, Morgan's colleague in the Senate from Alabama, had been a member of the Confederate Congress. Testifying before the Committee on the Condition of Affairs in the Late Insurrectionary States (Ku Klux Report), Pugh stated that he did not believe that there were a dozen Negroes in his home county who could call the names of their candidates when they went to the polls. This ignorance he laid to slavery: ''They were not allowed to read or write; they were kept in a state of utter ignorance to make them efficient as property.''[46]

The peculiar circumstances surrounding the social control of the Negro population lent themselves to rationalizing the protective measures taken by the white population on the ground that Negroes were incapable of being educated in a formal sense and that the institution of chattel slavery formed the best training ground for the limited capacities of the race. As the institution of chattel slavery dictated the type of education, or training, given to Negroes in ante-bellum days, it left an indelible stamp upon the attitudes which were to be social forces in determining the reaction of the whites to the education of Negroes in the future, after the institution itself had been abolished.

## CHAPTER III

## SOCIAL FORCES IN RECONSTRUCTION

The story of Reconstruction in Alabama, more than a twice-told tale, has become a commonly accepted pattern for the historical description of the South. In the definitive work of Walter Lynwood Fleming,[1] the central figures and facts are set forth with a conviction, and documentation, that for thirty years has closed the subject to further investigation.

The central figures in this stereotype are the shiftless, poor white scalawags; the greedy carpetbaggers; the ignorant, deluded, sometimes vicious, Negroes; and the noble, courageous and chivalrous Southrons who fought and won the battle for White Supremacy. The accepted facts are: the imposition of a corrupt carpetbagger-Negro regime on a proud State; the accumulation of a debt of $25,503,593;[2] the final victory of Honesty; and the shouldering of this immense debt by a war-ridden, despoiled people who toiled for generations under the incubus of fearful interest payments.

We enjoy, today, an advantage in perspective over Fleming, who was himself the son of a planter partially ruined by the War, and whose thesis, in some degree, was the expression of a class-attitude deeply affected by the events of the Civil War and Reconstruction, thinking in terms of ethical evaluations, and seeking, as even historians will, to fix blame. It is pertinent to remember that Fleming wrote, and published, less than thirty years after the occurrence of the events he described.

It is our purpose to take advantage of the perspective the passing of another generation allows us to enjoy, and to examine both the figures and the facts which compose the now stereotyped picture of Reconstruction in Alabama. It will not be possible to retrace the record of certain events which need elucidation; the record of elections, of politicians, even of the above-surface partisan conflicts and personalities, may be followed in any year-book, or in Fleming's work.

Whatever Reconstruction meant to Fleming, we may now agree that it involved social, economic, and political redefinition of the *status* of varied economic and racial groupings. The shape of future institutions was to be moulded, superficially by the partisan elements, fundamentally by the social and economic forces which gave those elements strength and direction. Our distinction between "social" and "economic" forces is one of convenience, rather than of logical discreteness. By "social forces" we mean here those social convictions, primarily derivative from economic groupings, which gave color to the social structures—attitudes—important for the definition of the rôle of the Negro in the new order. Such "economic forces" as may be identified cut athwart every social and racial alignment visible; and reference to them is made in a later section of this essay.

## SOCIAL FORCES IN ALABAMA RECONSTRUCTION

Significant social groupings—the source of social forces—involved in Reconstruction were, first, residual elements of the antebellum complex: the native whites, with their sub-division into slaveholders and non-slaveholders, and the Negro population. The War brought upon the scene the Federal Army and the Freedmen's Bureau, two intertwined socio-political entities representing social forces from the North. Particularly these latter two agencies becamè the instrument by which the theory of Northern Humanitarianism was made potent in the State.

*The Native Whites: The Aristocracy of Tradition.* At the end of the Civil War, as we are likely to forget, the sponsors of varied policies were actuated by an acute realism. No one should forget, as Garfield did not, that to expect "seven million men to change their hearts on the issue of a battle" is an absurdity.[3] It is clear that the former slaveholders never intended to accept the "freedom" of Negroes without the reservation that members of the race should continue to be wards, and under the tutelage, of the class which had owned them before the war. The slaveholders were realistic enough, and those who now view the figure of Thaddeus Stevens with such horror forget that, like the slaveholders, the Pennsylvanian was just as realistic, and pursued precisely the only course which he saw would nullify those firm reservations as to Negro status. In his inaugural address of December 13, 1865,

Governor Patton, newly elected Provisional Governor, said that "We shall not only extend to the freedmen all their legitimate rights, but shall throw around them such effectual safeguards as will secure them in their full and complete enjoyment. At the same time it must be understood that politically and socially ours is a white man's government."[4] The Negro, continued Governor Patton, "must be made to learn that freedom does not mean idleness and vagrancy." A cynic might have retorted that this is what freedom, precisely defined, *does* mean. A charge to a jury in Pike County is quoted by Fleming to show the "sentiments of the judiciary officers and members of the bar as well as jurists."[5] The charge was apparently an acceptance of freedom for the Negro; but it was *freedom* as conceived by Alabama planters:

We deplore the result as injurious to the country and fatal to the negroes, but we are in honor bound to observe the laws which acknowledge their freedom. . . . Nominally free, he (The Negro) is beyond expression helpless by his want of self-reliance, of experience, of ability to understand and appreciate his condition . . . (We must) convince the world of our good faith, get rid of the Freedmen's Bureau, . . . secure the service of the negroes, teach them their place, and convince him (sic) that we are their best friends.[6]

Fleming could have selected no better document to show prevailing "sentiments."

The restrictive legislation of the Provisional Assembly, and the numerous "Black Codes" of municipalities, are of the same nature. We need not concern ourselves here, as so many historians have done, with the "right" or "wrong" of these provisions. For our purposes, they are documentary evidences to a state of mind; they are exhibitions of attitudes which had force to motivate human action. The "aristocrats" had a tradition of righteous paternalism toward the Negro; and the issue of the battle had not changed the force of that tradition perceptibly. Indeed, many of those kindly disposed toward Negroes could not understand why their former slaves deserted their masters for the Yankees. It was, they reflected bitterly, final proof of an unregenerate, animalistic lack of gratitude.[7] Mrs. Clayton was convinced that the Southerners could have handled the Negroes without any trouble had it not been for the Carpetbaggers; the Southerners, she said, would have been able to keep the Negroes in their place.[8]  She was, undoubtedly, entirely right.   As a Union soldier in Alabama in 1865 reported, "I am frequently told by a planter, 'if we cannot whip the Negro, they and I cannot live in the same country.'  The revolution is so complete, the change so radical, that it seems impossible for them to comprehend it."[9]

*The Native Whites: The Non-Slaveholding Whites.*  It is generally agreed that the non-slaveholding whites of the South nourished a deep antipathy almost equally directed against the institution of slavery, the planters, and the blacks, all as symbols of an unfair economic competition they found it difficult, if not impossible, to sustain.  This antipathy was not so great, however, immediately after the War, as to keep the leaders of this class from agreeing to the extension of political rights and privileges to Negroes while they were achieving their own class interests. William R. Smith was one of the twenty-four members of the Convention of 1861 who refused to sign the Secession Ordinance.[10] With C. C. Sheets, another dissenter from the same general section of the North Alabama hill country, Smith helped organize the Republican party in 1866.[11]  The Alabama "scalawags" indorsed the Fourteenth Amendment in 1867, in a convention where the "hill and mountain" white people predominated.[12]  This indorsement was prior to the enfranchisement of Negroes in the State, but following the rejection of the Amendment by the Provisional Assembly, which, as noted above, was Conservative in tone.[13]  There were obvious economic grounds upon which could flourish a common sympathy between the Negro ex-slaves and the "poor whites," producing a unified political party that cut across lines of racial antagonism.  Both were poor; both were ignorant; both were so largely because of the planting oligarchy.  The poor whites by social heritage, and the Negroes by their recent emancipation, were equally aligned in economic antagonism to the interests of the former slaveholding class.  It is significant that all of the epithets hurled at the Republicans by Conservative opponents, immediately after the War, dealt principally with considerations of economic differentiation, and applied with equal force to whites and blacks.  The convention of 1867 was described by a Northern-born and reared, black belt planter as composed of "drunken, homeless, houseless knaves . . . . unknown native whites, worthless, ignorant Negroes . . . . The entire taxes paid by the members of the legislature were less than $100."[14]

The combination of poor whites and blacks was true throughout the South; it was marked in Alabama. "In short," says Russ, "it (Reconstruction) was a contest of radicals versus Conservatives in most of the States, rather than one of whites versus blacks, since thousands of the whites cooperated with the Negroes."[15]

It may even be true that the bitter antipathy supposed to have existed between the poor whites and the Negroes was the creation in great part of Conservative propaganda after the War. Charles Nordhoff, speaking of the attitudes of the poorer whites, said that "... this class lived in a dread of having social equality with the Negro imposed upon them. This fear has bred hatred of the blacks, to which, I believe, in the majority of cases, they were instigated by bad men of a class above them."[16]

*The Negroes.* The role of the Negro during Reconstruction has been given as many different interpretations as there are theories of racial psychology.[17] No esoteric explanation of their behavior is needed in this essay; it may be helpful to remember that the Negroes were ex-slaves and we know what the institution of chattel slavery consciously designed to produce as its labor force. That the masses were ignorant goes without saying; that they were disorganized and restless was inevitable.

And yet these masses—these ignorant and restless ex-slaves—knew exactly what they needed. Their slogan has been ridiculous for nearly seventy years, and probably will be so for eternity. What they asked of the Government which had set them free was, indeed, a monstrosity. They asked for a subsistence farmstead—for forty acres and a mule.

The leadership of this mass of ignorance was more important than the mass itself in directing its energies. This leadership has been alternately blamed and praised by partisans. Unfortunately, they left no documents which would help us understand what kind of men they were. We do know that they were persons with an education probably equal to that of the white politicians of their day, and that they had the same economic point of view.

The Mobile Creole community sent Ovide Gregory to the Constitutional Convention of 1867.[18] John Carraway, a prominent politician, was also from Mobile.[19] James T. Rapier was a mulatto of planting antecedents, a well-educated man with a cultural background probably unsurpassed in Alabama among his contemporaries, whether white or black.[20]

A significant fact about the Negro leadership prevalent during Alabama Reconstruction is that few were actually identified, in economic position, with the great mass of landless, utterly penniless Negro ex-slaves whom they purported to represent. The economic ambitions of the Negro leaders is reflected in Rapier's self-conscious pride in the ownership of a large plantation in North Alabama.[21] The Negro leaders of a "radical" party had little reason to advocate the economic radicalism of Agrarian Republicanism. They were bent on achieving, within the economic framework which favored them, the social and political privileges which were the dower of the white Conservatives whom they publicly opposed.

The Negro masses were in a revolutionary mood, willing to accept ideas because they were not articulate enough to force the ideas which were their own. That they were not as utterly impassive as many writers on the period have insisted is shown by the fervor with which they sloughed off their apparent loyalties to their former masters, who, in bitter disappointment, promptly called them "fickle." Governor Lindsay, elected as a Democrat in 1870, gives an exceedingly valuable picture of the disposition of the Negroes to change from docility as soon as they learned that they were "free."

They were disposed (he said) to get into a drunken disposition—I use that expression not in its literal sense—to assert their rights, thinking that such assertion was necessary to their maintenance . . . . (They would) rush right into a church, without any change having taken place, where the white people were sitting; not that they had no place to sit (i.e., the Negro pew) but simply to show their equality.[22]

One Democrat protested bitterly that his female servant refused to milk the cows after her husband began to vote, and generally began "to put on airs around the house."[23]

Negroes were even reported as striking white men, an offense punishable by death under the Code in force less than a decade before. At Selma the Negroes were alleged, by the Democrats, to have lynched a white man who had assassinated a Negro policeman.[24] At Tuskeegee a Negro politician was shot by a masked band, and another band, this time composed of Negroes, started out from Montgomery to retaliate.[25]

In this troublous time the Conservatives still felt themselves to be "the best friend of the Negro," but they insisted on preserving caste lines in dealing with him.  General Clanton was bitter because the Negroes in Montgomery refused to attend "a large barbecue got up of whites and blacks," the idea being to "harmonize and prevent a war of races."  He emphasized the fact that "the whites were going to march in to one table and the Negroes the other."  Yet he expressed the utmost scorn for the Republican tactics by which the Sheriff of Montgomery county solicited the Negro vote; the Sheriff "went out to a Negro baptizing about five miles from town, took a bottle of whiskey, let the Negroes drink first, and then drank."[26]

We have said that the Negro masses were agreed on the need for an agrarian reform that would assure them of control of the land.  The notion of "forty acres and a mule" appears to have had its origin in the Homestead Act of 1862, when Thaddeus Stevens brought into the debate on the measure the possibility of confiscating the estates of those in the "rebellious states" and dividing the land among the Negroes.[27]  This was Western Agrarianism applied to the South.  The creation of a Bureau for Refugees and Abandoned Lands in 1864 had implicit in it the idea of re-settlement for stranded white and black populations upon land sequestrated by the Government from former enemies.[28]

In Georgia Sherman, following the example of other Federal commanders along the sea-coast of Carolina, had assented to taking over the sea-island plantations abandoned by their owners, and had allotted parcels to the Negroes for cultivation.[29]  The first Freedmen's Bureau Bill of 1866 provided that unoccupied lands in Florida, Mississippi, Arkansas, Alabama, and Louisiana (not exceeding 3,000,000 acres of good land) should be set aside for refugees and for freedmen.  Allotments to individual families were not to exceed forty acres.[30]  Andrew Johnson vetoed the bill.  In the subsequent debate, Stevens and Trumbull expressed the opinion that the provision of "forty acres and a mule" was more important than the right of the franchise.  Stevens said, "Forty acres of land and a hut would be more valuable to him (the Negro) than the immediate right to vote."[31]  Trumbull agreed: "I believe a homestead is worth more to these people than almost anything else."[32]

We quote again from Fleming, who used the incident to give point to his story of the brutish ignorance and ridiculous hopes of the recently emancipated Negroes.  During the canvass for the Constitutional Convention of 1867, a Negro voter at Selma "held up a blue (Conservative) ticket and cried out 'No land! no votes! slavery again!' Then holding up a red (Radical) ticket he shouted 'Forty acres of land! a mule! freedom! votes! equal of white man!' "[33]

Our seventy years of perspective may lead us to wonder as to whether the Negro, or Fleming, who ridiculed him, was the wiser advocate of human betterment in the South and in the Nation.

*The Federal Army and the Freedmen's Bureau.*  These agencies have loomed large in the interpretation of Reconstruction, as self-motivating forces.  It is more important to recognize that the masters of the Bureau were the servants of the "Radical Reconstructionists," of whom Thaddeus Stevens was the dynamic leader.  There were many "Norths," as there were many "Souths."  These governmental agencies, for the brief space during which Congress brushed aside the Presidential authority, were the voice of a particular "North"; the North of New England Humanitarianism.  General O. O. Howard, Commissioner of the Bureau, is described by a friendly critic as "an honest man, with too much faith in human nature, little aptitude for business and intricate detail."[34]  It was, perhaps, more important that Howard was a product of Bowdoin College, a prime exemplar of New England's school of equalitarianism.

In Alabama the Bureau performed its tasks largely through the agencies of men who had formerly been Chaplains in the Union Army.[35]  This detail is significant when it is remembered that it was just this class of men who might have been expected, more than other officials of the Army, to be in sympathy with Northern Humanitarianism.  The early addresses of the Bureau officials were replete with moral homilies to the Negroes in the best New England Sunday School style:

You now have the sympathy of all humans and Christian people. . . . . Would you not also be glad to have their love and respect? . . . . It is (obtained) by good behaviour.  There is nothing that makes people so beautiful, whether they are white or black, as virtue . . . . Liberty alone is not happiness.  Self-support and self-control are required to make it pleasant.[36]

The Bureau in Alabama, according to Fleming, "was the least harmful of all in the South."[37] Yet, the Bureau there is severely criticised; and Fleming's strictures upon its work, aside from their value as historical appraisal, yield a perfect document as to basic attitudes toward the agency.[38]

| *What the Bureau Did* | *Result* |
|---|---|
| Landlords were prevented from evicting laborers until they were located elsewhere. (p. 431) | "Thus the negroes would do nothing and kept others from coming in their place." |
| General Swayne gave church property—used by Negroes before the war—to them, although the property belonged to white people. (p. 433) | "These buildings were used by . . . . missionary teachers and religious carpetbaggers who were instructing the negroes in the proper attitude of hostility toward all things northern." |
| The Bureau required landlords to make contracts with Negro farm tenants. (p. 436) | "Contracts caused trouble. . . . resulted in much litigation . . . . The negro . . . . did not feel free until he had a lawsuit with someone." |
| The Bureau maintained separate courts for Freedmen. (p. 438) | "The Bureau always took a negro's word as worth more than a white's . . . . encouraged complaints . . . . trials made occasions for lectures on slavery, rebellion, political rights of negroes, social equality. 'Proceeded upon the general principle that the negro was as good as, or better than, the Southern white.' Prominent men were hailed into court and 'before a gaping crowd of their former slaves were lectured by army sutlers and chaplains of Negro regiments'." |
| The Bureau cared for the sick. (p. 441) | A high death rate resulted; the relief work amounted to little. |
| The Bureau issued rations. (p. 442) | Bureau agents sold rations intended for free issue. |

| | |
|---|---|
| The Bureau caused demoralization. (pp. 441ff.) | By issuing rations, the Bureau created a situation where Negroes would not work. Negro women were told not to work, and they declared intention to "live like white ladies." The Bureau aroused false hopes of "forty acres and a mule." The Bureau was manipulated as a political machine, and "the Bureau agents, teachers, the savings-bank, and missionaries industriously carried on political operations." |
| The Bureau helped establish schools (pp. 464ff.) | "The white people came to believe, and too often with good reason, that the alien teachers stood for and taught social and political equality, intermarriage of the races, hatred and distrust of the Southern whites, and love and respect for the Northern deliverer only . . . . Violent . . . . incendiary." |

It is not necessary to deal, here, with the question of the justification of these charges. It is sufficient to observe that the Freedmen's Bureau probably appeared to contemporary white persons as it appeared to Fleming; and to note that in these things it was the agent of the force which had established it in operation.

*Northern Humanitarianism.* Carlton describes humanitarianism in terms of the residue of intimate, personal relations found in a "semi-paternalistic method of domestic economy, conflicting with modern industrial and city life."[39] Broadus Mitchell has suggested that only in contemporary times has Southern industrialization reached its adolescence.[40] It was, then, with a peculiar shock that the humanitarianism generated by a young, industrial North came into conflict with an agrarian system that had not taken even the first step toward industrialization.

Among the humanitarians arising from the youthful industrialization of the North, in the period from 1820-1850, were such figures as Henry Barnard, Orestes A. Brownson, James G. Carter, Ralph Waldo Emerson, Frederic Henry Hedge, William Ellery

Channing, James Freeman Clarke, Samuel Lewis, Horace Mann, Theodore Parker, Robert Rantoul, George Ripley, and Henry David Thoreau. These names would constitute, with few exceptions, a roll of leading anti-slavery agitators of their time. The age was noted for "integral reform." Horace Mann is an example of the integralist reformer; he left his work as First Secretary of the Massachusetts Board of Education to enter Congress, where he hoped to add his influence to the solution of the slavery issue. The abolition of slavery, he believed, was a moral issue whose solution was "preliminary to all questions respecting the best systems and methods for rendering education effective."[41]

The intellectual ancestry of the Northern missionaries, and of the Bureau agents, included the "integral reformism" of Mann and of the other Humanitarians. Control of Congress by Stevens and other radicals, and their consequent control of the Bureau, gave them an opportunity to advance, in the South, policies with reference to the Negro that were far ahead of contemporary Northern practice. Legislation regarding the education of Negro children in such states as Indiana and Illinois during the Reconstruction period was far less favorable than that which the Humanitarians, through the Bureau, urged to acceptance in the South. Not until 1869 did Indiana authorize the establishment of schools for Negroes, and then only in separate schools.[42]

Inasmuch as Thaddeus Stevens played so important a part in defining the course of Reconstruction legislation, for the South and so for Alabama, it may not be amiss to refer to him here. His personal character defies classification with the Puritan temper and habits of the persons usually listed as Humanitarians.[43] He entered Congress with Horace Mann after having defeated, in the Pennsylvania legislature, the bill intended to repeal the Free School Act of 1834.[44] He became a "Black Republican" in 1855, and was elected to Congress for that party in 1859.[45] He had already become widely known as an abolitionist through his defense of the Negroes involved in the Christiana Riot.[46]

During the Civil War he dominated much of the legislation leading to the successful culmination of the struggle by the North. From almost the beginning he advocated the confiscation of Southern property as an indemnity for the expenses of the War, and as a punishment for "treason"; and proposed that the property thus realized be given to the landless poor whites and to the Negroes.[47]   He submitted the 13th Amendment to Congress in 1864, and was, in great measure, responsible for the passage of the first Freedmen's Bureau Bill.[48]   He was the strongest figure in the prosecution of the post-war measures, culminating in the impeachment proceedings against Andrew Johnson, that included the final enactment of the "radical" Reconstruction legislation.[49]

This complex man was an iron-master himself, and an early advocate of a high tariff for that product; and yet in 1867 Henry Cooke wrote his brother, Jay, that the election of that Autumn, showing Republican losses, was tolerable to him because it represented the "purification" of the party, and promised ridding it of the influence of "the ultra infidelic rascals like Wade, Sumner, Stevens, *et id omne genus*" who were "dragging the Republican Party into all sorts of isms and extremes"; whose policy, Cooke continued, was "one of bitterness, hate and wild agrarianism."[50] When the question of admitting Alabama came up in Congress on March 17, 1868, Stevens spoke against the measure because to do so "would not be doing justice in legislation as will be expected by the people."[51]   In taking this view Stevens was in direct conflict with the industrialist, capitalist combine, represented in Congress by his Pennsylvania colleague, William D. "Pig-Iron" Kelley.   Kelley was a strong advocate of the admission of Alabama on its first application.   The Alabama government had been elected principally through the Union League Republican Organization, with John C. Keffer as its leading spirit.   Keffer petitioned Congress, with others, for action, and for the recognition of the Government and Constitution he had done so much to establish.[52] Kelley argued for admission, principally because, he said, only a *de facto* Republican administration could properly develop Alabama industrially.   Kelley had prospected in the State during 1867, in the course of which he had made several speeches to Negroes in cities, and visited the areas rich in mineral resources. Alabama, he said, was a State

. . . . in which gold, iron, copper, and various other metals are found along navigable streams and easily accessible for use . . . . And yet all that wealth is paralyzed, and all that capacity to afford cheerful homes to millions of people is shut against the immigrant from Europe or the overcrowded cities of the East . . . . closed forever if the Democratic Party of the State continues as refractory and turbulent as it has been.[53]

Mr. Kelley, long-time spokesman for the Pennsylvania coal and iron industries and their Philadelphia bankers,[54] was a prominent figure in the Philadelphia Union League, which backed Mr. Keffer's political activities in Alabama. Kelley's enthusiasm for the industrial development of Alabama under Republican auspices was probably not lessened by the fact that Keffer was Commissioner of Internal Resources and Immigration in the *de facto* Republican Government then clamoring for recognition.[55]

Yet, when the Omnibus Reconstruction Bill was reported, Stevens defended the admission of Alabama along with that of the other states.[56] He said that he went outside of the Constitution to attain this result, and that it had led through constant compromise; the recognition of Alabama, with the coterie still in charge of which he had before disapproved, may have marked one of the compromises upon which his entire Reconstruction program was built.[57]

At the least it is clear that the political and economic views surrounding the admisson of Alabama were not the same for such two Pennsylvania congressmen as William D. "Pig-Iron" Kelley, on the one hand, and Thaddeus Stevens, on the other. They were both Republicans; but so were Henry and Jay Cooke, and the "ultra-infidelics" Wade, Sumner, and Trumbull.

One may surmise that the Republican Party was never again the same, so far as its influence on Alabama was concerned, after the death of Thaddeus Stevens in the summer of 1868. If elections had helped "purify" it in the autumn of 1867, Henry and Jay Cooke must have been very grateful for the great purge that took away the *plus ultra* of all the economic infidels, leaving "Pig-Iron" Kelley as the leading Congressman from Pennsylvania, and John Keffer as Commissioner of Internal Resources in the newly approved State Government of Alabama.

## Chapter IV

# ECONOMIC FORCES IN ALABAMA
# RECONSTRUCTION

We have, so far, described certain social groupings in Alabama that were fruitful of attitudes with reference to the status of Negroes, and in the reconstitution of the new order. In doing so we have suggested that the stark and tragic stereotypes of familiar history may be divested of much of their high emotional and moral significance, and considered as the objective evidences of ways in which human beings have always reacted to given stimulations.

There is precedent for linking the long-favored figures of the Reconstruction history to the less romantic forces by which ".... the planting class was being trampled in the dust—stripped of its wealth and political power—(while)—the capitalist class was marching onward in seven league boots."[1] With an eye to what happened in Alabama, Russ says that the process of disfranchisement in the South "played an important part in producing modern Industrial America," through keeping the "exleaders of the South out of Congress until it was too late to change the new industrial order which had become firmly entrenched in the interim."[2] Whether these grand motives affected policy in Alabama, so far as internal politics were concerned, may be doubted.

What is doubtless is the value of the point of view for interpreting the record of Reconstruction in Alabama, for Alabama was more likely to witness the working of unsuspected economic forces than any other Southern state. Its natural resources were unique in the South; and, in an age when Coal was power, and Iron the other necessity for industry, it was already known that the Northern hill-country of Alabama had both in unexampled proximity. The bankers in Philadelphia and New York, and even in London, and Paris, had known this for almost two decades. The only thing lacking was transportation.

We propose to examine here the thesis, that the most important elements involved in the Reconstruction of Alabama were the
economic factors incident to the State itself and to the times.

*The Economic Disaster of War:* Sensational accounts of political and racial struggles during Reconstruction are inducement,
frequently, to forget that the Civil War was in itself a first class
economic disaster.  If we can imagine France after the Versailles
of 1871, or Germany after that of 1919, we may not need to rely
too heavily upon the stock figures of Carpetbagger or Negro to
explain the resulting social and economic prostration of the South.
The plantation system of cotton culture, disrupted during the
War, was not cured by Peace.  In Alabama the planters turned
from cotton to corn in the declining days of the struggle, when
markets had become invisible.[3]  Much of the desertion of the fields
by Negroes was a response to the internal decay of an economy
which no longer had use for a labor force.  The recruiting—in
most instances by force—of Negro labor by contesting armies was
another factor.[4]  One is inclined to suspect that planters, Negroes,
and governmental agencies were alike helpless and ineffective, not
so much as a result of their own failings, but because the entire
system had lost its structure.  High prices for cotton immediately
after the War smoothed the immediate shock, but when permanent
deflation came in 1873, the Black Belt suffered its final *coup de
grace*.  Census figures after 1870 show an immense increase in the
number of proprietors, and a decrease in the size of the farm unit
operated.[5]

As early as 1870-1871 Robert Somers, one of the keenest ob-
servers that England has furnished for the American scene, par-
ticularized specific economic reasons for the decline of cotton production, and of the Black Belt, where Fleming[6] and others attached blame to the "laziness" of the freed Negroes.  Somers said
that the entire economic system had been disrupted;[7] that the
"poor whites" of the upland country had begun to plant cotton
since the destruction of slave labor had enabled them to compete
with the Black Belt for the first time;[8] and in the development of
share-cropping he saw a profound social change in the life of
Negroes by removing family units from the communal "quarters"
around the big house to isolated cabins on isolated tracts of land.[9]

Local capital was almost annihilated by the War.  Vast sums
of money were lost through railroad investments charged off to

depreciated Confederate currency,[10] although stock holdings in these early lines became the nucleus for many of the bitter political struggles waged by Conservative Democrats. The emancipation of Negroes wiped out a class of capital investment estimated at $200,000,000 in 1860, a sum equal to one-half the assessed valuation of property in the entire State.[11] Banks were either ruined at the beginning of the War, or found their capital impaired by compulsory accumulations of Confederate currency.[12]

An assessment in 1860 of state property in the amount of $432,193,654 included the item of $152,278,000 for slaves.[13] The white counties, prior to the War, had forced the levy of taxes upon slaves so that this form of property paid most of the taxes in 1860.[14] In 1865 property was assessed at $128,846,475, and in 1870 at $156,770,387.[15] Taxation for the support of State government in 1860 was $530,107, for county purposes $309,474, and for towns and cities only $11,590, a total of $651,171, for all taxes levied for the support of state, county, and municipal government in Alabama in that year.[16] The State expended for common schools in 1860, $272,211, or slightly more than one-half of its total budget.

To maintain state or local expenditures in 1870 on the relatively simple scale of 1860 would have required the levying of taxes nearly three times as high as those collected in the former year. But the expense of maintaining new services set up by the Reconstruction Government required a State Budget for education alone which exceeded the total revenues of the State in 1860, when three times as much taxable property was assessed. With a 74 per cent decrease in assessed valuations, state levies increased 178 per cent, county levies 262 per cent, and town and city levies 3,385 per cent.

Both Democrats[17] and Republicans[18] during Reconstruction were fond of telling the people of the State that taxation in Alabama was, even at Reconstruction rates, lower than existing levies in other parts of the country. However true this may have been, it gave little comfort to the Alabama taxpayers of 1870 who were still in a position to remember their status in 1860.

Reconstruction loses something of its apparent simplicity as an entirely racial or sectional problem in view of but two aspects of this destroyed economic structure: (a) the possibility of tax exemption for various interests, or sectors of interests; and (b) the possibility of exploiting the only source of new wealth available in the State, i.e., its natural resources. Transportation was the key to unlocking these treasures; and so the railroads became the most important single factor in Reconstruction politics.

*Capital in Alabama—Railroads, Coal, and. Iron.* In 1850 the "Little Giant," Stephen A. Douglas, visited Alabama, spending most of the time in Mobile. The result of his visit was eminently successful; the Alabama congressional delegation, unanimously opposed to the Railroad Bill of 1848 as introduced by Douglas, in 1850 furnished the small majority by which it became law.[19] One reason for the change was that the 1850 bill made possible with later enactments a grant of 3,077,373 acres to various Alabama roads, in a compromise addition to the terms of the 1848 bill which specified a grant to the Illinois Central. The Alabama roads thus favored were the Mobile and Ohio, planned to make a juncture with the Illinois Central at Cairo; the Selma, Rome, and Dalton; the Alabama and Chattanooga; the South and North Alabama; and the Mobile and Girard.[20]

In 1852 a young man named Jabez Lamar Monroe Curry "traversed the counties of Talladega, Calhoun, and Randolph, making speeches, and obtaining rights of way and subscriptions" for the Alabama and Tennessee River Railroad Company, in which his father was a prominent stockholder.[21]

In 1853 this young man was elected to the State Legislature from Talladega county, and was immediately appointed Chairman of the Committee on Internal Improvements.[22] He held membership also on the Committee on Education. Curry sponsored legislation to give state aid to railroads from his Committee on Internal Improvements.[23] Two measures which had a prophetic relationship were also sponsored by Curry, future head of the Peabody and Slater Funds; one became the basis for the foundation of the first public school system in Alabama, and the second authorized the appointment of a State Geologist whose duty it was to survey "the mineral resources, their location, and the best means for their development" in the interests of the State of Alabama.[24]

A fellow member of the legislature of 1853-1854 was one Luke Pryor, who had been elected from Madison county. He was "pledged to the work of securing authority to subscribe two hundred thousand dollars to the capital stock of the Tennessee and Alabama Central Railroad, at Nashville and Decatur, and secured

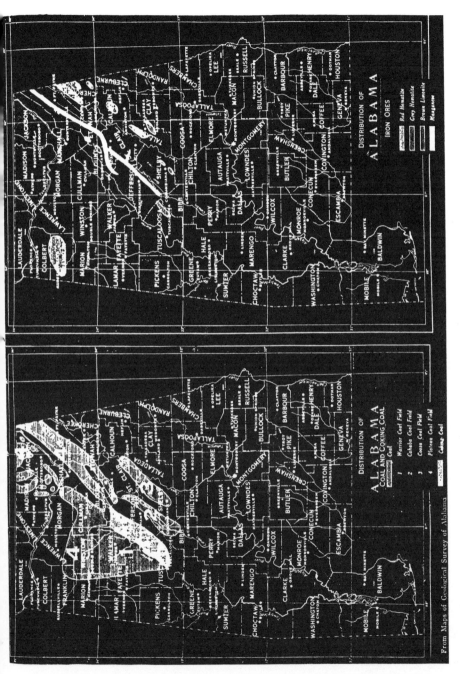

FIGURE 2. DISTRIBUTION OF COAL AND IRON ORES IN ALABAMA

the bill raising that tax, enacted over the veto of Governor Winston."[25]   Curry's biographers give to him the same credit; "his influence in the legislature, *or other undisclosed causes,* served to pass the State aid bills over the Governor's vetoes."[26]

The power behind Luke Pryor was James W. Sloss, described by Armes as Pryor's "side partner in railroad and commercial ventures."[27]   Sloss' name is unheralded and unsung in the more romantic annals of Alabama Reconstruction; and yet his influence, on close inspection, will be found connected with every important industrial and commercial enterprise in the State during the latter half of the nineteenth century.   Like Curry's father,[28] Sloss had accumulated capital for investment in railroads, not from planting, but from store-keeping.[29]   If the ventures of men like Sloss were less spectacular than those of the great planters of the Black Belt, and of his own Tennessee Valley; and if they are less known to history, it is because this was the Southern version of the new class of capitalists and industrialists, manipulating great affairs of State in the obscurity of public inattention while public officials basked in the outward gaze of the multitude.

In 1855 Sloss was president of the Tennessee and Alabama Central Railroad, and it was for this line that Luke Pryor "was sent to the State Legislature."[30]   Meanwhile, some five hundred miles to the North of Sloss' smaller principality, James Guthrie, President of the Louisville and Nashville Railroad, "was establishing that road as the political control of the State" of Kentucky.[31] The Louisville and Nashville early had visions of extending its empire to the South[32] and James Sloss' enterprise in Alabama stretched southward toward the "mineral resources" of North Alabama from Decatur, and northward toward Nashville, in the same direction which expansion for the Louisville and Nashville would, of necessity, involve.   It was, perhaps, no accident that James Guthrie, President of the Louisville and Nashville, in 1860 came into bitter conflict with the supporters of the "Little Giant" at the Charleston Convention.[33]   In 1860 the candidate for a presidential nomination was still the former protagonist of the Illinois Central and the Mobile and Ohio Railroads.   Could the feud, even thus early, have involved the ultimate goal of tapping Alabama's mineral wealth?

The Civil War left Alabama's railroads in poor condition; rolling stock, tracks, bridges, and other equipment were indiscriminately destroyed by contending armies in the ebb and flow of the tide of battle. Such disaster, however, does not seem to have overcome the fortunes of the North Alabama capitalists and politicians who were the associates of James Sloss. Robert Patton, a member of the Sloss North Alabama coterie, had a brother-in-law, J. J. Griers, who was in constant communication with General Grant during the war.[34]  Patton was later Provisional Governor under the short-lived Johnson regime, and during his tenure of office worked in close cooperation with the Sloss interests.[35] George Houston, who became Luke Pryor's law partner in 1866,[36] had a most uncertain record of loyalty to the Confederacy.[37]  Samuel Noble, later associated with Sloss in developing the mineral resources of North Alabama, and an ally of William "Pig-Iron" Kelly,[38] traded through the lines with the connivance of Confederate officials.[39]

The Louisville and Nashville Railroad also emerged from the war with enhanced prospects. As the direct carrier between North and South of the immense Federal business, the line had extraordinary profits during the war,[40] and its "wonderful prosperity" then attained continued until 1870.[41]  By the end of the war Sloss' railroad interests were already inextricably bound up with the Louisville and Nashville. In 1865 three small roads in North Alabama, including the Tennessee and Alabama, combined under Sloss' leadership.[42]  In 1866 Albert Fink, General Superintendent of the Louisville and Nashville, spoke in his Report to the Directors as though the Sloss roads were already a part of the Louisville and Nashville system, as, indeed, they probably were.

. . . . Decatur and Montgomery railroad. This road, when completed, will, by connecting Decatur with Montgomery, Alabama, form a most important link, in the through line from Louisville, to Montgomery, Mobile and Pensacola, and open to the enterprise of Louisville the rich country tributary to the above cities.[43]

By 1867 the Louisville and Nashville had come to terms with the Mobile and Ohio, negotiating a ten-year lease of the property.[44] But at Nashville the Louisville and Nashville found a strong competitor for the Alabama mineral regions' trade, in the Nashville and Chattanooga.[45]  The struggle between the competing interests may be simplified as follows: Should the Louisville and Nashville affiliates, by way of the Nashville and Decatur and the proposed

Montgomery and Decatur (later the North and South Railroad)
have access to Alabama's coal and iron, or should the Nashville
and Chattanooga, and its controlling capitalists, win the field
through extending a line from Chattanooga to the southwestward
along the Tennessee River Valley?

*Railroads and Reconstruction: First Phase:* Officially, in the
public eye and that of later historians, the actors in this dramatic
struggle were respectively Republicans and Democrats, fighting
for the slogans of ''White Supremacy,'' on the one hand, or
''Equal Rights'' on the other. Not apparent on the political stage,
but working powerfully behind the scenes, were such men as
James Guthrie, Albert Fink, and James Sloss of the Louisville
and Nashville; and V. K. Stevenson, the principal apparent
owner of the Nashville and Chattanooga.[46]  These men in turn
had their masters.  A local, but not altogether a minor capitalist,
was Josiah Morris, a Montgomery banker, who is listed as a large
stockholder and a director of all the Sloss railroad affiliates.[47]

V. K. Stevenson is said to have been supported by ''Boston
Financiers,'' made visible in the person of Russell Sage.[48]  The
Louisville and Nashville was financed largely by local Louisville
capital, with frequent and sizable contributions from the munici-
pality itself.  The name of August Belmont—and this suggests,
not only the activity of the Chairman of the National Democratic
Party, but also of the omnipresent and almost omnipotent Roths-
childs, of whom he was the American agent,[49]—was also linked to
the financing of the Louisville and Nashville especially in enterprises connected with the opening of Alabama coal fields.[50]

Sam Tate, a prominent figure in Tennessee railroad building
and politics, was also active in Alabama.[51]  Tate was the builder
and president of the Memphis and Charleston, a road traversing
North Alabama from the Mississippi line, on the West, running
just south of the Tennessee River to Decatur, where a bridge had
been built, and terminating at Stevenson, with a connecting line
from that point to Chattanooga.[52]  Like Albert Fink, of the Louisville and Nashville, Tate had the same vision of the possibilities
of exploiting Alabama's mineral resources:

*Decatur to Montgomery* is another important connection,
feeding your entire line with an abundance of iron and coal, within
seventy-five miles of your lines, from which tonnage for local consumption would alone be profitable, to say nothing of the immense

amount of Western produce you would carry over your lines to feed the thousands of operatives that will be employed in developing the vast resources of mineral wealth in the mountains south of Decatur. Your fostering aid and care should be extended to this road, too, as early as practicable, as it will be one of its most productive arteries.[53]

Indeed, at this time (1866) a close co-operation was in effect between the Louisville and Nashville, represented by Fink, and the Memphis and Charleston, as represented by Tate. Fink rebuilt the bridge for the Memphis and Charleston at Decatur which had been destroyed during the war.[54] Tate got the contract for building the road he and Fink had proposed.[55]

By act of February 19, 1867, the General Assembly of Alabama embarked on the adventure of giving the State endorsement to railroad bonds of certain extant companies,[56] in the amount of $12,000 a mile. This legislation was enacted in the face of impending congressional Reconstruction. This was the Provisional Assembly, with Governor Robert Patton, North Alabamian, and associate of Sloss, in control; and the endorsements included only those roads dominated by the coterie associated with Sloss. The South and North, the Montgomery and Eufaula, the Montgomery and Mobile, the Northeast and the Southwest, and the Wills Valley Roads were the beneficiaries.[57] An examination of the directorates of these railroads will show the presence of Sloss, of Pryor, of Houston, and of Morris; in short of the leading politico-financiers who figured in the Democratic (Conservative) Party during Reconstruction.[58]

When a Republican General Assembly was convened on July 14, 1868—the work of railroad endorsement had been done hurriedly in the closing days of the Provisional Assembly, when pending bills in Congress assured Republican control by the next year —a brief period ensued during which strange industrial and capitalistic bedfellows made political peace for mutual profit.

The Wills Valley and the Northeast and Northwest roads were combined and incorporated as the Alabama and Chattanooga. The formal date of the merger was October 6, 1868.[59] In a series of acts of the General Assembly during the session of 1868-1869, the State endorsement for railroad bonds was increased from $12,000 to $16,000 a mile.[60] The increased endorsement was not a "Republican" grab; for a brief period Sloss enjoyed a paramount

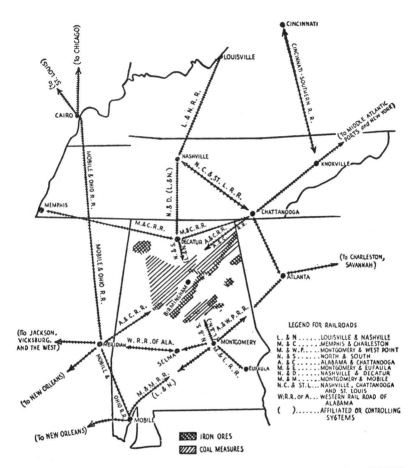

FIGURE 3.—THE CHIEF NATURAL RESOURCES OF ALABAMA, WITH
THE PRINCIPAL RAILROAD LINES (BUILT, BUILDING, OR PRO-
POSED) INVOLVED IN RECONSTRUCTION POLITICS

interest in the South and North, and the Alabama and Chattanooga, which became the particular beneficiaries of the raised indorsement.   Robert Patton, his associate in politics and business,
and formerly Governor under the Provisional Gvernment, became
a Vice President of the new Alabama and Chattanooga road, whose
bonds he had aided in endorsing shortly before as Governor.[61]
John T. Milner, engineer of the South and North, and John C.
Stanton, who held a like responsibility with the Alabama and

Chattanooga, joined in bribing members of the Assembly. A history of industrialization in Alabama, bearing the official approval of the Birmingham Chamber of Commerce, has this account of the manner in which the finances of the South and North were rescued under Republican rule.

> Mr. John T. Milner, Engineer of the Road, said that John Whiting, a Montgomery cotton factor, President of the South and North Railroad, told him he spurned the idea of getting among these Yankees at all, much less of paying them for their votes, but he said that I might do so if I felt like it. So I went.[62]

Milner's ventures were financed principally by Josiah Morris, the Montgomery banker. Stanton was the field agent of Russell Sage. The South and North, as an extension of the main line of the Louisville and Nashville, through 1868-1869 apparently had a working agreement with the Alabama and Chattanooga, through which the two lines were to be connected at a strategic point in the mineral region where a great industrial city would be built. The legislators were generous both with the South and North, planned to run from Montgomery to Decatur, there to connect with the Louisville and Nashville, and with the Alabama and Chattanooga, which was planned to run from Chattanooga across the state to Meridian, and from there, eventually, to New Orleans. In 1868 the South and North received the 2 and 3 per cent funds as a loan from the State.[63] By February 5, 1870, the Alabama and Chattanooga was loaned $2,000,000 by the State.[64]

A recounting of the liabilities assumed for these two railroad systems shows that between 1867 and 1871—under, first, a Provisional, "Conservative" government, and, later, under a "Radical" Republican government—the State incurred what have been called *debts* of approximately $17,000,000 in endorsements and loans. Of this amount Louisville and Nashville affiliates (the South and North, the Montgomery and Eufaula, etc.) accounted for $7,000,000; while obligations assumed for the Alabama and Chattanooga, and railroads represented in this merger, equalled approximately $10,000,000.[65] Since the Alabama "debt" at the end of Reconstruction has been estimated at a maximum of $30,-000,000 and $5,000,000 represented ante-bellum obligations, it is obvious how largely the manipulations of these two railroad systems alone entered into the final financial picture of the period.[66]

The apparent cooperation of the two groups of capitalists—

the Louisville and Nashville group on the one hand, and the Alabama and Chattanooga (Russell Sage) on the other—came to an end in November, 1870. The Democratic candidate for Governor, Lindsay, was elected over his Republican opponent, with a Democratic lower house and a Republican hold-over Senate. An agreement had been reached between the sponsors of the lines financed by the Louisville and Nashville, and the Alabama and Chattanooga, to locate the crossing of the railroad at a certain site in Jefferson County. The Stanton brothers, of the Alabama and Chattanooga (agents for Russell Sage) had taken options on the land surrounding the proposed crossing.[67] A group of Alabama capitalists, including Josiah Morris, W. S. Mudd, F. M. Gilmer, James W. Sloss, and others, took options on a new site, and, unknown to the Stantons, changed the route of the South and North so that it intersected with the Alabama and Chattanooga through the area which they controlled.[68]

The triumph of the local capitalists threatened to be of but brief duration. V. K. Stevenson and Russell Sage had acquired a majority of the $2,200,000 worth of bonds issued by the State in indorsing the building of the South and North.[69] They now (1871) threatened to foreclose their mortgage, demanding as an alternative that the South and North, already constructed from Montgomery to the Alabama and Chattanooga crossing, be turned over to the latter railroad for operation.[70]

In this crisis Albert Fink, said already to have had an agreement with James Sloss, ''and at all times a helper and cooperator, along with Luke Pryor[71] and George Houston,[72] of the South and North,'' met the backers of the Louisville and Nashville at a hastily convened conference in Louisville.[73] Perhaps ratifying a convention already in force, the Louisville and Nashville agreed to take open and complete control of the South and North, averted Russell Sage's threatened foreclosure, and dated the agreement as of May 19, 1871.[74]

The point of these inter-industrial feuds to our discussion is that they dominated every political maneuver that took place in the State during these troublous times. The Democratic and Republican Parties in Alabama, viewed from this angle, seem to have been only the obverse aspects of the Louisville and Nashville Railroad on the one hand, and the Alabama and Chattanooga Railroad on the other. The political tactics developed during this struggle were strikingly similar to contemporary developments in other states.

In Kentucky and Tennessee the Louisville and Nashville was said to "hide behind the city of Louisville" in its classic feud with Cincinnati. Promoters in the latter city proposed to build a road from Cincinnati to Chattanooga which would become the natural competitor of the Louisville and Nashville.[75] Unable to obtain capital elsewhere, the promoters managed to get a grant of $10,000,000 from the city of Cincinnati itself.[76] The Louisville and Nashville "ably supported Louisville in this fight," against the threatened competition from the sister city on the Ohio.[77] When proposed legislative aid to the Cincinnati-sponsored road was pending in the Kentucky legislature, ". . . . it was claimed by the friends of the bill that this gigantic corporation (i. e., the Louisville and Nashville) was the main source of opposition, trying to hide behind the city (Louisville)."[78] The Louisville and Nashville adopted as its principal tactical weapon in Kentucky, identification with the political, social and ideological pattern of the stricken South. "Isaac Caldwell, who was one of Louisville's staunchest defenders, accused Cincinnati of helping to vote Negro suffrage upon Kentucky, and then immediately coming and asking a special favor for doing so."[79] Louisville (i. e., the Louisville and Nashville) hired merchants ". . . . to go South and appeal to the disloyalty of their political record to seduce custom, and when they find that the South demands a better market than she affords, it again appeals to the more sectional feeling at home to prevent the South from getting to that market."[80] If there is any truth in this partisan accusation, it is the suggestion that capital —as represented by the Louisville and Nashville—preceded the politicians in appealing to racial and sectional interests. The fact that the Louisville and Nashville in Alabama was closey identified with local capitalists, while the Alabama and Chattanooga had such men as the "Stantons of Boston" in the chief place of prominence in operations, is an important key to politics in the State during the crucial years of Reconstruction.

### Basic Economic Factors in Alabama Reconstruction: Northern Capital and the Republican Party

The Republican Party in Alabama was organized through the agency of the Union League of America.[81] The League originated in Philadelphia, and among its charter members were Jay Cooke and William Kelley.[82] The League advertised its mission as that of carrying on a counter-propaganda to overcome the effects of "copperhead" agitation in the North.[83] The League contributed to relief work among Negroes and white refugees in Alabama during the latter part of the War.[84] Afterward, numerous branches were organized in Alabama. The head of the order, and the principal organizer in Alabama was John Keffer, a Pennsylvanian financed by the Union League of Philadelphia.[85] In the first efforts at the reorganization of political parties in Alabama in 1865-1866, the League spent most of its energies in the organization of whites in North Alabama.[86] With the assurance of Negro suffrage, the League turned to the organization of prospective Negro voters.[87]

The mother organization, at the termination of the War, declared that it would persist in its efforts to aid the work of national salvation, and defined the "vital issue" of national politics as the tariff.[88] It then began to devote itself, as the chronicler states, "to new and subtler duties."[89] Fleming betrays a delightful naïvete when he absolves the "aristocratic" mother clubs of Philadelphia and New York from full knowledge of, or participation in, the "excesses" attendant upon Alabama's internal Reconstruction politics;[90] he believed that these "aristocrats" could not possibly have known what their hirelings in Alabama were doing.

The John Keffer who organized the Union League in Alabama was a dominant figure in the Constitutional Convention of 1867,[91] and under the first Republican administration of Governor Smith, which was the period during which most of the railroad grants were made, served also as commissioner of the Bureau of Mineral Resources and of the Bureau of Immigration of Alabama.[92] The connection between the Union League and Eastern capitalists, and the Republican Party in Alabama, was close in other respects. We have noted, above, the activities, political and financial, of Congressman William D. "Pig-Iron" Kelley in Alabama during Reconstruction and afterward; the chronicler of the Union League refers to him as one "whose name was as closely associated with the protective principle as William McKinley's afterward came to be."[93] Kelley was among the first to bring to the attention of Eastern capital the glad tidings of Alabama resources;[94] and we have seen how he struggled against Thaddeus Stevens for the early admission of Alabama, with a "cabinet" including Keffer, and which he thought could be exploited profitably only if the *de facto* Republican government was accepted.[95]

In this connection nothing is more instructive regarding the peculiar mixture of humanitarianism and industrialism in the Northern interest in Alabama and the South than the activities of Congressman Kelley. A speech of his, to a mixed group of whites and blacks in Mobile on May 14, 1867, precipitated a riot.[96] An extract from this speech was included in a special textbook edited by the vigorous feminist and abolitionist, L. Maria Child, and intended especially for the use of the Freedmen.[97]

In Alabama the Union League, most often called the "Loyal League," furnished the political machinery for the manipulation of the Republican Party.[98] Fleming stated that the League at first favored the confiscatory program of Thaddeus Stevens.[99] The actual ritual of the organization was quite innocent, purporting "to preserve liberty, to perpetuate the Union, to maintain the laws and the Constitution, to secure the ascendancy of American institutions, to protect, defend, and strengthen all loyal men and members of the Union League of America, to demand the elevation of labor, to aid in the education of laboring men, and to teach the duties of American citizenship."[100] Certainly a program of expropriation would have been as popular among the poorer mountain whites as among the Negroes of the Black Belt plantations; after Stevens' death, the guiding hand of Cooke and his Philadelphia associates in the Union League must have worked in the direction of avoiding such dangerous "isms" along with Stevens' pernicious "greenbackery."

The League was effective politically in Alabama only during the period of the inauguration of the Constitutional Convention of 1867, and the adoption of the Constitution in 1868.[101] That it was a branch of the Republican Party, and, as such, was financed by the industrialists and financiers who composed the Union League in Northern cities and industrial centers, goes without question. The decline of the League after 1868 was due, probably, to two reasons:

1. With the Republican control of Alabama assured in 1868, the sponsors of the League might have thought their work well enough done.

2. The loss of the National elections in the fall of 1867 made the financial sponsors of the League unwilling to continue the more "radical" manifestations of the work in the South. As we have seen, the lost election had its consolation to offer the more Conservative wing of the party; the Republicans were promised "purification" of

. . . . the ultra-infidelic rascals like Wade, Sumner, Stevens, *et id omne genus* (who were) dragging the Republican Party into all sorts of isms and extremes. . . . Their policy was one of bitterness, hate, and wild agrarianism without a single Christian principle to give it consistency, except the sole idea of universal suffrage. . . . These reckless demagogues have had their day and the time has come for wiser counsels. With Wade uttering agrarian doctrines in Kansas and fanning the flame of vulgar principles, trying to array labor against capital and pandering to the basest passions; with Butler urging wholesale confiscation throughout the South and wholesale repudiation throughout the North so far as the National debt was concerned; with Stevens joining hands with the traitor Vallandingham and advocating the idea of a flood of irredeemable paper money sufficient in volume to drown the whole country; . . . . what wonder is it that the accumulated load was too heavy for any party to carry, and that it broke down under it?[102]

The Republican Party in Alabama after 1868 was fashioned more after the ideal of Jay and Henry Cooke than that of the "rascals" who fathered "isms." As the latter said, the only common basis for the Party had been Negro suffrage, and it is clear that the two wings sponsored this issue for very different reasons.

*Industrial Conflict and Debt, 1871-1876:* With this background both political and industrial conflict in Alabama during the latter stages of Reconstruction become understandable. Reference has been made above to the close cooperation existing between the officials of the affiliated lines of the Louisville and Nashville in Alabama, and the Democratic administration elected in the fall of 1870. According to the terms of state indorsements, the State was liable for interest payments in the event of defaults by the roads. The Alabama and Chattanooga defaulted payment of interest due immediately after the new Democratic administration went into office, as of January 1, 1871.[103] Governor Lindsay did not take over the road at that time, stating that to do so would acknowledge the validity of the grants to the Road, which his faction claimed had resulted from corrupt malpractice of the prior

Republican administration. When the railroad made its second default in June, 1871 (two weeks after the Lousville and Nashville had contracted to take over the South and North), Lindsay had different advice from his supporters; and he seized the road for the State, and appointed Colonel Gindrat and James H. Clanton as receivers.[104] Clanton was, at the time, Chairman of the Democratic State Executive Committee.[105] He was also a director of the Montgomery and Eufaula Road, soon to become officially an affiliate of the Louisville and Nashville system.[106] Among his fellow directors were Josiah Morris, of Montgomery, and Bolling Hall,[107] politician, director of the South and North, and one of the founders of the Elyton Land Company.

Clanton is frequently quoted in Fleming's work on Reconstruction as a paragon of pure political motive.[108] The Montgomery and Eufaula railroad, with the Alabama and Chattanooga, was a beneficiary of the extensive endorsements and State loans negotiated during the prior period.[109] In 1871 Clanton was killed in a brawl in Knoxville by one Nelson, who was employed by the Stanton, or Alabama and Chattanooga, interests. There is a certain irony in Fleming's eulogy of Clanton: "He was killed in Knoxville by a hireling of one of the railroad companies which had looted the state treasury and which he was fighting."[110]

The Alabama and Chattanooga dragged through a long period of litigation during the next few years. From July, 1871, to October, 1872, it was operated by the State.[111] The interest on the Alabama and Chattanooga bonds alone amounted to $500,000 a year.[112]

In 1872 David P. Lewis, Republican, was elected Governor of Alabama. Lewis immediately took steps to relieve the State of the devastating interest payments which had accumulated with successive defaults, following that of the Alabama and Chattanooga. By an agreement negotiated in the spring of 1873, the railroad companies, through an Act known as the "$4,000 a mile law," agreed to turn in their $16,000-a-mile-bonds, and to receive back $4,000-a-mile straight state bonds, thus reducing the State liability by 75 per cent.[113] In December of 1873, Governor Lewis stated that all of the roads involved had filed notice of their acceptance of the Act.[114]

It is strange that but little attention has been given to the effect of the Panic of 1873 upon the course of Reconstruction in the South. The failure of Jay Cooke removed from the scene, not only a heavy investor in Southern railroads, but also an "angel" of the Republican Party in the section; and left supreme in the field of these investments the combined forces of the Drexels and the rising Junius S. Morgan. While these circumstances may be of speculative interest here, they are worthy of study.

The majority of the Alabama and Chattanooga bonds had passed into the hands of a "group of English capitalists."[115] The accumulation of defaulted interest payments reached a peak in 1873, in the financial panic of that year. Even the Louisville and Nashville was completely prostrated. An operating deficit of $568,-362 for the entire system in 1873 was laid at the doors of the South and North. "The prostration of the iron industries has greatly retarded the development of the rich mineral resources along the lines of that road, which had been greatly relied upon for supplying it with a profitable business."[116] The result was that the Louisville and Nashville went into bankruptcy and the ownership of the line passed finally and completely from whatever local capitalists had shared in its major control before, into Eastern and European hands.

The financial crisis made the election of 1874 of paramount importance to the persons involved, who saw an opportunity to rescue from the general wreckage whatever salvage might be had. Industrial conflict, accordingly, was sharply focussed in political conflict. The strictly racial and sectional interpretation of the period by Fleming is likely to suggest that all of the corruption visible in Alabama was an outcome of Black Republican thievery.[117] We may say that the basic economic issue of the campaign of 1874 in Alabama was to determine which of the financial interests involved would be able to make the best possible settlement with a state government bankrupted by the earnest efforts of both. Certain facts add piquancy to the general notion that Reconstruction in Alabama was a tightly drawn struggle between Virtue, as represented by the Democrats, and Vice, as represented by the Republicans.

Henry Clews, an associate of Jay Cooke, and a heavy investor in Southern issues, was among the most prominent of the bankers holding the Alabama railroad bonds which lay in the scale of battle.[118] Clews boasted of having negotiated Dix's nomination as Governor of New York, which, he believed, made Grant's renomination certain.[119] His interest in Alabama, he said, was motivated by a noble-hearted impulse "to help the South and to help develop its resources."[120] He added, almost as an after-thought, that he had considered Alabama as the most profitable place for investment on account of its manifest industrial advantages over the North in the years immediately after the War.[121] Writing of the "repudiation" of Alabama issues owned by him, after the final victory of the Democrats, he laid it to "political manipulation."[122] In addition to investments in State issues, Clews was associated with Samuel Noble and William D. "Pig-Iron" Kelley in financing the Oxford Iron Works at Anniston, which lay along the right-of-way of the Alabama and Chattanooga, and he was a director of the Selma and Gulf Railroad (a railroad projected to run from Selma to Pensacola), advertised as forming "the most practicable route from the coal fields and valuable deposits of iron of central Alabama to the harbor of Pensacola."[123]

The election of 1874 determined the fate of the Republican Party in Alabama. George Houston, poetically represented in Democratic literature and in Fleming's account as "The Bald Eagle of the Mountains," and as the defender of "White Supremacy," was elected by a large majority.[124] Neither the campaign literature nor Fleming referred to his close cooperation and participation in the Sloss and Louisville and Nashville enterprises. Almost too innocently, Fleming states that: "The campaign fund was the largest in the history of the State; every man who was able, and many who were not, contributed; assistance also came from Northern Democrats, and Northern capitalists who had investments in the South or *who owned part of the legal bonds of the State.*"[125] As the "legality" of the bonds had not been determined at the time when these gentlemen made their contributions, the discrimination seems doubtful. Obviously the "Northern capitalists" who contributed to the Democratic fund did so *in the hope that with Democratic victory the bonds they owned would be declared legal by the new government.*[126] Nordhoff, a witness whose verdict was uncompromisingly against the Republican regime, said that "where conspicuous financial jobbery took place (in railroad legislation) Democrats have, oftener than not, been parties in interest."[127] Let us not forget what has already been noted; that as a specific effect of the Panic of 1873, it was the misfortune of the Republicans to enter the election of 1874 a year after the house of Jay Cooke had drawn Henry Clews with it to failure.[128]

There is a final incident to this industrial epic that may or may not have had a connection with the end of Reconstruction in Alabama in 1874, and in other states soon thereafter. On December 21, 1874, at Macon, Georgia, was formed what has been described as the "most efficient railroad pool in the United States, largely owing to the genius of Albert Fink as manager."[129]

Sharp competition first appeared after prostration by the Civil War, when it was soon discovered that there were more roads than available traffic. Agreements to restore and maintain charges alternated for a time with the most destructive rate wars. . . . Bankruptcy and ruin in railroad affairs were widespread. Permanent success was finally wrought out of such chaos by the first General Commissioner, who perfected an agreement in 1875 which proved lasting.[130]

The pool rejoiced in the innocent name of "The Southern Railroad and Steamship Company." It allayed competition, and facilitated the growth of several great systems where the highly individualistic small line had flourished theretofore.[131] Coincident with the formation of this pool, it is interesting to note certain changes in the directorates of many of the Southern lines as reported for 1875-1876, and contrasted with the same lists for 1868-1869.[132] J. Pierpont Morgan, in 1875-1876, appears as a Director for several of the Alabama and Georgia lines, including the Mobile and Montgomery, a Louisville and Nashville affiliate.[133] Josiah Morris appears as a member of the directorate of the Mobile and Montgomery, of the former Selma and Meridian, now the Western Railroad of Alabama (a Central of Georgia affiliate),. and the South and North (Louisville and Nashville affiliate).[134] H. B. Plant, founder of the Plant system, appears as Director of the Western Railroad of Alabama.[135]

The election of Governor Houston in 1874 provided an opportunity for the settlement of the "debt" of Alabama, as pledged by the winning party. The debt settlement is supposed to have been framed by a State Senator, Rufus W. Cobb, "and others."[136] Cobb, according to a biographical sketch, "devised the plan of readjustment for the state debt which Governor Houston submitted to the legislature after elaboration. He was the friend and admirer of Governor Houston during his administration."[137] Cobb was also President of the Central Iron and Coal Works at Helena, which was subsidized by the Louisville and Nashville.[138]  In addition, he was a local attorney for the Louisville and Nashville.[139]

Governor Houston began his administration with the expressed desire of settling the "debt." It should be kept in mind here that "debts" are either paid, or repudiated; and those who, following Fleming, state that the "Reconstruction Debt" in Alabama amounted to from $25,000,000 to $30,000,000, need to ask themselves how a "debt" of this size, existing at the accession of Houston in 1874, could become a "debt" of less than $10,000,000 through his adjustments without actual repudiation. Certainly the Alabama "debt" was *adjusted;* but there was no repudiation. It will appear in the following paragraphs that the Alabama "debt" of $25,000,000 to $30,000,000 was not, at any time, an actual "debt," but always a potential one; and that if it had been, or become, an "actual debt," the State would have owned all of the railroads endorsed by it as compensation for the "debt" assumed. The long-heralded triumph of Governor Houston's "debt settlement" actually will be seen to have consisted in relieving the State of its "potential debt," and the railroads of the threat of State foreclosure on mortgages held by it, on grounds highly advantageous to the railroads; or, at least, to those railroad systems with which the leadership of the Alabama Democracy was on a fairly intimate basis.

As his "debt commissioners" Governor Houston appointed Levi W. Lawler, T. B. Bethea, and himself as *ex-officio* chairman. T. B. Bethea does not appear as a director or stockholder in any published records of these facts.[140] Levi W. Lawler was reported in 1868[141] and 1870[142] as a director of the Selma, Rome, and Dalton, a competing road to the Alabama and Chattanooga; Peter Hamilton, listed with Rufus Cobb as one of the men responsible for the debt settlement before the Committee was appointed, was a Mobile and Ohio (a Louisville and Nashville subsidiary) director in 1868,[143] and in 1870-1871.[144] Houston was a director of the Nashville and Decatur (Louisville and Nashville affiliate) in 1868[145] and 1870;[146] his law partner, Luke Pryor, was a director of the South and North in 1870[147] and in 1875.[148]

The Report of the Debt Commissoners prefaced analysis of State obligations by saying that "The direct and contingent indebtedness of the State is $30,000,000."[149] This debt the Commission divided into four classes.

Class I was defined as including:

. . . . bonds issued or loaned to railroad companies (consisting) of bonds bearing five, six, and eight per cent interest; bonds issued for temporary loans; bonds hypothecated with and sold by the New York Guaranty and Indemnity Company, on account of a temporary loan; bonds hypothecated with and sold by agencies appointed by the United States District Court, in bankrupt cases; State obligations, bearing eight per cent interest; State certificates, known as "Patton money;" Trust funds, and some small claims against the State.[150]

This class of indebtedness amounted to $11,677,470, including $1,050,000 of unpaid interest. The great portion of this debt had accumulated prior to Republican rule in 1868; when this party had taken over control in 1868 the State bonded debt was $6,848,-400, with $2,494,654.87 of additional state funds which had been dissipated, but still involved the state in interest payments.[151] Obligations in Class I which might be laid to "Reconstruction extravagance" therefore accounted for approximately one million of the total.

Class I debts were "settled" by a refunding operation by which the State was granted a lower rate of interest and the cancellation of past due interest payments.[152]

Class II debts amounted to $1,156,000. They represented the liability of the State for railroad endorsements compromised under the law of 1873, in Governor Lewis' administration, when the railroads had exchanged $4,000-a-mile bonds for the prior bonds valued at $16,000-a-mile. By this means the State had, by 1874, reduced its liability by retiring $5,103,000 worth of endorsed bonds.[153]

Class II debts were "settled" by exchanging endorsement bonds for one-half of their face value; in other words, admitted the Commission, the "State accepted a clear loss of one-half." The roads so favored were the (James Sloss-George Houston-Luke Pryor) Louisville and Nashville affiliates, the South and North; the Grand Trunk; and the Savannah and Memphis.[154]

Class III debts are called by Fleming "the worst of all."[155] They totalled $2,573,093. These obligations included $600,000 of claims rendered by the South and North,[156] of which Governor Houston's law partner, Luke Pryor, was a director,[157] and of which, as we have seen, the omnipresent James W. Sloss had been from the first a prominent figure. Governor Houston himself had been a director of the affiliated Louisville and Nashville Company, the Nashville and Decatur, in 1868[158] and in 1870.[159] The South and North claims were actually Louisville and Nashville claims, since the company was a subsidiary of the greater line.

Regarding these claims, the debt commission, of which, it will be remembered, Governor Houston was chairman, stated: "It is not our province to make any suggestion in regard to the claim of the South and North. . . . They are not connected in any way with the bonded debt of the State, and do not come within the scope of our investigation and adjustment."[160]

But this $600,000 had been included in the "debt" as originally claimed by the Democrats, and as quoted by later historians. To disregard it was one of the simpler devices for "settlement" and "reduction" adopted by the Debt Commission.

The Commission dealt less kindly with $1,464,689 of obligations which involved the banking house of Henry Clews and Company. Clews, we have observed, was a banking associate of Jay Cooke,[161] and in Alabama had investments at Anniston in the Oxford Iron Works along with Samuel Noble, erstwhile trader-between-the-lines, and William D. "Pig-Iron" Kelley.[162] Clews' interests had been with the Alabama and Chattanooga, the Russell Sage, Republican sponsored road that was intent on invading the Alabama Mineral District from the direction of Chattanooga as the Louisville and Nashville was similarly bent on tapping this region from the North.

Mr. Clews' autobiography states simply, but eloquently, that the Debt Commission was motivated by "political manipulations" in disposing of his claims.[163] This was their solemn pronouncement regarding the Clews obligation: "The State is liable only for the amount of the debt which was due to Clews and Co., amounting to about three hundred and ten thousand dollars, with interest. This amount is all that we recommend to be arranged by the State; and as to which of the claimants it belongs we do not undertake to decide."[164] It was in this manner that another million of the "debt" was settled.

Class IV "debts" amounted to $14,641,000. They consisted of endorsed bonds on the basis of $16,000 a mile which had not been compromised under the $4,000-a-mile law. The total obligation, on inspection by the Commission, was scaled down to $11,-

597,000,[165] excluding $3,024,000 in loans due from the Alabama
and Chattanooga railroad and the Montgomery and Eufaula with
unpaid interest.[166]  The "scaled down" figure of $11,597,000 in-
cluded $5,300,000 worth of endorsements at $16,000-a-mile for the
Alabama and Chattanooga, $3,474,000 worth of unpaid interest,
and a $2,000,000 loan from the State to the Alabama and Chatta-
nooga.[167]

It has been pointed out above that Governor Lindsay, Democrat, had thrown the Alabama and Chattanooga into the hands
of the State in 1871.[168]  Extensive litigation had resulted, the
bondholders, most of whom were English, claiming that the State
had deliberately wrecked the road.[169]  Considering the fact that
Clanton, whom Lindsay appointed as one of the receivers, was
also Executive Chairman of the State Democratic Committee, as
well as a leading figure in the Louisville and Nashville affiliates,
the complaint had at least plausibility.  The Debt Commission compromised the claims of the English bondholders by (a) paying
them $1,000,000, thus disposing of the alleged nine million dollars
of indebtedness charged against the State in this connection,[170]
and (b) transferring to the owners of the railroads first mortgage
bonds on more than a half million acres of land, in the heart of
the rich mineral region, which later became the scene of extensive
industrialization in Alabama.[171]

The remaining items of endorsement, involving the Montgomery and Eufaula, the East Alabama and Cincinnati, the Selma
and Gulf, the Selma, Marion and Memphis, and the New Orleans
and Selma, were in litigation at the time of the Committee Report.  The Commission stated that the action of the court would
probably result in nullifying the purported liability of the State,
and that the interests of the bondholders would best be served by
"their acceptance of a transfer of the lien of the State created by
statute, and giving to the State a full discharge from those pretended claims against it."[172]  In other words, the "Debt" Commission itself denominated as "pretended claims" large amounts
which it afterward proudly claimed to have "settled," and which
historians have accepted as the "Alabama debt."

The final report of the Debt Commission stated that: "the volume of indebtedness of the State including State obligations will
be reduced to about $9,500,000 *exclusive of trust funds.*"[173]  Since
the Commission had begun its first report by stating that the

Debt amounted to more than $30,000,000, this immense reduction was hailed as a triumph of Democratic honesty over Republican extravagance. It has been so regarded by practically all historians. More interesting still, the myth of an immense debt of $30,000,000, crushing the people of Alabama for two generations, has persisted along with the paradoxical belief that the Democratic Party, immediately on its return to power, rescued the State from an immense load of debt. To all intents and purposes, the debt existed for purposes of Democratic propaganda in the election of 1874; it ceased to exist in 1875-1876 for the purpose of showing Democratic honesty; but it has always existed to show how great was the ruin wreaked upon the State by the Republican, Reconstruction government.

Fleming's conclusion to a discussion of the debt situation remains in evidence as *the* perfect document:

There was not an honest white person who lived in the State during Reconstruction, nor a man, woman or child, descended from such a person, who did not then suffer or does not still suffer from the direct results of the carpet-bag-financiering. Homes were sold or mortgaged; schools were closed, and children grew up in ignorance; the taxes for nearly twenty years were used to pay interest on the debt then piled up. Not until 1899 was there a one-mill school tax (until then the interest paid on the Reconstruction debt was larger than the school fund),[174] and not until 1891 was the State able to care for the disabled Confederate soldiers.[175]

Knight states that one of the reasons for the backwardness of Alabama in education was the fact that "upon Alabama was heaped a debt of $18,000,000."[176] Cubberly states, similarly, that the Reconstruction government caused backwardness in the schools through "wasting of resources."[177]

These statements may be seen to be exaggerated and incorrect, especially when they lay blame for immense "debts" upon "Negro," "Republican" regimes in Alabama. There was no "Negro" government; no such debts were left after Reconstruction; and what debts were created resulted from the activities of various capitalists working through both Republican and Democratic Party channels. The debt settlement of 1876 left the residual obligations of the State Government, including both bonded debt and the various trust funds for which the State was responsible, at approximately $12,000,000. It has been shown, above, that these same obligations in 1866, when the Reconstruction government took control, amounted approximately to $9,500,000.[178]

What is true is that in the negotiations leading up to the refunding of the debt, the holders of various State obligations drove a hard bargain with the Debt Commission regarding future tax policy. The Constitutional Convention of 1875 was in session while the debt negotiations were being held, and the articles adopted on taxation and finance were dictated by the arrangement with the bondholders. Considering their financial affiliations, it can be readily imagined that Governor Houston and his fellow-committeemen were all too eager to comply. On October 16, 1875, the Convention was reported on the verge of complete repudiation;[179] a combination of Black Belt Conservatives, not in the "ring," with hill country "radicals," were making trouble for the "debt" commission and its mission. The Committee on Taxation of the Convention reported that they had advised with General L. W. Lawler and Colonel T. B. Bethea, two of the three debt commissioners. These men were sanguine that the "debt" could be "reduced" from $30,000,000 to $10,000,000 through their negotiations, and advised the Convention to limit State tax levies to a maximum impost of .0075 (cents) on the dollar. If this were done, the debt commissioners believed that "Capital, seeing that our debt is reduced and our taxing power limited, will seek investment in our cheap lands, and population, always following capital, will fill up our waste places . . . . Capital (will see) that our property will enhance in value."[180]

In a letter written by the Debt Commissioners to the bondholders, dated December 30, 1875, it is revealed that the latter had made various suggestions regarding ways in which the expenses of the State could be cut, so as to allow payment of interest due on State obligations. One method suggested was to cut the size of appropriations made to the schools.[181] A second was to save money by cutting down the expenses of feeding prisoners.[182] In fact, the two fundamental anti-social weaknesses in Alabama's state government to comparatively modern times, i.e., poor schools and the convict lease system, were specifically suggested by the bondholders as possible sources of needed revenues.[183]

During debate, in the Alabama House, on a proposed tax bill, the estimate of the Debt Commission was taken as a guide for the House Committee. The Debt Commission estimated a total income of $1,066,000 would derive from a seven and one-half mill levy.  State expenses were estimated at:

| | |
|---|---:|
| State Government | $400,000 |
| Interest, Trust Fund | 100,000 |
| Appropriation, School | 100,000 |
| Interest, Univ. Fund | 24,000 |
| Interest, A. & M. Bonds | 20,280 |
| Interest, State Obligations | 154,000 |
| | |
| Total | $798,280 |

This would leave $267,720 to pay interest on the various debts.[184]  The refunding arrangement operated so that on several classes of obligations the interest began five years from the date of settlement, while on others interest was set at a low figure for the first few years.[185]  The only provision made for the support of schools was to provide (a) the "Interest on the Trust Fund"; this meant that the interest upon the fictitious literary fund which had been dissipated in the failure of the State bank twenty years before, would be appropriated by the Legislature yearly to the support of the schools; and, (b) a yearly appropriation of $100,-000 from the State Treasury.[186]  The Constitution imbedded in the organic law of the State a fixed state tax levy maximum.  This, together with the graduation of interest payments to increase over a period of years, and the Constitutional prohibition of local taxation for the schools, effectually estopped any major increases in appropriations for schools so long as the Constitution of 1875 remained in force.[187]

And so is completed an account of economic forces in Alabama Reconstruction.  How, finally, did they affect the schools?  The answer to that question is found in the account of educational legislation and accomplishment during the period that follows.

At the least we know that Reconstruction in Alabama began in a land laid waste by Civil War, and by the catastrophic reorganizations of the economic system made necessary by the abolition of slavery.

Even had the will to do so been present, it is obvious that the State did not have at hand the resources for supporting an effective school system.  The ruined agricultural structure—which was the only economic structure—could not have supported an expensive school system for either white or black children.

We are to trace, later, the course of political Reconstruction, and the course of educational legislation during the period. Economically Reconstruction in Alabama, from 1867-1875, was marked by the effort of local and Northern capitalists to bring about in a few years the industrialization of the State, and to control the form and direction of that industrialization. Given the War, given a disrupted economic system, given national economic and political struggles for power, the effort to industrialize Alabama in the period was no more heroic, and no less given to human foible and failure, than any other aspect of the period. If anything the efforts of industrialists and capitalists, of whatever faction, were as disruptive of an already ruined structure as the activities of humanitarians, politicians, Conservatives, Radicals, whites, or blacks.

How better it might have been, or how it might have been made better, is not our province here. If educational institutions require for their support wealth of the kind furnished by industry, we know that the economic penetration of Alabama by Capital in the period from 1867-1876 not only failed to furnish that necessary foundation, but, in fact, ended by protecting its failure through hamstringing educational progress.

What was done was to lay the foundations, in railroads, coal, and iron, of an industrial order in Alabama. Without moralizing we may conclude this story of aborted industrialization by saying that its failures were, after all, the inevitable failures accompanying the building of human institutions, and so were as necessary as they were inevitable.

## CHAPTER V

# THE COURSE OF POLITICAL RECONSTRUCTION, 1865-1875

## THE PROVISIONAL GOVERNMENT

On the 21st of June, 1865, Andrew Johnson appointed Lewis E. Parsons Provisional Governor of the State.[1]  A native of New York, Parsons had lived in Talladega County, in Alabama, since 1838.  Before the Civil War he had been elected to the Alabama legislature as an advocate of "internal improvements," and had been partially responsible for the first legislation in the State to subsidize, with State money, the building of railroads.[2]  In 1868 Parsons deserted the Conservatives and went over to the Republicans.[3]  In accord with the Johnson scheme of Reconstruction, Parsons set August 31, 1865, for an election for delegates to a Constitutional Convention, which was duly convened on September 12.[4] The convention numbered 99 members, of whom "about 63" were conservatives and the remainder "north Alabama anti-confederates."[5]

For our purposes, the negative activities of this Convention are as important as their constructive achievements.  The abolition of slavery was approved,[6] but neither Negro suffrage nor the education of Negro children received any favorable consideration.[7] It is also significant that representation in the General Assembly was placed on a basis of the white population, with thirty members of the Convention from the Black Belt voting against this provision.[8]

Under the new Constitution, Governor Robert M. Patton and the legislature elected under its provisions organized a government on December 13, 1865.  The Patton legislature did notable work in enacting what became known in the North as "Black Codes," for the regulation and control of Negro labor.[9]  On December 7,

1866, the Provisional General Assembly rejected the Fourteenth Amendment, and this denial of Negro suffrage was affirmed on two subsequent occasions when the question was submitted to the Alabama Legislature.[10]

On the 2nd of March, 1867, the First Reconstruction Act was passed over Johnson's veto, providing for the abolition of the provisional governments and for the division of the South into military districts for reconstructing the section in accord with the conditions set by Congress.[11] Alabama, with Georgia and Florida, was placed in the Third District, and General Pope appointed as military commander. He took office on April 1, 1867.[12] The Second Reconstruction Act was enacted on March 23, 1867. It provided for the registration of prospective voters ''without distinction as to race, creed, or color,'' and for the holding of a Constitutional Convention to establish a government under the conditions imposed by Congress. A prerequisite to registration was subscription to the ''Test Oath,'' a proviso aimed directly at individuals allied with Conservative Party interests in the South.[13]

The administration and results of the registration procedure are of interest. In later recriminations, partisans of the Conservative, Democratic regime claimed that the registration procedure was manipulated to exclude as many Southern whites as possible, and so to give a firm majority to the Republican side. More recent opinion agrees with Russ, who states that ''in short, it (i.e., Reconstruction) was a contest of Radicals *versus* Conservatives in most of the states, rather than one of whites *versus* blacks, since thousands of the whites cooperated with the Negroes.''[14] With a total registration of 165,813, an election was held from October 1 to 4 on the question of holding a Constitutional Convention, and for the election of delegates to such a Convention.[15] All of the figures dealing with registration are open to question as to their accuracy.[16] At the time of the election, it was reported that the total was racially divided between 61,295 whites and 104,518 blacks. Of 90,283 votes for a convention and for the delegates, 18,553 were cast by whites and 71,370 by blacks.[17] Of greatest importance to us here in interpreting the future course of Reconstruction is the aggregate of white votes cast for the Convention. They represented what was to become the pivotal margin in the elections of the next few years. In a state with a given majority of potential white voters the success of the Republican Party hinged on retaining the support of white voters.[18]

There was a total membership of one hundred persons in the Convention. The number of Negroes and "carpetbaggers" reported as members of the Convention varies with the sympathies of the individual describing it. One partisan Democratic source stated that there were twenty-six Negroes.[19] A Republican newspaper correspondent reported that there were seventeen.[20] A Republican member of the Convention, forty years after it was held, stated that the number of Negroes had been exaggerated, and that he could remember not more than twelve.[21] Fleming states that "the lists differ," but gives the names of twenty-two Negroes in one connection[22] while stating elsewhere that there "were eighteen blacks."[23] One name, that of J. H. Burdick, appears in Fleming's list both as a white "alien" "extremely radical,"[24] and as a Negro from Wilcox County.[25]

The Conservatives claimed there were only two Conservative whites in the Convention;[26] the Republicans, that there were four.[27] Fleming states that there were "thirty-seven or thirty-eight" carpetbaggers.[28] However, among those claimed to be Northern Carpetbaggers were "C. M. Cabot of (unknown)," "Joseph H. Davis of (unknown)," both of whom had been members of the Constitutional Convention of 1865 and had resided in Alabama before the War;[29] "Thomas Haughey of Scotland," "Whelen of Ireland," both of whom had lived in Alabama before the war.[30] With a maximum of twenty-one Negroes and thirty-eight *bona-fide* Carpetbaggers, there were at least forty-one "scalawags" in the Convention. The State was too young to give a "native" constitutional membership to any Party. Bromberg stated that the "native element" was in the majority in the Convention.[31]

A reading of the Convention proceedings, and of contemporary reports, reveals the strong influence exerted by John Keffer, the Pennsylvania agent for the Union League, who was Chairman of the Executive Committee of the Republican Party.[32] Keffer manoeuvered the working of the Convention so as to allay any racial difficulties that might arise between native whites and blacks, and to avoid radical economic measures distasteful to the economically Conservative North. The reporter for the *Chicago Tribune* wrote with horror of the action of a Negro delegate, Strother, who introduced a resolution instructing the Committee on Ordinances to report an ordinance to enable colored people to collect a fair equivalent for their labor from January 1st, 1863, to May 20th, 1865, from those who held them in slavery . . . . Its introduction is regarded as unfortunate. The object sought to be attained is impracticable, but it is feared it may be made out by demagogues to distract the Union Party. It is hoped that the Committee will allow it to go quietly to sleep.[33]

On the last legislative day of the Convention, Keffer presented a memorial to Congress in favor of an extension of the time for the completion of the railroads in the State. The memorial was defeated "by Bingham and the extremists, who desire Congress to revoke the grant of lands made to Southern railroads, and appropriate them to the education of the Freedmen."[34]

The minority of the Coburn Committee which investigated the State in 1875 complained that conditions in those Southern States where Government was in the hands of "tax-payers" was far better than in Alabama where "the political power of the State has been in the hands of the ignorant Negro and the non-tax-paying white man."[35]

Among the works of the Constitutional Convention, for our purposes the most important were those connected with the perpetuation of Republican Party rule in the State. Already the Republicans realized that their hold on power in the State depended on the precarious balancing of the North Alabama whites with Negroes, and the Convention compromised many racial issues accordingly.[36] Representation was fixed on the basis of population, a provision which, with Negroes voting, assured Republicans of power, but gave offense later to the white counties.[37] The Negroes were more moderate than the Carpetbaggers; under the leadership of Rapier, later Congressman, they voted with the Scalawags more frequently than with the Carpetbaggers.[38]

The Convention set February 1, 1868, as the date for the holding of an election on the adoption of the Constitution. The time for voting was later extended from the first to the fourth of February, and the registrars were instructed to keep the books open to that date. A full slate of officers was to be voted upon at the same time that the Constitution was submitted to the people.[39] The Conservatives adopted the strategy of defeating the Constitution by refraining from voting, since the Enabling Act passed by Congress provided that the Constitution should not be declared

in force until passed upon by a majority of registered voters.[40]
The vote on the adoption of the Constitution was 70,812 votes
for, and 1,005 votes against.   The Conservative strategy failed
when Congress admitted Alabama as a Reconstructed State in spite
of the fact that the original proviso had not been met.[41]

The new "Radical" General Assembly met on July 13, 1868,
and William H. Smith was inaugurated as Governor.[42]   A native
of Georgia, Smith had lived in Alabama since 1839.[43]   N. B.
Cloud, of Macon County, was elected Superintendent of Education.   Cloud had edited an agricultural magazine at Montgomery
before the War and was widely known as a scientific agricultural-
ist.[44]   The Senate was composed of thirty-two Radicals and one
Conservative.   Only one Negro was a member of the Senate.   In
the House there were ninety-seven Radicals, twenty-six of whom
were Negroes, and three Democratic Conservatives.[45]   The work
of this first Reconstruction legislature, "Radical" as it was called,
has been signalized principally by the measures taken to subsidize
railroad building in the State in the interest both of the legislators and of Alabama and Northern Capital.[46]   The Constitutional
Convention had made gestures toward measures designed to work
for the benefit of the poor white and Negro laborers.   Delegate
Strother, a Negro, had attempted to place a clause in the Constitution requiring payment of slaves for services rendered to masters.[47]   All church property used by Negroes was given to them.[48]
A tax exemption of $3,000 had received the support of the Scala-
wags and Negroes.[49]   The cotton tax was objected to by Negro
members on the ground that it worked a hardship on laborers.[50]
In general, however, one can look in vain for "radical" economic
measures in the Constitution of 1868, and the legislation of the
General Assembly of 1868 is even more barren of such items.[51]
George Spencer, a Carpetbagger, was elected by the Assembly to
Congress, where he became a notable associate of the high-tariff
interests of the Republican Party.   Spencer's re-election in 1873
was accomplished by the expenditure of immense sums admittedly
furnished by the National Republican Committee.[52]

## A Democratic Interlude

In 1870 the Democratic candidate for governor, Robert B.
Lindsay, a Scot by birth, defeated Smith by a vote of 76,977 to
75,568.   The Republicans carried eight white counties.[53]   Joseph

Hodgson, Conservation Democrat, was elected Superintendent of Education.[54]   The Republicans controlled the Senate, and the Democrats the House, during Lindsay's term.[55]   Behind the scenes of party politics appeared various alignments attached to financial interests which had acquired holdings in the State or in its railroad bonds.   General Clanton was the Chairman of the Democratic Executive Committee for the election of 1870, and is held up by Fleming as a paragon of pure political motives.[56] But Clanton was an attorney interested in the disposition of the railroad bonds involved in the election of 1870; and in 1871 he was killed in a brawl in Knoxville by one Nelson who was employed by the faction opposed to Clanton's.[57]   There is irony in Fleming's eulogy of Clanton: "He was killed in Knoxville by a hireling of one of the railroad companies which had looted the state treasury and which he was fighting."[58]   General Clanton was fighting "one railroad company," or rather, its financial backers; but he was also "fighting" in the interest of another set of financiers, as well as in the interest of the "state treasury."

THE REPUBLICANS REGAIN POWER—POLITICAL
STRATEGY DEFINED

In 1872 a Republican, David P. Lewis, defeated the Democratic candidate, Thomas H. Herndon, for the governorship, the vote being 81,371 for the Democratic candidate to 89,878 for the Republican candidate.[59]   After the victory of 1870, this was a shocking blow to the Democratic leaders.   The defeat was due in part, according to Fleming, to ". . . . the fact that some of the attorneys for the railroads were prominent Democrats who insisted upon the recognition of the fraudulent (i.e., railroad) bonds."[60] Besides illuminating the lines along which cleavages were drawn, the election of 1872 served to indicate to the Democrats that they had no chance to win another election in the State unless the support of the white voters of North Alabama was divorced from the Republican Party.   There were seventeen counties in Alabama where Negroes were less than 15 per cent of the total population in 1870.[61]   The Republican vote in these counties alone totalled 7,734 in 1872;[62] and this was more than the margin of victory upon which the Republican victory of 1872 turned.   It became plain that a Democratic victory in a "fair" election must transfer from five to ten thousand white votes in the State to the Democratic column.

The political situation between 1872-1874, culminating in a Democratic victory in the latter year, is highly illuminating with reference to the future history of the State. The Republican Party in Alabama, as we have seen, was "radical" only where the question of Negro suffrage was concerned. It had no "radical" economic program; on the contrary, it was a faction which was increasingly dominated by outside financial interests. Its constituency was made up of poor Negroes and poor whites; the first originally attracted by the prospect of free land, the second aligned against the planting class as of ante-bellum days. By 1872 there was no definte cleavage between the two parties on the basis of fundamental economic reform. What struggle there was came from opposed factions, one within the Democratic, the other within the Republican Party, aligned with different financial houses.

The "poor whites" were the balance of power, the prize sought after by campaign managers in such states as Alabama. Nordhoff said of politics in North Carolina:

The Republican Party . . . . is composed of the great body of the Negroes, and of a large mass of the poor whites in the western or mountain, districts. But these small white farmers dislike the Negro, whom they know little about, and are easily alarmed at the thought of social equality with them. The Democratic politicians very naturally worked upon their fears on this point, and thus they found their best argument put into their hands by those Republican leaders in the North who insisted upon this measure (the Civil Rights Bill).[63]

Fleming adds that "conditions were similar in Alabama." It has been a part of the tradition to emphasize the hatred of the poor white for the Negro: if Hinton Helper, in his *Impending Crisis*,[64] became the symbol of "the non-slaveholding whites of the South," so far as class hatreds were concerned, his later and less known book, *Nojoque*,[65] written "to write the Negro out of America," might well symbolize this hatred. Politics being the institution that it has always been, it is clear that the Democratic politicians would have been tempted to create racial hatred between poor whites and Negroes in Alabama, if it did not already exist. Their strategy is important for this narrative inasmuch as attitudes antipathetical to the Negro, strengthened or created by political campaigns, persisted far after the campaign itself had been forgotten.

## THE ELECTION OF 1874

In Alabama the Democratic strategy consisted in using the devices noted by Nordhoff. The Civil Rights Bill furnished the issue and "mixed schools," which had been soft-pedalled by the Republicans in Alabama as far back as the Constitutional Convention of 1867, were suspended threateningly over the heads of white Republicans in North Alabama counties.[66]  Other tactics were the hiring of Negroes to "arouse race prejudice" by applying at hotels for admission, and to make similar insistence on the enforcement of the law during the next year's canvass.[67]

The Republicans replied by stating that the Democrats were the "enemy of the public school system."[68]  The Democratic Party platform in 1870 had been innocent of any advocacy of public schools; the Republican claim to being the sole defender of the system forced the Democrats to pledge themselves to the continuation of the system.[69]  Further, the Democrats appealed to Negro voters in Black Belt counties while crying "white supremacy" in Northern white counties.  The house-servant of Governor Houston was employed by the Democratic State Committee to electioneer for his master.[70]  While the Democrats were accusing the Republicans of advocating "social equality," a Negro Democrat, H. A. Campbell, testified that he had ridden and eaten with the Democratic leaders while canvassing for the party.[71]  The Democrats accused the Republicans of buying Negro votes with a distribution of Government bacon; the Democrats gave elaborate suppers to Negroes who might favor their cause.[72]

Where persuasion seemed inadvisable the Democrats resorted to admitted coercion, using both the boycott and open force.[73]  In turn the Democrats accused the Republicans of intimidating Negro voters favorable to the Democratic cause in counties under Republican control.[74]

We have no necessity to establish here a case for either of the two contending political parties.  It is highly probable that both were guilty of all the malpractices charged.  What is important is that this political ferment illuminates basic attitudes; and was responsible for strengthening existing prejudices and, even, in creating others.

If the race issue was paramount in the appeal of the Conservative Democrats to white voters of North Alabama, the issue of economy and extravagance was barely secondary, and must have had great weight for persons of property aghast at taxes levied by the Republicans.  Two classes of persons were interested in lower taxes and smaller expenditures; first, the land-owners, the planters; and second, those financial interests which, if assured of recogniton of their securities by Alabama in lieu of opposing financial powers, would be in favor of safeguarding the budget of the State in order to protect what Fleming calls "the innocent bondholders."[75]

The seventh "plank" of the Democratic Party Platform of 1874 pledged the party "to reduce every public expenditure and to abolish and dispense with every office demanded by an economical admnistration of the government."[76]  The eighth and final "plank" pledged that "every dollar justly owing by the State shall be faithfuly and fully paid."  But, "at the same time it is principally determined that the welfare of the people of the State and the interests of its *honest* creditors shall not be put in jeopardy by the payment of unlawful or fraudulent claims of any kind."[77]

Henry Clews said afterward that he had been one of the "honest creditors";[78] but the election of 1874 was to define who were "honest" and who were "fraudulent" among the claimants. It is not strange, as Fleming reports, that "The campaign fund was the largest in the history of the State; . . . . assistance also came from Northern Democrats, and Northern capitalists who had investments in the South or who owned part of the legal bonds of the State."[79]

To add to Democratic prospects, the Republicans were hopelessly split.  In some sections the antagonism between factions split the party into "lily-white" and "black and tan" divisions;[80] in others, the split was between the "ins" and the "outs."[81]

The result was almost a foregone conclusion; Fleming reports, as an example of the fine organization of the Democrats in one county, that a pre-election forecast of votes in prospect for the Party was but two votes less than the number actually cast.[82] What with manipulation performed by both parties, the total summaries may or may not represent the number of votes actually cast.  The Democratic vote, electing George Houston at the head

of a victorious ticket, was 107,118; the Republican vote, 93,928.[83]
In the seventeen "white counties" mentioned above, the 1872
Democratic vote of 13,358 grew, by 1874, to 22,473; the Republican
vote only from 7,734 to 7,949.[84]

### THE POLITICAL AFTERMATH OF RECONSTRUCTION

As a result of the election of 1874, the Democrats controlled
all State administrative offices, and both houses of the General
Assembly.[85]  Early in March, 1875, the new legislature submitted
the question of a new Constitution to the people.  The question
carried, and the Constitutional Convention of 1875 met on September 6 for the purpose of carrying out the "mandate of the
people" as shown in the election of the previous year.[86]  In the
"abolition of unnecessary offices," and in the provision of opportunities for reduction of expenditures, the Convention majority
rigidly carried into effect the mandate of those responsible for its
election.[87]  The Republican cause, as a partisan power, was dead.

It is not difficult to find reasons for the failure of the Republican Party in the State.  It was an irreconcilable contradiction
founded on the promise of an economic revolution for the former
non-slaveholding whites and the emancipated Negroes.  It could
fulfill its revolutionary promise for neither of these two groups.
No sooner did another faction of the new northern industrialism
come to terms with the archaic planting aristocracy than the Republican Party collapsed.  With no genuine economic program in
accord with the natural interests of its two diverse supporters, the
Party fell a victim to its own internal corruption, contradictions,
and the alienation of white voters from its ranks resulting from
an appeal to race prejudices.

## Chapter VI

# THE BEGINNING OF AN EDUCATIONAL SYSTEM, 1860-1868

## Sectionalism and the Ante-bellum System

From its beginning public education in Alabama was involved in the sectional conflict that rose from the division of the white population into slaveholders and non-slaveholders, and the geographic distribution of the plantation system. In 1818 Congress devoted the 16th Section in the Alabama territory to school purposes.[1] With cotton cultivation as the economic basis of life, only those lands in rich cotton-producing areas were of much value, and, on sale or lease, realized any considerable income to the fortunate townships in which they were located.

The Enabling Act of March 2, 1819, by which Alabama was admitted as a State, confirmed this action.[2] The first educational legislation in Alabama providing for the establishment of a public school system was enacted in 1826.[3] Dealing particularly with Mobile County, the bill gave that local unit the right to establish a Board of Commissioners for the Public Schools; and endowed the Board with the right to raise funds from the proceeds of land grant sales, fines, and penalties, and "25 per cent of the 'ordinary' county tax."[4] This example was not followed elsewhere in the State. The Mobile public school funds were used principally to subsidize private schools.[5] Legislation of 1832 prohibiting the education of Negroes in the State resulted in a protest from Mobile County, indicating that among the schools aided there were several for the free "Negro creoles" of that community.[6] In 1852 an expenditure of $5,550 in aid of certain schools of Mobile County, specified as Methodist, Bethel, Catholic, and Trinity schools, included an additional item of $1,350 for "various other schools."[7] It is possible that the "Negro creoles" may have been schooled in these "various other schools," although current tradition in Mobile County has it that Negro creoles attended Catholic schools with white children until comparatively recent years.[8] The census of 1860, in spite of existing statutory prohibitions upon the instruction of Negroes, returned 114 "free colored" children in the city of Mobile as among those attending school.[9] The editor of a Reconstruction newspaper, Philip Joseph, was described as of "the creole class," "educated at a public school before the war, at the expense of the people of Mobile, and all the education he has is at their expense."[10]

The money derived from the distribution of the United States Surplus Fund in Alabama was dedicated to the schools, but invested in the State Bank. The Bank was directed to pay, after 1839, $150,000 annually to the schools.[11] The failure of the Bank, in 1843, left the State with a "fictitious" school fund which thereafter was to be paid actually from direct taxation and general state funds, on the theory that the State was paying the interest on the Educational Fund.[12]

It was not until 1853-1854 that the General Assembly of Alabama attempted to set up a state-wide public school system. The question of sectional rivalry immediately hampered the drafting of an effective law. The Black Belt representatives objected to a State distributive fund because their 16th Section income was already pledged, largely, to the support of private academies and other institutions through the section; and the assessment of a State Fund would necessitate pooling this income for distribution to all of the white children in the State.[13] The idea of an extra state appropriation was clearly recognized, and actually described as an "equalizing" fund thus early in Alabama's educational history. An elaborate formula for equalizing educational opportunity, through the distribution of a Fund, was adopted by the Assembly of 1853-1854. The township was the unit; and the State Superintendent was required, first, to estimate how much each township would realize from the 16th Section Fund. The appropriated educational fund was then to be apportioned so that the smallest amount received by any township through the 16th Section Fund was to be supplemented from the State Appropriation to make each Township share equally in educational benefits. The Superintendent was given wide discretion, as though the General Assembly realized how cumbersome was this legislation, to follow "this, or any other process which will attain the end of equalizing, as far as the residue of the educational fund will go, the inequalities of distribution produced by the 16th section fund ....."[14]

The next legislature clarified the law, and directed the Superintendent to pay to each township of the State a sum to be ascertained by multiplying one dollar and fifty cents by the number of children in such township within the educational age, and deducting from the result, the sum annually received by such township from the sale or lease of its 16th section.[15] There continued a bitter opposition to the law, manifested by the representatives of the Black Belt. In a protest made by the Senate in 1858, it was

.... demanded first that the method of apportioning the sixteenth section fund be changed. They demanded that the interest on the sixteenth section certificates be increased from 6 per cent to 8 per cent, and, although these certificates represented no real value, they insisted that this interest, raised by a general tax on all the counties, should be paid first of all out of the public taxes, and that after this was paid the remaining sum available for educational purposes should be distributed to all the counties "according to the number of children within the educational age within each county of the State."

.... It is the old story of the rich county, disliking to aid the educational work of the poor county. In their protest a table is given where it is shown that while 15 of the poorer counties paid $51,-983.92 in taxes and received $7,598.51 from the sixteenth section funds, they also received in 1856 for education in additon to the above, $61,281.41 from the State. On the other hand, while 15 of the wealthier counties paid the same year $394,262.74 in taxes and received $52,172.27 from sixteenth section funds, they were allowed from the general State tax only $45,112.18 in addition for schools.[16]

The method of apportionment remained the same, however, through the Civil War. But the "slaveholding element" continued to believe that public schools in Alabama were for "the laboring classes";[17] and the schools remained on a semi-subscription basis. In 1857 total expenditures of $564,210 were reported; "more than one-half of the cost of the schools was paid by the parents of the pupils attending the schools."[18]

### THE PROVISIONAL GOVERNMENT AND THE PUBLIC EDUCATION OF NEGROES—1865-1868

Weeks states that the period of the Provisional Government "was barren of educational results," so far as State action was concerned.[19] Knight, however, says the Alabama Provisional Assembly provided for an educational system, including Negroes, through legislation which

. . . . in February, 1867, created a creditable public school system open to every child between the ages of six and twenty years. School officers were appointed, and the schools were rapidly being brought into working order in a large part of the State when congressional reconstruction began.[20]

Fleming states that the Negro children were provided for by the Provisional legislature before the Reconstructionists took office:

the state schools . . . . largely outnumbered the Bureau schools.[21] The provisional government adopted the ante-bellum public school system and put it into operation. . . . The schools were open to both races, from six to twenty years of age, separate schools being provided for the blacks.[22] . . . The negro has no opportunities now that were not freely offered in 1865-1866, and the school system is not a product of Reconstruction, but came near being destroyed by it.[23]

The question is of some importance in defining the social attitudes involved in the later history of efforts to educate Negroes; for, if the Conservatives, as Fleming stated, offered educational opportunities freely to Negro children in 1865-1866, the later revulsion against schools for Negroes can be explained only as an outcome of Reconstruction.

The Constitution of 1819 had not mentioned race in the Article dealing with education, and none of the laws thereafter referred to Negro children in the sections defining those acceptable as students in the public schools.[24] The Constitution enacted in 1865 made but a slight change in the wording of that of 1819:

| 1819 | 1865 |
|---|---|
| Schools, and the means of education, shall forever be encouraged in this State; and the general assembly shall take measures to preserve, from unnecessary waste or damage such (school) lands. . . .[25] | The General Assembly shall, from time to time, enact necessary and proper laws for the encouragement of schools and the means of education; shall take proper measures to preserve from waste or damage such (school) lands. . . .[26] |

The Educational Bill of 1855-1856 read:

Article V, Section 2: Be it further enacted, that every child between the ages of six and twenty-one years shall be entitled to admission into any instruction in any of the free public schools in the township in which he or she resides, or to any school in any adjacent township. . . .[27]

When the Provisional General Assembly re-enacted the wording of the ante-bellum law, the use of the phrase "every child" must have been as inapplicable to Negro children then as before the War; and it is plain that the indiscriminate admittance of Negro children to the "free public schools" would have been unthinkable to the legislators of 1865-1866, else they would have hedged about the latter portion of the law with provisions for separate schools. But no such provision can be found in the Acts of these years. Furthermore, Superintendent Hodgson, Democrat, elected in 1870, criticised the educational legislation of the preceding Republican General Assembly for passing a bill making retroactive to July 13, 1868, certain claims of teachers "without distinction on account of race or color."[28] Hodgson added:

There were no colored teachers of State schools before July (1868). . . . It is not possible that before the inauguration of the present Constitution there were any colored public schools, or colored public school teachers, the colored people not being embraced in the school system.[29]

On the basis of this evidence it seems hardly possible to believe that the members of the Provisional General Assembly made any provision for the education of Negro children in Alabama prior to the advent of the Reconstruction Government, so far as public, tax-supported free schools were concerned.

There is a hint in the literature, however, that some provision was made for the welfare of Negro children; and this provision, if it was actually made as appears, is helpful in interpreting later Conservative attitudes toward the education of Negroes. A Mr. Mordecai Mobley, a witness before the Joint Committee on Reconstruction in 1866, reported a conversation with a member of the General Assembly in Montgomery.

Then we talked about our political problems. . . . "Now (he said) here is this great mass of negroes thrown upon us, and we must legislate in regard to them. And my view is . . . . that the best method under all the circumstances is this; now, there are three classes of people for whom I propose to legislate. I propose first to take the able-bodied class, and apply to them a vagrant law making no distinction between white and black. . . . Then I propose to take hold of the class of minors with an apprentice law, and provide that the masters shall educate these so as to read and write, and when they are of age give them a good suit of clothes, a horse and saddle and bridle, or a hundred dollars in money."[30]

An apprentice law was passed by the Provisional Assembly. It provided for the apprenticing

. . . . of all minors under the age of eighteen years . . . . who are orphans without visible means of support, or whose parents have not the means, or who, refuse to provide for and support said minors . . . . to some suitable and competent persons. . . .

Provided, if the said minor be the child of a freedman, the former owner of said minor shall have the preference . . . . . . . . . . . Section 2 . . . the said . . . master or mistress . . . shall furnish said minor with sufficient food and clothing, to treat said minor humanely, furnish medical attention in case of sickness, teach or cause to be taught him or her to read or write, if under fifteen years old. . . .[31]

Whether this law expresses the full intent of the members of the Provisional General Assembly regarding the education of Negro children or not, it is the only such reference in the public legislation of the period.

EARLY POST-WAR ATTITUDES TOWARD THE EDUCATION OF NEGROES

The supporters of the institution of chattel slavery in Alabama looked with favor on the religious education of Negroes, while frowning upon the instruction of the slave in formal subjects of instruction. In another connection reference is made to the content of education as sponsored by Conservatives for Negroes in the period from 1865-1868.[32]

There are several recorded instances of proposals made by prominent Conservatives to establish schools for Negroes by Southerners, but these efforts seldom appear to have gone beyond editorials, resolutions, and speech-making in favor of the general proposition. In 1865, "In Northern Alabama there are no old Alabamians who give it any encouragement at all. The educational interests are all in the hands of Northern societies."[33] In the neighborhood of Montgomery, there was no inclination among the white people to educate the Negro; "In fact, there is not much inclination to educate the whites who need it as much as the negroes."[34] One witness, testifying before the Joint Committee on

Reconstruction, believed the whites were utterly opposed to the education of the Negro, because "the negro would not work as well."[35] In Mobile, Dr. Josiah C. Nott was approached by General O. O. Howard, of the Freedmen's Bureau, for the use of the Medical School Building for a colored school. "I would rather see it burn down first," Dr. Nott was reported to have answered.[36]

Fleming classified as a favorable attitude toward the education of Negroes the action of the Conservative Party, meeting in Montgomery in 1867, in expressing the sentiment that "It is our earnest aim and purpose . . . . to instruct and aid in instructing them in a proper understanding of all their duties to themselves, to society, and to the country."[37] General Clanton and General Gordon advocated the education of Negroes;[38] and at Marion, Jabez L. M. Curry organized a mass meeting to forward the cause.[39] The Selma *Times* published an "appeal," which received wide circulation in the Conservative Press. It purported to come from the "leading Negroes of Selma." This remarkable document was addressed to

Dear friends and former masters:

We know there is a large number of widows and crippled men, who are well educated, and have no employment by which to make a living. These persons we would be pleased to see taking an interest in teaching our children, and training them up in the way they should go. We are greatly in want of schools, and to persons who will establish them, we will guarantee our undivided support. Our own people are the proper ones to teach us, and we sincerely wish them to do it. . . . And why should it be considered a disgrace now to make a living at this business in the South? We make our living out of the people here, and therefore we think it our duty to spend our money with those who have sustained and taken care of us.

The United States Government and your State Convention gave us our freedom, and we prefer you to any others to have the money derived from our daily labor for teaching our children. If you all stand back, strangers will come in and take the money from under your hands and carry it away to build up their own country. They are not ashamed to make money from any class of men.

In Mobile the colored schools are taught by strangers, and they are making large sums of money. In that city alone, not less than 1200 or 1300 colored children are at school, and all of them pay, with the exception of about ten or twelve. . . .[40]

The language of the "answer" to the "appeal" is in phrases
strikingly parallel to the letter of the "leading Negroes." The
editor said that the situation demanded that the Negroes "be
taught at least to read and write"; he even went so far as to say
that not only should opportunities for this education be provided, but that the white people "should compel them to avail
themselves of the proffered boon."[41]

General Clanton used the same arguments in advocating the
education of Negroes.[42] The Bishops of the Methodist Episcopal
Church said:

Under the Divine Blessing, our Church has done a great work for
this people. . . . It has accomplished more; it has materially contributed to their subordination and inoffensive behaviour through
the late defenseless and exciting times, when prophecies were confident and opportunities frequent for domestic insurrection.[43]

The Bishops concluded by urging the duty of continuing "religious education" of the Negroes. "Let special attention be given
to Sunday Schools among the colored people."[44] A Baptist organ
stated that "A large number of intelligent and pious missionaries
have been employed (1866) to preach to the freedmen of the
South . . . . and this is what they need—good, sound, theological
instruction."[45]

The Bethel, Alabama, Baptist Association was of the opinion
"that a large majority of the colored people do not really desire
the instruction of any white man."[46] Yet the Association was all
the more convinced that "the opposition or indisposition to receiving such instruction is a manifestation of their great need for
such instruction."[47] The message closed on a note of sober dedication to the gloomy inevitable:

They are a lamentably ignorant people—so ignorant indeed as
not even to know the value of proper instruction.
 . . . . We are of the opinion that our first duty is to give religious
instruction to the ignorant and destitute at our doors and in our
employ, and among whom we and our children are doomed to
live and die.[48]

As the result of Curry's mass-meeting a school for Negro children was established at Marion by Conservatives.[49] General Clanton was one of the many leading white people at Montgomery who
contributed money to establish a Negro school.[50] Buckley, Bureau
Agent, reported that he was assisted in teaching a Sunday-school

class of five hundred pupils by six young white men from a leading Baptist Church.[51] If the aim of education favored by the Conservatives was religious, their opponents, the Northern missionaries, set forth the same principle.[52]

## THE FREEDMEN'S BUREAU AND THE MISSION SOCIETIES

By the time the State of Alabama, under the Reconstruction Constitution of 1868, actually began public education for Negro children, many agencies had already made extensive efforts in this direction. Various mission associations of Northern churches had interested themselves in the welfare of the slaves and Freedmen whose life was unsettled by the struggle.[53] Frequent conflicts led to efforts to obtain unified activity.[54] In 1862 General Grant appointed Colonel John Eaton as Superintendent of the Freedmen in the West. His function was the consolidation and regulation of military and religious efforts to alleviate the condition of the Freedmen and the Refugees.[55]

In Alabama the first school for Negroes established under the conjoint auspices of a mission board and the Army was at Huntsville, in 1863, when that Tennessee Valley city fell into the hands of the Federal Army.[56] Chaplain W. G. Kephart wrote on May 9, 1864: "By the voluntary aid of chaplains, soldiers, and the Christian Commission, both a day and Sabbath school have been kept up during the winter, and I have been pleased to see the progress they have made."[57] Schools were also maintained at Stevenson and at other depots of the Federal Army in North Alabama within the area of the Chattanooga occupation.[58]

With the provision by Congress of funds for the educational work of the Freedmen's Bureau, this agency was able to lend resources to the extension of educational opportunities for Negro children in Alabama.[59] In most instances the Freedmen's Bureau assumed the responsibility of providing buildings in which schools could be conducted, while the mission societies selected and paid the teachers.[60] As of January 1, 1866, two schools aided by the Freedmen's Bureau were reported for Negro children in Southern Alabama. One was located at Mobile, one at Montgomery, and one at each of three North Alabama towns: Huntsville, Stevenson, and Athens.[61] These schools were reported to have fifteen teachers with 817 students.[62]

These first schools were supported, at least in part, by the payment of tuition fees. At Mobile the tuition was from twenty-five cents to one dollar and twenty-five cents monthly.[63] Alvord in his third report stated that Negro teachers were favored because they could easily make the schools self-supporting.[64] The report of July 1, 1866, showed 479 tuition-paying pupils out of a total enrollment of 3,338.[65]

Fleming[66] has referred to the difficulty of obtaining an exact idea of the extent of the work of the Freedmen's Bureau because of conflicting reports. The following summary from Alvord's successive reports may be as near accuracy as it is possible to come. Fluctuations in enrollment, and in other figures given here must be laid to inaccuracies in the reporting system then in vogue. On January 1, 1866, there were fifteen teachers and 817 students; on July 1, 1866, thirty-one teachers and 3,338 students; on January 1, 1867, sixty-nine teachers and 3,639 students; on June 30, 1867, students numbered 9,799; on January 1, 1868, 4,435; on January 1, 1869, 3,330; on July 1, 1869, 5,131; on July 1, 1870, 2,110.[67]

The missionary body which figured most largely in the early education of Negroes in Alabama was the American Missionary Association, the mission enterprise of the Congregational Church.[68] Before the Civil War the American Missionary Association was active in antislavery pamphleteering, and aided in the establishment of two schools, one at Oberlin, Ohio, the other at Berea, Kentucky, which violated all of the current racial orthodoxies by admitting Negroes as students.[69] While elsewhere in the South the Freedmen's Aid Society of the Methodist Episcopal Church, the American Baptist Home Mission Society, and the Presbyterians, Friends, and other denominations were active,[70] the work in Alabama was almost monopolized by the American Missionary Association. The Methodist Episcopal Church was active in North Alabama, but its educational activities were principally among white persons in the hill counties.[71]

In May, 1866, twenty-eight teachers were reported in Alabama under the auspices of various Freedmen's Aid societies, most of the support coming from the Congregational Church.[72] These teachers were located at Athens, Huntsville, Montgomery, Mobile, Selma, Stevenson, and Talladega. Night schools at Huntsville, Mobile, Montgomery, Demopolis, Greenville, Talladega, Gainesville, and Selma in August of 1866 reported an enrollment

of 2,606 students.[73] The teachers were supported by the Cleveland
and Chicago Branches of the American Missionary Association,
and the report was made to Chaplain Buckley, of the Freedmen's Bureau.[74]

In 1867 thirty-four teachers were listed in Alabama under
the support of the American Missionary Association.[75] They were
located at Valhermosa Springs, Montgomery, Selma, Girard, Athens, Demopolis, Marion, Mobile, and Talladega. The largest centers were at Mobile, with nine teachers; Marion, with four; and
Montgomery, with ten.[76] The school at Talladega was made a
Normal School for the training of teachers in 1867.[77]

From an inspection of these data it is evident that in Alabama the American Missionary Association was the dominant
church body through which the Freedmen's Bureau worked. The
charges of fraud against the educational work of the Freedmen's
Bureau in Alabama revolved around the relations of that Federal
Agency with the American Missionary Association. The following
sums were listed as having been paid to the American Missionary
Association by the Bureau from 1867 through 1869:[78]

| | |
|---|---:|
| December, 1867 | $4,000.00 |
| February, 1868 | 25.41 |
| October, 1868 | 584.85 |
| January, 1869 | 218.25 |
| April, 1869 | 683.53 |
| May, 1869 | 1,397.49 |
| June, 1869 | 95.87 |
| July, 1869 | 527.00 |
| August, 1869 | 857.61 |
| September, 1869 | 3,049.50 |
| November, 1869 | 3,469.50 |
| December, 1869 | 2,083.78 |

In addition, the sum of $20,000 was credited to the American
Missionary Association during this period on account of a building
located at Talladega, purchased by the Freedmen's Bureau and
donated to the American Missionary Association.

In early reporting of the combined American Missionary Association—Freedmen's Bureau educational ventures, the custom
was followed of counting each class maintained by a separate
teacher as a "school."[79] Seven "schools" were reported in existence in Montgomery, six of them under the operation of the
American Missionary Association. In Mobile this practice even-

tually led to the accusations of fraud against the principal of the "Blue College," a large school maintained by the American Missionary Association through the Bureau.[80] It was alleged that this man had reported himself principal of several "schools" and collected a salary as principal from each separately reported school.[81] In the first six months of 1867, the Bureau reported educational expenditures in Alabama of $28,685, divided between asylums, construction and rental of school buildings, and transportation of teachers.[82]

## The Mobile System: Example of Evolution of State Schools Independent of Bureau Schools

The city of Mobile set the example in ante-bellum times for the rest of the State in developing a public educational system. In the period immediately after the War a system of schools, supported partly by the city, preceded the development of a general State system for Negroes. The American Missionary Association, co-operating with the Freedmen's Bureau, had established a school for Negroes in Mobile as early as 1865.[83] On January 1, 1867, Chaplain Buckley reported to Alvord that a bill was pending in the Alabama legislature (provisional) by which "The Board of Directors of each township in the State shall establish separate schools for the education of negro and mulatto children, wherever as many as thirty pupils, in sufficient proximity for school purposes, claim the privilege of public school instruction, and the fund for that purpose is sufficient to support a school for four months in the year."[84]

Perhaps under the stimulation of this proposed law, the Negroes[85] of Mobile held a mass-meeting on May 2, 1867, in which a demand was made upon the School Commissioners for the extension of the system for Negro children.[86] In response to this meeting, the Commissioners appointed a Committee ". . . . to inquire whether our system of public instruction can be extended to colored children in Mobile, and, if so, to report in what manner; and by what means, such instruction can be most effectually accomplished."[87] In August, 1867, the Committee reported some correspondence with the American Missionary Association, which was fruitless. In the same month the Committee reported the formulation of a plan to establish three Negro schools in the city. Two schools were reported to have been opened for Negroes on

November 11, 1867.[88] The School Board approached the American Missionary Association at the same time with a proposition that the so-called "Blue College" building, formerly used in antebellum days as a medical college of the University of Alabama, be taken over by the Board, with the privilege of appointing the teachers and taking charge of the general administration. This the American Missionary Association declined to do.[89] The School Board evidently aimed to educate the Negroes on its own terms, and planned to substitute "native" teachers for the Northern teachers who had been imported by the Association. A member of the School Board testified before the Coburn Committee in 1875 that his niece had taught a Negro school in Mobile in 1867-1868.[90]

The schools supported by the Board were not, in 1867-1868, "free schools"; apparently the Board subsidized schools with small amounts which were supplemented by tuition charges. Barnas Sears reported in 1868 that he had promised $2,000 Peabody aid to the Mobile schools if they were made "free"; a tuition charge of $10 a year was then being made in the schools.[91] A resolution of the Board on January 10, 1868, directed its Secretary to "ascertain the amount of school taxes paid by the colored people, and to appropriate the entire amount, when ascertained, to the support of schools for colored children."[92] This acceptance of the responsibility of the State to support schools for Negroes only in so far as the Negroes themselves paid taxes had many precedents in the early evolution of tax-supported schools for Negroes in the District of Columbia and in the border states.[93]

There is a political background to the action of the Mobile City Board of School Commissioners which sheds light upon their partial acceptance of the principle of educating Negroes before the coming to power of the Reconstruction Government. The Mayor of the City was displaced by the Federal authorities early in 1867.[94] The old school board never co-operated with either the Freedmen's Bureau or the American Missionary Association before 1869, when the Negro school system was finally established. When a Reconstruction Government took charge of the State in 1868, the struggle for control of the Mobile Schools resulted finally in the ousting of the old school board by the State regime, under N. B. Cloud.[95] The State Board of Education, in displacing the "native" school board, gained complete control of the Mobile Schools and appointed as Superintendent the Freedmen's Bureau and American Missionary Association Agent, a member of the State School Board with whom the City Board had been at odds.[96] In 1869 Barnas Sears reported that the Mobile schools were free to Negroes, although tuition was still charged in the white schools.[97]

What the Mobile board would have done for the education of Negroes without the presence of the American Missionary Association must remain a matter of speculation. With the Association present as a competing and stimulating agent, the Board was led successively toward the development of a system of free schools for Negroes, by which the race might be kept under the patronage and influence of the native, Conservative element.

CHAPTER VII

# PUBLIC EDUCATION OF NEGROES DURING RECONSTRUCTION

## THE EDUCATIONAL WORK OF THE CONVENTION OF 1867

Seven members formed the Committee on Education and the School Fund of the Convention.[1] Gustavus Horton, of Mobile, was the chairman. Born in Boston, and educated at George Emerson's "English Classical School," he had located in Mobile in 1835 as a cotton broker. "He was one of the organizers of the public schools of Mobile and was the first president of the Board of School Commissioners. In 1867 he was mayor of Mobile. . . . A Jackson Democrat before the War, he was a Republican afterward."[2]

John Silsby is reported by Fleming as being from Massachusetts,[3] and elsewhere as "an Iowa man."[4] He had been a missionary to Siam under the auspices of the American Missionary Association, but returned to America in 1854.[5] On his return to America a letter appeared in the *Independent* accusing him of having employed slave labor while resident in Siam.[6] The circumstances of his return are explained as due to poor health, but it is probable that the slave charge resulted in his recall. His whereabouts from 1854-1858 are uncertain; in the latter year he appears as a home missionary of the Congregational Church in Wisconsin.[7] Silsby may have been in Iowa during the Convention of 1857. Skaggs, a populist leader of the next generation, says that Silsby was one of the "Good Carpetbaggers."[8] In 1875 he was an assistant professor in a "State Normal School and University for the Colored Race" established at Marion in 1873 by the Board of Education.[9] Benjamin Yordy was an official of the Freedmen's Bureau of unknown origin.[10] Peyton Finley, a Negro, "formerly doorkeeper of the House,"[11] is described by Fleming as "of no education and no ability, but he was a sensible Negro and was an improvement on the white men of the preceding Board."[12] C. W. Buckley, later Congressman, was born in New York in 1835. He moved with his family to Freeport, Illinois, in 1846; graduated at Beloit, with highest honors in 1860, and from the Union Theological Seminary in 1863. He was a Chaplain with the rank of Captain in a Negro regiment, and after the War served for two years as Superintendent of Education of the Freedmen's Bureau in Alabama.[13] In an autobiographical sketch Buckley claimed that "his efforts were especially directed to the work of framing into the Constitution that outline of a free public school system which, in its subsequent development, has brought the opportunities of a good common school education within the reach of every child in the State, without distinction of race, color, or previous condition."[14] Buckley was a prominent bank director, and the organizer of several coal and iron companies in the vicinity of Birmingham, after his retirement from Congress.[15]

B. W. Norris was born at Watertown, Maine, in 1819. He was a graduate of Watertown College (later Colby) and became a merchant. He was an early member of the Free Soil Party, and active in Maine politics before the War. All of his bills in Congress, where he served from Alabama in 1867-1869, had to do with land grants to railroad companies in Alabama.[16]

Littleberry Strange of Macon County was a white man, but there is no other record of him in the literature.[17] He was probably a "Scalawag"; his name does not occur in Fleming's list of Northern Carpetbaggers.[18]

Of the debates within the Committee we have no record. The Report of the Committee was not received until the final day of the Convention, and was disposed of in one afternoon of December 5, 1867, along with numerous other measures dealing with the adjournment of the Convention.[19]

The Article on Education, which was to be XI of the final document, was in fourteen sections, and was adopted as presented. It is instructive to note that the Article was taken almost directly from the Article on Education adopted by the Iowa Constitutional Convention of 1857,[20] with certain exceptions as to the power of the Board which were modified in the Iowa Convention when the original Report of the Iowa Committee was first presented.[21] Since the provisions of the Constitution of 1868 were to play so important a part in the future agitation over the deficiencies of Reconstruction plans, the Iowa document and the Alabama article are reproduced here in full.

## THE IOWA CONSTITUTION OF 1857

### ARTICLES ON EDUCATION[22]

Section 1. The educational interest of the State, including common schools and other educational institutions, shall consist of the Lieutenant-Governor, who shall be the presiding officer of the Board, elected from each judicial district in the State.

Section 2. No person shall be eligible as a member of said Board who shall not have attained the age of twenty-five years, and shall have been one year a citizen of the State.[24]

Section 3. One member of said Board shall be chosen by the qualified electors of each district, and shall hold the office for the term of four years, and until his successor is elected and qualified. After the first election under the Constitution, the Board shall be divided, as nearly as practicable, into two equal classes, and the seats of the first class shall be vacated after the expiration of two years; and one-half of the Board shall be chosen every two years thereafter.

Section 4. The session of the Board shall be limited to twenty days, and but one session shall be held in any one year, except upon the recommendation of two-thirds of the Board, the Governor may order an extra session.

Section 5. The Board of Education shall appoint a Secretary, who shall be the executive officer of the Board, and perform such duties as may be imposed upon him by the Board,

## THE ALABAMA CONSTITUTION OF 1867

### ARTICLE ON EDUCATION[23]

Section 1. The Common Schools, and other institutions of the State, shall be under the management of a Board of Education, consisting of a Superintendent of Public Instruction, and two members from each Congressional District.

Section 2. The Superintendent of Public Instruction shall be president of the Board of Education, and have the casting vote in case of a tie; he shall have the supervision of the public schools of the State, and perform such other duties as may be imposed upon him by the board and laws of the State. He shall be elected in the same manner and for the same terms as the Governor of the State, and receive such salary as may be fixed by law. An office shall be assigned in the Capitol of the State.

Section 3. The members of the Board shall hold office for a term of four years, and their successors shall be elected and qualified. After the first election, under the Constitution, the Board shall be divided into two equal classes, so that each class shall consist of one member from each district. The seats of the first class shall be vacated at the expiration of two years from the date of election, so that one-half may be chosen biennially.

Section 4. The session of the Board shall be limited to twenty days, and but one session shall be held in any one year, except upon extraordinary oc-

and the laws of the State. They shall keep a journal of their proceedings, which shall be published and distributed in the same manner as the journals of the General Assembly.

Section 6. All rules and regulations made by the Board shall be published and distributed, to the several counties, townships, and school districts as may be provided for by the Board, and when so made, published and distributed, they shall have the force and effect of law.

Section 7. The Board of Education shall have full power and authority to legislate and make all needful rules and regulations in relation to common schools, and other educational institutions, that are instituted, to receive aid from the School or University fund of this State; but all acts, rules and regulations of said Board may be altered, amended or repealed by the General Assembly.[26]

Section 8. The Board of Education shall have no power to lexy taxes, or make appropriations of money. Their contingent expenses shall be provided for by the General Assembly.

Section 9. The State University shall be established at one place without branches at any other place, and the University fund shall be applied to that institution and to no other.

Section 10. The Board of Education shall provide for the education of all youths of the State, through a system of common schools, and such schools shall be organized and

casions, when, upon the recommendation of two-thirds of the Board, the Governor may order an extra session.

Section 5. The members of the Board of Education, except the Superintendent, shall be elected by the qualified electors of the Congressional Districts in which they are chosen, at the same time and in the same manner as the members of Congress.

Secion 6. The Board of Educaion shall exercise full legislative powers in reference to the public educational institutions of the State, and its acts, when approved by the Governor, or when re-enacted by two-thirds of the Board, in case of his approval, shall have the force and effect of law, unless repealed by the General Assembly.[25]

Section 7. It shall be the duty of the Board to establish throughout the State, in each township or other school district which it may have created, one or more schools, at which all of the children of the State between the ages of five and twenty-one may attend free of charge.

Section 8. No rule or law affecting the general interest of education shall be made by the Board without the concurrence of a majority of the members. The style of all acts of the Board shall be, "Be it enacted by the Board of Education of the State of Alabama."

Section 9. The Board of Education shall be a body politic and corporate by the name and style of "The Board of Education of the State of Alabama." Said Board shall also kept in each school district at least three months in each year. Any district failing, for two consecutive years, to organize and keep up a school, as aforesaid. may be deprived of their portion of the school fund.

Section 11. The members of the Board of Education shall each receive the same per diem during the time of their session, and mileage going to and returning therefrom, as members of the General Assembly.

Section 12. A majority of the board shall constitute a quorum for the transaction of business; but no rule, resolution, regulation, or law, for the government of common schools shall be in force without the approval of the Governor of the State.

Section 13. At any time after the year one thousand, eight hundred and sixty-three, the General Assembly shall have power to abolish or reorganize said Board of Education, and provide for the educational interest of the State in any other manner that to them shall seem best and proper.[27]

2ND. SCHOOL FUNDS AND SCHOOL LANDS

(Provided in brief)

Section 1. (Control and management vested in the General Assembly.)

Section 2. (University fund defined.)

Section 3. (Land grant confirmed as source of income.)

Section 4. (Escheats, fines, etc., devoted to schools.)

Secion 5. (University land grant confirmed.)

be a Board of Regents of the State University, and when sitting as a Board of Regents of the University, shall have power to appoint the President and the faculties thereof. The President of the University shall be, *ex officio,* a member of the Board of Regents, but shall have no vote in its proceedings.

Section 10. The Board of Education shall meet annually at the seat of government at the same time as the General Assembly, but no session shall continue longer than twenty days, nor shall more than one session be held in the same year, unless authorized by the Governor. The members shall receive the same mileage and daily pay as members of the General Assembly.

Section 11. The proceeds of all lands that have been or may be granted by the United States to the State for educational purposes; of the swamplands; and of all lands or other property given by individuals or appropriated by the State for like purposes; and of all estates of deceased persons who have died without leaving a will or heir; and all moneys which may be paid as an equivalent for exemption from military duty, shall be and remain a perpetual fund, which may be increased but not diminished, and the interest and income of which together with the rents of all such lands as may remain unsold, and such other means as the General Assembly may provide, shall be inviolably appropriated to educational purposes, and to no other purpose whatever.

Section 6. (Financial agents provided for.)

Section 7. (Money apportioned for educables on the age basis 5-21.)

Section 12. In addition to the amount accruing from the above sources, one-fifth of the aggregate annual revenue of the State shall be devoted exclusively to the maintenance of public schools.

Section 13. The General Assembly shall levy a specific annual tax upon all railroad, navigation, banking, and insurance corporations, and upon all insurance and foreign bank and exchange agencies, and upon the profits of foreign bank bills issued in this State by any corporation (partnership or persons), which shall be exclusively devoted to the maintenance of public schools.

Section 14. The General Assembly shall, as soon as practicable, provide for the establishment of an agricultural college, and shall appropriate the two hundred and forty thousand acres of land donated to this State for the support of such a college, by the act of Congress, passed July 2, 1862, or the money or scrip, as the case may be, arising from the sale of said lands, or any lands which may hereafter be granted or appropriated for such purposes, for the support and maintenance of such college, or schools, and may make the same a branch of the University of Alabama for instruction in Agriculture, in the mechanic arts, and the natural sciences connected therewith, and place the same under the supervision of the regents of the University.

The Iowa Convention, after long debate, severely curtailed the powers of the Board contemplated in the Article which was adopted in Alabama almost without debate.[28]   A record of the *Journal* reporting action on the Education article follows.[29]

> Article X was taken up.
> The first six sections were adopted.
> The seventh section was read.
> Mr. Gardner moved to strike out "twenty-one" and insert "twenty."
> Mr. Smith moved that the motion be laid on the table.
> Agreed to.
> Mr. Semple offered an amendment as an addition, as follows:
>> And proper provision shall be made for the education of the children of white and colored persons in separate schools.

Semple was a native white, resident of Montgomery, the nephew of President Tyler.[30]   In presenting this amendment he injected the only issue which caused debate regarding the adoption of the Article on Education.   Section 7, it will be seen, stated that "It shall be the duty of the Board to establish . . . . in each township or other school district . . . . one or more schools which all of the children of the State between the ages of five and twenty-one may attend free of charge."[31]

This section, accordingly, left the maintenance of separate schools for the two races entirely in the discretion of the Board. Semple's amendment was intended to insure constitutional prohibition against the possibility of "mixed schools."

In the debate that followed, the Negro members stated that they wished the issue of separate schools left out of the Constitution because, while they did not want to send their children to school with white children,[32] the threat of mixed schools would remove the temptation from future officials to maintain inferior schools for Negroes.[33]   Delegate Carraway, a Negro from Mobile, offered an amendment to Section 7 as follows: "Should it prove expedient to have separate schools for white and colored children, the Board of Education shall cause an equal division of the school fund in such district where such division is demanded."[34]

The section was adopted by a vote of 47-26 when Keffer moved the previous question.   Unfortunately, no vote is recorded by name in the *Journal,* or in contemporary newspaper reports.   There was no debate on any other portion of the Article on Education.

There was some opposition to the Article on Education on the ground that it did not provide definitely for separate schools.

The strength of this opposition is difficult to estimate, because contemporary newspaper accounts, if Democratic, magnified it, and minimized it, if Republican. The *Tribune* said: "Mr. Semple of Montgomery presented a protest, signed by 15 members, some of whom are absentees. The protest was ordered spread on the *Journal,* but the names of the absentees who signed were stricken off. Two other members gave notice that they would present a protest tomorrow."[35]

But among the names of the "protestants" appears that of L. S. Latham, whom Fleming says was a Negro.[36] No protest involving the separate school item appears in the *Journal,* with the exception of one by J. P. Stow, whom Fleming classified as a Northern "alien," of unknown origin, but who was probably a "Scalawag."[37] Stow's protest stated: "I protest against the refusal of the Convention to provide expressly in the Constitution, for separate schools for the children of the two races, when necessary."[38] On paper, the Convention had fulfilled the prophecy of the Chicago *Tribune* reporter, who, at the beginning of the Convention, had said: "The black and white radicals are determined to have an efficient free school system, and they will have it. Mark that."[39] In summary, the Article on Education is notable for the highly centralized system it provided; for the immense variety of powers bestowed upon the Board of Education, which became a legislative body co-equal with the General Assembly; and for the ample financial support which was promised by its provisions. So far as Negroes were concerned it provided every promise of equal opportunities. The effectiveness of the schools during the period from 1868 to 1875, while the Constitution of the former year was operative, was dependent upon other factors incident to the enactment of the section and its functioning.

### The State Schools Build on Bureau Foundations

A general meeting of the various societies interested in the education of Negroes was held in New York on the 10th of September, 1867. A resolution was adopted at this meeting urging the substitution of state-supported schools for Negroes for the system then maintained by the Bureau and Mission forces.[40] The composition of the Bureau's official staff, the Mission Societies, and the State executive and legislative branches was so largely recruited from the same sources that collaboration was extremely easy.  Especially was this true in Alabama, where the Bureau and the teaching staff of the American Missionary Association contributed many persons to the Constitutional Convention of 1867, and to the General Assembly which convened at Montgomery in July, 1868.  This was also true of the Board of Education, which, with its extensive legislative functions, was even more important to the schools than the General Assembly.

N. B. Cloud, a "Scalawag," was elected Superintendent at the election in February which passed upon the Constitution formulated in 1867.[41]  The first Board of Education had but eight members, until August, 1869, when a special election was held to increase the number to ten.[42]  The initial Board was composed entirely of Republicans.  G. L. Putnam and Jessie Booth appear to have been "Carpetbaggers"; W. P. Miller, a native of Ireland, had lived in Alabama since 1840, and was a mechanic from Tuscaloosa, a hill county.[43]  A. B. Collins was born in the Tennessee mountain county of Rhea, and was reputed to be "the best mathematician" in Alabama.[44]  He had developed "several fine schools" in DeKalb County in ante-bellum times.[45]  T. A. Cook, added to the Board in 1869, was a native of Charleston, South Carolina, a graduate of Dr. Muhlenberg's institute in New York, and had been an Episcopal minister and teacher in the State in ante-bellum times.[46]  H. M. Bush, added to the Board in 1869, was a former official of the Freedmen's Bureau in Montgomery.[47]

The Board had comparatively little to legislate about at first; it was supposed to operate on an extremely ample budgetary basis, but the taxes which were to provide funds for the new system had to be levied by the Legislature, and funds were not available from the first year of Reconstruction revenue until late in 1869.[48]  One of the Board's first acts was "to secure cooperation with the Bureau of Refugees, Freedmen and Abandoned Lands, and the several aid societies."  The act provided

That so far as practicable the superintendent of public instruction shall be governed in the establishment of schools in the State, by the general understanding that for successful co-operation it is desirable
1st.  That the Freedmen's Bureau shall continue to aid in furnishing school houses either by renting buildings for school purposes or by assisting in their erection.
2. That the various associations and aid societies shall continue to select and send to the State competent teachers, and pay their transportation to and from their respective fields of labor.

3. That the State shall pay the teachers thus furnished, who shall be subject to the same examination as other teachers of free schools in Alabama, the same compensation when employed as received by other teachers of the same grade, from its educational fund.

Approved August 11, 1868.[49]

The Board also provided that the Superintendent should apportion the School Fund to the various counties, "according to the number of children in each over the age of five and under the age of twenty-one years."[50]  Cloud was faced with the difficulty of not having any money for the schools, and, even when money became available, there was no basis for distribution since no school census of the Negro children existed.  His report for the year ending September 30, 1869, states that it was not until May of that year that any apportionment could be made.[51]

On October 11 an Act of the Board was approved which set aside $45,411.46 to be applied "to the payment of teachers who rendered service in the public schools of this State since . . . . July 1st, 1868."[52]  It was this provision to which the next superintendent, a Democrat, took exception, declaring that the appropriation was fraudulent and intended for private schools; i.e., for the American Missionary Schools with which the Board had agreed to "cooperate."[53]

## POLITICAL PARTISANSHIP AND THE PUBLIC SCHOOLS DURING RECONSTRUCTION

It is not possible to understand the history of the public schools in Alabama apart from the virulent partisan strife that was going on between Conservatives and Republicans in the State during the period.  Even the documents upon which a record of the time should be based, are partisan documents, intended to discredit the work of the administration of the opposite faction.

These political changes are important in defining what took place so far as the schools were concerned.  N. B. Cloud, Republican Superintendent of Public Instruction, served from July 13, 1868, to December 1, 1870.[54]  At that time he was succeeded by J. H. Hodgson, Conservative.  From 1870-1872 the Governor and other state officials were also Conservatives, and the Conservatives held a majority in the House of Representatives of the General

Assembly.[55]   A Republican Administration was elected in 1872, and served until 1874, with Joseph Speed as Superintendent of Public Instruction.[56]   During all of this period the Republicans held a majority in the Board of Education.

The result was a constant warfare between these various factions, complicated by the fact that the General Assembly, whether Democratic or Republican, was jealous of the legislative powers vested in the Board of Education, and lost no opportunity to sabotage the work of that rival body. Even worse, the Reports of the Superintendents of Public Instruction were converted into political broadsides which in addition to being used as political fuel for their respective parties, were included in more respectable sources as bona-fide reports of the condition of the schools in the state. For this reason even the Reports of the United States Commissioner of Education are valueless for any correct statistical information on the period.

Regarding the attitude of the white people toward the education of Negroes, the following answers were quoted in Cloud's first report:

Coffee County:
    At the time I commenced appointing trustees, the prejudice of the people was general and strong against the free public school system . . . . The feelings of the people seem to have changed to a great extent on these subjects . . . .[57]
Sanford County:
    But I can safely say that the mass of the people were bitterly opposed to it (education of Negroes) . . . . and it was quite troublesome for me to get men to accept the position and act as trustees . . . .[58]
Marengo County:
    I found much prejudice among the people against colored schools, and it was with great difficulty that I procured teachers . . . . all such prejudices have now vanished . . . .[59]
Macon County:
    When I began operations in Macon County, I found great hostility to our free public school system, and it was a hard matter to find trustees in every township who would take sufficient interest to establish colored schools . . . . (All this changed) . . . . and I now find many people . . . . who believe it is fair and commendable to educate the colored children in our county.[60]
Dallas County:
    . . . . very few were willing to assist in establishing colored schools . . . . (all this changed).[61]

As though by way of rebuttal, J. H. Hodgson's first report made numerous accusations of dishonesty and incompetence in the administration of Cloud,[62] and listed reports from County Superintendents as gloomy as Cloud's had been optimistic.

Barbour County:
    There are no schoolhouses in my county owned by the townships .... for the colored ....[63]
Choctaw County:
    There are but few schools that are of much character .... The white people are generally opposed to the public school system, but as we have such a system they generally avail themselves of the schools and send their children while the schools are continued. I think that if the law was so altered as to give a *pro rata* share of the fund to all the children attending the schools it would be much more beneficial.[64]
Lowndes County:
    The attendance of the colored children in many places is fitful .... This annoying state of things is partly due to the exigencies of their parents, whose circumstances ofttimes require their assistance on the farm, but in many to a want of appreciation of their advantages.[65]

FINANCIAL SUPPORT OF SCHOOLS DURING RECONSTRUCTION

The financing of schools in Alabama from 1868-1875 may be discussed either from the standpoint of the amount of money which, theoretically, the schools received, and the amount which was actually paid them. The Constitution of 1868 provided ample sources of revenue for the schools.

There is no way to tell how much of this money was actually spent on schools. Hodgson[66] stated that there were so many irregularities in Cloud's management of the schools that it was impossible to tell how much money had actually been spent.[67] He complained, during his term of office, that the General Assembly was diverting money from the schools to other purposes.[68] His successor, Speed, complained of diversion during 1872-1873, and his last report confesses that no money at all was available for the schools.[69] Barnas Sears reports that no schools were operated by the State in 1873.[70] The following statements of diversion and expenditures are taken from various sources.

TABLE I

MONEY APPROPRIATED AND MONEY SPENT FOR ALABAMA SCHOOLS
DURING RECONSTRUCTION*

| Year | Money Appropriated | Money Received | Diverted |
|------|-------------------|----------------|----------|
| 1869-1870† ................ | $500,407 | $306,872 | $187,872 |
| 1870-1871 ................ | 581,389 | 320,480 | 260,908 |
| 1871-1872 ................ | 604,978 | 166,303 | 438,675 |
| 1872-1873 ................ | 522,810 | 68,313 | 454,496 |
| 1873-1874 ................ | 474,346 | ............ | 474,346‡ |

*Journal of the Board of Education, 1873; Weeks, History of Public School Education in Alabama, p. 104.

†Actually, this was the scholastic year; but the beginning of the fiscal year had been changed from January 1, 1870, to October 1, 1870.

‡Apparently, no state money was available for schools.

Yet the reports of Cloud and Hodgson list apportionments as though these sums were actually paid; and Hodgson's report specifies the number of teachers, with "rate of pay," for each racial group. Apparently the statements of salaries and expenditures in these reports are based upon the number of warrants issued; but these warrants in a number of instances were never paid.[71] Hodgson's report for the year ending September 30, 1871, gives a total of 2,497 teachers of white schools in the State, and 773 teachers of Negro schools.[72] With a monthly salary reported for both races approximating $43 a month, a slight calculation will show that Hodgson probably took the Apportionment figure for that year ($500,407), derived a number of teachers from an undefined source, and so arrived at a total expenditure for schools in a purely arbitrary fashion.[73] For he reports $493,336 in warrants issued for teachers' salaries, of which $211,217 were unpaid; while other sources give a total of but $306,872 received by the schools.[74] The result is that a reliable statistical basis for making an estimate of the extent to which the State schools reached Negro children during the administrations of Cloud and Speed is entirely lacking. During Speed's administration, by his own confession, the public schools were barely operative.[75]

NEGRO CHILDREN IN THE RECONSTRUCTION SYSTEM

Cloud gave no report as to the number of Negro children enrolled in the schools during 1868-1869. Hodgson, reporting for the part-period during which Cloud was Superintendent (through the latter part of 1869), states that the "attendance" of Negro children was 16,097.[76] Whether this figure refers to "average attendance" or to enrollment is uncertain. For 1870-1871 Hodgson reported an enrollment of 86,976 white children, and 54,336 Negroes, with 66,358 whites in average attendance and 41,308 Negroes reported as attending regularly.[77] There can be no doubt that both of these figures are exaggerated; the reported percentage of average attendance in 1869-1870 of Negro children was 76 per cent, as compared to 74 per cent reported in the year 1930 for the State, when a much more accurate accounting system was in vogue and the school laws put a financial premium on high attendance.[78] Whether the fault was in Hodgson's source reports, or in deliberate falsification in order to give a respectable showing compared to Cloud's, is uncertain. An inspection of individual teacher's reports during the period shows a reported average attendance of less than 35 per cent.[79]

The first enumeration of Negro children took place under Cloud's administration, and was made the basis for the first apportionment in 1869. The enumeration for this year was 223,482 white, and 164,671 Negroes.[80] In 1873 Speed reported an enumeration of 234,600 whites, and 169,139 Negro children.[81] Granting accuracy to the statement of the Negro enrollment, 32 per cent of the Negro children in the State in 1870 of school age, and 24 per cent in 1873, were enrolled in the State schools.

Under the method of apportionment to the counties on a strict per capita basis, there was every temptation to distort the enumeration of children within townships, in order to receive, from the State, a sum larger than actually warranted by the facts. This problem was to become at a later date a public scandal, where Black Belt Superintendents were openly accused of enumerating an excessive number of Negro children in order to receive a disproportionate amount of the school funds. Whether this procedure was followed in the Reconstruction period is not certain. The returns from the school census, in comparison with the United States Census of 1870, gives some startling results, although the same age-groups cannot be compared.

TABLE II

A Comparison Between School Census and United States Census
Enumerations in Alabama, 1870*

| County | White | School Enumeration 5-21 | | United States Census—5-18 |
| | | Negro | Total | Total |
|---|---|---|---|---|
| Autauga | 4,928 | 3,591 | 6,519 | 3,918 |
| Dallas | 2,128 | 9,276 | 11,404 | 12,638 |
| Lowndes | 1,979 | 5,711 | 7,690 | 8,440 |
| Wilsox | 2,859 | 6,534 | 9,393 | 9,581 |
| Mobile | 13,515 | 10,099 | 23,614† | 14,726 |
| Winston | 1,866 | 6 | 1,872 | 1,525 |
| Jackson | 6,785 | 1,205 | 7,990 | 6,934 |

*J. J. Hodgson, *Report for 1871*, Appendix, p. viii-ix; *United States Census of 1870, Population*, p. 623.

†With a total population of 41,131 reported by the U. S. Census, this would give Mobile a proportion of educables 5-21 which was 57 per cent of the total population.

THE EQUALITY OF EDUCATIONAL OPPORTUNITY
DURING RECONSTRUCTION

The growing acceptance on the part of the Conservatives of the idea of equal distribution of school monies to Negro children is significant. Hodgson's reports, even if manipulated, are valuable evidence of this tendency. Manuscript reports (See Figure 4) show that there was equal pay for equal services, in confirmation of figures published in the State Reports. The opposition that persisted among the white population was directed at high taxes, in the payment of which Negroes did not share, while, in Black Belt counties, receiving most of the benefit from them;[82] and at that provision of the school laws which discouraged private contributions.[83] It would appear that the Conservatives persisted in their older attitude that the public schools were for the pauper class; and, aside from the expense, believed that free schools of this sort were proper institutions for Negroes, as they had been before for the poor whites.[84]

Acceptance of equal expenditures may have been due to the number of white teachers who were serving in the schools. Fleming states that many whites taught in Negro schools, until the education of the race was discredited by the activities of the Mission

schools.[85] There is another explanation; that white teachers began
to be displaced when lower salaries were paid to teachers of Negro
schools, and it was a matter of economy to employ Negro teachers
for Negro schools in place of the white teachers, who would naturally insist on receiving the same amount of money received by
their white fellow-teachers in white schools. The white teachers
had their difficulties; the growing political and race consciousness
of their Negro charges made the task of adjustment a difficult
one.[86] The white native teachers employed were not of particularly distinguished ability. The Democratic Superintendent of Sumter County reported to Hodgson in 1871:

The public school is growing in favor with both races under the
present administration, and I am convinced the negroes cannot
be educated in any other way. The public school is their only
means of obtaining an education. I have induced moral, and highly
respectable *old men, who had taught the white children in former
years,* to teach the colored schools. Many who believed it a disgrace to teach under Radical Rule, are most efficient and faithful
teachers under the democratic.[87]

The same Superintendent Kinnard reported to J. M. McKleroy in
1875:

I have . . . . employed . . . . good, intelligent and efficient men and
women as teachers, who would not have been employed had I not
approached them on the subject. Gentlemen and ladies are teaching colored schools now, who a few years ago would have been
driven out of society for attempting such a thing.[88]

In 1875 the Superintendent of Marengo County, a Black Belt
County, neighboring Sumter, had little regard for the white teachers in his Negro schools, while he would not even employ Negroes.
The whites went into the schoolroom, he believed, "because it is
easier to sit in the shade than to plow; although from education
and physical culture they are better qualified for the latter."[89]

Another factor in defining the attitude of the Conservatives
with reference to the equal participation of Negroes in the school
funds was the fact that Negroes were politically active and their
support sought by Democrats and Republicans alike. Their political strength shows in the workings of the Board of Education, and
in the activities of Peyton Finley, the Negro elected to the Board
in 1870. The deliberations of the Board also show a consistent up-
holding of the theory of equality of apportionment between the
races.

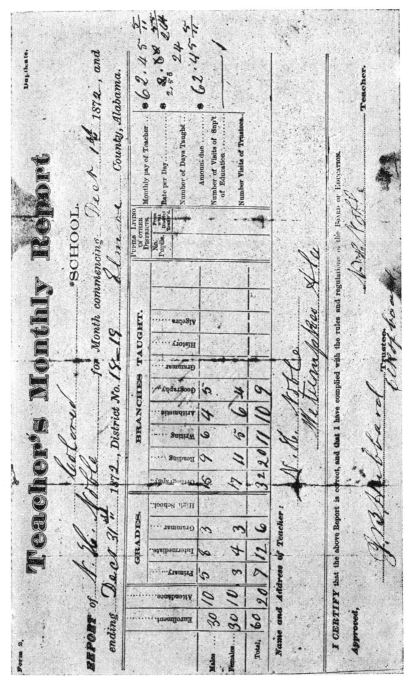

FIGURE 4.  A RECONSTRUCTION TEACHER'S MONTHLY REPORT

Under any sort of equable apportionment, the Reconstruction system gave Negroes a clear advantage over white children. The school population per capita payment basis established a system which actually enrolled only from 30 to 40 per cent of the Negroes while the percentage of whites enrolling would, in all probability, be much higher. A Negro school in a township might receive $1,500 from the state distributive fund for the education of one thousand children of school age. With only three hundred of these children enrolled, and with an average attendance of probably less than one hundred, the Negro school could afford a longer term and a better-paid teacher than the white school in the same township, where a higher percentage of educables would enroll and attend. As a result, the Negro schools in townships would frequently accumulate surpluses which were devoted to building schools from current funds, as in a Marengo County township where the Board of Education provided that

Whereas (the) colored school has been burnt, and a new one is needed, ''and the school fund apportioned to the colored schools in said township is sufficient to continue three schools for the colored race for the entire year'' and leave a surplus sufficient to build said school house, said funds amounting to the sum of $1,172.82, therefore

the trustees of the township were permitted to use their surplus for building a Negro schoolhouse.[90]    This differential in school needs of a racial group, less than a decade removed from slavery, with but few persons in advanced classes, early attracted the attention of those who objected to the payment of taxes to educate Negroes who were non-taxpayers.

The Board of Education maintained a special committee on Negro schools. Salaries were equalized by a provision which limited monthly salaries of rural teachers to $40, permitting the payment of $10 additional per month for each additional ten pupils over twenty.[91] The action of one township in maintaining two Negro schools with a teacher-salary of $50, while establishing a white teacher's salary at $60 a month, was the subject of special consideration in the Board, and explained on this basis.[92] Among many Acts of the Board is one appropriating $225 each ''for the relief of Mrs. Low Taylor and Mrs. C. M. Hopson'' for teaching, respectively, a white and colored school in the city of Talladega, ''. . . . to be paid out of any unexpended funds belonging to the townships in which said schools were located, appropriated to the respective races for which said schools were taught.''[93]

As each successive election added Democratic members to the Board, in 1870, 1872, and 1874, partisan lines were clearly drawn; but nowhere do they appear drawn on a strictly racial issue, as to equality of apportionment between the races.

### Normal and Higher Schools

The struggle for the establishment of normal schools in the State for Negroes furnishes an excellent index to the development of attitudes, and the effectiveness of various political forces.

In its first session in July, 1868, the Board of Education established ten normal schools, which were to be supported from the common school fund.[94]   This provision of support is important; for it did not require any additional appropriation from the Board, or from the Legislature.   Since the normal school money was taken from that race's share of the common school fund for which the normal school was established, there was less opposition to the support of a Negro normal or higher school than there would have been in the event that appropriations over and above the State fund had been utilized.   Money spent on Negro normals was taking money only from Negro children, where a fair apportionment prevailed.

The General Assembly of 1870, with the lower house under Democratic control, abolished these schools.[95]   Hodgson's report for 1871 states that sixteen normal schools were taught during 1870; these must have been ''classes'' or institutes connected with academies or large schools.   Included were schools for Negroes at Huntsville, which received $3,818; Talladega, $3,784; Marion, $486; Mobile, $1,328; Athens, $800; Montgomery, $593; and Selma, $800.[96]   The American Missionary Association had been maintaining schools for the Freedmen at all of these places; it is probable these payments represented an extension of aid in accordance with the *Act* of 1868 by which co-operation with the Bureau and the mission societies was guaranteed.

During the year 1870 nine ''normal classes'' were reported at six places, with Negro ''classes'' at Huntsville, Talladega, Montgomery, and Mobile.[97]   Superintendent Hodgson thought it unwise to have ''three times as many normal schools as the State of New York possessed for twenty-five years,'' and he ''had no infor-

mation as to the good they had done."[98]   But the superintendent
of Perry County said:

As regards public instruction, there is rapidly increasing interest
in favor of free schools.   The greatest embarrassment is the great
deficiency of competent teachers, and especially for our colored
schools.   But we have much to hope for from our normal school
at Marion, for it has already sent out six teachers, whose work
has been very satisfactory.[99]

Hodgson proposed that normal school education for Negroes would
be amply cared for by establishing "classes," in addition to the
one at Marion, in connection with the Swayne Academy in Montgomery, and another "with some colored academy at Mobile."[100]
The Swayne school was an American Missionary Association
school, and the only "colored academy" in Mobile at the time was
the Emerson Institute, also supported by the American Missionary
Association.

On the 27th of November, 1871, Peyton Finley, the Negro
member of the Board of Education, presented twin bills to provide four schools for white teachers, and four for Negro teachers.[101]   These bills were approved on December 20th.[102]   The bill
provided that $4,500 should be divided among the four white
schools, and $4,750 among the Negro schools.   The latter were to
be located at Montgomery, Sparta, Marion, and Huntsville; two
in the Black Belt, one in North Alabama, and one in South Alabama.   The schools were to be controlled by a Board of Commissioners for each institution, numbering three persons.   The Montgomery Board included Finley and two "Carpetbaggers."   On
the Marion board were two Negroes, Porter King and John T.
Harris, with Joseph H. Speed, later superintendent of Public Instruction.   The money for the schools was to be taken from the
common school fund before apportionment, and the balance apportioned to the several counties.[103]

Of the four white schools, three were placed in North Alabama, and the fourth in the "Wire-grass" section of Southwest
Alabama.   Not one was placed in the Black Belt.[104]

In 1872 an appropriation was made to three normal schools
for Negroes, Montgomery being excepted.[105]   The appropriations
for the school at Marion were made permanent.   On December 9,
1873, the school at Huntsville was established with an annual appropriation of $1,000 annually.[106]   The school did not open until
May, 1875.[107]

When a State Normal School for white females was established in 1873, Peyton Finley, a Negro member of the Board of Education, was appointed on the committee to locate it.[108]

## THE STATE NORMAL SCHOOL AND UNIVERSITY

During his two years of service on the Board Peyton Finley was a strenuous advocate of the establishment of a University for Negroes in the State, to do for the Negro what the University of Alabama purported to do for white persons.

During the first session of the Board which he attended, Finley presented a "preamble and resolution":

Whereas, the public good demands the establishment in this State of a University for the education of the colored race of this State;

And whereas, the present financial condition of the State University is such as to prevent much aid to a University for colored people for some time to come;

And whereas, the colored race have no desire or inclination, nor would they under any circumstances attempt to interfere with the action of the State University, by any claim or pretext of right thereto:

Be it therefore: Resolved, That the Superintendent of Public Instruction be, and is hereby authorized to make application as heretofore to urge upon the Congress of the United States, at the next session, in behalf of this Board, and the people of Alabama, for a grant of public lands in aid of such a University, and an additional grant in aid of the public schools of this State.[109]

Apparently nothing came of this Resolution. On November 28, 1871, Mr. Finley introduced an "act to establish a University for the education of colored students in the State of Alabama."[110] This was the day after he had introduced his bill to establish four normal schools for whites, and four for blacks. The bill was referred to the Committee on Revision, from which it was reported on December 2 by Mr. Booth. Mr. Comegys, a "Scalawag" from North Alabama,[111] spoke against the measure. He was in favor of educating the colored people; but he believed that establishment of a University for them was not needed at that time, and should be postponed.[112] His motion to lay on the table was lost, and the bill referred to a special committee composed of Finley, Booth, and Smith,[113] the latter a Democrat from Auburn who was working for the location of the Land-Grant College at that town.[114]

When the bill came up on December 11 Mr. Speed made a substitute amendment which passed, providing that the appropriation for the school at Marion be doubled in lieu of providing a University at that time.[115]

But Mr. Finley called up his bill again. The vote was six to six, three ''Scalawags'' joining with three Democrats against it. The vote being a tie, the President of the Board, who was Superintendent Hodgson, voted against it; so the bill did not pass.[116]

Then Mr. Finley introduced a resolution which directed a Committee of the Board to prepare a memorial to Congress asking for land for a University for the colored race.[117] The resolution was adopted on December 13.[118] Back of Finley's agitation was the fact that the General Assembly was then considering the establishment of a land grand college under the Morrell Act of 1862. So Finley presented another resolution asking the General Assembly in disposing of funds received from the United States for an Agricultural College to ''give a portion of it for the aid of the University for the colored race of this state.''[119] The resolution passed the Board, but apparently had no effect upon the General Assembly which established the Alabama Polytechnic Institute at Auburn without providing for Negroes.

The Commissioners of the State Normal School for Colored at Marion presented a report to the Board in 1873 which was an argument for the establishment of a Negro University. They reported that they had

. . . . introduced Practical Grammar, History, Physiology, Natural Philosophy, Higher Arithmetic, Algebra and Composition, and all this work has thus far been done by one teacher. There is three times the work now than there was at the organization of the school. We have been obliged to introduce the last named subjects, to satisfy the advancing condition of the colored race, and in view of the fact that they have no State University. The fact can no longer be evaded nor ignored, that if the colored people of the State have their just educational rights, they must have a University for higher instruction.[120]

Mr. Sears introduced a resolution in 1873 ''to locate a Colored University.'' The Board decided to memorialize the Congress of the United States to appropriate lands for maintaining a Negro University.[121] Mr. Finley was not a member of the Board, having lost his place early in 1873 when the Board drew lots according to law to select those men who should serve for two, or for four-year terms. The Committee appointed to memorialize Congress included two Democrats, Oliver, and Box, who was later to become State Superintendent of Public Instruction.

A bill to establish a "State Normal School and University" for the Negroes of Alabama was finally passed on December 5, 1873.[122] The Act had five sections: (1) The first provided that the establishment of the University was contingent on the donation to the State of the Lincoln Normal School, which had been operated by the American Missionary Association since 1866 at Marion. (2) The Act established "A State Normal School and University for Colored Teachers and Students." (3) Students enrolled were to pledge themselves to teach in the State for at least two years after graduation; however, the payment of tuition released the graduate of this obligation. The annual appropriation was $2,000, to be appropriated out of the common school fund for colored children. (4) A Board of Directors was specified, including Superintendent Speed, J. H. Sears, and five Negroes: Porter King, John Harris, A. H. Curtis, John Dozier, and John T. Foster. (5) The aim was expressed as follows: "the intent and purpose of this Act (is) to provide for the liberal education of the colored race in the same manner as is already provided for the education of the white race in our Universities and Colleges."[123]

The notable features of this legislation were: (a) appropriating money for support from the common school fund for colored children cost the State no extra appropriation; (b) the move was evidently a political one with the manoeuvering extending to both parties. There was no vote against it. It was designed to appease the Negroes by giving the name of "University" to a normal school. (c) The earlier attitude of the Board in sanctioning the idea of a University for Negroes showed a change, although the entire project was obviously an empty sham to delude the members of the race.

As a crowning example of the hypocrisy of the Board, on December 8 an Act was passed repealing the prior act of 1871 establishing Normal schools.[124] This cut the State appropriation for the higher education of Negroes from $4,000 to $2,000; and this small sum was to be taken from the Negro common school fund. However, the Board did establish a Normal School at Huntsville on the 18th of December, although this school did not open until 1875, due to diversion of the State Fund in 1873.[125]

In 1874 the officials of the "Normal University" reported one hundred students, who were to pursue a curriculum ranging from "reading, writing, Geography, Spelling" through Greek and Latin to "Trigonometry, Physiology, Natural Philosophy, and Chemistry."[126]   The President, Professor Cord, had raised funds for the purchase of "a complete set of Chemical and Philosophical Instruments, with a finely adjusted microscope magnifying 652,500 times (!) with which he is carrying on the work of his department with untiring energy."[127]   The building was "ample," and everything was on hand to "make our University first-class" with one exception.   The exception was the lack of money; two thousand dollars, reported the trustees, "is a very small amount with which to run a University."   They drew an invidious comparison with the $24,000 yearly income of the University of Alabama, and asked for two professors at $1,600, with two assistants at $600.   "We cannot run our University through this term without (sic) this is done.   We must have an appropriation of at least $5,000.   We can then publish to the colored people of the State that we have all the facilities for giving them an education in all the Departments of learing."[128]   With a Democratic Board of Education in 1874, the personnel of the Trustee Board was changed to give a Democratic majority, Negro Democrats being substituted for the Negro Republicans.[129]   The appropriation was raised from $2,000 to $4,000.[130]   In 1875 the Faculty was composed of three white persons; the Reverend John Silsby, the member of the Committee on Education of the Constitutional Convention of 1867 who helped provide for the Board of Education, is discovered by this report to be Assistant to the Principal, at a salary of $1,200 per annum.[131]

In 1875 John K. McKleroy, newly elected Democratic Superintendent, said: "The normal school at Marion is designed to become a University for the colored race in the State; and it is not doubted that its facilities for furnishing the higher education to this race will be amplified as the demand therefor becomes apparent."[132]

## CHAPTER VIII

## THE OBJECTIVES AND CONTENT OF RECONSTRUCTION EDUCATION

### THE CONTENT OF EDUCATION AS PROPOSED BY SOUTHERN WHITES

As no systematic effort was actually made to educate Negroes at public expense in Alabama prior to the inauguration of the Reconstruction Constitution of 1868, the content of education proposed by Conservative Alabamians for Negroes becomes largely a matter of speculative interest. Even so, it is an aid to understanding the violent reaction against Northern-sponsored education which took place.

Both Fleming[1] and Knight[2] assert that the State of Alabama would have undertaken the education of Negroes under Conservative control had Northerners not discredited the work. The objectionable features in Northern education were exemplified in the content of the instruction proffered. The advocacy of the education of Negroes by Conservatives "was a step towards securing control over the Negro race by the best native whites, who believed and will always believe that the Negro should be controlled by them."[3] The Northerners taught the Negro "to give up all habits and customs that would remind him of his former condition . . . . He must not take off his hat when speaking to a white person. In teaching him not to be servile, they taught him to be insolent."[4]

In May, 1900, toward the close of his life, J. L. M. Curry, whose official position as agent for both Peabody and Slater Funds gave him an immense prestige in the interpretation of the education of Negroes, made a blistering indictment of the content of education and the methods invoked by the missionary teachers in the South.[5] He was one of the original advocates of educating Negroes; his biographers say:

With the tenderness and affection for the black man which the typical Southern slaveholder preserved to the end, and which the typical Southern slave rewarded with a fidelity and devotion that is unparalleled in the history of the world—a tenderness which the alien will never comprehend, and a devotion which will never cease to astonish the outsider—Curry was, from the moment of the fall of the Confederacy, occupied in mind and heart with the probable future of these people. On May 15, 1866, he held a conference at Marion with Messers McIntosh and Raymond, the pastors of the local Baptist and Presbyterian churches, with reference to the education of the freedmen of the town.[6]

The resolutions adopted by the conference at Marion urged emphasis upon "the religious education of the Negro"; and asserted that since Northerners were coming into the State with the intention of educating Negroes, the Southern white people should undertake the task first.[7] The resolutions adopted by various religious bodies during the years 1865 and 1866 were in the same vein.[8] Chaplain Buckley, the State Superintendent of Freedmen's Schools, reported to Alvord that "there was unquestionably the alloy of prejudice and opposition to northern ideas in this recently developed friendliness and zeal for the education of the Negro," but he was charitable enough to add "better motives have also had their influence, and are destined to prevail."[9]

Curry left Alabama in 1867 to live in Richmond.

His recent experiences in Alabama had profoundly impressed him with the need of providing religious instruction for the newly-emancipated slaves; and we find him soon after his visit to Baltimore, and the accident to Mrs. Curry, addressing a mass-meeting of Baptists in Richmond, and urging upon his auditors the importance of the Southern people putting forth more vigorous efforts for giving the Negroes a proper religious education.[10]

Major General Thomas, whose testimony shows deep sympathy for the Southern point of view, said that the Curry-sponsored mass-meeting had ". . . . undertaken to establish schools for the religious instruction of the Negroes, and for education in the primitive branches of knowledge."[11]

Significant testimony is that of a witness before the Joint Committee of 1866 who spoke favorably of the plan of a representative in the Provisional General Assembly of 1868 regarding a bill for "the education" of the Negro which he wished to pass.[12] This bill would provide for the apprenticing of all Negro children to their former masters, and for compulsion on masters to teach apprentices how to read and write.[13]  This proposal for Negro children was probably derived from the idea of educational content for the lower white classes current in the South forty years before.[14]

Other testimony to the desired content of education for Negroes comes largely from negative statements regarding the effects of the missionary teaching on Negroes.  General Clanton qualified his advocacy of education for Negroes by saying that *"Now that the Negro is a voter, we would rather have him educated and intelligent."*[15] With education, continued, General Clanton, the white people believed that the Negro "will not steal as much."[16]  Clanton had been prejudiced against the content of schools for Negroes conducted by Yankees after attending a public examination where he saw "all sorts of caricatures to prejudice the Negro against the white man—pictures of the Negro as a slave and as a freeman."[17]  Another source of dismay to General Clanton was an address by a "radical reciting the wrongs against their race."[18] Congressman Peter M. Dox, a North Alabama Democrat, testified that his wife had taught her slaves to read before the War, and that a neighbor warned him to make her stop when she continued teaching her Negroes after the War.  He cited the case of an Elijah Fitch who had been beaten for teaching Negroes.[19]  Dox said that the objection to teaching Negroes was that they were getting out of their places; as an example, he had been obliged to black his own boots because the Negroes would not.[20] The Canadian teacher, Luke, was lynched because he had "made himself obnoxious to the white people . . . . seducing servants from the employ of planters."[21]  Bewailing the passing of the old regime, Mrs. Clayton said that "we (Southerners) could have managed them splendidly and without dissatisfaction or distrust on their part, had the so-called 'Carpetbaggers' kept out of their midst."[22] Mrs. Clayton cited the example of "her boy, Charles," a Negro retainer who was reported to be "as submissive as one of my old slaves, and as much attached to the family."[23]  Charles, in Mrs. Clayton's estimation, was a paragon; and this was due, she believed, to the fact that he had not been "educated."

One of my daughters undertook to educate him, and tried every evening for a whole winter to teach him, and at the end of the winter he did not know all of the alphabet, so she gave up his education in disgust.  Then another daughter began the task, and, after much trouble and patience, got him through the first reader. He is a bright boy, except in "book learning." He can count money, tell time by the clock or watch, and do an errand as intelligently as any boy. His father has been opposed to his being taught to read and write, because he says if he learns to write he will be in the penitentiary for some meanness, and Charley himself said, "Miss Mary, God did not make niggers to learn books." And it is true, many of the young boys that have grown up since the war have been sent to the penitentiary for obtaining money by the means of knowing how to write.[24]

If some of the opposition to Northern-controlled education of Negroes was motivated by social and economic reasons, there was also a tendency to furnish schools for economic reasons. General Clanton advised white people to teach Negro schools because it would furnish employment to needy white persons.[25] In addition, planters established schools for Negroes because the school was an economic asset to plantation management immediately after the War on account of the enthusiasm of Negroes for education. It was said that in Talladega County "many of the people want a school located near them as an inducement to laborers to settle and contract with them, not having any regard to the character of the school."[26] A Republican newspaper cited the case of Mr. Saunders, of Perry County, who

. . . . has employed a gentleman to teach a colored school on his plantation. Mr. Saunders bears all of the expenses of boarding and paying the teacher, and yet expects to be the gainer from having plenty of good, steady laborers well satisfied with their situation. That is to say, the mere prospect of being able to learn something is regarded as a temptation likely to be more powerful than any other on the minds of the freedmen.[27]

These sentiments indicate that the education of Negroes found favor with Southern white persons in a position to influence the course of legislation so long as it could be controlled and directed in favor of the maintenance of certain social and economic institutions. The violent reaction against the idea of educating Negroes visible after the assumption of power by the Reconstructionists can be understood only by an examination of the actual objectives and content of those who did, for a time, control the schooling of Negroes; and these people, as Southern whites feared, represented the "Radical Republicanism" of the Northern "Yankees."

## The Objectives and Content of Reconstruction Education

Education was clearly regarded as an instrument of social and economic policy by the different classes contending for control of Alabama in the years immediately following the Civil War. The extent to which the schools could be used for this purpose changed rapidly as political status changed; and educational objectives changed in turn. In the first year after the Civil War, before the participation of Negroes in politics was assured, the objectives of the missionaries were quite moderate. The scope of the work among the Freedmen was expressed as intended

> .... to make known the work of salvation—to gather and sustain Christian Churches—to instruct the people in all that pertains to life and goodness.
>
> Such have been the circumstances of the people, that in many places the school teacher, imbued with the spirit of Christ and love of souls, has seemed to be able to reach them with spiritual instruction, at least as well as the minister who did not teach.[28]

With the passage of the Amendments giving Negroes the vote, the mission bodies immediately struck a new note. The schools were now to help realize the noble slogan, "Let Us Make Man!"[29] The religious instruction stressed two years before was enlarged to include emphasis on "liberty, the ballot, and intellectual training."[30] Those who would now be called the "ideologists" of the work among Freedmen saw clearly that change in political status signalized by enfranchisement created a new social objective for the schools.[31]

In Alabama the personalities in control of the objectives and content of schools for Negroes were the officials of the American Missionary Association. They represented the strongest anti-slavery, "equalitarian" sentiment of the Abolitionist North.[32] Fleming concedes that "many of the Northern teachers were undoubtedly good people," but he says that "all were touched with fanaticism."[33] From the content of education, as well as from the objectives, it is easy to see how most Southerners would regard the American Missionary Association teachers as "fanatics."

The textbooks used in the missionary schools were standard Northern books, containing anti-slavery poems by Whittier, Holmes, and others; and a special textbook, *The Freedmen's Book*, was widely used as a reader. The editor of this book, L. Maria

Child, had been a vigorous anti-slavery worker for years before the Civil War.[34]   Among the readings included were:[35]

Ignatius Sancho
>(A story of a Spanish Negro who achieved distinction in letters in Europe in the 18th Century.)

Extract from the Tenth Psalm

Ethiopia
>(A poem by Frances E. W. Harper, a Negro Poetess.   The poem was descriptive of Ethiopia's strength, now unleashed —"And Ethiopia shall stretch forth her hands.")

The Hour of Freedom
>(A speech by the noted Abolitionist, William Lloyd Garrison, describing the wrongs of the Negro and discussing the possibilities of Freedom in no moderate terms.)

Toussaint L'Ouverture
>(A reading from an eulogy of the Haitian revolutionary, by Wendell Phillips.   Certainly a revolutionary document in the hands of ex-slaves.)

Bury Me in a Free Land
>(A poem by Frances E. W. Harper, giving the plaint of a slave who died under the lash, but wished his bones to lie in free ground.)

Madison Washington: The Story of the Creole
>(A story of a slave mutiny on the brig Creole, during which the slaves massacred all of the whites on board and finally brought the ship into a British harbor, free.)

John Brown
>(The story of the revolutionary, by L. Maria Child, praising his attempted insurrection in Virginia in glowing terms.   It will be remembered that this story was a part of the reading content of ex-slaves less than ten years after the South had been infuriated by Brown's exploit at Harper's Ferry.)

Several poems from Whittier
>(Accounts of the heroism of Negro soldiers in the Civil War, and of the victory of Negro troops over "Rebels.")

The book was dedicated to
>The Loyal and Brave
>Captain Robert Small
>Hero of the Steamboat Planter.

Small, a free Negro engineer on the Confederate steamer "Planter," had taken the boat out of Charleston Harbor during the Civil War and delivered it to the beleaguering Federal Navy outside the city.   It was not a dedication which might be expected to commend the volume to men like General Clanton, late of the Confederate Army.   The title page had a verse from Whittier,

O dark, sad millions,—patiently and dumb,
Waiting for God,—your hour at last has come.
And Freedom's song
Breaks the long silence of your night of wrong.

There was a curious mixture of political opportunism and high idealism, a working together of Northern, capitalist-sponsored political organizations such as the Union League, and the Northern religious, philanthropic bodies.[36] "Pig-Iron" Kelley, the darling of the Union League whose speech to Mobile Negroes resulted in a race riot and whose ever waking thought, besides Negro suffrage, was said to be a high tariff on Pennsylvania Iron, was represented in the Freedmen's Book by a speech to Freedmen. An excerpt read:

There are Southerners who are prejudiced against you; but you can find the way to their hearts and consciences through their pockets. When they find that there are colored tradesmen who have money to spend, and colored farmers who want to buy goods of them, they will no longer call you Jack or Joe; they will begin to think that you are *Mr.* John Black and *Mr.* Joseph Brown. (Great laughter from the Freedmen.)[37]

Interest in political activity extended to extra-curricular activities. In Montgomery, "The advanced grammar-class ended its lesson with the correction, on the blackboard, of a letter by a colored candidate for office, recently published; the class gave rules for its criticism and explanation."[38]

The teachers in these schools taught the children the social graces by precept, but also by example; part of their technique consisted in living with the Negroes, eating with them, and treating them in accordance with the equalitarian principles that were characteristic of their code. We have cited the case of William Luke, who was lynched because his white neighbors objected to his "fraternization," and teaching of the doctrines of "miscegenation" to Negroes.[39] A Negro, America Tramblies, of Chambers County, was allegedly killed because a white woman teacher was living in his house.[40] Allegations of "bad character" imputed to white teachers in Negro schools by white Alabamians in many cases appear to have been due to the practice of "social equality" —i.e., eating and living with Negroes—which was as much a shock to the native sense of propriety, and as much an index of "bad character," as a violation of the sex code would have been.[41]

Contrast this code of "social equality" with that of Mrs. Clayton. Impoverished after the Civil War, she would occasionally visit one of her ex-slaves who had prospered in freedom, and who took these opportunities to give his former master and mistress a needed full meal: "They never thought for one moment of sitting down to the table with the 'master's' folks. She and 'Sonny,' as she called her boy, would wait on us while we were eating, and when we had finished our dinner and gone into the sitting room, the family would sit down and eat their dinner."[42]

The missionaries and Mrs. Clayton typify these two different worlds which came into conflict in Alabama after the Civil War; both intolerant of the other, sure of its principles of life, and utterly unable to speak the same language where racial conventions were concerned.

For the rest, the content of Negro schools in these early days followed the conventional pattern known to the teachers imported from the North. Much was made of temperance instruction, and a society, "The Vanguard of Freedom," pledged the young Freedmen to "abstain from all intoxicating drinks, the use of tobacco in any form, and from all profane and vulgar language."[43] In the last-named category were such names as "fool," "liar," "thief," "nigger," "as well as stronger epithets."[44] Silsby, a missionary teacher, in a Mobile speech advised the Freedmen not to drink whiskey. "You don't find," he said, "such men as General Howard, General Swayne, or the martyred Lincoln, whiskey drinkers."[45]

The school at Mobile, opening in May, 1865, "by 1866 . . . . had classes in all the different readers, from the pictorial Primer to the Rhetorical Fifth Reader. One class is now in intellectual Arithmetic, reciting in reduction; other classes are well advanced in English, Grammar and Geography."[46]

In Montgomery a total enrollment of 700 was, in 1867, divided as follows: 68 studying the Alphabet, 360 "who read and spell easy lessons," 270 in the advanced reader, 145 in Arithmetic; 175 in Geography, 277 in Writing. This teacher also reported that she had "received from Boston more than 1,000 Temperance tracts and copies of the Lincoln Temperance Pledge."[47] A school opened at Talladega in 1867 by the American Missionary Association, although endowed with the name of "College," instructed students "in the rudiments of two or three of the most needed branches and by practice in drilling the young pupils in these branches.''[48] In 1869 a newspaper report of the closing exercises at the Swayne School in Montgomery stressed the "surprise" and "delight" of the visitors in finding the pupils

. . . . especially ready in mental arithmetic . . . . Similar proficiency was shown in other branches and the recitations exhibited far more than the ordinary exercise of memory witnessed at such times. The singing and general deportment of the pupils gave abundant evidence that with the more solid elements of education the graces of life are not neglected.[49]

Those critics of Reconstruction education who apply the epithet "fanatic" to the Northern missionaries neglect the fact that the kind of education sponsored by the missionaries for Negroes during Reconstruction was the natural outgrowth of a social and political theory diametrically opposed to that of the Conservative whites. Opposition to the education of Negroes was crystallized by the clearly drawn issue between two different social and economic systems, while the school was logically regarded as an instrument of social control. Prejudice against educating Negroes developed from the identification of the school with the Northern humanitarian program of social revolution in Alabama.

## Chapter IX

# COTTON AND STEEL: ECONOMIC CHANGES IN ALABAMA, 1865-1900

### The Reorganization of Agriculture After the War

The Freedmen's Bureau had first attempted to substitute a system of paid labor with wages paid weekly or monthly, for the slave system.[1] This effort was foredoomed to failure. The planters had little capital, and were unable to obtain more. With the approval of the officials of the Bureau, cotton culture fell into the only system of financing agricultural production through free labor which was left to it; the system of share-cropping, by which the laborer agreed with the owner to work a crop through the course of the year, the hire of the laborer to be paid from the anticipated returns on the crop when sold.[2]

Since the available labor on the old plantations was totally without resources of any sort, the planter, in order to insure himself of a supply of labor throughout the year, was obliged to make "advances of such necessary farming utensils and necessities for food and clothing" as the laborer and his family might require until the crop was harvested and sold.[3] The planter had no more capital than the laborer; as the "cropper" could furnish only his labor, the employer had only the land upon which the "cropper" might work. To obtain the necessary capital with which to "furnish" the laborer, the employer had to have recourse to a third person, the merchant, who advanced to the planter the supplies needed for the tenants on a plantation.[4]

Somers reported that the share-cropping system was fully developed by 1871, and at that early date he called it a "miserable" system. The fault, he believed, lay with "the sheer excess of privilege and license" accorded to the croppers.[5] But Somers talked principally to the planters in obtaining his information. By 1875 even an apologist for the system was conscious of the role of the merchant. "The planter usually, and I may say nine times out of ten, does not get a dime. The merchant has got him in debt, and applied (sic) the proceeds; and if there is any over—if the negroes are entitled to any—they get it.''[6]

The share-cropping system thus took on the characteristic form of pure exploitation which it has borne ever since.

The system in its incipiency had nothing in its intent discommendable, but it afterward grew into the strongest engine of power, political and civil, as turned against the colored laborer and the poor white. The profit to be derived from such an occupation, in which total ignorance had to compete with panoplied intelligence, soon caused numerous small merchants to set up small stores on every plantation cultivated. In most instances the merchant was also landlord, and in this combination commenced a system of usury, unrivalled by the Jews of Lombardy of ancient times. The poor, ignorant, colored and white man, renting small farms and relying on the merchant for advances to make his crop, were and still are compelled to pay the exorbitant interest, frequently of fifty per cent and not unusually of seventy or ninety per cent. A coat which cost the merchant one dollar, was frequently sold for two; a pound of meat that cost six cents was sold for twelve; a hat which cost fifty cents was sold for $1.50; so likewise with shoes and other things. . . . I have seen colored men whom (sic) having a large crop, and at the end of said year, after paying such debts to the merchants as were incurred in making said crop, not have enough money to buy a suit of clothing for anyone of the family. I have also seen the taking of all of the crop by the merchant, and also, the horse or mule and other chattels which were given as collateral security for the debt in making a crop in one year.[7]

This exploitative system did not end with the local merchant. Holland Thompson says that ''in spite of the apparently exorbitant percentage of profit, few country merchants became rich.''[8] The hazards of this precarious hierarchy of credit resulted in a banking system that charged much higher interest rates than elsewhere in America;[9] and the banking system in turn was bound to Eastern capital by bonds as onerous as those which shackled the tenant to the planter.[10]

To bulwark this unsound system it became necessary to have control over legislation in the State, and over the police power locally. To this end the planters and the merchants worked in the General Assembly for a system of laws by which labor could be controlled. The device which found greatest favor in Alabama was a system of crop mortgages and liens protected by law which could be enforced by the planter and merchant in courts controlled by them.[11] These oppressive laws fomented discontent on the part of the heavily burdened white and Negro masses. A system of peonage frequently resulted which affected both whites and blacks. In one case in South Alabama ". . . a white man and his entire family were held in peonage by another white man. There had been a 'fake' trial before a Justice of the Peace 'specially elected for the business.' A fine was imposed which the unfortunate man was not able to pay and he was 'turned over to work out his fine'."[12]

This exploitative system, transferring power slowly but surely from the planter to the merchants, was bound to result in the transfer of intelligence and leadership from the old planting aristocracy of the Black Belt to the new mercantile class. But there were other economic forces at work which hastened the decline of the Black Belt. The slave system had progressively exploited fertile lands from East to West, and had paid no attention to the replenishment of these lands, finding it more economical to expand the cotton belt continually to the Southwest and transfer the labor force in slaves to new areas than to keep up the soil.[13] Although Alabama's Black Belt had been in cotton for only four decades at the time of the Civil War, the wasteful methods of the plantation system had already brought even the rich waxy soil of that section to the edge of exhaustion by 1860.[14] After the War, with the mercantile class depending upon exploitation of the labor force through stores and supplies as much as upon actual agricultural productivity, little effort was made to preserve or enhance the fertility of the soil.[15]

The result was that throughout the South, and in Alabama, the decadence of the Black Belt was accompanied by a partial transfer of cotton productivity from the older areas to the "sand barrens" and the foothills.[16] This change was facilitated by several factors. One was that the system of tenure in the hills was based on small farms individually owned and tended by the owner with occasional hired labor.[17] These farms, peopled by "poor whites" or by yeoman farmers, had been unable in ante-bellum times to compete in cotton production with the slave labor and fertile soils of the lowlands. Now by the use of commercial fertilizers the hill country found itself able to raise cotton more profitably than the Black Belt with its demoralized labor system and the fantastic

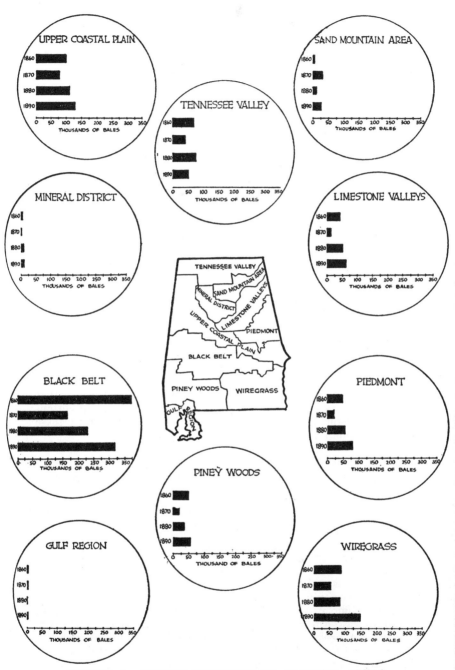

FIGURE 5.  COTTON PRODUCED IN ALABAMA AREAS,
1850, 1870, 1880, 1890.

financial structure based on share-cropping.[18]  By 1880 Smith reported that the center of cotton production in Alabama had shifted definitely to the uplands.[19]  A system of poor agriculture, absentee direction, and the prohibitive cost of fertilizers on rundown lands were held partially responsible; but the system of advances and crop-liens was even more disastrous.

In addition to these, the system of advances or credit, so prevalent through the cotton-producing sections of the State, is not without its evil influence, for the laborer, and too often the owner of the land, is obliged to get advances of provisions from their merchants, for the payment of which the crop is mortgaged; and as cotton is the only crop which will always bring ready money, its planting is usually insisted on by the merchants making the advances and selected by the farmers as a means of providing for payment. In this way cotton comes to be the paramount crop, and there is little chance for rotation with other things. . . .

In the other agricultural regions of the state, and in most of the counties also of the Tennessee and Coosa Valleys, the farms are, as a rule, small, and cultivated by their owners, with the assistance of such labor as may be hired, from time to time. In all these cases provisions are produced on the farm, and cotton is planted as a secondary crop. There is thus some chance for selection of the soils and for rotation of the crops; and when a man cultivates his own farm fertilizers are in more general use so that with the soils naturally much inferior to those of the main cotton-producing regions the average per acre is much higher in these regions of small cultivation.[20]

John Milner, hard-headed industrialist who played a prominent part in the development of industry in Alabama, believed that the economic decline of the Black Belt was linked to a degeneracy of the intelligence and spirit of its potential leadership. In that section, twenty years after the War, there were

No fences, no hogs, no cattle, no agriculture, no nothing. . . . The white people here now all belong to the now super-abundant non-producing class and will work nowhere in the fields. They are educated and born non-producers, and cannot and will not labor in the fields. The product of the soil of Alabama does not sustain and support the population of the State at this time. The large farmers are broke everywhere. Not one in a hundred makes a crop now without a mortgage for his year's supplies and support. Farm after farm, acre after acre, is eaten up in this way, until now it is hard to ascertain to whom the lands in Alabama really belong.[21]

The reorganization of agriculture in Alabama after the Civil War, then, had these immediate results: (1) The development of the system of share-cropping as the basis for cotton production in the Black Belt demanded exploitation of the labor force and effective measures for its control. (2) The effects of the destruction of the old system were felt in the growing decadence of the planting class and the rise of a class of merchants to take its place. (3) The decline of the Black Belt as the center of cotton production shifted cotton culture to the uplands and brought the yeoman white farmers to the front. (4) As a result of these economic and social changes the yeoman farmers assumed an importace in the economic system which was speedily transferred to activity in political fields.

### The Beginning of Industrialization and Urbanization

In 1860 Alabama was almost purely agricultural.[22] Only 4.2 per cent of the Negro slaves and 5.7 per cent of white persons lived in towns with a population of over 2,500. By 1900 the State was still primarily agricultural, with only 11.9 per cent of the Negroes living in cities and forming 45.3 per cent of the total urban group as compared to 45.2 per cent of the total rural population.[23] By this same token the industrialization of the State was in its infancy. It was not until after the turn of the century that urbanization, accompanying industrialization, became socially significant.

Yet it was during the period now under discussion that the foundations of industrialization in Alabama were laid. However infantile this growth by 1900, it had assumed sufficient importance in combination with agricultural change to warrant consideration here.

The immense mineral wealth of the Northern portion of the State was discussed, and plans made for its exploitation, as early as 1840.[24] Coal mining began in 1840 in Jefferson County.[25] Small collieries and foundries were located at Selma, Tuscaloosa, and at other points in North Alabama in ante-bellum times. During the Civil War Negro slaves were used in Jefferson County furnaces and mines, the Negroes being assigned to the rough labor while the mechanics, foremen, and skilled operatives were detailed from the Confederate Army.[26]

The realization of the natural wealth to be tapped in Alabama's "Mineral Region" led to the spirited struggles detailed above in the Reconstruction legislatures, for it was seen that control of railroads leading into the region made profitable utilization of these resources possible.  The industrial history of Alabama properly begins with the completion of the two lines into the area; the South and North (now L. & N.), from the North, and the Alabama and Chattanooga (now Southern) from the Northeast.[27] These two lines met in Jefferson County near an old town known as Elyton, but named Birmingham in prophecy of its industrial future.[28]  The new town was located in one of the most fortunate areas possible for an industrial community; with an iron mountain on one side, coal measures all around, and limestone beds in a neighboring chain of hills.[29]  The land company which set out to exploit this location was called, by one of its satellites, "A Corporation with a Soul."[30]

The phenomenal development of this region is reflected in the coal and iron production in the State from 1870 to 1900.  These data are given in Table III on the next page.

These developments were for the most part in those counties of Northern and Northeastern Alabama which were described above as falling within areas I, III, IV, and V.  In the Tennessee Valley the cities of Sheffield, Tuscumbia, and Florence, the "tri-cities" of the Muscle Shoals region, were favored on account of their location at the head of navigation of the Tennessee River.[31]  Gadsden,[32] in Etowah County, Anniston,[33] in Calhoun County, and Decatur in Morgan County were rapidly growing centers of mining and smelting industries before the end of the century.

On the Northeastern border of the State, along the Georgia line, was the beginning of a textile industry that never employed many Negroes, but became a powerful magnate for the white population of the surrounding rural regions.  Owens gives as explanation for the failure of the mills to use Negro labor the reason that the Negroes could not learn how to use the intricate machinery.[34]  The poor whites, he continues, entered the mills to avoid the competition of the Negro in the cotton fields.

A more probable explanation lies in the fact that in Alabama, as elsewhere in the South,[35] the textile industry was popularized through an appeal to humanitarianism for the poor whites, and capital was sought locally on this basis.  In Sheffield $35,000 was raised in 1890 by subscription among citizens of all ranks to purchase machinery for a cotton mill.[36]  Later it was reported that

TABLE III*

COAL, IRON ORE, AND PIG IRON PRODUCTION IN ALABAMA, 1870-1900

| Year | —Production in Thousands of Tons— | | |
| | Coal | Iron Ore | Pig Iron |
|------|------|----------|----------|
| 1870 | 13 | ------- | ------- |
| 1871 | 20 | ------- | ------- |
| 1872 | 30 | 22 | 11 |
| 1873 | 44 | ------- | ------- |
| 1874 | 50 | ------- | ------- |
| 1875 | 67 | 44 | 22 |
| 1876 | 112 | ------- | ------- |
| 1877 | 196 | ------- | ------- |
| 1878 | 224 | ------- | ------- |
| 1879 | 280 | ------- | ------- |
| 1880 | 380 | 171 | 68 |
| 1881 | 420 | ------- | ------- |
| 1882 | 896 | ------- | ------- |
| 1883 | 1,569 | ------- | ------- |
| 1884 | 2,240 | ------- | ------- |
| 1885 | 2,492 | 505 | 203 |
| 1886 | 1,800 | ------- | ------- |
| 1887 | 1,950 | ------- | ------- |
| 1888 | 2,900 | ------- | ------- |
| 1889 | 3,572 | ------- | ------- |
| 1890 | 4,090 | 1,897 | 816 |
| 1891 | 4,759 | ------- | ------- |
| 1892 | 5,529 | ------- | ------- |
| 1893 | 5,136 | ------- | ------- |
| 1894 | 4,397 | ------- | ------- |
| 1895 | 5,693 | 2,199 | 854 |
| 1896 | 5,745 | ------- | ------- |
| 1897 | 5,893 | ------- | ------- |
| 1898 | 6,509 | ------- | ------- |
| 1899 | 7,484 | ------- | ------- |
| 1900 | 8,504 | 3,095 | 1,155 |

*Owens, *op cit.*, I, 284, for coal production; *ibid*, II, 796-97 for iron ore and pig iron production.

"Citizens of Huntsville have subscribed $125,000 for the erection of a cotton mill plant."[37] The humanitarian argument used by capital held the cotton industry up to the local citizenry as a means by which the poor whites could be elevated from their lowly position and given a regular income. As a result, Negro labor was barred.

POPULATION CHANGES AS A RESULT OF AGRICULTURAL AND
INDUSTRIAL CHANGES

The urban movement was not particularly marked in Alabama
prior to 1900. The beginning of industrialization joined with the
shift of cotton culture away from the Black Belt to the Uplands to
effect a redistribution of population in the State. This demographic
change affected both whites and Negroes. The change in the location of the white population is of more importance here as it created
new political and educational problems which were to affect the
Negro more by indirection than through personal participation in
the motivating events.

In Area III the white population was 3.8 per cent of the total
white population of the State in 1860. By 1900 the three counties
in this "Mineral Area" included in their population 11.7 per cent
of the total state white population. The Negro proportion meanwhile increased from .7 per cent in 1860 to 7.4 per cent in 1900.
In 1860, 12.3 per cent of the white people in the State lived in
Area VII, the Black Belt. By 1900 this percentage had decreased
to 7.9 per cent. The Negro percentage in the same period decreased
only from 39.1 to 38.0 per cent.

Changes in other areas with relation to the total State population reflect the decreasing importance of the areas with large Negro
populations—the old centers of the planting aristocracy—and the
transfer, first of population, and then of power, to the areas where
formerly the white population had been inarticulate and impotent.
These population changes are of great importance in reflecting a
transfer of the educational burden for white children.

POLITICAL CHANGES RESULTING FROM ECONOMIC CHANGE,
1865-1900

The key to politics in the period from 1875-1900 is to be found
in the same kind of sectionalism which disturbed the State in ante-
bellum times. Reconstruction was a brief interlude during which
the vote of Negroes in the Black Belt had destroyed the sectional
balance which had previously obtained between the white voters.
The Constitution of 1875 had not disfranchised Negroes. The election machinery had been so rigged that it was almost impossible for
the Republicans to win; but the right of the Negro to full civil
and political equality had been guaranteed by the Democratic Party
before and during the Constitutional Convention of 1875.

On the theory that Negroes were to be voters, representation in
the legislature was still based upon the number of people resident
within certain counties; the Constitution of 1875 made no change in
the provisions of the Constitutions of 1865 and 1867 regarding representation. In ante-bellum times[38] representation had been fixed
on a "white" basis, although the Black Belt struggled for the Federal Basis which would have counted the Negro as 3/5 of a white
man. The Constitution of 1875 placed the Black Belt Democrats
in the most enviable position of any faction in the history of the
State. If the Negro vote could be controlled, the Black Belt Democracy would have a disproportionate share of representation in the
General Assembly, because Negroes, voting or not, were counted
for that purpose; and in addition the Black Belt Democracy,
through manipulating the potential Negro vote, could insure continued control over the Democratic Party, for representation in the
party convention was based upon the number of votes cast in
the prior election.

The election of 1874 had been won on the issue of the fear of
"Negro domination." This stereotype, says Clark, held the Democrats together long after they would have split under normal circumstances.[39] The whites from the "white counties" were suppressed in the Party and in State elections by ". . . . basing the
representation in the Conventions of the party and in the legislature upon an apportionment embracing the disfranchised blacks in
the Black Belt counties and thereby prohibiting the control of the
party or the legislature by the white counties of the States."[40]
Frequently the number of ballots cast exceeded the number of potential voters. In every election huge majorities were returnd for
the Democratic candidates; and in the Black Belt these huge votes,
registered even when the outcome was absolutely sure, assured control of subsequent Party Conventions. Typically, in 1890 Dallas
County had thirty delegates in the State Democratic Convention;
while Cherokee County had ten. The population of Dallas numbered
9,285 whites, while Cherokee had 18,080.[41]

The shifting of economic power from the Black Belt to the
"white" counties, year after year, accentuated the contest which
was in process, and the discontent of the "white" counties. The
political discontent first took form in 1878 when the "radical" remnants of the white Republicans in North Alabama sponsored a
"Green-Back-Labor" party which was also called "The People's

Anti-Bourbon" party.[42] It is probable that the combination ruling the Democratic Party represented two classes: first, the planters from the Black Belt interested in low taxes and economical administration of affairs; and, second, the clique of railroad interests which were aligned with the Democratic Party as against the factions controlling the old Republican Party. George S. Houston was elected Governor for two terms, in 1874 and 1876. He was widely heralded in the first drive to win the State for the Democratic Party as "The Bald Eagle of the Mountains," sworn to uphold White Supremacy.[43] We have seen that Houston was aligned with Sloss, Leeds, and Pryor, all railroad and coal and iron magnates, against the Russell Sage interests.[44] The Democratic candidate in 1878, R. W. Cobb, was a local attorney for the Louisville and Nashville, the same railroad in which Houston and Sloss were interested; and Cobb had played a leading part in the negotiations in 1874 which had "adjusted" the State debt through "compromise" with the various claimants, "fraudulent" and otherwise.[45]

The Greenback-Labor Party polled 42,343 votes for the Reverend James Pickens in 1880 against 134,411 for R. W. Cobb.[46] The size of the Democratic vote gave notice that the Democrats in the Black Belt were either voting the Negroes, or counting fictitious Negro votes into the State total.[47] This year marked the first definite division of the white vote since the end of Reconstruction.

The insurgent voters needed an organization to work against the powerfully entrenched Black Belt Conservatives. This organization was furnished by the appearance in the State of the Populist Party, whose organization in Alabama was known as the Alliance, or Farmers and Laborers Union.[48] As an organization of farmers the Alliance was preceded in Alabama by the Grange of the Patrons of Husbandry. But the Grange appears to have been composed of planters, and, in the State, to have succeeded in some degree to the political and economic workings of the Ku Klux Klan.[49] The Alliance reflected the will of the men from the hills and uplands where cotton culture had migrated since the Civil War.

The Grange was a friend to education; the Alliance made education one of their principal planks. The industrial portion of the Alliance never developed strongly in Alabama; the young industrialism had no urban mass, as yet, who might aid the embattled farmers. The Knights of Labor had organized several locals in Alabama, one of which was a Negro assembly at Birmingham.[50] At the St. Louis Convention in 1889 when the Alliance came to terms with the remnants of the Knights of Labor, a strong stand was taken on the political and economic rights of the Negro.[51] Faced with the threat of disruption of Black Belt control by the rising tide of Populism, the Conservatives raised the issue of race supremacy again, stating that the Populist program as adopted in St. Louis was "subversive to white supremacy."[52] The action taken by the St. Louis Convention and the consequent raising of the race issue in Alabama is said by Clark to explain the failure of the Populists to gain control of the State government there.[53]

The leader of the Alliance in Alabama was Reuben J. Kolb. Kolb was an ex-Confederate soldier and lived in the Wiregrass section of the State.[54] As Commissioner of Agriculture he built up a powerful political organization within the Democratic Party. Meanwhile, the Alliance was making steady inroads in the General Assembly, finding both Republican and Democratic support in the "white" counties. In 1889 the Alliance controlled the House of Representatives.[55] In 1892 Kolb ran for Governor on a Populist platform, having failed to gain the Democratic nomination in 1890 and 1892. His opponent was Thomas G. Jones, a Montgomery lawyer and typical Black Belt Conservative.[56] The manner of this election is described by one of Kolb's supporters, in terms to which later critical historians have given assent.[57]

In a State election where Captain Kolb, an ex-Confederate soldier, was an independent candidate, the "Democracy" was "saved" by immensely padded returns from the sixteen Black Belt counties in Alabama populated largely by blacks, and enormous fictitious majorities from these counties were employed to overcome and to annul the majorities honestly polled by the whites in the forty-five white counties of the state—counties populated almost exclusively by whites. Returns were recorded for the "Democracy" from Black Belt precincts where the polls were not in reality opened, and where the formality of an election was dispensed with. Upon the day of the "official" count the majority of votes for Kolb were scaled down in the white counties, where the "Democracy" controlled the returning boards, by the throwing out of the vote of many precincts voting Kolb majorities; and this was necessary to overcome the revolt against the machine, even though the Black Belt had already "done its duty." There is not an informed man in Alabama who will not, perhaps, confess to the election of Kolb in 1892 by a tremendous majority. The supporters of the Kolb ticket were mocked at and defied. The Bourbon leaders boastingly asserted: "Yes, we counted you out and we will do it again, if necessary, and what are you going to do about it?"[58]

After the election of 1894, the Populist movement in Alabama dissolved. As a radical movement of the yeoman white farmers of the State, it failed precisely for the same reason that the agrarian radicals who co-operated with the Negroes during Reconstruction had failed—an inability to make economic issues paramount to the race issue. "Becoming, as it did, a question of the 'Solid South' and a choice between 'white supremacy' and a third party, white supremacy won in the 'nineties' as it had in the 'seventies'."[59]

Yet the revolt of the Populists was not without its effect upon legislation, nor upon the status of the Negroes in the State. They played a powerful part in educational reform; and the peculiar manner in which this was effected was of vital importance to the Negro schools. By 1896 Populism in Alabama had "lost its props," because Democrats had enacted legislation to meet "populite" demands—among which were "diversified agriculture," as well as general and technical education.[60]

### Changes in the Centralization of Wealth

In the year 1852 state taxes in Alabama amounted to $548,-340.[61] To some extent the assessment of taxes is a measure of wealth in the state. Taxes on slaves realized $224,822, or 41 per cent of the total. In 1853 the fourteen counties in which Negro slaves were more than fifty per cent of the total inhabitants, paid $256,389 out of a total State levy of $590,224.[62]

The Reconstruction legislature of 1868 under the Constitution adopted that year could find in this agricultural State no other basis for the tax burden than that utilized by the ante-bellum taxing machinery. The result was the imposition of heavy taxes upon real and personal property. In 1870 total State receipts of $1,378,168 included $1,171,486 derived from taxes levied upon the land.[63] These taxes still bore heavily upon the Black Belt, leaving the "white counties" almost as lightly taxed as before the War. The rise of urban centers is evidenced by the fact that the four counties containing urban centers in 1870—Dallas, with Selma; Madison, with Huntsville; Mobile, with Mobile; and Montgomery, Montgomery—together paid $380,674, or 32 per cent of all of the state taxes collected in that year.[64] Dallas and Montgomery were in the Black Belt; their importance in the financing of the State reflected the development of mercantile centers, rather than the rise of industry; Huntsville, in Madison County, was still the center of the Tennessee Valley cotton industry.

The pattern of the distribution of wealth, in so far as it is measured by the payment of taxes on State assessments, shows by 1880 a close approximation to the pattern of the ante-bellum years. The Conservatives reduced both taxes and expenditures sharply, but 90 per cent of all money for the expenses of running the State departments was still derived from the taxes on real and personal property.[65] How much *true* wealth escaped this land levy is uncertain; but the process of general industrial growth of the State, still in an agrarian stage of development, may allow us here to take the distribution of taxes paid as a true index to the distribution of wealth.

It is not until 1890 that a definite shift in the center of wealth as shown by taxes paid develops in the returns from counties. In that year Jefferson County, in which was located the new city of Birmingham, appears for the first time as a center of taxable wealth of great importance to the finances of the State government, with the payment of 15 per cent of the total taxes collected by the State.[66] Calhoun County, with its county seat at Anniston, a new creation of the new industry, appears as an important center of taxable wealth along with Montgomery and Mobile. The center of wealth as measured by tax collections in 1890 had moved definitely to the Northeastern portion of the State along with population.

TABLE IV

PERCENTAGES OF TAXES PAID TO THE STATE BY AREAS OF ALABAMA IN
1852, 1870, 1880, AND 1890

| Area | 1852 | 1870 | 1880 | 1890 |
|------|------|------|------|------|
| I | 11.5 | 13.4 | 14.5 | 12.3 |
| II | 17.2 | 13.0 | 11.2 | 11.1 |
| III | .8 | 1.7 | 3.3 | 17.9 |
| IV | 1.3 | 1.6 | 2.0 | 3.6 |
| V | 4.2 | 5.8 | 8.4 | 10.9 |
| VI | 6.2 | 3.7 | 3.3 | 4.7 |
| VII | 36.7 | 34.6 | 28.1 | 21.3 |
| VIII | 4.9 | 3.6 | 3.3 | 4.4 |
| IX | 7.9 | 8.9 | 7.0 | 7.9 |
| X | 10.3 | 13.7 | 18.9 | 5.9 |

A grouping of tax returns by specific areas within the State indicates even more clearly than data by counties the transference of taxable wealth to certain definite areas of the State (Table IV). In 1870 more than one-third (34.6 per cent) of all State taxes collected in Alabama came from the ten "Black Belt" counties included in Area VII. Only 1.1 per cent came from the three counties included in the Mineral Region, Area III. By 1900 the proportion of State taxes collected from the Black Belt had decreased to one-fifth of the total, while the percentage for Area III had increased to 17.9 per cent. Each successive decade was to show a larger proportion of taxes coming from the Mineral Region, and a smaller amount from the Black Belt.

The economic changes represented by these data were accompanied by a growth of political aggressiveness on the part of the residents of the counties whose contribution to the treasury of the State was increasing. Schools were also affected; the "newly rich" counties began to be more vocal with reference to the school fund, of which they were paying an increasing proportion. They demanded the privilege of local taxation, free from the restrictions of the 1875 Constitution, as their ability increased.

## Chapter X

# ECONOMIC AND POLITICAL CHANGES AS AFFECTING THE EDUCATION OF NEGROES, 1875-1900

A discussion of the education of children in a Northern State might be limited to a survey of basic economic patterns and the description of the manner in which these economic factors were translated into political action, with a final analysis of the educational institutions arising from direct political influences. The discussion of the education of children in a Southern state demands a more extended derivation of forces. With dual systems of schools in theory deriving support from the same source, the development of Negro schools is obviously dependent upon the demands which the system for white children makes upon public support; and the mere physical existence of Negro children is vital to the financing of schools for white children.

We have to discuss in this chapter, then, two varieties of influences. The first has to do with the manner in which economic and social forces, working through political action, affected the educational demands of white children as competitors of the black for public educational funds.

The second variety of influence concerns the rôle of the Negro in the determination of educational policy. Among the sub-categories apparent here is the exercise of direct political power by Negroes. Another is concerned with the effect of social and economic forces in defining the status of the Negro in the community, and so defining his relation to educational needs in the minds of those responsible for public legislation.

## POLITICAL REVOLT AND THE EDUCATION OF WHITE CHILDREN, 1875-1900

The Constitution of 1875 had severely restricted the amount of money available for the schools.[1] This economy was in accord with the pledge of the Conservatives during the election of 1874, and in calling for a constitutional convention.[2]  The scarcity of school monies under the Constitution of 1875 and its effect upon the work of the school system was immediately noted by the Superintendent.[3]

Between 1874 and 1888 the number of white children increased from 91,202 to 159,671.  At the same time Negro children enrolled increased from 54,595 to 98,919.  With the increasing popularization of the school, the need for more revenue became apparent.  Barnas Sears of the Peabody Fund said that the remedy was a local tax:[4] but the Constitution limited the municipalities and made local taxation impossible for school purposes.

Where, then, could revenue for the schools be found?  With a dual system, one for white, and one for Negro children, it was patent that additional money for the white system might be derived from the money spent upon the Negro system, thus increasing the facilities for white children with no addition to taxes. The history of the movement to make the State reach this commitment to inequality in school expenditures covers a long period and deserves extended attention as the vital decision for the future support of Negro public schools.

The Greenback-Labor Party in 1880 marked the first decisive division of the white vote.  The third plank of the party platform denounced the ineffectiveness of the school system and demanded that more money be spent for the schools.[5]  The legislature of 1882-1883 added $100,000 to the State Appropriation for public schools, bringing the school fund to a total of $506,499.[6]  But the rising enrollment in the schools kept pace with increased appropriations.

At the third Annual Meeting of the Agricultural Society in 1888 strong resolutions were passed demanding additional school funds.[7]  The Agricultural Society had been organized among Alabama farmers by Reuben Kolb, then Commissioner of Agriculture. Most of the leaders of the Society later became ''Kolbites'' and ''Populites'' when the third party movement took root in the State.[8]  The Alliance or Populists organized in Alabama in 1887, and one of their basic purposes was the promotion of education.[9]

During this agitation in the 1880's the school fund rose by virtue of these appropriations from $392,904 in 1882 to $511,540 in 1885 and to $646,893 in 1890.  But by the last-named year the

enrollment of white children had reached 180,495 and that of
Negroes 101,649.  On the basis of enrollment the State distributive
fund in 1874-1875, the last year of Reconstruction school finance,
had amounted to $3.85 per child enrolled.  In 1889-1890, in spite
of large additions to the distributive fund, the per capita available was only $2.29.

In addition to the agrarian discontent at insufficient schooling provided by the restricted school fund, a strong sentiment in
favor of larger appropriations and local taxation was evident in
the developing urban centers.  Weeks[10] points out that the levying of local school taxes was clearly unconstitutional; but the
General Assembly persisted session after session in the creation
of new separate school districts endowed with the taxing power.
The first such district was created at Oxmoor in Jefferson County
in 1877.[11]  By terms of this legislation the school trustees were
permitted to levy a tax ''on all property, both real and personal,
within the bounds of said school district, not to exceed half of one
per cent, for school purposes; and for the first and second years,
half of one per cent for building purposes.''[12]

The idea of separating taxes for the support of schools on the
basis of race appeared first in the school district law creating a
separate district at Auburn in Lee County, approved February
17, 1885.[13]  However, the statute provided only that ''the mar-
shal shall keep separate lists of the assessments made against the
property of each race.''[14]  The implications of this law were made
explicit in that creating a separate school district at Opelika approved February 22, 1887.[15]  This law provided that ''the amount
collected from the white race shall go to the support of the white
schools, and the amount collected from the colored race shall go
to the support of the colored schools.''[16]

In 1887 the State Supreme Court declared unconstitutional
the creation of separate school districts where the taxing power
was vested in local corporations.[17]  The question of a racial division of taxes was not reviewed by the Court.  The decision barred
the way to any further hope for finding new sources of revenue for
the schools through local taxation unless the Constitution was
changed.  In his annual Message to the General Assembly in 1890
Governor Seay said that he regarded local taxation as necessary as
ballot reform.[18]

The linking of educational with political reforms is significant.

As the Black Belt politically dominated the white counties through the control of the Negro vote, the Black Belt also stood in the way of local taxation for the schools.  The claims of the Negro for a share of the public school fund were to affect white schools, while the needs of the white schools were to affect vitally the type of legislation enacted in the State in the next few years.

## THE NEGRO IN POLITICS, 1875-1901

While Negro voters after 1875 were firmly controlled by Democratic politicians in the Black Belt, they remained an important political force in the State for some years.  Either in an effort to reassure the North, to obtain Negro support, or as an honest conviction, the Democrats continued to pledge "equality before the law" to Negroes.  The Party Platform of 1876 declared that "We now pledge to all the colored people of this State the protection and maintenance of all their rights to equality before the law, and we are glad to recognize that the more intelligent and better class of them are awakening to the fact that their best friends are the white people of Alabama."[19]

In the course of the election of 1876, the *Advertiser,* organ of the dominant Black Belt Conservatives, took great delight in calling attention to the number of Negroes voting the Democratic ticket.[20]  The Livingston *Journal,* another Black Belt periodical, referred to 500 Negroes in the county voting the Democratic ticket, adding "We compliment them on their good sense, and assure them that they shall find no cause to regret having done so."[21]  The Demopolis *News-Journal* boasted "About 1,000 sensible colored men showed that they are free indeed, and voted the Democratic ticket openly, without fear or favor.  All honor to our colored friends who stood up for the good of the State."[22]  The Macon County *Mail* called attention to a large Negro Democratic vote there in the election of 1876, and gave an admonition to fellow white Democrats to "teach them that in the hands of the Democratic Party, as it is known today, every interest and right of the citizen is to be sacredly protected."[23]

On August 14, 1876, a triumphant procession in Montgomery celebrated the victory of Governor-elect Houston over his Republican opponent.  A large Negro Democratic club was a prominent feature of the parade.[24]  The Democrats, said the *Advertiser,* wanted the aid of the Negroes in "building up and retaining good government." Yet no matter how the Negroes chose to vote, "they should be protected to the fullest extent of their right of suffrage."[25]

Both before and after Reconstruction the Republicans asserted that the Democrats were opposed to the education of Negroes. The Democrats stoutly resisted this allegation. A letter of Wade Hampton to the South Carolina Democrats became a campaign document in Alabama.

We are bound alike by every consideration of true statesmanship and of good faith to keep up in the State such a system of free schools as will place within the reach of every child, the poorest as well as the richest, black as well as whites, the means of acquiring an honest and honorable education. I shall look with confident hope to your aid in carrying out and fulfilling pledges to which we are solemnly committed.

Now that all the Southern states are under the administrative control of men who have the good of all the people at heart, the school money, instead of being squandered, as was the case under the radical rule, will be properly used and made the means of doing vast good to the children, for whose benefit the appropriations were made.[26]

The direct influence of Negro voting upon educational affairs concerning the race is discernible in several instances. The State Board of Education, under Republican control, had provided that the poll tax be devoted to the race by which it was paid. When the Democratic General Assembly of 1874-1875 changed this law in order to have the poll tax money retained in the counties where collected, a proviso was written into the law by the Negro members of the Legislature which declared as public policy that

. . . . it is hereby expressly declared that the true and only intent and purpose of this Act is to secure the "free public school money" so that it may be promptly applied exclusively to the support and maintenance of the public schools, and that this Act shall in no wise interfere with or alter or change in any respect the apportionment of the free public school fund, *pro rata,* to the white and colored children of this State, within the educational age as now provided by the existing laws of the Board of Education.[27]

Tuskegee Institute was founded as a State Normal School in fulfillment of a pledge made to a Negro politician of Macon County, Lewis Adams, who became one of the first Trustees of the

Institute.[28]     Adams had been a prominent Republican in Reconstruction times and was a member of a Republican Negro convention that assembled in Montgomery in 1874.[29]     In 1880 a white
candidate for the General Assembly on the Democratic ticket
promised Adams to introduce a bill setting up a State Normal
School at Tuskegee in return for his political support.[30]

During the Populist schism in the nineties, the Negroes assumed an important position between the warring white factions.
The leadership of the Negroes appears to have been almost entirely
corrupt and venal.     In part the Negro Democrats were financed
by the growing industrial concerns in the industrial section of
Northern Alabama, working hand-in-glove with the Black Belt
Democrats against the Populist revolt.     The *Advertiser* claimed
that Governor Jones received 31,593 Negro votes against Kolb in
1892;[31] and the newspaper was a Jones advocate.     These claims,
of course, were made to shield the tremendous fraud being practiced in the Black Belt to defeat the fusionists; but the presence
of the Negroes as a political force is undeniable.

A conference of Negro Democrats was held in Montgomery
in December, 1892.[32]     The General Assembly invited them by formal resolution to take seats in the gallery as special guests.[33]
That these Negroes were the willing tools of the Black Belt "oligarchy" is shown by their resolutions.

We respectfully urge upon the Afro-Americans of the State
to act with that class of men who have stood for them in time of
need—men who have supplied them with the necessities to make
their crops, have assisted the race to accumulate over $250,000,000
worth of real property, and who now pay 90 cents out of every
dollar for the education of the colored children.     For a Negro to
vote against these men, would be for him to go against himself;
to vote with these men would be to go for his own interest, and to
down race prejudice and race antagonism.[34]

It is interesting to note that the leader of this conference,
H. C. Smith, of Birmingham, had the year before severely condemned Booker T. Washington for an alleged "radical speech"
which the latter had made against the school apportionment bill
of that year.[35]     In later years Smith was financed by the mining
interests of Birmingham and vicinity to fight the organization of
Negro workers in the United Mine Workers in the North Alabama
coal fields.[36]

He declared that he made his living by doing "welfare work" and that the "industrial institutions" around Birmingham contributed between $3,700 and $4,000 for his work so that he did not "have to worry for support." He edited a paper, now defunct, known as the *Southern Industrial Fraternal Review*, organ of a paper organization called the Southern Afro-American Industrial Brotherhood.[37]

The Populists made efforts to enlist the aid of Negroes, a portion of their platform in 1892 pledging the party to ". . . . the protection of the colored race in their legal rights . . . . encouragement and aid in the attainment of a high civilization and citizenship . . . ."[38] But the Populists could never overcome the advantage possessed by the Black Belt Democrats in their control of the fictitious Negro vote. Skaggs, a Populist leader, calls attention to the fact that the vote for a Constitutional Convention pledged to disfranchise Negroes was successful because of the huge vote for the proposal registered in certain counties on the margin of the Black Belt. Leading Negro Democrats worked vigorously for the calling of the Convention.[39]

The Negroes are to be recognized, therefore, as a political force which declined steadily after 1875 but which nevertheless exercised some control over legislation. For the most part, however, the Negro vote, especially in the period after 1885, was a fictitious entity manipulated by Democratic politicians for the purpose of maintaining the Conservative Black Belt white leadership in control of the State.

THE DEFINITION OF THE NEGRO STATUS IN THE NEW ECONOMIC
ORDER AND ITS EFFECT UPON EDUCATIONAL THEORY

It appears that both Conservative and Radical arguments for the education of Negroes during Reconstruction were based on the theory that the Negro was to be inducted into the new social order with the same standing as whites and with the same social and economic stratification. With the elaboration of the share-cropping system of tenant farming earlier arguments for the education of Negroes lost their force and meaning. Under such an exploitative system as described in a preceding chapter it is obvious that an educated labor force, intelligent regarding rates of interest, cognizant of even the simplest methods of accounting, would be a distinct liability to the system rather than an asset.

The result was that the Negro tenant again figured in the agricultural scheme as he had before the war as a slave. He was a labor item, engaged in crude processes which required no special intellectual training; and, indeed, it was thought he would be unfitted for his rôle by the educational process. In the course of the debate on the Blair Bill in the U. S. Senate, in 1888, John Tyler Morgan, Alabama Senator whose home was in the Black Belt county of Dallas, argued that the amount of money which his county might receive from the Blair Bill fund would seriously disturb the labor conditions of his community.

Evidently, Alabama could only use double the sum now employed in common schools in Dallas County, either to double the length of the school term, making it one hundred and forty-six days, or to double the salaries of the teachers . . . . seventy-three days out of a crop is a large item in a cotton country.[40]   One hundred and forty-six days would ruin a crop.[41]

If the Negro was to have a place only as a peon on a cotton farm, there was the danger that "education would spoil a good plow-hand," and that it would make the Negro "get beyond himself," i.e., beyond his status as fixed by the economic system.[42] After the long agitation leading up to the Constitutional Convention of 1901 a planter said that there was no fear of the illiterate Negro, but of "the upper branches of Negro society, the educated, the man who after ascertaining his political rights forced the way to assert them."[43]

It is difficult to separate the rationalizations from considered opinion. Yet it is clear that the growing antagonism to the "younger, educated generation" which was exhibited during the period was associated with a conflict between a status assigned to the Negro in the economic and social system and the threat that education might unfit the Negro for that status. The literature exhibits many documents expressing complete satisfaction with the Negro "in his place," while questioning the behavior and attitudes of the younger generation which was "getting out of its place." The process of education was logically regarded as a disturbing factor, granted that the economic system relegated the Negro to use as a labor implement only. "Old South," a frequent contributor to newspapers of the period, reflected the view of many regarding the relation between economic and social status and education.

Editor, *Advertiser*:

The "New South" humiliation having made itself nauseous to the dwellers in our benighted section, we are next to be begrimed with the hogwash of the hopeful "nigger" and his prospects here in the South.  Reasonable speculation and study of the questions as to what is to come of it if the negro gets strong enough to have a controlling influence in legislation, not to say in social arrangements, in a white civilization, is all well enough and proper.  If the inquiry were put to a genuine Yankee whether it woud advance the cause of liberty, personal morals, individual and national greatness, and general universal loveliness, to flood this country (not with niggers, but) with free Patagonians, or Feegians, or Hottentots, or even the "Heathen Chinee," or Cossacks, or Turks, or the freedom loving followers of the Mahdi, he could and would answer you most promptly, No.

. . . . He would say to you that these people are not of us nor like us in any kind or degree; that physiologically, psychologically, constitutionally, they differ from us; that to absorb them would be to mongrelize and debase to a lower level the masses of our own.

. . . . He would tell you that education, whatsoever else it might do, will not bring forth the fruits with those races that it does with us.

. . . . In our dismay . . . . we turn tail and fly to education. "Wo! Is me, Alabama!"  Well, of course, let education go on. It serves our purpose: it appeases, a little, political masters and religious cranks.  But it is a stupendous farce and a snare.

. . . . When sycophants of the Tom's Cabin sort and slobbering milksops, who mistake themselves for philanthropists, would mislead the mind of the Southern youth with that fallacy of fallacies that education can make the Negro their equal, we should denounce the false teaching, as wicked as false.

OLD SOUTH.[44]

It was in vain that advocates like Jabez Lamar Monroe Curry argued for the education of Negroes on the ground that education affected Negroes just as it did whites.  In answer to the argument that education made Negroes "get out of their place," he retorted "I have never heard of a graduate of the University of Tuscaloosa going between the plow handles."[45]

But the dominant agricultural system envisaged no place for the Negro except "behind the plow-handle."  Prevailing sentiment had no desire to see the Negroes transferred into a landowning population: even an anticipated change in the plantation system was not expected to change his status as crude labor.  The *Advertiser's* ideal of agrarian reform was a 40-acre farm owned by a white man and worked by a Negro on shares.  ". . . . The thousand-acre plantation will . . . . be diverted into forty-acre farms, cultivated as they should be by white owners assisted by Negro wage laborers. Every Negro now here and many more will be needed when ten acres to the plow constitute the average, and his political power will be neutralized beyond the danger line.''[46]

It is doubtful if Curry's arguments made much if any impression on his hearers; for the social and economic system was defining the proper place of the Negro as ''between the plow-handles,'' while reserving other places for the graduates of ''The University at Tuscaloosa.'' The difficulty lay precisely in the fact that education affected Negroes exactly as it did whites.

### The Education of the Negro in an Industrial Community

Southern industrial history like that of the agricultural system has been characterized by efforts to expand productivity while maintaining competitive advantages over other sections.[47]   The industrial corporations engaged in the exploitation of the natural resources of Alabama had the advantage of cheap production ''because of the low standard of living among both Negro and native white'' workers.[48]   These corporations, then, unaffected by any philanthropic considerations, were interested in labor from the standpoint of profits returnable from their investment.   The use of Negro labor in Alabama industry was strictly in accord with the economic advantages to be derived in national and international competition.

The presence of the Negro laborer added a social element to the relations between labor and capital which were early appreciated by both in terms of national competitive advantages or disadvantages.   Trade unionism in the North in the two basic industries of Alabama, coal and iron, discovered that it could not enforce demands for higher wages and better working conditions in its own section while Industry could maintain production in its southern units for the supply of national needs.   Industry in Alabama increasingly followed the example of Southern railway management which frankly used Negroes to weaken white unions and to depress wages.[49]

By 1890 there were 3,687 Negro mine operatives in the bituminous fields in Alabama compared to 2,787 native whites and 1,492 foreign-born whites.[50]   By 1900 the Negroes had increased to 9,735, the native whites to 5,984, and the foreign-born whites only to 1,573.[51] In steel mills Negroes were employed in 1907 only as ".... pipe fitters' helpers, engine tappers, or helpers about the blast furnaces, or blacksmith helpers .... The Negro in Birmingham industry was used largely for common labor."[52] After 1907 Negroes were used as skilled workers and supervisors. The change was made when the United States Steel Corporation purchased the Tennessee Coal and Iron Company which previously had been in the hands of a local management.[53] This change is important because it introduced a more sophisticated conception of the status of the worker in an industrial community than had existed in Alabama before, and in turn this new conception of labor management introduced new concepts of Negro education in Birmingham and the industrial communities generally.

Besides its cheapness, the advantages of using Negro labor as insurance against labor troubles was early recognized. The industrial scheme called for a labor pyramid with a mass of black common labor, with an intermediate layer of white skilled workers and middle class "white collar" employees, and with the financiers and capitalists of these enterprises at the apex. The development of such a structure called for a definition of the social status of the Negro, and prescribed a definite type of education needed for the race. An early "booster" of industrialization in Alabama said:

About 40 per cent of the total city population of Birmingham is Negro. About 90 per cent of the labor employed by all the furnaces, near Birmingham, is Negro.

Besides the Negro furnace labor, much of the labor employed by the city manufacturing industries in iron, such as the rolling mills, foundries, etc., is Negro. Increasing relative employment of it is the rule with all the hard labor enterprises.

*The manifest result of the presence of the Negro labor here is that we have a more intelligent and orderly white laboring population than otherwise might be anticipated.* The Negro of Birmingham fills the industrial position which elsewhere in great manufacturing towns is filled by a low class of whites. The Negro here is satisfied and contented; the low whites elsewhere are dissatisfied and turbulent. *The white laboring classes here are separated from the Negroes, working all day side by side with them, by an innate consciousness of race superiority.* This sentiment dignifies the character of white labor. It excites a sentiment of sympathy and equality on their part with the classes above them, *and in this way becomes a wholesome social leaven.*[54]

From the industrial complex flowed an argument for education based solely upon the contribution which it could make to greater industrial productivity. In this system, the two races were to receive an education appropriate to their status.

. . . . The complex mechanical agencies of our commerce, the varied mechanism entering our trades and industries, are too powerful and intricate to be manipulated by the unschooled and illiterate masses. These considerations alone, to say nothing of the duties of intelligent citizenship, amply justify the maintenance of a system of public education in an industrial center like Birmingham, and the flourishing condition of her public schools furnishes the most convincing evidence of the fact that . . . . she has not been unmindful of her duty.[55]

The definition of the Negro as needed by the industrial community solely as raw labor in the lower brackets of manufacturing skill led inevitably to differentiations in the educational system provided by Birmingham. For Birmingham white children, there were three "elegant grammar school buildings and one high school building"; for Negroes "two comfortable and well arranged buildings."[56] The white school was furnished with "the elegant 'new Paragon' single desk," the colored schools with the "Andrews Triumph Desk," the latter a double desk.[57]

This thinking was general in Alabama. In 1900 a conference of industrial promoters described the labor force of Alabama as made up to the extent of one-third of Negroes, "who are well adapted for common labor, and in some instances can be satisfactorily used for semi-skilled capacities."[58] A paper read by D. A. Tompkins listed the need for technical schools to train textile workers for the growing textile industry, but no reference was made to Negroes except as potential raw labor for crude operations.[59] Although Negroes had performed most of the skilled operations on the plantations in ante-bellum times, the new economic setting called for a re-definition of the Negro's ability to perform such labor. The *Advertiser* said: "The undeniable truth is that the Negro is not fitted to perform successfully any work which requires skill, patience, or mental capacity. There is something lacking in their brain and in their body. Their minds cannot comprehend the intricacies of fine mechanical work and their hands canot be trained to accomplish it.[60]

This conception of the Negro status, transferred to education, was vigorously affirmed by J. H. Phillips, Superintendent of the Birmingham schools. "Whatever anthropologists may report," said Superintendent Phillips, "the black race is to all intents and purposes a young race; therefore it is imitative." The practitioner of educational method should remember, he added, that the Negro child might appear to better advantage in rote learning than the white child, "but in anything that requires reasoning—in mathematics for instance—the Negro soon falls behind."[61] The needs of industry in Birmingham and the capacity of the Negro child thus neatly coincided.

In defense the advocates of the education of Negroes were obliged to argue for funds on the same economic ground, that education would equip Negroes for profitable employment in industrial communities. Attention to these arguments will be deferred to a later section.

## Chapter XI

# RACE, CLASS, AND THE SCHOOL FUND, 1875-1900

## The Legal Basis of School Support in 1875

By way of recapitulation, the Constitution of 1875 had provided for the support of schools in the State by a State School Fund. Local taxation was prohibited for school purposes and the provision that local public corporations might make appropriations to schools from their general tax funds was rendered ineffective as a source of large aid from municipalities by another provision which prohibited the municipal corporations from levying a tax higher than thirty cents on the hundred dollars of assessed valuation. The municipalities were strained to support their other responsibilities within this limited levy.

The State School Fund thus became almost the sole public source of support for the schools. This Fund was to consist of income from U. S. land grants; escheated and intestate estates; a poll tax of $1.50; and income from the surplus revenue.[1] A Constitutional provision restricted the amount of money which could be spent for any school purpose other than the salaries of teachers to 4 per cent of the total Fund.[2] There was, therefore, to be no local taxation, very little money for administration, and none for building schoolhouses. As the State School Fund was a purely fictitious claim upon the State because of the loss of the Fund in ante-bellum times, the entire finance for the system was to be derived from State taxation.

The law governing apportionments directed

The Superintendent of Education . . . . (to) apportion the educational fund to the respective townships or school districts subject to the provisions of the preceding section, according to the latest official returns of the enumeration of the townships or other districts which have been made to his office; and he shall also apportion the fund for each township between the races therein.[3]

The apportionment was to be strictly on a per capita child population basis. With the Constitutional injunction that schools

should be provided throughout the State "for the equal benefit of
the children thereof," this law left no discretion to any official to
discriminate racially for or against either racial group.[4]   The
county superintendent was to be notified by the state superintendent of the amount of money due each township; and the county
superintendent, in turn, was to notify the township trustees of
the amount of money available for them.[5]   One phrase of the law
reads as though a loophole had been provided by which discrimination could be practiced.   The county superintendent was

.... in making such apportionment, (to) have regard to the number of children of his district within the educational age, *who
will probably attend each school,* and apportion the district fund
to the several schools of his district *as nearly per capita as practicable,* so that all children who attend the public schools established for them shall receive equal benefit from such fund.[6]

### EFFORTS TO OBTAIN MORE SCHOOL MONEY

The Act of 1875, providing for the payment of the poll tax
to the school of the race represented by the taxpayer, recognized
the principle of dividing the taxes.[7]   This Act did not take effect
on account of what the Superintendent called "clerical mispri-
sion."[8]   By Act approved February 8, 1877, the statute was made
operative.[9]   In 1879 the superintendent reported a large poll tax
delinquency which was much greater among the Negroes than
among the whites.[10]   Undoubtedly this delinquency was due to
the practical disfranchisement of the race.

In the General Assembly of 1876-1877 an effort was made by
Black Belt representatives to change the Act, which then provided
for the payment of the apportionment to the counties and townships on a quarterly basis, to a yearly basis, and to eliminate from
the Act the term "free schools."   The Constitutional Convention
had inserted in the Article on Education a section[11] which prohibited the payment of any of the public school money to sectarian
schools.   Fleming says that this section was aimed at the co-
operative arrangement which obtained between the State and
American Missionary schools during Reconstruction.[12]   Former
Superintendent McKleroy, a Democrat, representative in the General Assembly from Barbour County, condemned the bill because
it was intended to subsidize private schools by paying only once a
year.[13]   Few colored schools, he added, would be allowed to run,

because the yearly apportionment would be made when the Negro schools were not in operation.[14]   The sponsor of this legislation was S. J. Doster, from Dale County.   In a letter to the *Advertiser*, he explained:

It is the object of the law to apply and to utilize the school funds for the education of the children of the State—to re-establish the grand old schools of primary, academic, and collegiate; (sic) to restore local self-management to parents, teachers, and to trustees . . . .

The strongest opposition to the "substitute" came from members, who represented "school districts" of the old law, and from colored members, frightened at the loss of monthly pay for teachers.[15]

In 1882 the Superintendent of Education took cognizance of the growing agitation for local taxes and discontent at the share of the state apportionment received by Negroes.   In his report he suggested:

If it can be constitutionally done, which it is the province of the General Assembly to determine, I would recommend the enactment of a law, giving to counties, cities, towns, and separate school districts, the power and authority, by a vote of the people resident therein (with proper restriction), to levy and collect a special school tax, not to exceed four mills on the dollar, to be used for the purpose of purchasing school sites, the erection of schoolhouses, and the payment of teachers, as a supplement to the amount appropriated by the State; the amounts so raised by each race to be applied to the use and benefit of such race.[16]

The General Assembly did endow local corporations with the taxing power for school purposes, but the State Supreme Court ruled this procedure unconstitutional in 1887.[17]   It was not until the same year that the law establishing the separate school district of Opelika provided for the segregation of taxes according to race.[18]   Superintendent Armstrong repeated his recommendation for a segregated school tax in his report for 1884.[19]   His successor, Solomon Palmer, stressed the need for more school revenue in his first report for the year ending September 30, 1885.   "There will have to be," he said, "an increase of school funds to meet the demands of our rapidly increasing school population."[20]   He reported that patrons were supplementing the school fund by private contributions and by the payment of tuition fees so that the amount of money reported paid to teachers was not even "an approximation of what the people of Alabama are paying for the education of their children."[21]

In 1887 the per capita apportionment for white children decreased from 73 to 72 cents, while that for Negroes decreased from 73 to 66 cents. The difference was explained by the fact that the General Assembly was making more generous appropriations for the support of Negro Normal schools; but these appropriations were deducted from the Negro share of the total school fund.[22] It was therefore possible for the legislature to establish and support these higher schools as political "log-rolling," at the expense of the Negro common school fund but at no added expense to the State.

The Supreme Court decision had "blasted" the hopes of Superintendent Palmer and other advocates of education "that a sentiment favorable to local taxation for school purposes might be awakened in the minds of the people of the State . . . . as the best available means to make a public school system efficient."[23] It was a year of crisis for the Negro schools, for the Court decision, in barring the way to increased revenue for the white schools from local taxation under the Constitution of 1875, left as an only resource the money appropriated to Negro children. Increasingly it was realized that "the great need of our school system is more money. Our school population increases each year, making an annual increase in appropriations for schools necessary if we hope to meet the demands upon us and to keep pace with the progress of the times."[24]

In the course of the year before the session of the General Assembly of 1888-1889 a determined campaign was waged to add support to the advocates of an increased school appropriation. In the background of this agitation were the rising Populists in the white counties[25] and the stand taken by the Agricultural Society in the summer of 1888 for increased educational facilities for white children.[26]

The legislative session was preceded by a newspaper campaign for and against an increased fund which clearly shows the decisive factor of the Negro participation in school benefits. The Montgomery *Advertiser,* historic organ of the Conservative Black Belt Democracy, took a strong stand for the adoption of an increased fund. The objections to such an increase were listed and discounted.

Here in the Black Belt, where the country white people pay the taxes and the negroes go to school, there is considerable sentiment to the effect that taxation for public schools is a burden to the white people, not a benefit. Whether the Selma *Times* and Eufaula *Times* will succumb to this remnant of opposition to public schools, we have been hitherto unable to forecast.[27]

The Selma *Times and Mail* quickly asserted its stand against any increase in the state appropriation. It objected to the poll tax as "oppressive to the farming classes," because "the white people pay the taxes and the Negroes go to school."[28] The *Advertiser* answered that the property tax and not the poll tax was the crucial point of issue. "It is the property tax, here paid by the whites and enjoyed mainly by the Negroes, that constitutes the burden."[29] The *Advertiser* recognized the justice of the complaints made by Black Belt property owers, saying that "no people less enlightened, less generous and less far seeing" would continue to pay taxes for schools. The *Advertiser* slyly continued ". . . . but for our own knowledge of their high aims and purposes we should ourselves wonder that the opposition is not greater than it is."[30] After all, the *Advertiser* concluded, the opposition to more liberal appropriations was only "grumbling," and when the time came to vote for higher appropriations the men of the Black Belt would ". . . . go down for progress in education as in all things because in their hearts and consciences they know that civilization demands it and it is wisest and best."[31] This was pure wishful propaganda as the next session of the legislature was to show.

### THE DEBATE ON AN INCREASED SCHOOL FUND

When the session convened the argument against the school fund increase was concentrated more and more in opposition to giving the Negro non-taxpayers more money for their schools. From North Alabama an editorial voice counseled:

Now, don't give us any of the old chestnuts—"Educate a negro and you spoil a good field-hand"—"a man ought to educate his own children"—"The State of Alabama devotes a larger proportion of her revenue to educational purposes than does any other State."

We have heard all this, over and over, and yet we believe in our heart of hearts that it is right to enlighten every human being into whom God has breathed the breath of life, and the public good demands that the State aid in this work to a reasonable extent.[32]

The debate on increasing the school fund appropriation began and ended in the House on December 3, 1888. The school bill provided for an increase of $55,000. Mr. McLeod, of Clarke County, moved that the amount be raised to $100,000.[33] Mr. Paine, of Macon County, spoke against the increase.[34] Coming from a Black Belt county, he could not, he said, support the increase. The people of the Black Belt were paying for the education of three Negro children to one white child, such was the distribution of the fund. Did it strike any man's mind as fair for the whites to pay the taxes and the Negroes get the education? The whites, he said, paid three dollars and educated three Negroes, while the Negroes paid only one. He was willing to divide the fund and he asked where was the justice of the appropriation asked for when it worked injustice to the whites. He was willing to do what was right.[35]

Mr. White, of Geneva County.[36] pointed out that this was a Democratic legislature, and since the inauguration of Governor Houston in 1874 the Democratic Party was committed to the education of the Negro. "Were we," he asked his fellow legislators, "to refuse education to the Negro and cut off the white children, too?" He was willing to go to Dallas County and pay his taxes and educate the Negro if by so doing he would educate the white children of the white counties.[37]

Mr. Cunningham, of Lauderdale County,[38] wanted more school money. He sympathized profoundly with the Black Belt, but that section could not be separated from North Alabama. He did not believe any member of the House would vote against the bill because it educated the Negro. The people of North Alabama would not always take a stone when they asked for bread. The people of North Alabama paid more taxes under Democratic than under Republican rule. Promises would not always do and nothing but the 15th Amendment ever kept them from voting the Republican ticket. "Kinky" heads did not look half so obnoxious to the people as they used to. The Democratic State Convention promised to increase the fund to the fullest ability of the State. If the promise were not kept, instead of having seven Republicans in the House, they would have a controlling interest in the next House.[39]

Mr. Adams of Bibb County[40] wanted to bring one question before the House. What does this thing resolve itself into? It was a question of whether the Negroes and the whites should grow up ignorant together, or be educated together. Should we then say to the people, because a few ignorant, depraved Negroes were ignorant, we shall shut off the white boys and girls of the State? The House owed it to the children of the whole State to increase the appropriation, and he would support Mr. McLeod's amendment.[41]

Mr. Summers of Colbert County[42] favored Mr. McLeod's amendment. There should be no discrimination, but all should be educated, white and black, male and female. He was here to ask for more money to dispel ignorance and prejudice. Educate and elevate every son and daughter of the State. He wanted the House to understand the gravity of the situation. He loved the Jeffersonian and Jacksonian Democracy and his father was a Democrat and bore arms for his country. He was a dyed in the wool Democrat.[43]

Mr. Lowe, of Jefferson County,[44] thought Mr. Paine was mistaken in opposing the increase because it meant more money for Negroes. The fact was that there were over 100,000 more white people in the State. This was not local and when the appropriations were made it was given to the whole State and the white people got the larger share of the appropriation. He should be unwilling that one race should drag another race down to ignorance because of a difference in color.[45]

The notion to increase the appropriation by $100,000 was voted down, 45-41.[46] The Black Belt voted almost solidly against the measure; the counties of Autauga, Barbour, Bullock, Dallas, Greene, Hale, Lowndes, Macon, Marengo, Montgomery, Perry, Pickens, Russell, Sumter, and Wilcox "hit it with an almost solid shot of 27 votes."[47] But on the next day the vote was reconsidered, and the increase was agreed to without a record vote.[48] The *Advertiser* had declared on the evening of the first vote that it was a contest between "property rights" and the rights of children, and asked the question "Have the white children of the white counties no claims which property is bound to respect?"[49] A statement by Mr. Wiley, of Montgomery County, is significant. He showed that the amount of taxes paid by North Alabama had increased greatly within the last few years, and that the section, therefore, was now paying a much larger proportion of the State taxes.[50]

## The Tax Rate and the State School Fund

It is also of interest to note that the legislature of 1888-1889 was attempting to lower the tax rate, and the State School Fund represented a levy upon property valuations because the taxing machinery depended almost entirely upon a property levy for state income.   In the debate over the increased school fund reference was frequently made to the high tax rate and to other "obligations" of the State.[51]   One of these obligations was represented by a Confederate soldier lobby working for pensions.   The situation, then, was immensely complicated for the politicians, with property-holders clamoring for lower taxes, Populists clamoring for more money for the schools, Negroes possessing some political power, and the Confederate soldier pension grant in the offing.   By 1890 the direct State appropriation (including the 16th Section fund) amounted to $455,658.[52]   In the same year the amount of general taxes in the State amounted to $1,042,618.[53]   Adding in appropriations for the various educational institutions of higher grade, more than fifty per cent of total state taxes were thus devoted to educational uses.   Table V indicates the relationship between valuation, taxation, and the educational fund in Alabama from 1875-1900.   The Democrats had boasted of their economy as compared to Reconstruction "extravagance."   Now the increasing demands for schools threatened to raise the tax levy in spite of a greatly increased tax valuation.

TABLE V

Valuation, Taxation, and Appropriations for Schools in Alabama, 1875-1900 (By Five-Year Periods)

| Year | State Property Valuation | Tax Rate, Mills | | | Amount of General Taxes | School Appropriations |
| | | General | Special Soldiers | Special School | | |
| --- | --- | --- | --- | --- | --- | --- |
| 1875 .......... | $135,535,792 | 7½ | .... | .... | $1,016,518 | $348,891 |
| 1880 .......... | 139,077,328 | 6½ | .... | .... | 908,678 | 337,320 |
| 1885 .......... | 172,528,933 | 6 | .... | .... | 1,041,897 | 511,540 |
| 1890 .......... | 258,979,575 | 4 | .... | .... | 1,042,618 | 498,698 |
| 1895 .......... | 242,537,176 | 5½ | ½ | .... | 1,135,597 | 738,577 |
| 1900 .......... | 270,408,432 | 5½ | 1 | 1 | 2,028,063 | 916,059 |

## The Change of the Method of Apportionment

In his report for 1890 Superintendent Palmer introduced his discussion of the school problem by saying that "Alabama must

—by some means—largely increase her school fund if she keeps pace with other states, and meets the growing demand of her school population."[54]    He then proceeded to review the complaints "against the way in which the school funds are apportioned and used." The two principal ones were, first, that Negroes in the Black Belt received all of the money while paying no taxes; and, second, that the Negroes were not mentally advanced to the point where they needed as much education as the white race, and therefore did not need as much money for their education.[55] Palmer would not go "into the discussion of the question"; "I desire to say that under the present system of apportionment of the school fund there are cases of peculiar hardships that can be, and in my opinion should be, remedied by a different and more simple form of apportionment."[56]    The present system, he stated, called for the apportionment of money to the schools so that sometimes "one or the other of the races has funds which for lack of numbers cannot be used by that race, so that at the end of two years it has to be reapportioned into the general fund of the county.  Now," continued Palmer, "in order to remedy this and other evils, the school fund should be apportioned by the Superintendent's office to the different counties and townships without regard to race." The township trustees were then to take responsibility for apportioning the fund, and establishing schools for the number of children "who will probably attend each school." He also recommended that the legislature pass a certificate law, making salaries contingent upon the grade of certificate granted.  It was clear that this provision was aimed at the Negro schools, as was the first: ". . . . under our present apportionment of funds such is frequently the case that the poor teacher of the colored race gets much better salary than the well qualified white teacher."[57]

Palmer's program called for the placement of the school funds in the hands of local authorities to be spent at their discretion. With what degree of sincerity it is difficult to judge he added,

Allow me to say here that I have no sympathy with those who would deprive the colored race of an equal participation in the benefits of the public school fund.  I believe that it is not only our solemn duty but best interest to see that the colored race is educated and elevated so as to fit him for good citizenship, of which, in my opinion, there is not the slightest probability that he will be deprived.[58]

Neither did he favor the segregation of taxes for school support: "Such a law . . . . would be declared unconstitutional as being against the public policy and contravening the spirit and policy of the 14th Amendment."[59]  His plan would "go far towards remedying the evils complained of" and would be on "sound principles," i.e., constitutional, "that teachers should be paid in proportion to the quality of the work performed by them."[60]

Palmer's plan was introduced in the House by Mr. Steele, as House Bill 504.  Its purpose was immediately recognized there and widely applauded.  Mr. Smith of Russell County thought the bill was the best measure ever introduced in the Alabama legislature. He thought that the author of the bill "deserved a vote of thanks from the *white* people of the State."[61]  Mr. Davis of Fayette County stated that the author of the bill was Professor J. W. McAdory, Superintendent of the Jefferson County Schools.  The House gave no further debate to the bill, and it was ordered to third reading and passed without a dissenting vote, 65-0.[62]

Coming after the long debate on the bill of 1888, where so many members protested an interest in equal opportunities for the education of Negroes, this precipitous passage through the House gives rise to speculation.  As the bill was intended to aid the Black Belt it is probable that the white county representatives had made a compromise agreement with the Black Belt, agreeing to let them have the advantage of a diverted school fund from Negroes if the Black Belt in turn would agree to raising the amount of money appropriated by the State for schools.

In the Senate the bill encountered opposition.  The probable reason for this is highly significant in the interpretation of the status of public schools for Negroes during the period.  The bill passed the House on February 2.  On the next day there convened in Montgomery a "Colored Convention," intended "to discuss subjects which would benefit the Negro race in Alabama."[63]  The personnel of this Convention included the names of all the prominent politicians among the Negroes of the State.  The topics set for discussion were "The rights of the Negro with regard to railroads and common carriers," the "treatment of convicts and the lease system," the "necessity of supporting newspapers published in the interest of the Negro race."[64]  A bill was pending in the General Assembly to segregate Negroes on the railways; this "Convention" was intent on moderating legislation hostile to Negroes.

On the first day a Committee was appointed "to appear before the legislature and urge the passage of such measures as will be of benefit to the negroes of Alabama."[65]

In the evening session of the Convention, a speech was made by Professor B. T. Washington, of the Tuskegee Normal School, described by the reporter as a ". . . . bitter speech against the legislature for apportioning the public school fund as it had. He denounced the bill now pending in the House with reference to separate cars for negroes. His entire speech was aimed at the Legislature."[66]

The Negro Democrat, H. C. Smith, followed Washington. His remarks as quoted by the *Advertiser* illustrate why he was on the Democratic payroll and was later to be on the payroll of anti-union industrialists in Birmingham.[67]

H. C. Smith, the Birmingham negro lawyer, advised the Convention to proceed with caution. Denunciations had never yet resulted in any good. If the Convention really wanted measures enacted into law, which would benefit the negro race in Alabama, they must go about it in a manner different from the method which Professor Washington inaugurated. It was also through the instrumentality of Smith that action on the Force Bill was laid aside. His idea was that the less this Convention had to do with the Force Bill the better it would be for all concerned.[68]

In a dignified answer to this article, Washington wrote the *Advertiser* that the report was "calculated to do me injustice regarding the speech I made before the Colored Convention." He denied nothing and affirmed nothing except to state that "so far from denouncing anybody as being bitter, I should have been willing for the whole legislature or all of the citizens of Tuskegee to have heard all that I said."[69]

The Convention sent a delegation to see Governor Jones regarding current legislation affecting Negroes. They were reported to have gone away from their conference with this politician "mightily pleased," and "saying that such talk as his would soon make them all Democrats." Jones told them that the purpose of the school bill was not to discriminate against Negroes, but ". . . . to do away with the hardships in some townships, where the number of one race was so great that the children in a minority received practically no benefit. It was a different proposition, he added, from the proposed amendment to the Constitution to which he had already alluded in his inaugural.''[70]  The bill ''was a different proposition''; as noted above, it was a proposal for discrimination so worded as to remove its unconstitutional features, and to deceive the trusting Negroes.

In the course of the Senate debate eighteen counties, all ''white,'' were tentatively excluded from the provisions of the bill. Mr. Milner said that he ''did not see how the bill could hurt the white counties, and it would help the black counties, and he was willing to do all he could for those peope.''[71]  Mr. Inzer objected to it on Constitutional grounds.  The Constitution, he said, required that the funds be expended per capita.  Mr. Hargrove moved an amendment to make the bill constitutional.  It was to insert after the words ''. . . . equitable, the words 'and for the equal benefit of the children thereof'.''[72]  Mr. Skaggs opposed changing the system.  The present law, he thought, provided a just and equitable method for apportioning the fund.  The people of the Black Belt could do what they wanted to with the school fund, but the people of North Alabama had some rights that ought to be respected.[73]  Mr. Milner

. . . . said he didn't have much to do with the public schools and possibly did not know much about them, but he saw no justice in having the schools for negroes open nine months in a year and the schools for white children open only about one month in two years.  The school fund is intended for the equal benefit of both races, and he was in favor of the bill because he wanted the schools for the whites opened for the same length of time as were those for the  negroes.[74]

Mr. Crampton called for a ''bold and united front, in behalf of the proper distribution of the school fund.''[75]

The appeals of the majority resulted in the withdrawal of exceptions to the bill, by a vote of 19-8.  The bill then passed without a further record vote.[76]

### The Effect of the Apportionment Act of 1891

The significance of House Bill 504 lay in two changes from the former system, as an examination of the two acts will show.  These changes were as follows:

| APPORTIONMENT PROVISIONS OF FORMER LAW | APPORTIONMENT PROVISIONS OF NEW LAW |
|---|---|
| The Superintendent of Education (shall) apportion the educational funds . . . . *between the races therein* . . . . so that all children who attend the public schools established for them shall receive *equal benefit* from such fund.[77] | . . . . the superintendent of education (shall) . . . . apportion the public school fund . . . . according to the entire number of children of school age. . . . . *the township trustees* . . . . shall apportion to each school . . . . such an amount . . . . *as they may deem just and equitable* . . . .[78] |

These changed provisions gave to the local officials entire discretion as to what they should consider "just and equitable" amounts. In an opinion asked for by Superintendent Palmer to clarify the meaning of the act the Attorney-General said:

Under said act the Superintendent of Education is relieved of apportioning the school fund between the races; otherwise, the duties of that officer with reference to the apportionment and disbursement of the school fund as prescribed by the provisions of the code hereinbefore quoted, are in no way changed. In brief, the effect of the act, is to amend the existing law by erasing the words hereinbefore *italicised*.[79]

In other words the Act was intended only to allow discrimination between the races. The opinion continued by saying that a "*per capita* apportionment is not indispensable in a system which secures equal benefits to all children." Equality of educational opportunity did not require an equal per capita payment; the Trustees could satisfy "equal benefit" provisions of the Constitution by providing schools for the two races identical in term "equally suited to the educational wants of the children of each race."[80]

Superintendent Harris emphasized the purpose of the law in his comment on the opinion. "One teacher may be secured to teach a certain school at one price, while another teacher may be employed to teach a different school at a greater or less sum. Trustees must use their very best judgment, looking to the highest interest of all the children to be taught."[81]

It is difficult to get a statistical measure of the alacrity with which the local officials hastened to "use their very best judgment" in apportioning the funds "with justice and equity." The

State Report for 1891-1892 discontinued the printing of expenditures by race; the student can find only a statement of the amount of money apportioned to the counties, with no record of what was done with it afterward.[82]  The fact that the State Report did not resume printing these data until 1908 is in itself a significant testimony both to the result anticipated and to that immediately obtained.  It also indicates that the state officials felt a reason for concealing the result of the law; and from whom?  Presumably from the Negroes.  It follows, from the delayed resumption of reports at a time when the disparity had grown extremely great, that there was no longer any fear of the publication of these data so far as the Negroes were concerned.  Indeed, other circumstances lead one to believe that the publication of the financial data by race, showing an aggravated condition of discrimination, was prompted as an argument for local taxation and to reassure the white citizens that Negroes were not receiving then any significant portion of the public school fund, and would, therefore, not be likely to receive any of the money to be provided by local taxation.

If the reports were discontinued because the State officials proposed to keep the Negroes in ignorance of what was happening, it indicates to what degree the political power of the Negroes was feared.  By 1908 Negroes had been thoroughly disfranchised in the State.

Despite the lack of itemized accounts the reports yield some indication of what happened as soon as the new law was in force.  The Superintendent of the Wilcox County Schools where above 85 per cent of the educables were Negroes reported in 1891 that in anticipation of the working of the new law, "Wilcox never had such a boom on schools.  The new law has stimulated the whites so that neighborhoods where no schools had existed for years, are now building houses and organizing good schools.  The attendance for 1892 will far exceed that for 1891."[83]  In his message to the legislature in 1892 Governor Jones said that "the number of schools during the past two years has been greater than ever before, and the attendance better."[84]

It is evident that salaries were first reduced, after which the length of the term was curtailed.  Other data show that the number of Negro teachers was reduced while the number of white teachers was increased.  In the Black Belt one township with a heavy Negro population was reported by a State Superintendent

TABLE VI

EXPENDITURES AND SCHOOL POPULATION IN THE BLACK BELT COUNTY OF
WILCOX, BY RACE, 1876-1930

| Year | Expenditures for Teachers' Salaries | | School Population | |
|---|---|---|---|---|
| | White | Negro | White | Negro |
| 1876-1877 | $2,136 | $6,055 | 2,403 | 7,357 |
| 1877-1878 | 2,368 | 5,936 | 2,113 | 6,559 |
| 1878-1879 | 2,307 | 5,154 | 2,113 | 6,559 |
| 1879-1880 | 2,538 | 5,997 | 2,021 | 6,190 |
| 1881-1882 | 2,142 | 6,064 | 2,057 | 6,457 |
| 1882-1883 | 2,155 | 6,181 | 2,057 | 6,457 |
| 1883-1884 | 2,370 | 6,574 | 2,057 | 6,457 |
| 1884-1885 | 2,603 | 8,044 | 2,046 | 7,456 |
| 1885-1886 | 2,326 | 8,607 | 2,046 | 7,456 |
| 1886-1887 | 2,689 | 7,753 | 2,250 | 7,675 |
| 1887-1888 | 2,596 | 7,309 | 2,250 | 7,675 |
| 1888-1889 | 2,468 | 6,850 | 2,322 | 7,719 |
| 1889-1890 | 2,379 | 7,157 | 2,322 | 7,719 |
| 1890-1891 | 4,397 | 6,545 | 2,482 | 9,931 |
| 1907-1908 | 28,108 | 3,940 | 2,285 | 10,745 |
| 1908-1909 | 27,679 | 3,844 | 2,111 | 10,155 |
| 1909-1910 | 30,612 | 3,339 | 2,000 | 10,758 |
| 1910-1911 | 30,294 | 3,569 | 2,000 | 10,758 |
| 1911-1912 | 30,129 | 3,750 | 1,884 | 10,677 |
| 1912-1913 | 29,135 | 3,225 | 1,884 | 10,677 |
| 1913-1914 | 34,127 | 3,480 | 1,985 | 10,263 |
| 1914-1915 | 34,127 | 3,580 | 1,985 | 10,623 |
| 1915-1916 | 33,289 | 3,462 | 1,868 | 9,872 |
| 1916-1917 | 33,289 | 3,462 | 1,868 | 9,872 |
| 1917-1918 | 39,924 | 4,055 | 1,791 | 9,054 |
| 1918-1919 | 40,917 | 4,959 | 1,791 | 9,054 |
| 1919-1920 | ......... | ........ | ........ | ........ |
| 1920-1921 | ......... | ........ | ........ | ........ |
| 1921-1922 | 56,231 | 4,762 | 1,865 | 8,946 |
| 1922-1923 | 55,360 | 4,300 | ........ | ........ |
| 1923-1924 | ......... | ........ | ........ | ........ |
| 1924-1925 | 57,478 | 4,600 | 2,022 | 8,636 |
| 1925-1926 | 65,342 | 4,423 | 1,978 | 8,626 |
| 1926-1927 | 57,437 | 4,661 | 1,978 | 8,626 |
| 1927-1928 | 64,622 | 5,090 | 2,167 | 8,927 |
| 1928-1929 | ......... | ........ | ........ | ........ |
| 1929-1930 | 57,578 | 8,176 | 1,865 | 8,483 |

(No data as to expenditures for teachers' salaries available, 1891-1907.)

not only as having run ".... its public school eight months with a first-class teacher," but as also having defrayed "a considerable portion of the expenses of boys and girls off at college."[85]

An inspection of expenditures for teachers' salaries for 1890 and for 1930 indicates that the per capita expenditure for Negro children in the latter year was in several counties not much larger than it had been in the former year. By placing the state appropriation in the hands of local authorities the Act of 1891 irretrievably doomed the Negro schools of the Black Belt to an inferiority which widened constantly as the years passed.

The Act did more. It gave the resources of a diverted school fund from Negro children to the politically powerful but minority white population of the Black Belt. As a result, that section no longer clamored for local taxes; and for the next twenty-five years every effort, on the part of the "white counties," to obtain legislation permitting local taxation, was estopped by the Black Belt. There are few new patterns apparent in the educational systems for Negro children in the rural, Black Belt of Alabama since 1890. For such changes as have occurred, we are obliged to turn to the urban centers, meanwhile studying the peculiar and complicated situation by which the diversion of the school fund from Negro children in the Black Belt was to retard education generally elsewhere in the State, and so affect, again by this curious indirection, the education of Negro children in other sections.

## Chapter XII

# THE CONSTITUTIONAL CONVENTION OF 1901: PUBLIC OPINION OF THE NEGRO

The legislature in session in 1900-1901 authorized the holding of a Constitutional Convention. When submitted to the people the proposal carried by a vote of 70,305 to 45,505.[1] The customary heavy majorities for any administration measure were polled throughout the Black Belt, indicating, as the Populists pointed out, that the Negroes were voting for their own disfranchisement.[2]

The Convention assembled at Montgomery on May 21, 1901, and remained in session for eighty-two legislative days. For the student of education, the records of this Convention are especially valuable. A stenographic report was preserved of all debates. This report is utilized here, first, to yield an approximation of the prevailing sentiments regarding Negro social status, and, second, to give the background of the constitutional and legal framework now represented by existing statutes under which the schools for Negro children in the State have been administered since the Convention of 1901.[3]

## THE SETTING OF THE CONVENTION

The Constitutional Convention of 1901 was not a phenomenon peculiar to Alabama. Rather it was a culmination of a series of events, economic, political, and social, which had parallels in each of the other states of the lower South during the same period. The atmosphere of the section has led one Negro historian to refer to the two decades from 1890 to 1910 as ''The Vale of Tears.''[4] The years in which various conventions were held represent significant social barometers to measure cumulative pressures of racial and economic conflict, exploding in the form of conventions. Mississippi held her Convention in 1890. South Carolina moved to revise her basic law in 1895. Louisiana's point of maximum pressure may be dated by the Constitutional Convention of 1898. North Carolina called her Convention in 1900, and Virginia and Alabama held concurrent Conventions in 1901.[5]

The period was one marked by discriminatory legislation enacted against Negroes in each of the States, following a kind of social contagion transmitted to legislative bodies.[6] Throughout the two decades mentioned the years were punctuated by frequent and bloody instances of race riots and lynchings. In 1892 two hundred and fifty-two Negroes were lynched in the United States, the largest number on record for any year.[7] In Alabama extralegal executions in this category reached their peak in 1893, when twenty-seven persons of the Negro race were lynched.[8] Incidents of inter-racial violence were given lurid and lengthy emphasis in the newspapers.[9]

It is probable that the incessant and morbid preoccupation of the press with such matters, which was the mark of journalism of the period, acted as an additional inciting factor to new and more outrageous incidents. Nor can it be doubted that these stories were powerful agents in building up a body of public opinion which became increasingly hostile to the Negro. Agitation of politicians was another source of propaganda which must have had far-reaching effects upon public opinion.

Racial violence and open conflict were symptomatic, not causal. The deep roots of inter-racial difficulties, so far as they were economic and social, have been traced elsewhere in this volume. It is certain that the Alabama Constitutional Convention of 1901 was of the same order of symptoms, and represented a climactic point for Alabama. Specifically, the Convention climaxed (a) conflict between white and Negro workers, (b) appeals to the Negro issue in politics and in industrial conflict, (c) the dissolution of the Populist Party and the absorption of many of its elements into an insurgent Democratic faction founded on racial, not economic, radicalism, and (d) tensions between industrial and political factions for control of the State.

Since the same pattern followed in Alabama was paralleled in other states due caution is necessary in assigning any specific, local causes. Sentiment and action in Alabama were part of a sectional, almost national fever. As such the phenomenon deserves detailed examination in search of what the consequences were for Negroes and for their schools.

The Debates of the Convention require caution in interpretation. At the very beginning of the Convention there was a spirited discussion regarding the advisability of making a stenographic record of the proceedings. Some of the members believed that the Convention would incriminate itself by its discussion of expedients intended to disfranchise the Negro. John T. Heflin, who later became United States Senator from Alabama, in 1901 was a youthful delegate to the Convention bent upon making his mark in public life. He was among those opposed to printing the stenographic report. His reasons against publication were expressed as follows: "There will be, Mr. President, when the battle comes between the Anglo-Saxon and the African, things said here that we do not want to go before the Court of the United States . . . . We will say things down here in our Southern way, and in the great old commonwealth of Alabama, that we do not want read and criticized day after day."[10] The delegates were speaking with one eye on the United States Supreme Court, with the other cocked at public opinion elsewhere in the nation. They were also talking for home consumption. Mr. J. T. Long, a wry-tongued member from Walker County, accused the members of introducing useless ordinances in order to see their names in print. "The first thing they do when they get the *Advertiser* after introducing a resolution or an ordinance on the day previous is to swell with pride like a toad frog swells with wind."[11]

The motive for calling the Convention has been variously defined, both by commentators, and by the delegates themselves. Fleming states that the white people of Alabama were tired of the corruption necessary to manipulate or suppress the corrupt Negro vote, and so desired disfranchisement in order to assure the State of clean elections thereafter.[12] Scroggs says that the white counties saw that there was no way to unseat the Black Belt unless the fictitious Negro vote was legally abolished.[13] Yet Skaggs, a Populist, believed that the Convention was the work of the "Black Belt Oligarchy."[14]

It is probable that the Convention, like any other outcome of the political mind, was a compromise compounded of all of these notions on the part of those who voted for it. It is important to recognize the variety of factional sympathies which was present in the Convention. This variety was reflected in comments on the status of the Negro, and must be taken into consideration in interpreting the meaning of individually expressed opinions.[15]

### The Status of the Negro as Reflected in the Debates

The majority of the 155 delegates to the Convention were pledged to disfranchise the Negro, while committed to the principle that no white man should be deprived of the ballot. It might therefore have been expected that sentiments expressed would reveal a generally limited conception of the status of the Negro in public and social life. The Convention, however, was so permeated with extremist convictions that ex-Governor Oates was led to declare, toward the end of the Convention:

It is most startling to me, remarkable under the change in public opinion in regard to the status of the Negro in our State (sic). Why, Sir, thirty years ago, when I was a member of the House of Representatives here, right over there between those two columns, I witnessed a fight between a leading carpetbag member of the legislature from Montgomery—Stroback and Bob Arrington, a negro employee of the House, and I stood over them myself and kept anybody from interfering until the negro gave him a good beating which he deserved, and I never incurred the disapproval of a single one of the Democratic members of the House. Why, sir, the sentiment is altogether different now, when the negro is doing no harm, why, people want to kill him and wipe him from the face of the earth.[16]

This changed sentiment Oates thought the more remarkable because many of the men whose bitterness was extreme had, in his opinion, less reason than he had for their feeling.

I have cause for a greater grievance against the race, politically, than any delegate in this Convention. In 1870 when I was elected to the Legislature a negro ran against me. In 1872 when I ran as the Democratic nominee for Congress in this district, I was defeated by a negro, Rapier, the only time I ever was defeated in a race before the people, but these occurrences do not warp my judgment nor bias my sense of justice.[17]

The extremists were drawn from Oates's contemporaries as well as from the younger generation of delegates.[18]

The men who expressed the more moderate attitudes toward the Negro in the course of debate included ex-Governors Oates and Jones. Delegates Case, Cofer, and Freeman, with other Populists and Republicans, exhibited a kind of professional sympathy for the Negro and voiced criticism of the Democratic leaders intent on disfranchisement. The ex-Governors were of the old Conservative wing of the Democratic Party. They spoke usually in terms of a paternalistic responsibility which, they asserted, was the portion of the "white man's burden" in dealing with the Negro.

The populists and Republicans, all of whom represented white counties, spoke in terms of abstract justice and right. To this extent the debates do not warrant the belief that there had been a development of anti-Negro sentiment in the counties almost entirely populated by white persons. The most virulent anti-Negro speakers were from the Black Belt or from counties bordering on the Black Belt; and from counties where the new industrialization was developing. Prominent in this latter group were Delegates Burns, of Dallas, a Black Belt county; J. Thomas Heflin, of Chambers, a marginal county on the fringe of the Black Belt with a rapidly developing textile industry; J. T. Long, of Walker, a coal mining county in the Mineral Region that had been the scene, just five years before the convening of the Constitutional Convention, of bloody conflicts between white and Negro miners; and Williams of Marengo, a Black Belt county.

It is not without significance that both Oates and Jones had been in the higher circles of the "oligarchy" which had ruled the State since 1875. These two men had some reason to be grateful for the Negro vote, fictitious or real, through which their party machine had been perpetuated in control of the State. They were in the forefront of the struggle against the Populist schism of the early 'nineties, when the anti-Negro propaganda had been the greatest single asset of the Conservatives. In one of his Convention speeches Oates grew reminiscent regarding extra-legal means he had used in 1874 and 1875 to disfranchise Negroes.[19] Apparently many of the older members of the Convention had carried on, for a lifetime, political campaigns based on the race question in which they had constantly expressed sentiments that were purely political shibboleths which they did not, themselves, take too seriously. What was shibboleth to them, however, must have had a profound effect upon the opinions of their followers.

## NEGRO PETITIONS

With no members of the race represented in the Convention four groups of Negroes availed themselves of the right to petition in support of the claims of their people. The reception of these petitions was not especially respectful and the necessity for resort to this technique in itself reflects the changed status of the Negro in Alabama political and social life. If the Negroes of the Reconstruction period had been "impudent" and arrogant in their public assertions, by comparison the petitioners of 1901 were humble, conciliatory, and even subservient to the point of abject apology.

The first petition was presented on the 7th legislative day just after Mr. Bulger of Tallapoosa County had moved to adjourn. The delegates were weary and in no mood for "trifling." Mr. Coleman, of Greene County, asked "Who is the author of this petition?" The presiding officer replied, "I see it is signed by Booker T. Washington." Mr. Samford of Montgomery immediately asked for an adjournment. There were cries of "Read it!" from the floor. Mr. Coleman argued that Booker T. Washington was "the most noted man of his race in the State, and perhaps in the South . . . . and I, for one, would be pleased to hear it read."[20] The petition was finally read over the protests of several other delegates.

The petition bore, in addition to that of Booker T. Washington, the names of fourteen prominent Negroes in the State. V. H. Tulane was a Negro real estate dealer in Montgomery. Three Negro physicians, Dungee of Montgomery, Steers of Huntsville, and Washington of Montgomery, were in the list of signers. Others were W. R. Pettiford, President of a Negro bank in Birmingham; W. H. Councill, formerly a Negro politician, and for the period from 1875 to the date of the Convention president of the State Normal School and land grant college for Negroes at Huntsville; and J. R. E. Lee, director of the Academic Department at Tuskegee Institute.[21]

The petitioners explained their pleas as the only way by which Negroes could present their views to the Convention, since no Negroes were included in its membership. They were not, they said, "stirrers-up of strife between the races." Each represented himself as a good citizen and as a taxpayer. Their race, they said, had been brought to America forcibly, but had benefited from slavery. Negroes had rendered much service to the white people; they had nursed "you and your children," and shown deep loyalty during the war when treason would have meant the immediate collapse of the Confederacy. Negroes had already been disfranchised in Alabama for twenty years; there was no need for additional measures which would serve no useful purpose aside from humiliating the race.

The Negro was declared to be at the mercy of the delegates.

The white man in the South claimed to be the Negro's best friend; now the Convention had a chance to prove the claim. The petitioners objected to disfranchisement, and added that they feared that the Convention would take public school opportunities away from their race. They understood that certain members of the Convention proposed legislation by which Negro schools would be "virtually blotted out."[22]

Other petitions received from Negroes in the course of the Convention were signed by A. F. Owens, Negro minister and school principal at Mobile;[23] Willis Steers, Negro physician, of Huntsville; and W. H. T. Holtzclaw, principal of a Negro school at Snow Hill in the Black Belt county of Wilcox.[24] The latter petition contains an interesting appeal to the economic interests of certain of the delegates and illustrates the usual technique of the Negro leaders in appealing to the employing class among whites:

And if you of the dominant race will be generous in your dealings with us, generous in the matter of education, you will ever have at your door a people who *will not trouble your sleep with dynamite nor your waking hours with strikes.* This is the people that appeal to you today to make a suffrage law (though the test be the severest that is consistent with reason) that will operate for all men alike.[25]

The Negroes might have saved themselves the trouble of their artful petitions had they been as realistic as Delegate J. T. Long of Walker County. Mr. Long was violently anti-Negro, but his frank statements have for our purpose the great virtue of needing not too much extrapolation regarding their fundamental honesty of conviction. In another connection he said, "I know I am up against a shell game, and it will do me no good, but I am here to speak my protest against a property and educational qualification."[26] It may be that the Negro petitions were addressed to the Convention in the same spirit of futility.

### THE SUFFRAGE PLANK

The debate on Negro suffrage served as a forum for the lengthy discussion of the capacities of the race and of the implications of the "race problem" in general. It had been argued that the Black Belt wanted a limited Negro suffrage in order to be able to continue in control of the state political machinery. Several

Black Belt delegates vigorously denied the charge. Only a few Populists and Republicans spoke in favor of full Negro suffrage. Mr. Case of Dekalb County, a Populist, was one. He proposed that the first article of the Convention should read: "That all men are equally free and independent; that they are endowed by their Creator with certain inalienable rights."[27] He was howled down. Mr. Lowe of Jefferson County argued that the Convention had not met to disfranchise Negroes and to insure white supremacy, but to secure honest elections for the State.[28] The insurgent Democrats proposed a Grandfather clause and a Board of Registrars as the instruments of Negro disfranchisement. Mr. Lowe expressed the belief that the talk regarding "white supremacy" was designed to shield from public view the fact that the proposed Board of Registrars would create a political machine which it would be impossible to defeat in the course of future elections.

Mr. Freeman, a Republican, was against the idea of a Constitutional Convention from the very inception of the idea. Any scheme of disfranchisement would lead, he believed, to eventual corruption of the body politic.[29] Mr. Banks, ex-Governor Jones, ex-Governor Oates, and others, were for a qualified Negro suffrage. Oates argued that there were some Negroes better qualified to vote than some white men. He recalled an incident of the Battle of the Wilderness, when a body servant seized a rifle and fought shoulder to shoulder with his company while one of the white soldiers ran to the rear.[30] Mr. Burns of Dallas County promptly called him to task. Did Oates, he asked, mean that any Negro was better than a white man? The speaker, he added, could have found better examples of the conduct of white men during the Civil War, when the boys in gray fought for their homes and their freedom.[31] Mr. Oates was obliged to apologize; he had been in twenty-seven battles for the Confederacy, he believed in White Supremacy, and his devotion to the cause was unassailable.

Mr. Long of Walker County was opposed "to the enfranchisement of any Negro in the state of Alabama, let it be Booker Washington or anyone else."[32] Senator Morgan, Senior Senator from Alabama, opposed the Grandfather Clause in a letter read to the Convention. He did favor an ordinance to bar all Negroes from holding public office. The Grandfather Clause, in his opinion, was palpably in conflict with the Federal Constitution. The insurgents hinted that he opposed it because the Conservatives wished to use the Negro vote in the next few years while solidifying their position under the new Constitution.[33]   Ex-Governor Jones joined in opposition to the Grandfather Clause on constitutional grounds.

Mr. Coleman of Greene County, who previously had defended Booker T. Washington in his right to petition, spoke for the Grandfather Clause, and asserted his support would go for any other clause which served totally to disfranchise the Negro.   He lauded the Negro as a slave; he, too, had fought in the Confederate Army, and his body-servant had tended him nobly when wounded.   Negroes had been faithful and obedient immediately after the war. But the Carpet-baggers had made savages of them.[34]

Mr. Greene reviewed the horrors of Reconstruction.   The Convention ought to disfranchise Negroes to prevent a recurrence of such a period.   The State and the white people did not need Negro disfranchisement now; the Negro was already under control.   Disfranchisement, however, was needed to insure the perpetuation of the white people in control of the State.[35]

Mr. Cunningham of Jefferson County was for the Grandfather Clause.   So was Mr. Knox of Calhoun, the President of the Convention.   Knox was Joseph J. Johnston's campaign manager in 1896 and in 1898, and it was said currently that Johnston planned to contest Morgan's senatorial seat in 1902.[36]   Mr. Knox believed that Negroes were in need of suppression throughout the South. He cited an editorial from a Negro newspaper in Wilmington, North Carolina, which had precipitated a bloody race riot there. Total disfranchisement would help prevent such incidents in Alabama.[37]

Mr. Jones of Wilcox County in the Black Belt stated that his people were just as much in favor of the disfranchisement of Negroes as any in the State.   Mr. Hundley of Randolph County said that he was from a county where there were 1,400 white Democrats, 1,200 white Republicans, and 800 Negroes.   The Negro vote could be bought; and both Democrats and Republicans among the white people wanted Negroes disfranchised because it was getting too expensive to have to buy the Negroes, who had raised their prices recently.[38]

Mr. Williams of Marengo County said that it was time for one of the younger men to speak, one who had come up since slavery.   He thought that there was no Negro as good as "the least, poorest, lowest-down white man he ever knew."   He was

from the Black Belt, but still he was for complete disfranchisement of the Negroes. He asked the Convention "to place the
white man, be he ever so lowly, above the negro, be he ever so
high and exalted among his own people."[39]

The speech of Delegate J. T. Heflin, of Chambers County, is
interesting as another specimen of the sentiments expressed by
the younger leaders in the Convention. Mr. Heflin was to figure
as a prominent political force in Alabama during the next three
decades, and his rise was facilitated by an appeal to his constituency on the basis of race prejudice and an assumed economic
identity with the interests of the "man lowest down" among
white persons.

In the debate on Negro suffrage in the 1901 convention, Heflin
said: "I believe as truly as I believe that I am standing here that
God Almighty intended the negro to be the servant of the white
man."[40] The Negro, thought Mr. Heflin, should be disfranchised
because he could be bought "for twenty-five cents and a drink of
whiskey." In answer to the argument put forward by ex-Governor Oates concerning the faithfulness of the old time Negro, Mr.
Heflin said:

That, Mr. President, was the old-time slave of over thirty years
ago. That, Mr. President, was the negro that had been brought
up in the back yard and in the kitchen, and brought up to reverence and respect his master. There was a spirit of fear that went
about him; reverence for his superior, and a feeling of humility
and obedience on occasions like that was innate, and we are glad
that they did so well. I am not an enemy of the negro; I am a
friend to him in his place. My father owned more slaves than
any man in Randolph County. I love the old-time Southern negro. He was in his place as a slave, and happy and contented as
such; and, Mr. President, I love to think of the old black mammy,
as Governor Taylor says; I believe the time will come when the
South will erect a monument to the old black mammy for the lul-
labies she has sung. We like to think of all these things . . . . We
love to go back and bring them back to memory; but you take the
young negro of today, and put them in the same position that
their fathers were in, and, gentlemen, a quarter of a century from
now you would not be on a floor like this singing their praises. I
tell you that the old negroes are passing out and the young bucks
that are coming in have got to be attended to. I like to think of
the negro from the old fashioned Southern standpoint. I like to
tell him you do this, or you do that, John, and here is a quarter;
you black my shoes, or catch my horse, and you do this and that,
and all is well; but when I have to walk up to him and say, John,

come down off that telegraph pole that Governor Oates spoke of on yesterday, where he is setting telegraph poles through the city;[41] come down, I want to talk to you about the tariff question, and sit down with him at my side, just light up our cigars and talk . . . .

Is not that a sad state of affairs? Why, Mr. President, I saw this morning a little fellow coming down the street, and the negro was as happy as could be, with a piece of watermelon in one hand and a set of cane quills from the swamp tied together with a string, in the other, blowing "Boogoo Eyes." You see them now and then in a blacksmith shop with a squeaking bellows, and with the hammer and anvil making music sweet. That is his home; that is where he ought to be, and that is where he must be.

A man goes out and buys a section of land, or inherits it from his father, and in the midst of the place he builds a magnificent home, and there he rears a family, and a negro comes along through the country and builds himself a little house out in the woods, and becomes the servant of the white man and looks after his horses, and stands at the door with his hat off, and asks, "Boss, you want your shoes shined?" and all is well. He stays in the kitchen where he belongs.[42]

### OTHER DEBATES ILLUSTRATING NEGRO STATUS

The brief debate on the convict lease system, which was an enterprise highly profitable to the State and to the private companies engaged in the business, casts an interesting sidelight on the technique by which the Negro issue was used to defeat every proposed economic or social reform. Mr. Pillans of Mobile, and Mr. Beddow of the city of Birmingham in Jefferson County, were for the abolition or moderation of the lease system. Mr. Beddow represented trade union sentiment; the convicts on lease in Jefferson County furnished an impossible competition to the union miners in Alabama as elsewhere in the South. Mr. Cunningham of Jefferson County defended the lease system.[43] He believed that, contrary to assertions, it was an eminently humane system; and after all, most of the men affected were Negroes. Mr. Beddow nevertheless thought the system a disgrace to the State. Mr. Rodgers of Sumter County defended the use of the lash, which Mr. Beddow wanted to outlaw. Mr. Rodgers said that he had a Negro ex-convict in charge of his plantation at home in Sumter County. The ex-convict had told Mr. Rodgers, "Yes, Boss, they do whip them up there, and they ought to be whipped." Mr. Rodgers added:

Now, everybody knows that the great bulk of convicts in this State are negroes. Everybody knows the character of a negro, and knows that there is no punishment in the world that can take the place of the lash with him. He must be controlled that way. He inherited that peculiarity from his ancestors, when he came from the shores of Africa, where they provide that kind of punishment, and if we take away the lash from this convict system, we will destroy the efficiency of the system.[44]

The convict system was left inviolate by the Convention.

Booker T. Washington was not entirely popular with several of the delegates. Mr. Cobb of Macon County, in which Tuskegee was located, introduced a measure to remove schools holding more than two hundred acres of land from tax exemption. Tuskegee and the white college for girls situated at Montevallo had recently received federal land grants totalling twenty-five thousand acres for each school. The Tuskegee land was located in Walker County. Mr. Long of Walker County wanted to know if the ordinance "would affect Booker Washington's school, owning fifteen or twenty thousand acres of land in this State?"[45] Mr. Cobb thought that it would. Mr. Long stated that he hoped so. Mr. Cobb stated that there were private institutions chartered in Alabama "that have vast amounts of money coming to them year after year, and they are buying every acre of land they can put their hands on."[46] Mr. Greer of Calhoun County thought that the State would be taking a backward step if it removed Tuskegee from the tax exemption list and Mr. Spears agreed with him. Did the gentleman from Macon County (Mr. Cobb) want to tax Tuskegee Institute alone, and not the white schools in the State? To do so would be unconstitutional.[47] Mr. Lomax thought the measure "a deadly blow at higher education."[48] Undoubtedly the measure could not escape taxing the University of Alabama. Mr. Lomax thought further that even if the white schools were not affected the measure was unwise. "Are we," he asked, "going to pass this amendment to put a tax upon the school of Booker T. Washington? Why should we tax that more than any other school?" After other objections had been raised by Robinson, Lomax, and Bulger, Mr. Cobb withdrew his amendment.[49]

Mr. Long from Walker County then submitted a similar amendment raising the tax exemption for private schools to fifteen hundred acres. He stated that much of Tuskegee's tax-exempt land was located in his county and that it crippled the tax-raising

possibilities of the communities including the property. Mr.
Burnet asked, ''Are you aiming at Booker Washington's school?''
Mr. Long replied that he was not, specifically. People had been
turned off the land which had been donated to the University at
Montevallo, and to Booker Washington's school. ''In the name of
the Lord,'' asked Mr. Long, ''ain't fifteen hundred acres enough?''
On motion of Mr. Browne, Chairman of the Committee on Taxa-
tion, Mr. Long's amendment was then tabled.[50]

During the course of the final debate on suffrage, Mr. Burns
of Dallas County introduced a measure which by implication was
aimed directly at Booker T. Washington.[51] The proposed ordinance read:

> *Whereas,* mixed bloods seldom inherit even the impaired vir-
> tues of their progenitors, and in every section of our country are
> always found among the most vicious and vindictive classes of our
> citizens, and
> *Whereas,* this Convention was called with the understanding
> and for the purpose that white boys of Alabama should not be
> forced to compete with any others, whose only qualifications for
> suffrage lies in their ability to memorize .... and .... therefore,
> *Be it Ordered,* by the People of Alabama, in Convention as-
> sembled, That all bastards whose disabilities as such have not been
> removed by the Governor, or Circuit or City Judge, shall not be
> allowed to register or vote in this State.[52]

Mr. Burns's ordinance was referred to the Committee on
Harmony. The only argument attempted against it by the friends
of Washington in the Convention was the oblique one that it would
also disfranchise several hundreds of white men in the State.[53]
When the Article on Suffrage came up for final passage, Mr.
Burns brought up his ordinance again. His speech was in reference to the influence of Washington, and of Tuskegee Institute,
as he saw it:

> We were sent here to kill snakes. When I was a boy I was a
> snake hunter (laughter) and I have killed a good many innocent
> black snakes, and coach whips, and chicken snakes, and house
> snakes that will sleep with you and not harm you; but I always
> hated to bruise the head of one of these, but it was always my de-
> light to find a rattler with his mouth open and his fangs ready, a
> rattler who has control of nearly all of the other snakes, especially
> of his color and of his pedigree, a rattler educated and warmed at
> home by the fires, by smiles, by the approbation of the best white
> citizens, Democrats, and supported at the North by white Republi-

cans who have never had any use for Alabama, or the Democrats in Alabama.   That rattler with his mouth open, but his tail not giving you warning, his fangs are here, and he sends out young rattlers every summer, twelve or fifteen hundred, two thousand, yea, and more.

Those young ones come out and among them gather a great quantity of damsels—some from Massachusetts, some from Rhode Island, some from Cuba, and from other places.[54]

## CHAPTER XIII

# THE CONSTITUTIONAL CONVENTION OF 1901: TAXATION AND EDUCATION

In his introductory message to the Convention, President Knox reviewed preconvention pledges not to raise the taxes in the State, which were accompanied by other pledges "to take no backward step in education."[1] On the floor of the Convention it was frequently asserted that the white counties were more interested in obtaining more money for education than in the disfranchisement of the Negro. The speech of President Knox reflects the conflict between the taxpayers and the friends of education, and the solutions proposed in the Convention.

Illiteracy, he said, retarded the growth and the development of the State. Education increased its productive power; Massachusetts was cited as an example of a state where production was in proportion to education.[2] A good school system would encourage immigration in order to meet the industrial needs of the State for skilled labor. The new Constitution, he prophesied, would probably enact literacy and educational qualifications for the vote, and so the State should provide a good school system for those who otherwise would be unable to qualify for registration.[3] Some opposition to the Convention, continued Knox, had arisen from those who believed that the Convention would adopt a "suffrage plan" which would offer to the Negro an incentive to obtain an education, while the child of the white man would be without a like stimulus because protected in his right to vote without regard to the density of his ignorance. This, he said, was not the purpose of the Convention. If it wished to do so it could make literacy a qualification for the vote. If so there was all the more reason for providing a good school system.[4] "I believe we should keep faithfully the pledges we have given not to increase taxation, but this should not deter us from making every effort to rid our State of the disgrace of illiteracy."[5]

The delegates did not seem to conceive of any other source of revenue for governmental purposes other than the time-honored *ad valorem* tax upon land.[6]   The maximum tax rate had been set by the Constitution of 1875 at 7½ mills.   The appropriation annually made for the schools had, by 1900, reached $807,000. This was equivalent to a three mill levy on the State property, assessed at $276,000,000 in that year.   In addition, a special tax of 1 mill had been levied since 1896 for the benefit of Confederate veterans. With a State levy set at 7½ mills, only 3½ mills would be left for the general expenses of the State.   The politicians in the Convention faced the problem of bettering the schools, pleasing those who wanted a tax reduction, and providing at the same time for the general expenses of the State.

## TAXATION

What the State would do for education depended upon the degree to which limits were set, by the Convention, on the taxing power.   The Committee on Taxation made its first report on the 32nd day of deliberation.   There were two provisions affecting education directly : one, in a section which proposed that the State tax limit be reduced from 7½ to 6½ mills, and the other, Section 5 of the proposed Article, providing that counties be allowed to levy a special tax for education not to exceed 1 mill.[7]   This proposal simply menat that the 1 mill levy detached from the General State Tax was to be given to the counties for school purposes.   The General State Tax had previously provided a lump sum which, theoretically, could be tapped for school support through general appropriations by the Assembly.   These state appropriations, apportioned on a per capita child basis, gave a distinct advantage to the Black Belt counties.   The reduction of the tax levy from 7½ to 6½ mills therefore reduced the total anticipated income which was susceptible to appropriations to the distributive school fund, and, to this extent, was prejudicial to the interests of the Black Belt counties.   Permission to levy a 1 mill county levy for schools counterbalanched this loss to the total school monies available in the State; but since the county levies would be expended within the county, the schools for white children in the white counties stood to receive under the new system a larger share from this local levy than they had before received from the State levy.

The constitutional limit for county and State taxes, since

1875, had been a total of 12½ mills for both purposes. The new proposal was to allow 6½ mills for the State, and 5 mills for the county, with 1 additional mill to be levied by local county option. Since the decision on taxation depended on what disposition was made of the educational system, the final disposition of Section 5 of the Article on Taxation was put over until the report of the Committee on Education had been received.[8]

The matter came up again, however, in connection with the definition of qualifications for voters in special elections for local levies. Mr. Browne of the Committee on Taxation wished to limit the voting on such levies to a "majority of values"[9] in a given local unit, and to require in addition that three-fifths of such voters favor the proposal. Whether Mr. Browne was using a real or imaginary club to frighten the Convention, he stated, "I am told that under the most rigid suffrage law that can be enacted, in some counties there will still be almost a majority of colored voters, who are non-taxpayers."[10] This might just as well have been a fear of non-taxpaying white voters disguised under the convenient Negro issue.[11] Mr. Heflin of Chambers, Mr. Long of Walker, and Mr. Reynolds of Chilton were all against the proposal to "let property decide." In each of these counties there was a large number of white persons who were small taxpayers. The speakers emphasized the fact that tenants paid taxes as well as owners. Peculiarly enough, Mr. Heflin spoke here in the interests of the white tenant. In further debate where Negro schools were concerned he argued that Negroes paid no taxes, and therefore should receive no school money.[12]

The Convention finally agreed to set a limit upon State taxation of 6½ mills. The consideration of education then shifted to proposals intended to segregate taxes for school purposes according to race.

## THE SEGREGATION OF SCHOOL TAXES

At no time during the Convention did the issue of Negro schools come squarely to the front. In a similar convention in Mississippi, Noble has argued that the refusal of the Convention to accept a proposal to segregate school taxes by race was a great victory for the friends of Negro schools.[13]

But the issue was not so simple either in Alabama or in Mississippi. The representatives of the white counties wanted local

taxation for their schools.  The Black Belt counties had already a
sufficient fund, derived from discrimination against Negroes, for
operating the white schools without local taxation.  Representatives from these Black Belt counties argued that local taxes would
give money derived from taxation principally of white property
owners to the majority Negro population.  To surmount this argument the representatives of the white counties said in effect, "If
you let us have local taxes, we will safeguard the white property
owners of the Black Belt so that local taxes in that section will go
to white, and not to Negro, schools."

It is probable that many of the men from the Black Belt who
finally voted against the proposal to segregate taxes by race did
so, not for love of the Negro, nor for the sake of abstract justice,
but because they did not want to hazard local taxation of schools
under any condition.

The issue was raised soon after the beginning of the Convention, with the presentation of numerous resolutions designed to
permit local taxation with taxes paid by Negroes going to the
support of Negro schools, and those paid by white persons going to
the support of white schools.  These resolutions differed principally in minor details of the language employed.  Mr. Ashcraft
presented a full resolution including a complete prospective Article on Education.  The section on local taxation proposed that
separate districts be drawn for whites and Negroes, the white
property to be taxed for white schools, and the Negro property
to be taxed for Negro schools.  The question arose as to how to
deal with corporate property, which was not locally owned either
by whites or by blacks.  Mr. Ashcraft proposed that each company
involved be required to list its stockholders by race, and that taxes
collected from such corporations be divided according to such
racial evidence of ownership.[14]  This bizarre proposal was later
modified by Mr. Ashcraft when it appeared in later discussion.

The Black Belt representatives presented resolutions which
proposed, as the only change from the old Constitution, the substitution of the phrase "just and equitable" for that in the Constitution of 1875 which required that all funds be apportioned "for
the equal benefit of all the children."  They were also willing to
accept a provision that schools should be maintained for the two
races of equal length.[15]  This was the language of the law of 1890
which had proved satisfactory to the Black Belt in every respect.

Not all of the preliminary ordinances reflected a desire to discriminate against Negroes. Ex-Governor Jones of Montgomery presented a resolution obviously aimed at those proposing tax segregation.

The fundamental principles of justice and free government are violated, when the benefits the citizen derives from money raised by taxation are ascertained and measured according to the poverty or riches of the class to which he belongs, or the proportionate amount of taxes paid by the race or class to which they (sic) belong.[16]

Another section of Jones's resolution declared that it was unconstitutional to segregate the taxes by race.[17] Since all of these resolutions were submitted to committees, their purpose was principally argumentative and Jones's was no exception to the rule.

The question of segregated taxes arose again when the Committe on Taxation resumed its report in the Convention on Section 5 which dealt with tax limitations for minor civil bodies. Mr. Browne moved an amendment to the county taxation proposal which would have required all funds to be divided in a "just and equitable" fashion. He made it quite clear that his intention was to permit county authorities to divide the school fund "unequally," but not to permit any phraseology which would be unconstitutional.[18] Mr. Foster asked if the phraseology would not permit the County Commissioners to divide the fund "unequally." Mr. Browne answered, "No, sir; to divide it equitably."

Mr. Foster. "What does 'equitably' mean?"

Mr. Browne. "Some commissioners' courts would construe it one way and some another."[19] He believed that the decision in the case of Claybrooke vs. Owensboro (16 Fed. Rep., 302) released officials of the duty of making exact per capita expenditures. So long as the terms for the two races were identical in length, the requirement of equal benefit was satisfied. "There is no necessity for paying a teacher for a colored school the same amount you pay to white school teachers, because you can get them at much less salary. Under the present laws of Alabama, if the law is carried out, the colored pupil gets the same amount of money per capita as the white pupil, and that is not justice."[20]

Mr. Ashcraft proposed an amendment to Section 5 which was, in essence, his Ordinance, refined now of some of the crudities which had accompanied it on first introduction. Instead of requiring corporation taxes to be levied on, and the income so obtained distributed according to the race of the stockholders, he now proposed that the income for corporation property be distributed according to the proportion of each race resident in the district where the corporation property was located.[21]   In support of his amendment he repeated his belief that local taxation was a more important issue to the people of North Alabama than the disfranchisement of the Negro.[22]

Mr. Ashcraft's amendment was tabled to await the report of the Committee on Education.[23]

### The Work of the Committee on Education

The Committee on Education included nineteen members. Whether intentionally or not, the Committee was "packed" with Black Belt representatives.   Fourteen committee members represented counties in which Negroes constituted over 50 per cent of the population.   Six members of the committtee represented five counties where Negroes were in excess of 80 per cent of the total population—Wilcox, Sumter, Dallas, Hale, and Bullock.

The Committee had two reports.   The Minority report was submitted by Mr. Ashcraft and was signed, besides, by Earl Pettus, Henry Opp, and W. P. Hodges,[24] accounting for all of the Committee members from counties with a white majority population with the exception of Mr. Bulger.

The report of the Majority of the Committee was given by its Chairman, Mr. Graham of Talladega.   The old Article on Education in the Constitution of 1875 was re-submitted with the exception of Sections 1, 5, and 12.   The change in Section 1 was intended to remove all doubts as to the Apportionment Act of 1890 by rewording the Constitution so as to use the language of the Act which had permitted discrimination through giving broad discretionary powers with respect to apportionment of funds to the local county commissioners.[25]   Section 1 of the old Article, accordingly, had been amended by "striking out the word 'equal' as a basis for apportionment and substituting in substance and fact the provision for a free school term of equal length as the basis of division of the school fund in the respective townships and districts."[26]   Section 1, as reported by the majority of the Committee on Education read as follows:

The public school fund shall be apportioned to the several counties in proportion to the number of school children of school age therein and shall be apportioned to the schools in the districts or townships in the county as to provide, *as nearly as practicable, school terms of equal duration in* such school districts or townships.[27]

Section 5, the Committee report said, "presents apparently the greatest change, yet in fact is largely a change in method only."[28] The former method of supporting the schools had been by providing for such an appropriation from the General Fund as the legislature thought advisable. The recommendation of the Committee was to substitute a provision for a special State levy for schools (within the limit of the 6½ mills) which would probably yield as much income as the appropriation for the year 1900. The legislature had appropriated for schools for the scholastic year 1900-1901 the sum of $550,000. There was a special 1 mill levy which had yielded $257,000. The Majority report "substituted an annual 3 mill levy" for the appropriation. This new levy was estimated to produce approximately the same amount as formerly furnished by an appropriation since the State assessment for 1900 was reported to amount to $276,000,000.

Section 12 was described as follows: "a new section which is a modification of an amendment offered to the Article on Taxation by the Chairman of the Committee. It provides for a 1 mill local tax, with the county as a unit, to be voted in the respective counties by 60 per cent of the qualified electors voting at such election."[29]

As noted above this provision for local taxation was a "snare and a delusion," since the limit of State taxation had been reduced from 7½ to 6½ mills. It favored such a county as Jefferson, by placing the 1 mill reduced from the State levy at the disposal of wealthy counties. But the provision retired from availability to the poorer white counties 2/15 of the levy which formerly had been distributed over the State. Furthermore, the county tax limit was set at 5 mills, excluding the potential school levy of 1 mill. A county voting the maximum 5 mill county levy for general purposes; the 1 mill school levy; and with a State levy of 6½ mills, was thus limited to the imposition of 12½ mills for all purposes as before.[30]

The Minority of the Committee on Education realized this

fact quite clearly. With the prevailing temper of the times they saw no way to obtain the approval of a local tax by the Convention unless it hurdled the race issue. What, therefore, was apparently a movement directed against the education of Negroes, is to be interpreted more correctly as an effort on the part of the white county delegates to attract support for local taxation through the popular strategy of making the issue a race issue.

The Minority report differed from the Majority report principally on the issue of local taxation and the segregation of taxes according to race, which was a piece of strategy incidental to the main purpose of obtaining local taxation. These principal differences were as follows:

| SCHOOL TAX PROVISIONS OF MAJORITY REPORT | SCHOOL TAX PROVISIONS OF MINORITY REPORT |
|---|---|
| 1. A county 1 mill tax (optional) | 1. A county 1 mill tax (optional) |
| 2. A 3 mill state tax (to be apportioned according to school population). | 2. A 3 mill state tax (to be apportioned according to school population). |
| 3. State taxation for all purposes limited to 6½ mills. | 3. State taxation for all purposes limited to 6½ mills. |
| 4. County taxation limited to 5 mills for general purposes, with 1 mill school tax additional. | 4. County taxation limited to 5 mills for general purposes, with 1 mill school tax additional. |
| 5. Maximum state and county tax for general and school purposes set at 12½ mills. | 5. Maximum state and county tax for general and school purposes set at 12½ mills. |
| 6. *No provision for local district tax.* | 6. *The provision of a local district tax of 1 mill, optional, with the machinery of districting prescribed, and with taxes segregated according to race.* |

The substitute of the Minority of the Committee was badly drawn. Unlike the ordinance which preceded it the first paragraph as printed in the *Proceedings* directed the County Superintendent "to organize the white people into white school districts," but made no reference to Negro school districts. Whether clerical or not this error is significant; for the oversight is indicative of the real interest of the Committee.[31]

The Minority defended their proposal by saying that they wished to stimulate "both local and race initiative." This may or may not mean anything; the protested advantages to accrue to Negro schools were probably a part of the program to show how the Minority Report was not discriminatory and therefore not unconstitutional.[32]  So the development of separate districts for Negroes was calculated to give the Negro

an opportunity to do something as a race. (He will) . . . . no longer be in the position of an absolute mendicant, and will have the opportunity of showing himself worthy of the large share he receives from the general fund.[33] He will have the opportunity of cultivating self-respect and self-reliance.[34]  Race pride and race fraternity will take the place of that suspicious envy which now manifests itself in the commission of these crimes,[35] which shock humanity.[36]

On account of these advantages the proposed section would not be discriminatory or unconstitutional.  The Minority referred to the Cummings Case (175 U. S., 528),[37] the Owensboro case (1 Fed. Reporter, 297), the Pruitt Case (94 N. C., 709) ; arguing that what was contemplated in Alabama was not invalidated by these decisions.[38]

### THE DEBATE ON THE ARTICLE ON EDUCATION ON FINAL PASSAGE

The Article on Education in the Constitution came up for final passage on the 71st day of deliberation.  Mr. Graham, the Chairman, again retraced the changes made in the Constitution of 1875 and the reasons for their recommendation by the Convention.  The law of 1890 was cited and the new portion of Section 1 declared to be a device to bring the Constitution into harmony with that law.  Proposals to segregate the taxes by race, he continued, had been regarded by the Committee as unconstitutional. The Committee had provided instead: ". . . . that equal benefits of the school fund of the races shall be equal as nearly as practicable, and thereby meet all the requirements of the Constitution of the United States and of justice between the races in Alabama.''[39]  No other changes had been made in the Article on Education as it had been reported and debated on the 43rd day.[40]

Section 1, directing the State Legislature to establish a system of public schools, separated by race, and maintained "as to provide, as nearly as practicable, school terms of equal duration,'' was read and adopted without debate.  Section 2, which set up and described the distributive school fund, was also adopted without debate. Section 3, adding bequests and estates to the school fund, was also adopted without discussion, as was Section 4, referring to the poll tax.

Section 5 referred to the setting aside of 3 mills of the total State tax levy for schools and contained a statement regarding the total limitation of all State taxes to 6½ mills. Mr. Watts, Mr. Cobb, and Mr. Walker, all from Black Belt counties, thought that it was a "dangerous thing" to give the schools 3 of the 6½ mills allowed for state taxation. Mr. Graham denied this probability. The State assessment, he said, was growing steadily; income from other sources such as corporation taxes and the income from licenses would amply protect the State. Mr. Sanford retorted that the only adequate basis for figuring the State income was with reference to property taxes; all other sources of income were speculative.[41]

Section 5 was then adopted as read. Section 6 (limiting administrative expenditures to 4 per cent of the distributive fund), Section 7 (establishing the office of the State Superintendent as the principal educational officer of the State), and Section 8 (prohibiting appropriations to sectarian schools) were adopted without debate.[42]

Section 9 referred to the management of the University of Alabama, and was debated at length. Section 10 (concerned with the location of the University and of the A. and M. College), and Section 11 (requiring the taking of a school census) were adopted as read.[43]

The climax of the debate on education was reached on the 72nd legislative day, when Section 12 came up for final passage. This was the section referring to local taxation; the majority report favoring a 1 mill county levy optional with the county, Mr. Ashcraft and the minority report favoring a district tax in addition to the county tax and segregating districts in order to avoid segregating taxes by race.[44] This ruse, which Mr. Ashcraft thought would remove constitutional objections to his proposal, was clearly perceived by the adherents of the Majority report. Local taxation by districts was obnoxious to the Black Belt and to industrial interests. The debate apparently hinged on the abstract issue of justice to Negroes; but men who formerly in the Convention had argued against granting Negroes any advantages under the new dispensation now joined with the most ardent advocates of Negro rights to show the unwisdom and unconstitutionality of the Minority report.[45]

The final form of the Minority proposal was changed in several aspects from that in which it had been originally introduced as an Ordinance by Mr. Ashcraft. County Superintendents were to be permitted to set up two kinds of districts, one for whites, and one for Negroes, "without regard to each other as to territorial boundaries."[46] These districts, then, were to be a sort of incorporeal entities; a definition necessitated both on constitutional grounds, and on account of the fact that it would be impossible to draw districts geographically so as to include in one all white, and in the other, all Negro, children. These districts would be permitted "to levy a special assessment of not more than $\frac{1}{4}$ of 1 per cent[47] in any one year upon the property of a white person situated in a white district or upon the property of colored persons situated in a colored district."[48] The approval of 3/5 of the registered voters was required to levy this tax. Only whites were to vote in white districts, and only colored in colored districts. Corporate property was to be taxed "in such proportion of the value therein as the number of colored children or white children bears to the whole number of children of school age in the county."[49] Mr. Ashcraft said that this substitute did not discriminate; it gave to Negro children every advantage open to white children. He desired not to "take away from the negro, but to give to the white people freedom for action for and on behalf of our own people. . . . It would be beneficial to the negro; it would develop his race pride." The Minority report wished to make it possible for local communities to levy a local tax and so enable them to escape from the dead hand of the Negro.[50] The following colloquy took place:

Mr. Reynolds (Chilton County): In the districts where negroes are disfranchised, how can they vote for it (i.e., a local tax upon their districts)?

Mr. Ashcraft: If there are any districts that do not contain negroes who can vote they will have to wait until they could vote. Of course it is absolutely a voluntary matter with the white people whether they will tax themselves, and with the negroes whether they will tax themselves, and if there be a single community of ngroes without a man capable of voting they will have to wait until they can educate men who can vote.[51]

Mr. Jones of Wilcox County, a member of the Majority of the Committee, stated that Mr. Ashcraft's legal reasoning was awry.

The Cumming's case "decided nothing of the sort" that Mr. Ashcraft had claimed.  Mr. Ashcraft had not quoted several decisions that made his proposal clearly unconstitutional.  "In North Carolina in the case of Markham vs. Manning, 96 Carolina, the Court decided that taxes for schools open to the children of only one race is (sic) unconstitutional as denying equal privileges and immunities."[52]  He ridiculed Ashcraft's claim that Negroes wanted separate districts.  "I have never heard of a Negro from Booker Washington to a bootblack asking any member of this Committee to set aside the taxes of their race for themselves."[53]  If the Minority proposal was constitutional with reference to school districts, taxes could be segregated for other purposes in larger units.  The cases cited by Mr. Ashcraft in support of his proposal actually meant just the opposite.[54]

Mr. Williams of Barbour County was against both the Minority and Majority reports where they favored local taxation.  The taxpayer was too heavily burdened already.  Taxation was heavy in the agricultural sections and the owners could not, he said, afford to let the non-taxpayers saddle any more taxes upon them.[55]

Here was a typical Black Belt attitude, stripped of verbiage or subterfuge for political effect.

Mr. Coleman of Greene County, also in the Black Belt, was surprised that Mr. Ashcraft should look so little into the direction of the cases he cited.  The proposal was clearly unconstitutional.[56]  Mr. Pettus, of the Minority of the Committee, said that the proposal was a matter of expediency.  He said that no one in the Convention actually believed that Negroes should receive an equal benefit of the school fund.  The Minority report was a new idea and its constitutionality should be left to the courts to decide.  The Convention should let the white people progress as they wished without delay or hindrance from the Negroes.[57]

Mr. Brooks of Mobile was against the Minority report.  It posed a question not merely of expediency, not merely of constitutionality, but of justice.  There should be no discrimination against Negroes because they paid no taxes.  If there was, why not discriminate against the white non-taxpayers?  The Negroes were taxpayers, though not directly.  The Negro was here and here to stay; and when he reached the point where "he will be able to defend himself against the cupidity of the white man to swindle him," he would be a self-respecting, valuable citizen.[58]

Mr. Cunningham of Jefferson County favored local taxation and an "equitable" distribution, but he was against the Minority Report. He thought it would be unconstitutional. "I contend, Mr. President, that it would be a violation of the fundamental principles underlying the whole question of taxation for public schools."[59] If the Minority Report was correct in principle, why tax Jefferson County to educate the children of Limestone County, from which Mr. Ashcraft came? He hoped the Convention would provide for local taxation with the county as the unit.[60]

Mr. Heflin of Chambers County made the final, as well as the longest, argument for the Minority report. The segregation of the races into districts was perfectly constitutional and proper. "It is the old Southern idea that the Negroes should go to school to themselves, and that the whites should attend school to themselves." Then why not logically extend the principle to separate districts? The convention should think of the men who fought for the Stars and Bars, and who fell in the defense of the old flag; and the Convention should think of their sons. "I ask if it is right to tax them to educate the Negroes of Alabama?" The proposal was not wrong so far as the Negroes were concerned. In fact, the Negroes were getting ahead too rapidly now through education.[61]

They are being educated very rapidly. Why, they will attend school with but few garments to wear and with but little to eat, when the child of the white man would be kept at home because he hasn't good clothes to put on and good victuals to send with him to school as his neighbor has. Pride oftentimes will keep him back. It is wrong, but it is true, nevertheless. The negroes are being educated very rapidly, and I say in the light of all history of the past, some day when the two separate and distinct races are thrown together, some day the clash will come and the survival of the fittest, and I do not believe it is incumbent upon us to lift him up and educate him and put him on an equal footing that he may be armed and equipped when the combat comes. I favor the minority report and shall so vote.[62]

Mr. Browne of the Committee on Taxation was against the Minority proposal. At the beginning of the Convention, he had introduced an ordinance to segregate the taxes according to race; but since that time he had been convinced that the proposal was unconstitutional. The case of Davenport vs. Cloverport (a Kentucky case, 72nd Federal Reporter), had not been cited. But it was the strongest argument against the proposal. In this case the white people had tried to avoid the constitutional difficulty by levying a tax on white property only. This device had failed, the Court promptly ruling it unconstitutional.[63]

Ex-Governor Jones of Montgomery County made a final speech against the adoption of the Minority Report. However unlike in sentiment, the speech, like Heflin's, is a valuable document deserving citation here. His opposition was for two reasons.

> One is that, after thorough investigation, I find the plan is plainly, and palpably, and manifestly unconstitutional; but I do not rest my opposition upon that ground solely. I remember seeing it related somewhere of Robert E. Lee, when he was asked why he took so much interest in a worthless soldier, and why he seemed to have a solicitude for his welfare, that grand old man answered, "Because he is under me." The negro race is under us. He is under our power.[64]

The Convention had disfranchised the Negro; in return, it was obligated to extend to him "all the civil rights that will fit him to be a decent and self-respecting, law-abiding, and intelligent citizen of the State." Negroes were taxpayers, indirectly.[65]

The crowning argument for the education of Negroes, concluded Jones, was that the Negro had a soul. "We ought to teach the negro at least enough to enable him to read his Bible, to understand the laws that he is to obey, and to understand the contract he signs."[66]

The debate concluded. A motion was put to table the Minority Report, and this motion was carried, 90-31. The Majority Report was then adopted without further debate.

### THE AFTERMATH OF THE PROVISIONS OF THE CONSTITUTION OF 1901

The debate on Education during the Constitutional Convention, as noted above, at no time forced a decisive vote on the issue of the education of Negroes. The political strategy behind the Minority report gives the semblance of such an issue to the disposition of Section 12, but on closer examination it is obvious that the proposal to segregate taxes by race was more a Black Belt-White County contest than a clear consideration of the right of Negroes to share in tax-supported funds. Section 1, providing for a "just and equitable" apportionment, was more significant; and it passed with little or no opposition.

The overwhelming defeat of the proposal to establish local districts and so segregate taxes by race appears to have been due to a combination of (a) Republican, Populist, and Conservative Democratic representatives favorable to the Negro with (b) representatives from the Black Belt and industrial centers inimical or indifferent to the Negro, who were opposed to the principle of local taxation, and who were not led away from their position by the semblance of the race issue contained in the Minority Report.

So far as the education of Negroes was concerned, the provisions of the law of 1890 which permitted local officials to control apportionments and so discriminate against Negroes were engrafted into the Constitution. The enactment of this proposal was attended by little debate and encountered little opposition. This provision derives its importance from its further commitment of the State to the policy of discrimination in expenditures.

The suffrage provisions of the Constitution were of vital importance to the education of Negroes because they focused attention on the necessity of educating white children, and made the expenditure of school funds even more a matter of competition between the two separate systems. Throughout the debates on the suffrage clause the injustice of disfranchising white illiterates, and the great amount of illiteracy among white persons, was stressed on all sides. Knight has argued that the revival of education in Alabama after 1900 resulted from the propaganda activities of certain educational leaders in Alabama.[67] But the work of these men would have been largely ineffective had it not been for the cumulative force of economic and social change directed, by the work of the Convention, into a realization of the inadequacies of the educational equipment of white persons in the State.

From 1901, with Negroes thoroughly disfranchised, all emphasis was laid on the education of "white" children in the State. Official *Reports* specified this interest; so far as educational campaigns were concerned, Negro children did not exist in the State. In 1922, an exposition of Alabama's deficiencies, preliminary to a new program, emphasized "White" children.[68] The Constitutional Convention of 1901 definitely committed the State to this policy.

Two other factors affecting all education in the State, and so that of Negro children, were the provisions regarding local taxation and regarding limitations upon the tax-levying powers of the

General Assembly.   Of the first, the Education Commission of 1919 said:

It can be stated with substantial accuracy that there was no provision for local taxation for educational purposes in the State of Alabama from 1875 until 1901. . . .   In so far as education is concerned, therefore, the Constitution of 1875 marks a change from a Constitution providing as liberal a method of support for schools as existed in any State of the Union to a Constitution with the most illiberal and inadequate method of support to be found in any state.

In the Constitution of 1901, a material change for the better is to be noted. . . .   Although conditions were improved by this tax privilege (i.e., 1 mill county tax), the relief was entirely inadequate, as the results have clearly shown.[69]

The provisions of the Constitution of 1901 which limited taxation have been described by the Brookings Institution as resulting in a "warped and distorted" revenue system.[70]   The assessment of all species of property "at one and the same proportion of value, and its taxation at the same and uniform rate is impracticable and unsound."[71]   The policy of limiting taxation in Alabama has proved "defective, detrimental, and unsound."[72]

In the financing of the general school system this "obsolete" taxing machinery has influenced schools for Negroes in Alabama as it has schools for white children.   More important is the fact that the taxing machinery continued to emphasize property values. As a result, expenditures for Negro children were directly connected with direct land taxes; and any expansion of facilities for Negro children had to meet the full brunt of the old opposition of the "taxpayers" versus the "non-taxpayers."

A final indirect factor resulting from the Constitutional Convention of 1901 was the final disappearance of the Negro as a political power.   However this move may have contributed to the cleansing of the franchise, it left the Negro population totally at the tender mercies of the white population where almost every conceivable grant of privilege or citizenship was concerned.   By 1905, under the new Constitution, only 3,654 Negroes out of 181,474 of voting age were registered, as compared to 205,278 out of 224,212 whites.[73]   The number of Negroes registered is known to have decreased by 1930, although exact lists for the entire State are difficult to obtain.[74]   The Negroes were not only without any political power to influence public officials; the very suspicion of friendliness on the part of a politician toward the Negro became a deadly weapon in the hand of a political opponent.[75]

After 1901, the development of Negro schools was even more than ever at the mercy of stark social and economic influences, divorced of any ameliorating effect which the exercise of the franchise may have introduced in the past. For many reasons, therefore, the Constitutional Convention of 1901 is the definite climax of the problem of educating Negroes in the State at public expense.

## CHAPTER XIV

# THE INFLUENCE OF PERSONALITIES ON THE PUBLIC EDUCATION OF NEGROES IN ALABAMA

Whatever importance be assigned to the role of personalities in the historical process, our habit of thinking and writing of social processes in terms of individualities makes the subject significant. In Alabama the presence of a commanding personality and the school which was "his lengthened shadow," requires detailed attention to this force in the interpretation of education of Negroes in the state.

Booker Taliaferro Washington was born in Virginia at sometime in the middle 'fifties of the nineteenth century.[1] His life, he said, "had its beginning in the midst of the most miserable, desolate, and discouraging surroundings."[2] He entered Hampton Institute in 1872, finishing the course of instruction there in 1875.[3] After teaching in West Virginia for two years he spent a fruitless year at Wayland Seminary, a classical school in Washington; returned to Hampton Institute as an assistant in charge of the Indian boys domiciled there, and later served as instructor in the Night School for work students.[4] In May of 1881 Samuel Chapman Armstrong, Hampton Principal, received a letter from Alabama asking him to recommend a principal for a new school to be established at Tuskegee in Macon County.[5] Washington was selected; and he arrived in Alabama late in June, 1881, to take up his new duties.[6]

## INTELLECTUAL BACKGROUND OF BOOKER T. WASHINGTON

Hampton Institute was a foundation of the American Missionary Association and of the Freedmen's Bureau, as were so many of the colleges for Negroes established in the South immediately after the Civil War. As such it was a product of New England humanitarianism. It was unique in its principal, Samuel Chapman Armstrong, the son of missionary parents resident in the Sandwich Islands.[7] Armstrong was graduated at Williams College in 1862, during the presidency of Mark Hopkins. "Whatever good teaching I may have done," said Armstrong, "has been Mark Hopkins' teaching through me."[8]

More important than the Williams' background in Armstrong's educational planning appears to have been his youthful experience in Hawaii. Unlike other "missionary" teachers Armstrong had a perspective including the application of humanitarianism to a "folk"; and there can be no doubt that this colonial experience affected the adaptation of humanitarian theory which he invoked at Hampton. In explaining his work at Hampton he acknowledged his debt to the institutions established for natives in Hawaii.

There were two institutions; the Lahainaluna (government) Seminary for young men, where, with manual labor, mathematics and other higher branches were taught; and the Hilo Boarding and Manual Labor (missionary) School for boys, on a simpler basis, under the devoted David B. Lyman and his wife. As a rule, the former turned out more brilliant, the latter, less advanced but more solid, men. In making the plan of the Hampton Institute, that of the Hilo School seemed the best to follow.[9]

At Fisk University in Nashville, Erastus Milo Cravath instituted a curriculum taken bodily from the classical course of study at Oberlin College where he had studied. At Atlanta University Edmund Asa Ware and Horace Bumstead adopted without change the curriculum which they had studied at Yale. General O. O. Howard, head of the Freedmen's Bureau, was a graduate of Bowdoin College; in inviting Armstrong to establish a school at Hampton he doubtless had in mind the same sort of institution which his New England agents set up elsewhere in the South. But Hampton under Armstrong became a school with a "policy of only English and generally elementary and industrial teaching."[10] As a product of such a school Booker T. Washington, aside from his talents of intellect and of personal force, differed radically from the hundreds of young Negroes in the immediate postwar period who flocked to the mission schools in the South in search of an education.

### The Origin of Tuskegee Institute

It is a significant reflection of his policy that Booker T. Washington never published the complete story of the founding of Tuskegee Institute. In his *Autobiography* he says:

I found that a year previous to my going to Tuskeegee some of the coloured people who had heard something of the work of education being done at Hampton had applied to the state Legislature, through their representatives, for a small appropriation to be used in starting a normal school in Tuskegee. This request the Legislature had complied with to the extent of granting an annual appropriation to two thousand dollars.[11]

In a description given by a less subtle historian[12] of this event, the "application" of the Negroes for a school is further illuminated.

It came about that in the year 1880 in Macon county, Alabama, a certain ex-Confederate colonel conceived the idea that if he could secure the Negro vote he could beat his rival and win the seat he coveted in the State legislature. Accordingly, the colonel went to the leading Negro in the town of Tuskegee, and asked him what he could do to secure the Negro vote, for Negroes then voted in Alabama without restriction. This man, Lewis Adams by name, himself an ex-slave, promptly replied that what the race most wanted was education, and what they most needed was industrial education, and that if he (the colonel) would agree to work for the passage of a bill appropriating money for the maintenance of an industrial school for Negroes, he (Adams) would help to get for him the Negro vote and the election. This bargain between an ex-slaveholder and an ex-slave was made and faithfully observed on both sides, with the result that the following year the Legislature of Alabama appropriated $2,000 a year for the establishment of a normal and industrial school for Negroes in the town of Tuskegee.[13]

When Washington arrived at Tuskegee he found that the appropriation was limited to the payment of salaries only. Washington in later years frequently referred to the "generosity" of the Alabama Legislature in appropriating the initial sum. The money was appropriated out of the Negro public school fund, and, according to constitutional restrictions, not more than four per cent of any money from the fund could be appropriated for any purpose other than that of teachers' salaries.[14]

On the 4th day of July, 1881, Washington opened his school in a "little shanty and church."[15] From this beginning flowed an international reputation for the man and for his school, grown great in the course of the years. A recent appraisal cited him as follows:

. . . . leader of his race, and friend to all races : who achieved for himself and the Negro people a genuine freedom through service : great teacher of the dignity of humble labor. . . . Washington's plan consisted chiefly in teaching that the way to authentic freedom lay in doing well the work at hand.[16]

The manner in which this personality affected the education of Negroes in Alabama can best be understood through the medium of contemporary individualities and forces with which it was associated.

### JABEZ LAMAR MONROE CURRY

J. L. M. Curry was born in the state of Georgia in 1825.[17] His biographers record certain youthful incidents that may have significance for his future career. His father owned a number of slaves and his boyhood companions were Negro children.[18] A mulatto preacher, Adams, frequently officiated at the "Double Branches" Church where the Curry family attended religious services. "For a colored man to preach to white congregations was no offense."[19] In 1838 the family moved out to "the frontier," to a new plantation in Talladega county, Alabama.[20] In 1845 Curry graduated from the University of Georgia, where Benjamin Harvey Hill, Joseph LeConte, and Linton H. Stephens were among his fellow-students.[21]

Following graduation from college, Curry entered the Dane Law School of Harvard college in September, 1843.[22] Rutherford B. Hayes was a classmate.[23] As a student he attended public meetings where he listened, among others, to Frederick Douglass and Wiliam Lloyd Garrison, "The negro and white abolitionist agitators."[24] He followed with interest the controversy between Horace Mann and the Boston school masters.

Mann's glowing periods, earnest enthusiasm and democratic ideas fired my young mind and heart; and since that time I have been an enthusiastic and consistent advocate of universal education.[25]

Following his graduation from the law school in 1845 Curry entered the practice of law and the pursuit of politics in his home county in Alabama.[26] In 1847 he campaigned for the General Assembly as a Democrat, voicing particular support for free schools and for the University.[27] In the sessions of 1853-1854 he was a member of the Committee on Education, and helped perfect and carry through the legislature the law establishing a system of public schools in Alabama.[28]   He was a prominent advocate of internal improvements, and voted for the measures to subsidize the railroads which characterized the session of 1855-1856.[29]   In all the interlocked web of political and business interests apparent in this survey, nothing is stranger than the fact that Curry's father was a director and large stockholder of the Tennessee and Alabama Railroad, and that Curry was, himself, an agent for the road in obtaining subscriptions for its extension.[30]

Elected to the United States Congress in 1856, Curry resigned in 1861, and during the Civil War served the Confederacy both as a member of the Confederate Congress and in the field as a soldier.[31]   After the War he served as president of Howard College at Marion, Alabama, for a brief period.[32]   In 1866 he called a committee which "prepared and introduced resolutions favoring the education of the colored people by the white people of the South."[33]

Following a period of preaching and teaching in Richmond, Virginia, Curry's application for the Agentship of the Peabody Fund was answered by a letter from his former classmate, Rutherford B. Hayes, announcing his "unanimous election."[34]   This election was in February, 1881—three months before the appointment of Booker T. Washington as principal of Tuskegee.

### BOOKER T. WASHINGTON AND J. L. M. CURRY

The career of Washington at Tuskegee was peculiarly bound to the same social and economic class to which Curry belonged, and to the work of the latter as General Agent of the Peabody Fund. Washington's initial appropriation of $2,000 was increased in 1882 to $3,000 by the General Assembly;[35] Curry's first speech as Agent of the Fund was delivered before the General Assembly of that year.[36]   Busy with plans for expansion, Washington obtained a grant of $500 from the Peabody Fund in 1882, and $1,000 from the Slater Fund, with which Curry was closely associated.[37]

From his first report Curry lauded the work of Washington at Tuskegee, and the emphasis he placed on industrial education.[38] Washington himself always referred to Curry in the most glowing terms.[39]   To Washington the attitude of Curry toward the education of Negroes seemed all the more remarkable on account of the fact that, as he told Washington, "he had been bitterly opposed to

every movement that had been proposed to educate the Negro''
immediately after the War.  He added that after visiting several
Negro schools he had become an advocate of the education of
Negroes.[40]

As the General Agent of the Peabody Fund, and, later, as the
administrative head of the Slater Fund, devoted exclusively to the
education of Negroes, Curry's chief activity became that of an
educational propagandist.  Much of his time was spent in making
public speeches before citizens and legislative bodies in an effort
to influence favorable action toward public schools.[41]  Curry addressed the Alabama legislature during the sessions of 1882-1883,
1885-1886, 1889-1890, 1896-1897, and 1900-1901.[42]

There is an interesting conflict between the dual rôle of J. L.
M. Curry as the representative of a dominant social class, and
J. L. M. Curry as the advocate of public, tax-supported education.
He defended the theory of taxation responsible for the poor con-
dition of Alabama schools in an article published three years after
assuming the administrative leadership of the Peabody Fund.[43]
The enjoyment of property rights was endangered, he said, ''by
bad men, and chiefly by injustice and tyranny of governments.''[44]
There were two dangers that tax-payers in the United States
needed to guard against.  They were:

1. The power of combined wealth.
2. Universal suffrage may often imperil property rights.
   Agrarianism and communism are seen, not merely in strikes
   and ''bread or blood riots,'' but in the growing heresy that
   government must provide labor for the unemployed. . . . .
   It seems to be the very acme of injustice for a man who
   pays no taxes to vote taxes on all the property around him
   for an alleged public good and a resulting private benefit.
   When the Sultan of Turkey confiscates private property we
   condemn the act in no honeyed phrase, but is it any the less
   an outrage for men who bear none of the burdens of taxation to impose taxes wantonly for other men to pay?[45]

To protect property against these dangers, Curry described
the limitations which had been placed on expenditures in several
Constitutions, and approved them as measures designed to prevent
''the contraction of public debts and the extravagant appropriation of public money.''[46]  ''The state should tie its own hands.''[47]
''Jealousy of excessive taxation is a test of liberty.''[48]

We may be permitted to conclude that Curry, like modern

Alabama men of kindred opinions, had a deep and fundamental
distrust of democracy. He thought of education as a cure for
the dangers of the mass mind placed in control of property.
"Property must pay a ransom for the privilege it enjoys, and it
will find it to its advantage to provide insurance against the risks
to which it is exposed, to guard against the perils of ignorance,
agrarianism, nihilism, and dynamite."[49] The perils of "agrarianism" in Alabama were represented during Curry's lifetime by the
Populist party.

### Curry's Arguments for the Education of Negroes

To no small degree Curry, when arguing for the education
of Negroes, was arguing against himself; the man who said it was
an "outrage" for non-taxpayers to tax other men was, in his new
rôle, arguing that Negro non-taxpayers should receive public tax
funds derived from taxes on other men. The resolution of this
fundamental conflict is of interest as it appears in Curry's published speeches on the problem.

Although Curry's efforts were cast in a period of steadily rising economic and political discontent in the South, his whole argument was directed to the political masters the Populists called
"the Oligarchy." When he spoke before legislatures he asked
the aid of "the intelligent and more refined class of the white
people," on whom the Negroes had depended in the past and in
the future must depend "to prevent a widening of the breach between the races and to bring about their higher advancement."[50]
Two principal reasons were given for extending this aid to the
Negro. The first was in the spirit of *noblesse oblige.* White Supremacy was an inevitable law of nature and in the best interests
of the Negroes. "History demonstrates that the Caucasian will
rule. He ought to rule."[51] The education of the Negro must be
undertaken as a part of the white man's burden. "The Caucasian
. . . . made our Constitution; he achieved our independence; he is
identified with all the true progress, all high civilization, and if
true to his mission . . . . he will lead out all other races as far and
as fast as their good and their possibilities will justify."[52]

A moral obligation to assist in the education of the Negro
grew out of his inferior status. "It must be eternally right to
Christianize and to educate the Negro."[53] Since it was to the

best interests both of the Negro and of the white man, that the Negro remain in an inferior position, education should be controlled and administered by Southerners, rather than by "agitators provoking strife and racial conflict."[54]    Curry felt very bitterly toward the missionary teachers from the North who had established schools and colleges for Negroes during Reconstruction.

It is not just to condemn the negro for the education which he received in the early years after the war.    That was the period of reconstruction, the saturnalia of misgovernment, the greatest possible hindrance to the progress of the freedmen, an unmitigable curse, the malignant attempt to use the negro voter as a pawn in the corrupt game of manufacturing members of Congress.    The education was unsettling, demoralizing, pandered to a wild frenzy for schooling as a quick method of reversing social and political conditions.    Nothing could have been better devised for deluding the poor negro, and making him the tool, the slave of corrupt taskmasters.    Education is a natural consequence of citizenship and enfranchisement, I should say of freedom and humanity.    But with deliberate purpose to subject the Southern States to negro domination, and secure the states permanently for partisan ends, the education adopted was contrary to common sense, to human experience, to all noble purposes.    The curriculum was for a people in the highest degree of civilization; the aptitudes and capabilities and needs of the negro were wholly disregarded.    Especial stress was laid on classics and liberal culture, to bring the race *per saltum* to the same plane with their former masters, and realize the theory of social and political equality. . . .    Colleges and universities established and conducted by the Freedmen's Bureau and Northern Churches and societies, sprang up like mushrooms, and the teachers, ignorant, fanatical, without self poise, proceeded to make all possible mischief.    It is irrational, cruel to hold the negro, under such strange conditions, responsible for all the ill consequences of bad education, unwise teachers, reconstruction villainies and partisan schemes.[55]

The second general reason for the education of Negroes Curry found in the self-interest of white men.    If the white men of Alabama did not assume the responsibility for lifting the Negro, he prophesied the race "will drag you down to hell."[56]    The same economic arguments for the education of white children applied to Negroes with even greater force.    "Education," Curry said, "is the fundamental basis of general and permanent prosperity.    Poverty is the inevitable result of ignorance.    Capital follows the school-house."[57]    In their ignorant condition the Negroes furnished to the South only "brute force"; education was the only means by which their productivity could be raised to a profitable level.[58] "If you do not lift them up they will drag you down to industrial bankruptcy, social degradation and political corruption."[59]

It is, of course, impossible to say precisely to what extent Curry's propaganda activities aided Negro schools, or, indeed, white schools. The Alabama public school could not obtain more money until the limitations on taxations imposed by the Constitution of 1875 were removed. It is immensely significant that it was not until the white opponents to the "intelligent and more refined class of white people" in Alabama got control that tax limitations for schools were revised. In increasing, through developing public opinion, the demand of the white people for schools, it might even be said that Curry was increasing the danger to the Negro schools. In 1894 Curry wrote to both the democratic and populist candidates for Governor, asking their aid for the proposed amendment to the Constitution submitted to the people in that year.[60] This so-called Hundley Amendment provided for an optional county tax of 2½ mills:

Possible hostility for the fear that the propertyless might avail themselves of the opportunity to levy educational taxes on the rich was disarmed in advance by the requirement of a local vote for the enactment of the law; the fear that negroes might get too much was met by the provision that each race might, if it was so desired, receive what it paid.[61]

In his letter, Curry said the schools in Alabama were handicapped "by a clause in the constitution limiting local taxation to an extremely low figure."[62] It was a clause which he had defended strongly ten years before. The Amendment failed to receive a majority of the votes cast at the election, and so was lost.[63]

### BOOKER T. WASHINGTON AND WILLIAM H. COUNCILL

During the time when Booker T. Washington was establishing a reputation at Tuskegee Institute, he had an important rival for the favor of the state and of philanthropic agencies in William H. Councill, president of the State Normal School at Huntsville.[64] John Temple Graves, prominent Birmingham, Alabama, publicist, referred to Councill in a speech at the University of Chicago in 1898 as follows:

The wisest, and most thoughtful, and the most eloquent Negro of his time—as discreet as Washington, a deeper thinker, and a more eloquent man.    But for one hour of the Atlanta speech, Councill, of Huntsville, might stand today where Washington, of Tuskegee, stands—as the recognized leader of his race.[65]

Councill,[66] like Washington,[67] and Washington's successor at Tuskegee, Robert R. Moton,[68] had begun his public life as a politician.    The school which he headed at Huntsville had been established in 1874 by the same kind of political "log-rolling" which six years later was responsible for Tuskegee Institute.[69]    The interests of Tuskegee and of the Huntsville school conflicted in numerous ways, and frequently gave rise to political manoeuvering between Washington and Councill.    With the acceptance by the state of the conditions of the Second Morrill Act of 1890 by Alabama in 1891, there was spirited competition between Tuskegee and Huntsville for the allocation of the Negro share for a land-grant college to either place.[70]    Councill, at Huntsville, was successful.[71]    During the legislative session of 1896-1897, Washington and Councill both lobbied vigorously to obtain for their schools the state appropriation for an agricultural experiment school which was provided in the legislation of that session.[72]    Tuskegee was successful on this occasion.    In the same year there was much agitation to take the land-grant from Councill's school and bestow it upon Tuskegee.[73]

Councill is important in interpreting Washington because his career exhibits in aggravated degree all of the opportunistic characteristics which some critics have ascribed to the more prominent man.    This "discreet" man, "deep thinker," and "eloquent" orator was plainly an adroit and shrewd student of the foibles and prejudices of his white contemporaries, and bent his educational and public career to take best advantage of the susceptibilities of his masters.    An accomplished orator, he used all of the shibboleths dear to the hearts of romantic white persons.    It was a gospel of sweetness and light.    It is difficult to recognize the protesting politician of 1874 in the man who said, in 1900: "The love and attachment between the races of the South are more than wonderful when we consider the untiring efforts of busy and meddlesome enemies—the politicians, the newspapers, the magazines and even the pulpit seeking to scatter seeds of discord and break up our peace."[74]    Councill, like Washington, clearly discerned class differentiations among white persons, and staked his appeal for support on this basis. "When the old, gray-haired veterans who followed General Lee's tattered banners to Appomattox shall have passed away, the Negro's best friends shall have gone, for the Negro got more out of slavery than they did."[75]  His "Reports to the State Superintendent" are, one and all, interesting documents, artful to the extreme.  He made a point of trying to have none but ex-Confederate officers on his trustee board.[76]  Constant emphasis was given to the "practical" nature of the school, and of the "training in race relations" which the school existed to impart.  The reports of Washington, from Tuskegee, and Councill, from the A. & M. College at Huntsville, made so much of "industrial education" that the white President of the Normal School at Montgomery, W. B. Paterson, wryly stated in his report for 1899-1900:

> For several years there has been much discussion as to WHAT the Negro shall study, whether industrial or the so-called higher education best adapts him for success in life.  The importance of the HOW, or the manner of education, has been forgotten, and the result has been numerous failures both in the Industrial Schools and Colleges.[77]

### "A School Built Around a Problem"

Up to this point we have mentioned the personalities of J. L. M. Curry, Booker T. Washington, and W. H. Councill, so far as they impinged more particularly upon the social problem of race contacts and not on educational problems *per se*.  It is, in fact, impossible to disentangle the rôle of Tuskegee Institute and Washington as educational agencies, and as self-conscious social forces. Washington himself always indicated that Tuskegee "was built around a problem."[78]  The problem included three classes of people: the Negroes, whom he hoped to educate and to aid in achieving progress; the Northern white people, whom he depended upon to finance the school; and the Southern white people, whose support was essential, first, in order to permit such an institution as he envisioned to exist in the heart of the South, and, second, to make a success of the demonstration in better race relations which was his ultimate goal.[79]  "I saw," he said, "that in order to succeed I must in some way secure the support and sympathy of each of them."[80]

It was a task easily seen to require the most consummate skill, amounting, in Washington's case, to a peculiar genius. Educationally it had the misfortune to depend so much upon his personality and upon a refined technique of racial strategy that whatever educational outcomes were derivative from his work could easily be swallowed up in an ocean of individual and racial deceit. It has an additional disadvantage for the student of educational structures. Since the school was an instrument of a social policy, it is difficult to tell where it was primarily an educational institution, and where a social device.

One appraisal of Washington disregards the contribution he is ordinarily thought to have made to education. He was important, "not because he became a great man, or a great Negro, or rose from slavery, but because he embodied the survival elements of the Negro race in an environment hostile to its ultimate objectives."[81] From this standpoint his work at Tuskegee is interpreted as that of "a social strategist," giving a common sense demonstration of what a student of human behavior might prescribe today as the technique of social adaptation in a situation immensely complicated by age-old social structures.[82] Given an acute sense of the power of social and racial attitudes, an indomitable will to achieve ends to which these attitudes were barriers, the attainment of ultimate objectives could follow either the pathway of direct assault upon the interposed barriers, or that of careful, tedious, skillful indirection. Washington is seen as having chosen, with utter clarity of vision, this latter course.[83]

Whether "strategy" or no, the educational work of Washington in Alabama is reflected intelligibly only by reference to the social and economic influences with which he was associated and frequently aligned. When he spoke of "the white people of the South," he appears to have been talking of that social and economic class dominant in the state when Tuskegee Institute was established, and not of the turbulent, discontented folk who were later to figure so largely in the administration of public affairs.

A speech delivered at the Atlanta Exposition on September 18, 1895, is generally credited as the fortuitous circumstance which enabled Washington to project himself before the Nation as the recognized representative of his race.[84] Ex-Governor Bullock of Georgia announced in advance of the Exposition that its purpose was to prove to Northern capitalists that the "free-silver lunacy'' and anti-Negro agitation were ''silly hobbies,'' not truly representative of the South.[85]    He explained further to the New York Chamber of Commerce:

. . . . one of the good effects of our Exposition will be to dissipate the political usefulness of the color-line bugaboo and set our white people free to form and act upon their best judgment as to governmental policies, uncontrolled by prejudices engendered by issues that are now happily of the past.[86]

The Board of Directors was described, with a highly significant sense of values, as ''made up of fifty men, who are the best of our city—bank presidents, wholesale dealers, manufacturers and retired capitalists.''[87]    He concluded by assuring the New York business men that all was well in the South, and that ''the colored labor in our section is the best, safest and most conservative in the world.''[88]

Several incidents given wide national publicity during the month of August, 1895, may or may not shed illumination upon Washington's Atlanta speech.    On August 1, at the Brookside Mines in Jefferson County, near Birmingham, there was a riot between white and Negro miners.[89]    The whites were striking for higher wages; the Negroes refused to quit work.    On August 4, at Princeton, Illinois, began a race riot lasting for several days between Italian and Negro coal miners.[90]    The Negroes were strikebreakers imported from the South.

Washington said afterward that he felt he ''had in some way achieved'' his object, which he described as ''getting a hearing from the dominant class of the South.''[91]    In composing the speech, he said, he kept in mind that his audience would be composed largely ''of the wealth and culture of the white South.[92]

An examination of the document shows Washington's mastery of the art of opposing shibboleth to shibboleth.    ''Social Equality'' had been the stereotype by which the ''dominant class'' to which he now addressed himself had won the support of the poorer whites and overturned the Reconstruction governments.    Washington met the issue with skillful phrases: ''The wisest among my race understand that the agitation of questions of social equality is the extremest folly, and that progress in the enjoyment of all the privileges that will come to us must be the result of severe and constant struggle rather than of artificial forcing.''[93]    In all things that are purely social we can be as separate as the fingers, yet one as the hands in all things essential to mutual progress."[94]

He invoked the shade of the traditional, paternalistic relationship so dear to the romantic picture of the ante-bellum South. "As we have proved our loyalty to you in the past, in nursing your children, watching, by the sick-bed of your mothers and fathers, and often following them with tear-dimmed eyes to their graves. . . . ."[95]  Washington said the Exposition would introduce "a new era of industrial progress" to the South.[96]  The white people were advised to "cast down your bucket where you are," and not to "look to the incoming of those of foreign birth and strange tongue and habits for the prosperity of the South."[97] The Negroes were described as the "most patient, faithful, law-abiding, and unresentful people the world has seen,"[98] who could be depended upon to "buy your surplus land, make blossom the waste places in your fields, and run your factories."[99]  The Negro would continue to labor "without strikes or labor troubles."[100]

In his speeches before mixed audiences, Washington employed the oratorical device of addressing the white and Negro divisions of his audience alternately.  Only one brief paragraph of the Atlanta speech was so directed to the Negroes.  They were advised: "We shall prosper in proportion as we learn to dignify and glorify common labor and put brains and skill into the common occupations of life."[101]  They were to remember that "there is as much dignity in tilling a field as in writing a poem."[102]  Negroes must begin at the bottom and not at the top.[103]

The effect of the speech was as dramatic as the circumstances surrounding its delivery.  Clark Howell wired the *New York World* that "the whole speech is a platform upon which blacks and whites can stand with full justice to each other."[104]  Grover Cleveland thought that the speech justified holding the exposition.[105]  It made Washington the arbiter of matters affecting the Negro, not only in education, but in social, economic, and political affairs as well.  It also gave him an opportunnity to reach more persons of wealth in the country and obtain more money for Tuskegee Institute.

### THE FRIENDS OF WASHINGTON AND TUSKEGEE

As Washington, in his Atlanta speech, frankly addressed himself to "the dominant class in the South," his whole career was bound up with a successful appeal to the sympathies of that class, both in the South and in the North, among white people.  His course has significance for the education of Negroes in Alabama because it meant that much depended on the persistence of this class in control of public affairs.  It also meant that Washington and the Negroes generally were allied with the dominant social and economic class as they had been, in the thinking of the poorer whites, during slavery.  It may have been that Washington believed it was fruitless to cultivate the class of white persons who were on the lower levels of society; that he thought the antipathy of this class to the Negroes was too through-going to overcome. Whatever the reason, Washington definitely allied himself to "the better class of white people" incarnated in the powerful and wealthy of his period.

In Alabama Washington sustained relations of the most friendly sort to the leading politicians of the "oligarchy," up to the time when the line was overturned by insurgent Democrats. Governor Thomas Seay (1886-1890) was a "friend and champion of the Negro's rights."  Washington is quoted as saying that Seay was "the best friend the Negro race ever had."[106]

Seay's successors, Thomas Goode Jones (1890-1894), and Governor Oates (1894-1898), were elected over Populist opponents by various political devices.[107]  Jones was one of the staunch defenders of Negro rights in the Constitutional Convention of 1901. On September 14, 1901, Theodore Roosevelt wrote to Washington, asking him to come to the Capitol for a conference on Southern political appointments.[108]  On October 2, 1901, Washington wrote to Roosevelt:

Judge Bruce, the Judge of the Middle District of Alabama, died yesterday.  There is going to be a very hard scramble for his place.  I saw ex-Governor Jones yesterday, as I promised, and he is willing to accept the judgeship of the Middle District of Alabama.  I am more convinced now than ever that he is the proper man for the place.  He has until recently been president of the Alabama State Bar Association.  He is a Gold Democrat, and is a clean, pure man in every respect.  He stood up in the Constitutional Convention and elsewhere for a fair election law, opposed lynching, and he has been outspoken for the education of both races.

Yours truly,
BOOKER T. WASHINGTON[109]

Jones' appointment to the position was announced on October 14, 1901. When it became noised about that Booker T. Washington was responsible for the appointment a storm of criticism was levelled at Jones, Washington, and Roosevelt.[110] Jones denied this, saying that he owed his appointment to Grover Cleveland. Under the Administration of Governor Comer (1907-1911), the Alabama legislature passed several laws intended to effect rate-making on Alabama railroads.[111] Jones ruled in a series of decisions handed down from 1909 to 1911 that the regulatory laws of the Alabama legislation were "confiscatory" and unconstitutional.[112] Each of his several decisions was reversed by the Circuit and United States Supreme Court.[113]

Now, the same "anti-railway" legislature of 1906-1907 promptly passed a joint resolution asking the Governor to appoint an accountant to investigate the business affairs of Tuskegee Institute, and all other departments which he saw fit to inspect.[114] The spirit of the proposed investigation was so hostile that Washington was unable to make his "usual Northern trip seeking contributions in the winter of 1907."[115] It was "designed to reveal the shortcomings of the school and thus to bring reproach upon Northern ideas concerning Negro education."[116] Washington succeeded in bringing enough pressure to bear upon Governor Comer, so that the latter appointed as investigator a friend of Tuskegee whose report was favorable to the school.[117]

This incident is an illustration of the possible defect in the appeal of Washington and J. L. M. Curry to "the dominant class of the South." In application to the common schools it meant when that class lost its political dominance the Negroes had no friend at court. It is entirely possible, of course, that no other strategy was feasible for Washington and Curry.

Jones' successor as governor, Oates, was a staunch friend of Booker T. Washington, and, like Jones, defended the rights of the Negroes in the Constitutional Convention of 1901. There is an incident connected with Oates that reflects Washington's invariable skill in handling difficult situations. Washington invited Oates to speak at the Tuskegee Commencement of 1894 and to share the platform with a Negro, John C. Dancey, who was later appointed Collector of Customs at Wilmington, North Carolina, through Washington's influence.[118] Dancey was an eloquent speaker. He paid "a glowing tribute to the New England men

and women who had built up Negro schools in the South."[119]
Oates, the next speaker, arose in obvious agitation.

I have written this speech for you (waving it at his audience) but
I will not deliver it.  I want to give you niggers a few words of
plain talk and advice.  No such address as you have just listened
to is going to do you any good; it's going to spoil you.  You had
better not listen to such speeches.  You might just as well understand that this is a white man's country, so far as the South is
concerned, and we are going to make you keep your place.  Understand that.  I have nothing more to say to you.[120]

The audience, composed for the most part of the teachers and
students at Tuskegee, was plainly nettled.  Another speaker was
scheduled to follow Oates.  But Washington arose and said:

Ladies and Gentlemen: I am sure you will agree with me that we
have had enough eloquence for one occasion.  We shall listen to
the next speaker at another occasion, when we are not so fagged
out.  We will now rise, sing the doxology, and be dismissed.[121]

Oates' speeches in favor of the education of Negroes and for
a just treatment of the race in the Constitutional Convention of
1901, might have lacked much of their fervor had Washington been
less tactful.

Washington's relations with the Alabama politicians who were
themselves so deeply implicated in industrial and financial developments in the State were duplicated by his experience with national leaders of industry.  The task of raising money for Tuskegee was said to have consumed two-thirds of his time, "and perhaps even more of his strength and energy."[122]  His frank appraisal of the men to whom he appealed, and the methods he employed, may have been either incredibly naive, or as consciously
artful.[123]  As, when he spoke of the "white people" of the South,
he was speaking of the "dominant class," the "best white people"
of America were those who had money to give to Tuskegee.  The
drudgery of raising money had its compensation, he said, in that
it gave him an opportunity to meet "some of the best people in
the world—to be more correct, I think I should say *the best* people
in the world."[124]  "My experience in getting money for Tuskegee," he said, "has taught me to have no patience with those who
are always condemning the rich because they are rich, and because they do not give more to objects of charity."[125]

In the rôle of defender of the rich Washington was superficial both in appraising the nature of criticism directed at them and in his answers to that criticism. "Those who are guilty of such sweeping criticisms do not know how many people would be made poor, and how much suffering would result, if wealthy people were to part all at once with any large proportoin of their wealth in a way to disorganize and cripple great business enterprises."[126]   His preference as to an audience was for groups of "strong, wide-awake, business men, such, for example, as is found in Boston, New York, Chicago, and Buffalo."[127]

It is probably without significance that the men who contributed most largely to his work at Tuskegee also had, in most instances, large business and industrial interests in Alabama; for they were men who participated in industrial development everywhere in the United States.   Andrew Carnegie made numerous gifts to Tuskegee, including a personal donation of $600,000, the interest from which was set aside, at the request of the donor, to free Washington, during his lifetime, from any care or anxiety regarding his personal expenses.[128]   Carnegie called Washington "a modern Moses and Joshua combined."   "No truer, more self-sacrificing hero ever lived; a man compounded of all the virtues. It makes one better just to know such pure and noble souls—human nature in its highest types is already divine here on earth."[129]

Washington had tried for years, without success, to interest Carnegie in the work at Tuskegee.   One day, while playing golf with Frank Doubleday, the publisher called his attention to *Up From Slavery*, which Doubleday's firm had just issued.   After reading the book Carnegie wrote to Washington and expressed his willingness to help to the extent of a donation of $20,000 for a new library building.   Knowing how significant was this first expression of interest, Washington carefully estimated the cost of erecting a building, with student labor, at $15,000.   "Mr. Carnegie was amazed that so large, convenient, and dignified a building could be built at so small a cost."[130]   From this time on, Carnegie remained a firm friend to Washington.

H. H. Rogers, Standard Oil and railroad financier, was another large contributor to the work at Tuskegee.   In defining the attitudes of the different wealthy men to whom he appealed for funds Washington said that Rogers regarded Negroes as "part of the resources of the country which he wanted to develop."[131]

Like Carnegie, Rogers' first interest in Tuskegee was said to have come from reading *Up From Slavery*.[132]  Washington said that he received his first gift from Rogers, amounting to $10,000, on the morning after a New York speech delivered by Washington.  The first gift was to aid Negroes in the rural regions surrounding Tuskegee to build school houses,[133] a conditional grant that was later taken up by Rosenwald.[134]  While Rogers was building the Virginia Railway from Norfolk, Virginia, to Deepwater, West Virginia, he planned with Washington "a wide reaching work in agricultural education among the Negro farmers living within carting distance of his road."[135]  "Booker T. Washington had demonstrated to his satisfaction that by increasing at the same time their wants and their ability to gratify their wants he would be building up business for his railroad."[136]  Before his death in 1909 Rogers arranged for a speaking tour by Washington along the line of the railroad, giving him a special train for the purpose. The tour was carried out and Washington, in a climactic address at Suffolk, described the previous arrangement and lauded Mr. Rogers to several thousands of the members of both races.[137]

Collis P. Huntington gave Washington $2 when first solicited.[138]  Washington persisted, however, and Huntington's last gift to Tuskegee was $50,000.  Mrs. Huntington gave large sums to Washington after the death of her husband.[139]  William H. Baldwin, for years the Chairman of the Tuskegee Board of Trustees, was general manager of the Southern Railroad when Washington first interested him in his work.[140]  Morris K. Jesup and Robert C. Ogden were already affiliated with the Peabody and Slater Funds when Washington first met them.[141]  Henry Clews, New York financier whose early political and economic interests in Alabama during Reconstruction were numerous, was a friend and collaborator of Washington.[142]  So, too, was Julius Rosenwald, who, in addition to giving large sums of money for Negro schools at the solicitation of Washington, helped raise money for Tuskegee from his financial associates.[143]

A list of "exceptional men" that Washington gives as "types" is illuminating.  No white farmer or laborer of the lower economic classes is given in this list of his "friends"; a white railroad conductor marks the nadir of the social and economic classification represented.[144]  Henry Watterson and J. L. M. Curry are given as representatives of the old aristocratic South.[145]  John

M. Parker of Louisiana, planter and cotton broker, is described as "a man who has no special sentiment for or against the Negro, but appreciates the importance of the Negro race as a commercial asset."[146] The future of the Negro in the South, thought Washington, depended largely on men like Parker, who "see the close connection between labor, industry, education and political institutions, and have learned to face the race problem in a large and tolerant spirit."[147] Three exceptional men in the North were H. H. Rogers, interested in Negroes as natural resources;[148] Robert C. Ogden, interested in Negroes as "human beings";[149] and Oswald Garrison Villard, who was interested in Negroes as objects for the application of the principles of abstract justice.[150]

Washington met the problem of the unionization of Negro workers with silence, until just before his death. In 1904, when the effort to organize the Chicago Stockyards was defeated by the importation of Negro strikebreakers from the South, the officials of the unions appealed to Washington "to use his influence to prevent Negroes from working in the plants until the strike was settled, and to address a mass-meeting of colored citizens in Chicago on the subject: 'Should Negroes become strike-breakers?' "[151] Washington pled a previous engagement in stating his inability to address the mass-meeting, and never issued the appeal requested.[152] In 1913 he published an article which by implication discouraged the unionization of Negro workers.[153] Negroes generally, he said, looked to their employers as their friends, and did not understand or like "an organization which seems to be founded on a sort of impersonal enmity to the man by whom he is employed."[154]

## INDUSTRIAL EDUCATION

J. L. M. Curry was a firm believer in the virtues both of industrial and manual training in the schools.[155] His election to the position of Field Agent for the Peabody Fund in 1881, in the same year that Washington came to Tuskegee, may have been responsible for the great vogue this theory of education immediately began to enjoy in schools for Negroes. The Slater Fund for the education of Negroes, incorporated in 1882, was placed in the hands of trustees, two of whom were also on the Peabody Board.[156] Curry was consulted in making plans for the disposition of the Fund. A Southern minister, Atticus G. Haygood, was made the General Agent. On Haygood's election to the Bishopric of the

Methodist Episcopal Church, South, in 1890, Curry was given his place. He thus combined, for all practical purposes, the work of the two funds.[157]

The degree to which these foundations were able to effect educational policy in the Negro schools and colleges is obvious. It became a stipulation of both that no aid was to be granted unless the school maintained a department for training in the industries.

At Hampton Institute Washington had become thoroughly imbued with the "practical" educational principles instilled in him by General Armstrong. As Washington described it, the school which he attended from 1872-1875 had no formal courses in the industries.[158] It was a school with an "English" normal curriculum, where students were given an opportunity to work their way through school.[159] In his own account of his education at Hampton, Washington nowhere mentions having studied any specific "industry" or trade. He did learn "a valuable lesson at Hampton by coming into contact with the best breeds of live stock and fowl."[160] This was incidental to the general understanding that every student was supposed to work. Washington's principal job as a student was one as janitor.[161]

At Tuskegee he said that each industry had grown gradually; "We began with farming," he said, "because we wanted something to eat."[162] The students were desperately poor; and, besides, he believed thoroughly that no person should dislike manual work. In his first report he referred to industrial beginnings as follows: "In order to give the students a chance to pay a part of their expenses in work, to teach the dignity of labor, and to furnish agricultural training, the friends of the school have bought a farm."[163] The term "Industrial Education" appears to have been borrowed by Washington from its current popularity as an innovation in American schools. Washington referred to it first in a speech before the National Educational Association in 1884.[164] Curry took up the phrase in his report for 1882.[165]

The second "industry" was begun in 1882 when bricks were needed for a new building and the school had no money with which to purchase them.[166] A brickyard was started.

Lewis Adams, the Negro trustee and political figure who had helped obtain the appropriation for the school, was a tinsmith.[167] One of the next "trades" started was that of tinsmithing.[168] After the brickyard had begun to produce bricks the trades of carpentry and brick-masonry were begun in conjunction with the building of the proposed structures.[169] "Practical housekeeping" was begun for the benefit of the women. Dormitory life was essential because the students could learn nothing of "proper" home life in the homes then present at Tuskegee.[170]

Stripped of phrases, the early program at Tuskegee Institute was derived from a glorified common sense amounting in this instance to genius. The elaborations of "Industrial Education" came later. The students were raw, uncultivated, undisciplined country youth; Washington started to induct them into the American culture through a discipline based on the fundamentals which they lacked. That was the process which had touched him when, as a ragged, hungry boy, he had applied for admission to Hampton Institute, and had been asked to sweep a room as his entrance examination.[171] In all of his speeches and writings Washington exhibited a deep contempt for "Latin and Greek" as the subjects of instruction in Negro colleges.[172] It was his misfortune to have attended, after leaving Hampton, one of the pretentious institutions for the higher education of the Negro, Wayland Seminary, in the District of Columbia.[173] But if Washington had attended Talladega College, or Fisk University, or Atlanta University, he would have met there men and women from New England who possessed the same idea as to disciplinary regimentation of the plantation Negroes which he found at Hampton. He would have found, in all of these schools, men and women with New England ideas of cleanliness and order.[174] He would have been in school with fellow-students who were as poverty-stricken as he, and who worked their way through school with the same eagerness to learn he showed at Hampton. At Tuskegee the use of the tooth-brush, the daily bath, the absence of grease-spots from clothing, neatness and order—these evidences of what Washington called "civilization"—were as important, in the writing, and perhaps of the thinking, of its founder, as "Industrial Education."[175] The brick-yard which he established at Tuskegee was preceded by one set up at an American Missionary School in Athens, Alabama, for the same purpose—furnishing work for students, and necessary bricks which the school was too poor to purchase.[176] In 1853 Frederick Douglass, the runaway slave who became a leading figure in the abolitionist agitation, had asked Harriet Beecher Stowe to go to England to raise funds with which to establish an industrial, trade school for Negroes.[177]

The principal difference does not wholly lie in the kind of subject matter which the leaders of these schools believed in as fundamental media for the required discipline.  Armstrong, the Hawaiian-born, New England-educated, ex-soldier, believed in the general discipline of "military training," and in the dignity of labor for members of an "undeveloped" race.  Cravath, at Fisk, and Ware and Bumstead at Atlanta, believed in the discipline of Latin and Greek.  With all their belief, however, in the virtue of the "classic," they established these curricula as goals to be achieved rather than as immediate studies.  Established in 1867, it was not until 1881 that Talladega College in Alabama gave its first college degree,[178] and not until after 1920 did the "college" number more than twenty per cent of the entire student body.[179]

The difference between these two types of school—the "Industrial" and the "college"—was indubitably affected by the fundamental attitude toward racial equalitarianism.  The strict humanitarians were, to this extent, "misguided fanatics," as Curry called them.  They were placed in an alien environment and they refused to compromise with it.  There is a profound educational significance in the effect of these personalities, whether "fanatical" or "practical," upon the habits and attitudes of the young Negroes who came to them from slavery, and who received from both types an impress that was revolutionary.

It is important also to remember that both Curry and Washington saw "Industrial Education" as a technique to be used to obtain support from people who otherwise would have been op posed to any kind of education.  Washington said Industrial Edu cation "kills two birds with one stone"; it secured the coopera tion of the whites, and "does the best possible thing for the blacks."[180]  Curry hoped that industrial education would reduce "idleness, pauperism, and crime," and thereby meet "prevalent and plausible objections to general education."[181]  The motives of Washington in appealing for money for the support of industrial education may not always have been the same as those of the men who gave him money.

EDUCATIONAL INFLUENCE OF WASHINGTON AND TUSKEGEE
IN ALABAMA

There are certain intangibles connected with the life of Booker T. Washington which cannot be statistically evaluated.  The school was operated as a propaganda agency; the effects of this propaganda in influencing public opinion favorable to the education of Negroes cannot be measured.

One outcome of Washington's work is obvious. His assured position made him the arbiter of affairs bearing on the Negro. The philanthropic organizations consulted Washington, not only with regard to the education of Negroes, but also regarding certain schools for white persons in the State. An excerpt from a diary of Mr. Wallace Buttrick follows:

*Southern Trip*—May 19, 1902, to June 2, 1902. . . . (In Atlanta) At 11:30 A. M. I returned to the station and met Principal Washington of Tuskegee, making plans for the afternoon and evening and for the following day.

. . . In the afternoon I attended the exercises of the Negro conference at Atlanta University . . . I also had a further interview with Mr. Washington, particularly with regard to Dr. Massey's school in Tuskegee.[182]

. . . Wednesday morning, 5 A. M., started for Montgomery. Mr. Washington and Mr. Scott, his secretary, being with me on the way to Cheehaw. I went over our card catalogue of the schools of Alabama with Mr. Washington, indicating his opinion regarding the several schools by notes on the margin of the cards.

Thursday morning in the early part of the day I had interviews with two or three of our Negro friends, including Prin. Edwards of Snow Hill.[183] At 10:30 A. M., attended a conference of educational leaders at the rooms of the Y. M. C. A. The meeting was presided over by State Superintendent of Public Instruction John W. Abercrombie. The Governor was present, but evidently was not quite happy, and escaped at the earliest opportunity.

Friday morning, 6 A. M., started for Tuskegee, where I arrived at 8 o'clock. I was met at the train by Mr. Washington. After a long talk with Mr. Washington over matters of common interest, with him I visited his new children's home, it being evident that he had some ulterior designs of which we shall hear later.[184]

Since Tuskegee theory was that the school should begin first in its own community to transform the life of the people, various efforts were initiated in this direction by Washington. In 1896 he said that many Tuskegee graduates were ''showing the people how to extend the school term to 4, 5, and even 7 months, when before they went there the school term was only three months.''[185] At this early date he had the conception of philanthropic aid to communities which twenty years later developed into the Julius Rosenwald Fund. He claimed Tuskegee graduates "are very seldom in a place long before they secure a good schoolhouse which is usually built by the contributions of the country people themselves in labor and money."[186] H. H. Rogers gave his money to aid Negro communities in Macon county build rural school houses; and, through aid given by Rosenwald, Washington said in 1912 that "forty-seven school buildings have been erected in Macon county by colored people themselves."[187]

The stimulating force in this school-building program was furnished by the Extension Department of Tuskegee Institute. Washington was, indisputably, a man of the folk.[188] The written speeches printed as having been delivered by him can give no hint as to the wealth of anecdote and ready sympathy, while talking to plantation Negroes, for which he is still remembered.[189] He wished to make all of the country folk thoroughly at home at Tuskegee Institute. He organized a Farmers Conference to which Negroes from the surrounding countryside came, as they still do, "in ox-carts, mule-carts, buggies, on mule back and horseback, on foot."[190] Free forage for animal and food for man was provided in limitless quantities for the visitors.

The matters considered at the Conference are those that the colored people have it in their own power to control—such as the evils of the mortgage system, the one-room cabin, buying on credit, the importance of owning a home and of putting money in the bank, how to build school-houses and prolong the school term, and to improve moral and religious conditions.[191]

The agricultural extension department sent speakers and teachers into the rural areas to teach Negroes better methods of agriculture. This work was inaugurated as early as 1897.[192]

Washington was a ceaseless educational propagandist. On the platform, through periodicals and in the white and Negro press, he lost no opportunity to plead for education. In a series of annual letters published in white and Negro newspapers in the South, he gave advice to Negroes on the improvement of their schools. Where Negroes were being discriminated against in the distribution of the school fund, they were advised to "bear in mind that we are citizens," to make "a direct appeal to the public school authorities for a more just distribution of the public school fund." If the authorities did not immediately give the Negroes a fair share of the fund they should ask until they did receive it.[193]

### Appraisal of the Effect of Washington on Education in Alabama

The effect of Booker T. Washington's personality on school improvement for Negroes in Alabama was possessed of certain qualities not susceptible to measurement. Physically it is possible to obtain some indication of the degree to which public schools for Negroes were influenced in Tuskegee's county, Macon, as a result of the work of the Tuskegee principal.

Washington said that he found the teachers in the rural schools "miserably poor in preparation for their work," with the schools in session from three to five months. "There was practically no apparatus in the schoolhouses, except that occasionally there was a rough blackboard."[194]

Perhaps for the reason that Booker T. Washington obtained his money to improve schools from practical business men who expected an immediate demonstration of returns from their investment, Washington and his colleagues were not hesitant in claiming substantial improvement in educational affairs for Negroes in the counties surrounding Tuskegee. In 1911 he claimed, as a result of the Tuskegee program, "a model public school system, supported in part by the county board of education, and in part by the contributions of the people themselves."[195] What had been done was an "actual experiment" to show "what a proper system of Negro education can do in a country district toward solving the racial problem."[196] "We have," added Washington, "no race problem in Macon county; there is no friction between the races; agriculture is improving; the county is growing in wealth."[197] His secretary, Emmett J. Scott, made the statement that "the better class of Negro farmers has greatly increased during the past thirty years, until at present from 90 to 95 per cent of the 3,800 Negro farmers in the county operate their own farms either as cash tenants or owners."[198]

It was frequently argued that educating Negroes would take them from the soil and deprive the plantations of labor.[199] In rebuttal Washington claimed that the graduates of Tuskegee went directly into agricultural and industrial occupations in the rural regions of Macon county, and helped keep the Negro on the land.[200]

It is possible to obtain some indices to indicate the degree to which these claims were justified.

### The Rural School as an Agent in Keeping the Negro on the Farm

The Negro population of Macon county increased from 18,874 in 1900 to 23,039 in 1910. At a time when the population of Black Belt counties generally was decreasing, the Tuskegee adherents claimed this fact as a recommendation for the school; it made for a contented and satisfied labor force.

In a survey of 612 Negro rural families in Macon county, made in 1931, Charles S. Johnson[201] found three members of the communities studied who had learned trades at Tuskegee.[202] The successful heads of families were those with an average education corresponding to the third grade in school. They were "neither too illiterate to take advantage of their surrounding," nor did they have "more schooling than is demanded by their dependent economic position."[203] The school has been an agent in equipping some members of the community with abilities and ambitions which they cannot satisfy in "the shadow of the plantation"; and so the Negro rural school, instead of creating a settled class of Negro peasant proprietors, seems, particularly since the World War, to have conspired with other tendencies to hasten the movement from the rural South to the Northern cities.[204]

### The Influence of Tuskegee and Washington in Changing the Economic System

The Tuskegee program aimed to "create a settled class of Negro peasant proprietors," i.e., owners of small, self-sufficient farms. But Macon county was not only in "the shadow of Tuskegee"; the survey quoted above refers also to the more powerful "shadow of the plantation" system which has been a more powerful resistant agent to educational, social, and economic progress than the school itself has been a catalytic one. Making due allowance for exaggerations made by Washington and others in justifying the too-early success of their program, the results after fifty years are somewhat unsatisfactory. There were a few members of the community who had returned to their communities from Tuskegee and who were working at their trades with no great distinction. Booker T. Washington "was remembered and liked by some of the older individuals";[205] in the Sambo community "the cabins had been whitewashed in preparation for a visit from him about

twenty years ago. He came—a great man with a personality
which took them in, which understood them, and which they could
understand."[206]   An association to purchase land financed partially by H. H. Rogers and William H. Baldwin, which had been
one of the glowing hopes of Washington, was no longer active.[207]
Negro tenancy in the selected communities studied was as high as
elsewhere in the Black Belt of Alabama, and the South.[208]

THE INFLUENCE OF TUSKEGEE AND WASHINGTON IN IMPROVING
THE EDUCATIONAL SYSTEM

This melancholy picture is supplemented by figures referring
to the physical condition of the schools. The official State Reports,
unfortunately, during a portion of the time report the condition of
the rural schools separately from the elementary schools connected
with Tuskegee Institute, while combining these figures since 1925.
The number of children enumerated by the school census, in Macon
county, increased from 6,868 in 1898-1899 to 7,145 in 1929-1930.
During the same period the number of children enrolled arose from
3,045 to 4,444. The percentage of children of school age enrolled
in school increased from 44 to 62 per cent.[209]  In 1904-1905, thirty-
one per cent of the school population was reported in average
daily attendance. In 1929-1930, this index showed a moderate improvement to 40 per cent.[210]  The percentage that average daily
attendance was of enrollment decreased from 67 per cent in 1904-
1905 to 63 per cent in 1929-1930.[211]

The length in days of the rural school term supplied by the
public school funds was 69 in 1898-1899, 100 in 1904-1905, and
94 in 1924-1925, excluding Tuskegee.[212]  Expenditures for Negro
teachers' salaries were $8,974 in 1909-1910, and $11,550 in 1924-
1925.[213]  The Negroes' share of the State apportionment in 1909
was $18,341; 64 per cent of this amount was spent on Negro schools
in that year. The Negro share of the State apportionment in
1929-1930 was $37,196, of which 80 per cent was spent on Negro
schools. The situation is much more serious than the increased
percentage of state apportionment indicates, because it shows that
with the addition of local taxation in the interim Negro schools
in Macon county do not yet receive their full share of the State
apportionment, and nothing at all of the funds derived from local
taxation.[214]

What progress has been made in Macon county is not exceptional in comparison to other counties in Alabama. Macon county ranked 60th among 67 Alabama counties in 1930-1931, in the percentage of Negro children in average daily attendance of the entire number enrolled; and 45th in the A. D. A. of the total school census.[215]  Current expenses per Negro child in average daily attendance for the State of Alabama in 1929-1930 were $10.06; and, for Macon county, $10.49.[216]  In this index Macon county was the median county of 66 operating Negro school systems. Forty-four per cent of Negro children of school age were enrolled in school in Alabama and in Macon county in 1900-1901; a percentage of 62.4 per cent for the State in 1929-1930 compares to one of 62.2 per cent for Macon county in the latter year.

At the least it is possible to say that the claims made by Washington and by others for the influence of Tuskegee upon the schools, and, through the schools, upon the life of the Negroes of Macon county, are hardly justified by facts pertinent to their present status. The effect may have been a negative one. In occasional reports to the State Superintendent the county officials show not only perfect willingness to let philanthropy assume the responsibility of the county and the State, but a sense of jealousy which stimulated the requirements of the white children for schools. Thus in 1906 Superintendent Stevenson commented as follows:

We think the next legislature should allow the County Board of Education to use any surplus money on hand to assist the patrons in building and furnishing our school houses. The Negroes are building quite a number of school houses and painting them. I don't know where they get this money from, but suppose it to come through the Normal Colored School at this place.[217]

The "surplus money" the Superintendent had in mind would have come from State Fund appropriations diverted from the general appropriations sent into the county on the basis of educables of both races to the peculiar needs of the white schools. It is probable that the law of 1907, appropriating money for the purpose of building school houses in the counties,[218] was stimulated by Washington's demonstration for Negroes in Macon county. The appropriation in Macon county was used to build white schools, seven new buildings having been erected between 1907-1909 with the aid of the State Fund. The first agitation for this law is to be found in Superintendent Stevenson's reports.[219] Through the State Schoolhouse Fund the white schools found State money to do what Rogers, and later Rosenwald, did for Negro schools. It is, of course, fruitless to speculate regarding the degree to which Negroes might at any time have shared in the State Fund for schoolhouse construction had not philanthropy aided the race.

## BOOKER T. WASHINGTON AND THE "GREAT MAN THEORY" OF EDUCATIONAL HISTORY

Appraisals of Booker T. Washington may easily fall into the common error of attributing momentous social and economic changes to the impress of a great personality whose life was contemporary with these changes. Such great men, because they are identified in time with social change, come to be regarded as essential causative factors when more correctly their lives merely illumine, through their numerous contacts, the slow and sub-surface movements of human events.

There is another error as fundamental; and it is to decry the positive contribution of great personalities because we have no adequate statistical measure of their effect upon human history. Such statistical measures as we have might give the impression that Booker T. Washington lived and died in Macon County without leaving behind him any permanent impress upon the educational institutions supported at public expense by the citizens (and, politically defined, this means "white" citizens) of that county. But this impression would be a gross under-estimation. There is a dim and shadowy area of social forces which, from lack of perspective, we have no adequate means of presenting to the imagination. In this survey, in addition, little reference has been made to the immense influence which Booker T. Washington had upon private philanthropy, and so, through these agencies, upon public education for Negroes. The building of Tuskegee Institute, the service of its many graduates throughout the South, the profound effect upon public opinion of the man himself; these are among the positive, immeasurable influences generated by this great personality, which in themselves constitute unique social forces, transcending the spheres of his own and our generation, and giving promise of increasing power through successive generations in an undiminished flow into the future.

It would appear that the evidences of greatness are to be found, not in immediate institutional results, nor even in those claims upon which the personality itself rests its petition for present and future acknowledgment; but in the long-time contribution which that personality can make to the area of thought and feeling and opinion. It is so with Booker T. Washington. Another generation may evolve more delicate instruments for such appraisal; until that time, the historian of educational events may find in the life of the builder of Tuskegee Institute perhaps the most illuminating point of departure from which to evaluate the times and the social and economic forces in which he was involved. In his own time Booker T. Washington was a vivid, towering personality; even in our time he has become a legend.

And who shall deny the importance of legends, as social forces, in affecting the course of human history?

CHAPTER XV

COTTON AND STEEL: ECONOMIC CHANGES
IN ALABAMA, 1900-1930

In previous chapters the economic background of education
in Alabama to 1900 has been described. That year furnishes a convenient point of division, principally because the Constitutional
Convention of 1901 symbolized the culmination of a decisive political era in the history of the State. The political climax was obviously a superficial manifestation of more fundamental movements taking effect in the realm of social and economic change.

It is the purpose of this chapter to review like changes which
transpired in the period from 1900 to 1930. The terminal date
may be adjudged at some future time to have logical significance
in the history of the development of institutions within the State.
From our present brief perspective it appears that the onset of
economic depression, notable in Alabama industry as early as 1928,
coincided with the closing of an epoch which flourished in the late
nineties of the last century and the first decade of the present one.

AGRICULTURE

In 1900, 89.1 per cent of all Negroes in the State of Alabama
were reported as living in rural communities. In 1930 this percentage had dropped to 71.6. The profound social change suggested by this fact has roots in forces intimately connected with
the fate of the agricultural occupations in which these rural inhabitants found a livelihood. Agriculture in Alabama in 1900
meant principally the production of cotton. From 1900 to 1915 the
percentage of all farm land devoted to the production of the staple
in Alabama ranged from 35 to 45 per cent. In this period the
great cotton producing counties of Alabama were those located in
the Black Belt and in the Tennessee Valley areas, where Negroes
formed an overwhelming proportion of the population.

Of paramount importance in the period was the appearance
in Alabama in 1912 of the boll weevil. The weevil struck Alabama

like a plague, particularly in the area of concentration of Negro farm operators, the Black Belt. Between 1912 and 1917 cotton acreage in the State was reduced from 3,770,000 to 1,970,000. The yield per acre in Alabama was cut 31 per cent as a result of the first weevil infestation.[1]

The catastrophe was aggravated because the first onslaught of the weevil coincided with a period of low prices in cotton. For a long period the Southeastern cotton area had been on the verge of complete financial prostration. The Southwestern cotton area, first infested, was the first also to recover from the ravages of the pest; and with the destruction of the Southeastern area as a competitor came the opportunity for the expansion of the cotton area in the Southwestern states of Oklahoma and Texas.[2]

The Southeastern area eventually recovered from the effect of the boll weevil, or developed methods of control; but from the effects of the first invasion there could be no recovery. The effects of the weevil in Alabama may be noted in (a) a shift in cotton production within subregions of the State, with the Black Belt suffering losses once more to the hill areas, apparently less susceptible to the ravages of the weevil; (b) continued financial decay of the Black Belt, and consequent decline of its political and social influence in the State; and (c) a transfer of population within subregions of the State, and between states, as the devastated areas suddenly found themselves with greatly reduced acreage and a surplus labor force.

Coupled with this domestic force in weakening the foundations of the agricultural system in Alabama and the Southeast generally, was the slow development of cotton culture in foreign countries to the point where they began to compete for the world cotton market.[3] This factor has been more notable in the period since 1920, and its final effects cannot as yet be gauged. By 1926 foreign and Southwestern competition had made cotton culture in the Southeast a precarious enterprise affecting the lives of the millions of blacks and whites living in the area. In 1923 L. E. Long and others[4] estimated that the cost of producing a pound of cotton in two typical Alabama counties, Madison and Chilton, was, respectively, 32 cents and 25 cents, compared to net costs of 17 cents, 13 cents, and 10 cents in three Texas counties. Differentials for cotton raised in foreign countries are probably even more decisive in favor of the latter. The net effect of such a sit-

uation is to require, for continued cotton culture, perpetuation
of the thoroughly disorganized, exploitative system so far in vogue
in the Southeast and in Alabama.

### TENURE IN ALABAMA

The effect of these forces has been to perpetuate and
strengthen the grip of farm tenantry upon the Southeast. Since
1880 the number of Alabama farms operated by tenants has
shown an increase at each decennial census with the exception of
the period from 1910 to 1920. By 1930, 64.7 per cent of all Alabama farms were operated by tenants, as compared to 46.8 in 1880.
The percentage of acreage farmed by tenants has increased from
34.2 per cent of the total in 1910 to 44.5 per cent in 1930.[5]

This general increase in tenantry has characterized both black
and white in the Southeast, a fact that but recently has excited
comment in the face of a general opinion that tenantry was particularly a Negro problem. In 1925, 51.1 per cent of all tenant-
operated farms in Alabama were operated by white tenants, as
compared to 48.9 per cent by Negro tenants.[6]  By areas the percentage of Negro tenant-operated farms ran consistently higher
than that for white persons, ranging from the Black Belt where
91.9 per cent of all tenants were Negroes, to the Sand Mountain
area where only 1.9 per cent of the tenants were Negroes.[7]  Para-
doxically enough, the areas of highest percentage of Negro tenant-operated farms are also those highest for Negro owner-operated
farms. Negroes owned 48.2 per cent of owner-operated farms in
the Black Belt in 1925. The average holdings of Negro owners,
however, were small, and far below the value of the holdings of
white owners.

In the period to 1910 a remarkable increase in Negro land
ownership was noticeable throughout the South. This fact furnished a text for Booker T. Washington's most fervent claims regarding Negro progress.[8]  Between 1900 and 1910 the land in
farms owned by Negroes in Alabama increased from 1,216,813 to
1,466,719 acres.[9]  The areas of acquisition by Negroes, however,
were principally in what are today classified as "submarginal"
areas, either on the fringes of fertile population areas, or in the
"pineywoods" section where much government land was acquired,
through homestead entry, by Negroes. With depression in agricultural prices these small owners on unfruitful land speedily suc-

cumbed to the general decadence of the Southeast as a center for cotton culture. The percentage of Negro-operated farms owned by Negroes was 15.4 per cent in 1910, 18.1 per cent in 1920, and 17.0 per cent, a decrease, in 1930.[10]

Between 1920 and 1930 Negro farm owners in Alabama decreased 7.4 per cent; the land in their farms showed a decrease of 10.8 per cent; and the value of farms reported as owned by Negroes decreased 14.0 per cent.[11]

This gloomy picture where Negroes are concerned is intensified when one realizes that Negroes were a part of an agricultural system that showed the same general trends for white persons. No peculiar racial misfortune overcame them; it was the common lot of an entire region, and such institutions as Negroes possessed were subject to economic instability to the degree that the entire area was affected.

The general decadence of rural life, as a result of an almost continual state of depression, has already been described. It was not possible in the period after 1900 for the tenant farmer to advance beyond the status fixed by the system prior to that time. This condition of institutional status in tenant communities in Macon County, Alabama, in 1930, has been summarized by Charles S. Johnson as follows:

The community studied reflects a static economics not unlike the Mexican hacienda, or the condition of the Polish peasant—a situation in which the members of the group are "muffled with a vast apathy." It is unquestionably the economic system in which they live, quite as much or even more than the landlords, that is responsible for their plight.
. . . . The social results of the economic system in this area, past and present, have been positive and unmistakable. The traditions, supported by what remains of the plantation structure, has given a measure of equilibrium to the social relations existing within the structure. From the nature of the external conditions determining the early social organization of this group it has taken form, naturally, outside the dominant current of the American culture . . . . The situation is one clearly of isolation and cultural lag.[12]

## INDUSTRIALIZATION

With the turn of the century in Alabama came reorganization of small independent industrial units, locally owned, into great enterprises connected with affiliated concerns owned and operated

from distant points, and interwoven into a veritable national net-
work of kindred or identical interests.   With new capital the industrialization of Alabama went on apace.   The State was rapidly
transformed from an economy dominated by agricultural interests into one in which the new industry was the paramount factor.

The great steel producing companies of America had interests
in the Alabama area from the first.   It was not until 1907, however, that the Tennessee Coal and Iron Company, the largest producer of coal, iron, and steel in Alabama, was purchased by the
United States Steel Corporation.[13]   The Corporation introduced
what amounted to a revolution in its attitude toward, and treatment of, the Negro as a worker.   Before the advent of United
States Steel the practice of using Negroes only as unskilled laborers had been established in the coal and iron industries.   The *Advertiser* explained the tradition in the following terms:

The undeniable truth is that the Negro is not fitted by nature
or habits to perform successfully any work which requires skill,
patience, or mental capacity.   There is something lacking in their
brain and in their body.   Their minds cannot comprehend the
intricacies of fine mechanical work and their hands cannot be
trained to accomplish it.[14]

The Alabama Industrial Board stated that the Negroes were "well
adapted for common labor, and in some instances can be satisfactorily used for semi-skilled occupations."[15]   A historian of the
steel industry in 1907 made the statement that "Generally speaking, the colored worker of Alabama is not a success when he is
taken from the cotton fields and harnessed to the chariot of coal
and iron."[16]

These opinions, so characteristically a part of the thinking
convenient to the past, changed when management of the larger
enterprises shifted to Northern capitalist groups.   Judge Elbert
Gary introduced in Alabama the labor techniques which he had
found so practical in other portions of the country.   A friendly
biographer said:

There was nothing to do but import this labor from Europe
or develop it from the material at hand.   The policy of the Corporation has always been to take what you had on hand and work
with that and that was what Mr. Crawford did.[17]   When the contract with the state for convicts ran out, he took up its renewal
with Judge Gary.   "Think of that!"   I have heard the Judge
say, "I, an abolitionist from childhood, at the head of a concern

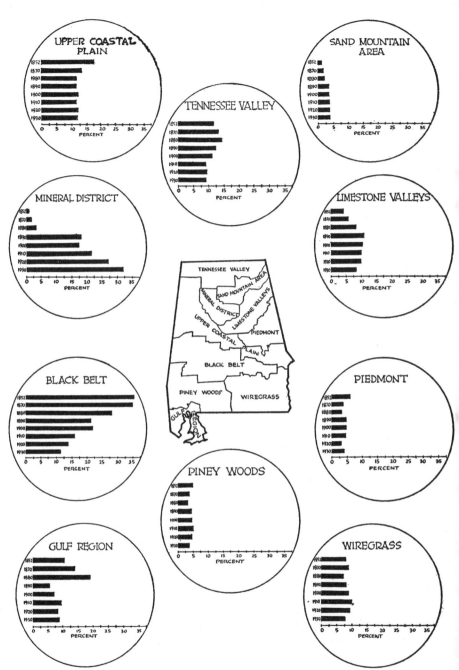

FIGURE 6. CHANGES IN THE CENTRALIZATION OF WEALTH IN
ALABAMA AS SHOWN BY THE PERCENTAGE OF ALL STATE TAXES
PAID BY EACH AREA, 1852, 1870, 1880, 1890, 1900, 1910, 1920, 1930

working Negroes in a chain gang, with a state representative punishing them at a whipping post!" "Tear up that contract," he ordered. "It is not necessary to consult anybody. I won't stand for it."[18]

Before the United States Steel Corporation entered Alabama Negroes were employed as skilled workers only in mining with a "few handy men about the mines or plants, such as pipe fitters' helpers, engine tappers, or helpers about the blast furnaces, or blacksmiths' helpers."[19] The Corporation gave Negroes opportunities to enter many lines of work which had before been closed to them, "as motormen, blacksmiths, masons, machine runners, linesmen, rockmen, machinists, pipe men, etc., which were formerly considered white men's jobs."[20]

One needs to be wary in attaching too much of a sentiment of equalitarianism to the new policy of the Corporation in Alabama, or even to that "abolitionist" spirit in which Judge Gary claimed to have been nurtured. Various students of labor problems in Alabama have suggested that the policy of United States Steel in the Birmingham area was in actuality a long-time insurance plan against labor difficulties. To one writer, it appeared that the Company embarked on a "deliberate policy of flattering the Negro workers," and that the device of inserting Negroes into the skilled levels was both cheap, and conducive to furthering the open-shop policy.[21] The Birmingham area was a most important link in the national scheme of the United States Steel Corporation, and its attitude toward labor was conditioned by the union problem in other areas and the desire to maintain in its Southern workings a reserve productive source which could be depended upon at all times for cheap production; and in times of labor crises elsewhere, for uninterrupted operation in Alabama. In both coal and iron ore mines "the labor cost of the Southern territory was cheaper because of the low standard of living among both Negro and native white miners."[22] The use of Negro labor in the higher brackets of skilled employment may reasonably be considered one means by which the Corporation sought to achieve its end, as we may likewise regard the various social services, including the provision of schools, which will be described later.[23]

The new industrialization in Alabama resulted in a shifting labor force from white to black, whereby "Mining as a whole . . . . is slowly becoming a Negro occupation."[24] Spero and Harris lean to the interpretation that this resulted from abortive efforts to unionize the mines by the United Mine Workers, efforts met sternly by mine operators who realized that the Alabama mines furnished a key point in the struggle against unionism on the national front. In the iron and steel industries the percentage of Negroes employed rose steadily after the entry of the United States Steel Corporation on the scene; "the proportion of Negro iron molders in Alabama rose from 10 to 24 per cent of the total between 1910 and 1920."[25] In 1923 Negroes constituted 52.7 per cent of the miners of Alabama.[26] Every effort was made to unionize the coal mines and the steel industry in Alabama in the period from 1890-1900.[27] It is significant that this organization period coincided with the rise of Populism in the State, and that the first union effort foundered on the race question, Governor Jones calling out the militia to "protect Negro miners" who were "scabbing" in certain mines in Jefferson and Walker counties. The mine operators nationally were united against the unionization of the Alabama Negro miner because these skilled men were frequently used elsewhere as a reserve of strike-breakers; and the unions wished to enter the Alabama field for the same reason.[28]

In 1918 an attempt was made to organize the steel industry in Alabama. At this time Negroes were approximately 70 per cent of the labor force of the ore mines, and from 40-45 per cent of the workers in steel plants.[29] The metal trades unions were all white, but realized that in order to win their demands the Negroes would have to be included. In turn the companies fought the strike principally by playing up the race issue. Negro organizers were beaten severely and generally given harsher treatment by the police than white organizers.

The great steel strike of 1919 found no support in the Birmingham area, and may have failed largely because of the far-sighted vision of the larger corporations in diversifying their plants and their labor force in this section. "The Negroes took no part at all in the second walk-out. They had been so thoroughly intimidated during the first strike that they refused to have anything whatever to do with the second."[30]

The industrial changes to which attention has been called in the preceding sections are important for several reasons where education is concerned. In the first place, they worked, in combination with a decadent agriculture, toward a redistribution of

the population of the state; and so re-defined the focus of educational effort for whites and blacks directly, and for Negroes indirectly so far as changes in the white educational system had a
reflex action upon the separate Negro system.

In the second place industrialization established new sources
of taxable wealth that could be exploited by educational institutions supported by public taxes.    Finally, the industrialization
of sections of the State resulted in a changing of certain attitudes
with reference to education in general, and specifically with regard
to the education of Negroes.    A more detailed analysis of these
results will be given in another connection.

### THE REDISTRIBUTION OF POPULATION

With continued depression in the agricultural areas and a
rapid tempo of industrialization, Alabama from 1900 to 1930
witnessed a fundamental redistribution of her population, including both whites and Negroes.    This population change for Negroes
involved migration from the State, and within the State from
rural to industrial and urban centers.

The migration of Negroes to various Southwestern states was
noted in Alabama as early as 1874.[31]    In every instance of migration contemporary accounts indicate some effort made by white
persons to meet the complaints of the migrants in order not to lose
too large a proportion of their labor force.    The greatest of these
migratory movements began in Alabama early in 1916.[32]    A wide
variety of reasons was given for the mass movement which resulted
in taking thousands of Negroes from Alabama.

On September 27, 1916, the *Advertiser* reported that daily
trains were leaving Eufaula packed with Negroes.    The *Advertiser*
laid the migration to the ruin wrought in crops by the spring floods
of that year.    Bullock County was said to have lost one-third of its
Negro population as a result of the exodus.[33]    In October, 1916,
it was reported from Mobile that ''two trainloads of Negroes were
sent over the Louisville and Nashville Railroad to work in the railroad yards and on the tracks in the west.''[34]    In the same month
''the exodus from Dallas County had reached such alarming proportions that farmers and business men were devising means to
stop it.''[35]    The Montgomery City Commission passed an ordinance
fining ''any person who would entice, persuade, or influence any
laborer or other person to leave the city of Montgomery for the

purpose of being employed at any other place.''[36]    The ordinance also forbade the distribution of any literature which might be disseminated with a view to encouraging the migration of Negroes. Throughout the state labor agents were arrested on technical charges.

In the efforts exerted by planters and by city employers to retain their Negro labor the services of Tuskegee Institute were called upon.    Authorities at the school conferred with neighboring bankers and planters in an effort to deal with the situation.[37]

The twenty-sixth annual Negro conference at Tuskegee gave an opportunity for another effort on the part of this institution to stop the migration then in process.    It is significant to note that the efforts of the Negroes to co-operate with the white people in ''stopping the migration'' also gave the Negroes, perhaps for the first time, an opportunity to register certain complaints regarding what they considered unfair treatment in the South.    Accordingly, the Tuskegee Conference issued declarations reciting ''the distress and suffering impelling the Negroes to migrate,'' and specified as impelling forces in the movement the prospect of better treatment at the North and ''better protection under the law and better school facilities for their children.''[38]    The *Montgomery Advertiser* insisted, however, that the Negro was migrating ''because of economic conditions which he cannot help and which he cannot overcome . . . . The Negro is going because he is the most unfortunate of the victims of the combined disaster this year of the flood and the boll weevil.''[39]

Negro leaders generally took the opportunity to rebuke the white South in a manner never before or after permitted to them. A Negro minister wrote to the *Advertiser* as follows:

Why should the South raise such objections to the jobless man seeking the manless job, especially when it has held that jobless man up to the ridicule of the world as trifling, shiftless, and such a burden to the South?    Now that the opportunity has come to the Negro to relieve the South of some of its burdens, and at the same time advance his own interests, a great hue and cry is started that it must not be allowed, and the usual and foolish method of repressive legislation is brought into play.[40]

W. J. Edwards, Principal of the Snow Hill Institute in the Black Belt County of Wilcox, wrote a lengthy letter to the *Advertiser* in which he recited many of the ''wrongs'' done to his race, emphasizing poor educational facilities as a major injustice.[41]

Between 1900 and 1930, the Negro population decreased substantially in the Black Belt, remained practically stationary in the Tennessee Valley, Sand Mountain, and Piedmont areas; showed moderate increases in the Upper Coastal Plain, the Limestone Valleys, Southwest Alabama, and the Wiregrass; increased by half in the Gulf Region, and was nearly tripled in the Mineral Region. Between 1910 and 1930 only the Mineral Region shows a large increase of Negroes, while in this twenty-year period alone the Negro population decreased by more than fifty thousand persons in the Black Belt. This inter-area shifting of population was an urban movement; the increases within areas can easily be explained by the development of cities there which paralleled industrial and manufacturing progress in the State. The concentration of the Negro population increase in Area III is easily explained by the presence of Birmingham with its constellation of smaller cities and industrial units. Area I had Huntsville, Decatur, and the Muscle Shoals tri-city center to retain as many Negroes as it did. The Upper Coastal Plain had Tuscaloosa and Opelika; the Limestone Valleys, Anniston, and Gadsden; and the Gulf Region, Mobile. It is significant that the great loss of the Negro population from the Black Belt was in spite of the presence of two of the largest cities in the State, Selma and Montgomery.

TABLE VII

PERCENTAGE OF NEGROES LIVING IN CITIES IN ALABAMA—1890-1930*

|  | Year | | | | |
|---|---|---|---|---|---|
|  | 1890 | 1900 | 1910 | 1920 | 1930 |
| Percentage ........ | 10.3 | 11.9 | 17.2 | 21.9 | 28.4 |
| Number ............. | 69,607 | 98,154 | 156,603 | 196,833 | 268,450 |

*Negroes in the United States, passim. United States Department of Commerce, Bureau of the Census, Bulletin 129. Washington: Government Printing Office, 1918. Negroes in the United States, 1920-1932, p. 53. United States Department of Commerce, Bureau of the Census. Washington: Government Printing Office, 1935.

The percentages of urbanization do not convey accurately the degree of the movement among Negroes in Alabama; the rigid census definition of an urban community as one with a population in excess of 2,500 obscures the fact that practically all of 175,853 Negroes reported as living in the Mineral Region (Area III) in 1930 were living in industrial communities closely approximating the conditions of urban life.

## OCCUPATIONAL CHANGE

An examination of principal occupations employing Negroes in Alabama in the period 1910-1930 shows changing status resulting from urbanization, the decline of agriculture as a principal reliance for subsistence, and the general effect of the industrial com-

### TABLE VIII

PERCENTAGES OF NEGROES GAINFULLY EMPLOYED IN ALABAMA, 1910 AND 1930, BY SELECTED OCCUPATIONS AND BY SEX*

| Occupation Employed In | Per Cent of All Gainfully Employed | | | |
|---|---|---|---|---|
| | ——Male—— | | ——Female—— | |
| | 1910 | 1930 | 1910 | 1930 |
| All Occupations | 100.0 | 100.0 | 100.0 | 100.0 |
| Agriculture | 67.7 | 53.8 | 70.8 | 46.4 |
| Laborers in Blast Furnaces and Rolling Mills | 1.6 | 1.7 | ---- | ---- |
| Draymen and Teamsters | .9 | .6 | ---- | ---- |
| Chauffeurs, Truck and Tractor Drivers | ---- | 1.7 | ---- | ---- |
| Operatives in Coal Mines | 3.8 | 4.5 | ---- | ---- |
| Operatives in Iron Mines | 1.3 | 1.1 | ---- | ---- |
| Servants | 1.5 | 1.4 | 11.6 | 26.5 |
| Laborers in Saw and Planing Mills | 1.8 | 3.2 | ---- | ---- |
| Laborers on Steam Railroads | 2.1 | 2.1 | — | — |

*Negro Population, 1790-1915, pp. 517-21; Negroes in the United States, 1920-1932, p. 303.

plex in the state.  The sharp decline in the percentage of workers engaged in agriculture is perhaps the most notable transformation in the period.  By 1930 Negroes in Alabama were principally employed as agricultural workers, as laborers, and as domestic and personal servants.  The presence of most gainfully employed members of the race in these poorly paid, unskilled occupations, has interesting implications for educational policies which will be explored in a later portion of this thesis.

### REDISTRIBUTION OF WEALTH AS SHOWN BY TAXES

In the ante-bellum period more than forty per cent of the State revenue was derived from taxes levied on the counties now included in the area designated here as the Black Belt. Inadequate as tax collections are for a measurement of true wealth, they have value in suggesting the tremendous shifting of wealth which took place in Alabama in the period after the Civil War. An analysis of Table IX indicates an acceleration of the trend toward industrialization in the period after 1900 as a source of taxable wealth.

In 1900 the three counties in the Mineral Region—Jefferson, Walker, and Winston—were paying nearly one-third of all State taxes. Ninety-two per cent of this total derived from Jefferson County. The latter county in 1930 alone paid nearly three times the amount of state taxes collected from any single area in the State.

TABLE IX

PERCENTAGE OF STATE TAXES PAID BY DIFFERENT AREAS IN ALABAMA,
1900-1930*

| Area | 1900 | 1910 | 1920 | 1930 |
|---|---|---|---|---|
| I. Tennessee Valley | 11.0 | 9.2 | 9.7 | 9.1 |
| II. Upper Coastal Plain | 11.9 | 11.4 | 11.9 | 11.6 |
| III. Mineral Region | 17.0 | 21.4 | 26.6 | 31.8 |
| IV. Sand Mountain | 3.6 | 3.6 | 3.6 | 3.7 |
| V. Limestone Valleys | 10.3 | 9.8 | 9.6 | 8.1 |
| VI. Piedmont | 4.6 | 4.5 | 3.0 | 4.2 |
| VII. Black Belt | 21.6 | 15.9 | 13.6 | 11.3 |
| VIII. Southwest Alabama | 4.6 | 5.0 | 4.5 | 3.8 |
| IX. Wiregrass | 8.5 | 9.8 | 9.4 | 7.8 |
| X. Gulf Region | 7.0 | 9.4 | 8.1 | 8.6 |
| Total | 100.0 | 100.0 | 100.0 | 100.0 |

*Annual Report of the State Auditor of Alabama for the Fiscal Year Ending September 30, 1900, p. 5. Montgomery: A. Roemer, 1900. Annual Report, Year Ending September 30, 1910, p. 52. Montgomery: Brown Printing Co., 1910. Annual Report, Year Ending September 30, 1920. Montgomery: Brown Printing Co., 1920. Annual Report, Year Ending September 30, 1930. Montgomery: Wilson Printing Co., 1930.

The implications for education involved in this transfer of sources of taxation—wealth—extend beyond changes in taxing methods made in the period. By 1930 the industrial areas of Alabama had far surpassed the historic center of political, social, and economic life in Alabama, in population, and in wealth. What this meant for the education of Negroes in the State will be discussed in the following chapter.

CHAPTER XVI

# COTTON PLUS STEEL EQUALS SCHOOLS, 1900-1930

In a prior chapter[1] it was shown that up to the first decade of the twentieth century Negroes found a place in Alabama industrial development only as laborers furnishing unskilled work. Skilled occupations were regarded as the natural province of white workers. When great national accumulations of capital entered the Alabama area the larger industrial concerns, especially in coal and iron, changed their policy to allow Negroes to reach slightly higher occupational levels.

## OBJECTIVES IN THE EDUCATION OF NEGROES FOR THE NEW INDUSTRY

The educational implications of this changed policy are illustrated by the self-conscious planning for industrial development in Alabama instituted by the Tennessee Coal and Iron Company in its history since 1906 as a subsidiary of United States Steel. The principal labor in the mines was formerly furnished by Negro convicts, farmed out to private companies by the State of Alabama.[2] With no "decent houses, no decent schools," the situation was described as "terrible" for George Crawford, installed as managing president, "who had a complicated metallurgical and developing problem thrust upon him and who needed steady, trustworthy labor if he was to succeed."[3] The large industrial corporations were also faced with the problem of labor trouble; and the elevation of the Negro in the industrial scale seemed to promise, in the Birmingham area, a respite from a continuation of such difficulties in Northern centers.

The Tennessee Company began at once to build up complete industrial and housing units, fitted with hospitals, welfare centers, and schools, by which means it was frankly hoped to regularize the uncertain Negro labor.[4] It was officially stated that this was not a philanthropic movement: "The Steel Corporation is not an eleemosynary institution," and its first object was "to make money for its stockholders."[5]

240

The peculiar racial situation of the Alabama workers permitted the development of a paternalism unmatched elsewhere in the country.  While a semblance of self-control was permitted the inhabitants of company towns in Minnesota, Ohio, and Pennsylvania, it was "necessary for the Tennessee Coal and Iron Company to manage directly the affairs of the settlements of its workers."[6]  In those localities "where municipal, county or state educational facilities are poor," in the words of a less hard-headed eulogist, "it has gladly assumed the burden."[7]  The paramount difficulty which the Tennessee Company found, after its acquisition by United States Steel, was the ignorance, and poor educational facilities of Negro workers.[8]  Especial attention was given to "dilapidated buildings" in Jefferson County, and to the "inadequate pay offered teachers (which) failed to attract men and women competent to train the youthful mind."[9]

The Tennessee company made an agreement with the authorities of Jefferson county by which the company was to build and equip a sufficient number of school houses in the neighborhood of its plants and mines.  The county authorities agreed to turn over to the company the annual appropriations received from the State for teachers' salaries.[10]  The result was that the Tennessee Coal and Iron Company was able to operate an educational system for its workers, using State funds, but supplementing them, free of any regulation from local school officials.[11]  A self-appraisal of results is not exaggerated: "the instructors in charge are of a high average type and the schools are recognized as having no equals in the South."[12]  The 1919 Survey of Alabama Schools described the T. C. I. system as follows:

One of the most interesting educational experiments in the bituminous coal region of the Appalachian system is conducted by the Tennessee Coal, Iron and Railroad Company.  The work is done in complete cooperation with the county school board, which apportions funds to the mining town school on the same basis as to other schools.  The superintendent of the schools in the mining towns is an assistant county superintendent, but is paid entirely by the company.

Social work is required by the company, and special stress is placed on personality and fitness for this additional service.  The classroom work is of splendid quality.  The teaching staff shows good organization, enthusiasm, loyalty, and a high degree of professional spirit.

As a whole it is an object lesson in efficiency which may well be studied by other mining communities. It shows conclusively what can be done by the expenditure of reasonable funds, business encouragement, and professional service . . . . What can be accomplished here can be accomplished elsewhere, with similar management and expenditure.[13]

The educational system of the T. C. I. interests was joined to an extensive program of community service and welfare work. The Company generally preferred to establish towns for workers entirely owned by it. One of the "model" examples of such company-owned communities was Westfield, Alabama, where houses equipped with modern conveniences, a community house, athletic fields, and school houses have been constructed by the Company within a kind of general compound which has no equal in the South for the comfort of living provided for industrial workers.[14]   A general hospital for T. C. I. employees is maintained at Fairfield, and through this institution, according to Ida Tarbell:

. . . . Judge Gary himself has given the highest endorsement possible to the Employee's Hospital of the T. C. and I., by going there himself for treatment and rest.   Under the same roof with him, *though out of his hearing*,[15] Negro and white mothers bear their babies, Negro and white workers are treated for burns and broken bones, Negro and white children are nursed through measles and mumps.[16]

The policies of the United States Steel Corporation in Alabama with reference to employer's welfare have admittedly been taken in self-interest, and have not escaped severe criticism.  Confessedly not "an eleeymosynary" institution, it is probably true that "in building 'model' company towns, the companies have one leading motive, namely, to cut down labor turnover while at the same time continuing to pay low wages.'"[17]   It is further alleged that the policies of the Corporation in giving decent living and educational quarters to Negroes were in line with a careful, long-range policy to keep Negro and white workers apart, and labor subordinated, by exalting the Negroes as competitors of the whites.  From this view, the welfare work for Negroes was "a deliberate policy of flattering the Negro workers," by building Negro schools from the same plans as the white schools, and admitting Negroes to "the pretentious base hospital at Fairfield on payment of the usual fee, and of course strictly on a Jim-Crow basis."[18]   In contrast to the glowing accounts of magnanimity in the descriptions of Tarbell and Cotter, Davis says the company "achieved its aim, cut down turn-over, and wages of laborers in the Alabama steel industry remained at a level of about 60 per cent of that of the steel industry in Chicago, and Pittsburgh."[19]

The Tennessee Company issues no specific reports by which the sources of its income for this work, and the exact distribution of funds, can be traced.[20]  It is, therefore, impossible to see to what degree the welfare services contributed by the Company are paid for out of the "cuts" usually deducted from the workers' weekly pay checks.

Yet the superiority of the T. C. I. schools was undeniable.  In 1930 the writer, in conjunction with Clark Foreman,[21] had occasion to visit all of the Negro schools in Jefferson County, Alabama. Tests were administered to all of the children enrolled in the third and sixth grades.  Comparative scores indicated a considerable superiority for the children of the T. C. I. system by comparison with the Negro children enrolled generally both in the other county and city schools and in the South at large.  The average educational score made by the third grades in the T. C. I. schools was the normal score for that grade.

One interesting reflection of the status of the Negro as indicated by educational opportunities provided in the T. C. I. schools is the fact that the system provided education only up to the high school level.[22]  Apparently it was believed that this moiety of education sufficed for the industrial purposes to which the Company intended to set its Negro labor.

### President Harding on Socio-Economic Status of Negro and Education

An excellent example of the social and educational philosophy derivative from the industrial setting of Negro labor in the Birmingham area was furnished by the speech made in that city in 1921 by the late President Warren G. Harding.  President Harding, it may be agreed, represented the industrial North.  To some extent his speech was a document resembling that of Booker T. Washington at the Atlanta Exposition in 1895.

The Negro, said President Harding, should be allowed to vote "when he is fit to vote.  I would," he continued, "insist upon equal educational opportunity" both for white and for black. Both should "stand uncompromisingly against every suggestion of social equality.'' This was because of a ''fundamental, eternal, inescapable difference.'' By bringing Negro labor to the North the World War had made people of that section cognizant of the problems which the South had always faced. The proper course of race development would emphasize equal opportunity of a cultural and economic nature, while recognizing ''physical difference'' and paving the way for the ''natural segregations'' noticeable in the South.[23]

There should be equal educational opportunity; but ''this does not mean that both would become equally educated within a generation or two generations or ten generations.'' Negroes should not, by implication, necessarily receive the same education that white people receive.

I would accept that (sic) a black man cannot be a white man, and that he does not need and should not aspire to be as much like a white man as possible in order to accomplish the best that is possible for him. He should seek to be, the best possible black man, and not the best possible imitation of a white man.[24]

Every consideration led back to the question of education. There was skillful double *entendre* in this section of the President's speech.

When I speak of education as a part of this race question, I do not want the States or the nation to attempt to educate people, whether black or white, into something they are not fitted to be. I have no sympathy with the half-baked altruism that would overstock us with doctors and lawyers, of whatever color, *and leave us in need of people fit and willing to do the manual work of a workaday world.*[25]

Mr. Harding envisioned a continued ban on foreign immigration, and of a draft upon the South of black labor for Northern industry. To keep its labor present in the South, that section would be obliged, he thought, to offer greater educational opportunities.

If the South wishes to keep its fields producing and its industry still expanding it will have to compete for the services of the colored man. If it will realize its need for him and deal quite fairly with him, the South will be able to keep him in such numbers as your activities make desirable.[26]

The speech is more than the skillful phrasing of a politician; to no small degree it was the philosophy behind the establishment and maintenance of the T. C. I. system. It was ''enlightened'' industrialism speaking to a section in the process of industrialization.

Our survey has shown little change occurring in the status of the Negro in the agricultural system. One might therefore expect that no change in the education of Negroes took place in agricultural areas. Yet change took place, not as a result of fundamental influences incident to the culture itself, but proceeding from external philanthropy. These influences will be traced in another chapter. We have seen that the migration of Negroes, threatening the basis of agriculture in the State, was used by the Negro leaders to obtain more money for Negro schools. This strategy may have been successful; the transference of large numbers of Negroes to urban communities is explanation enough for the increases in educational expenditures within the State in the last three decades covered by this study.

There are even occasional indications of a survival of the oldest conceptions regarding the rôle of the Negro in rural society, and the type of education befitting him. In a curious pamphlet published in 1933,[27] there occurs the following statement:

The taxing of poor white people to furnish "HIGHER EDUCATION" for negro wenches and sassy bucks, is an OUTRAGE upon the WHITE and an injury to the negroes. The schools and colleges are turning loose on the country thousands of negro men and women who have been taught the smattering of the higher branches and who, in consequence, consider it beneath their dignity to work with their hands. There is absolutely no place in this land for the arrogant, aggressive, school-spoilt Afro-American, who wants to live without manual labor.[28]

The author was opposed not only to the support of higher education for Negroes but also to "taxing the white man to educate negro children."

You can go on with your foolery, Mr. Politician and Mr. Philanthropist, insisting upon a high grade of education for the negro, whether he is fit or not. We people of the South are perfectly willing for our brethren who do not agree with us to take care of the so-called Afro-American, and we of the South will be glad to have those who only have sense enough to fear God and obey the laws of the land.[29]

It would, of course, be a mistake to assume that these sentiments are too widely shared by Southern whites in view of the development in recent years of county training schools offering high school work.

A sober student of the plantation economy believes that the situation in plantation areas today is not far different from that of ante-bellum days when "Literacy was not an asset in the plantation economy, and it was not only discouraged but usually forbidden."[30]  In Macon County expenditures for Negro teachers' salaries have tripled since 1915, amounting to $27,813 for 7,145 children in 1930, as compared to 9,545 expended for 7,853 children in the former year.  The result has not been a widespread enlightenment of the population; on the contrary, the school has to some degree served as a disruptive social agency.  Those who receive what education the community has to offer become migrants from the community to the small towns and cities.  The illiterate are left behind.  The Black Belt setting is described as one "that bred few land-owners, tolerated few innovations, and placed a penalty upon too much book-learning."[31]  The most successful individuals in the plantation economy are those "neither too illiterate to take advantage of their surroundings, nor (those who) have more schooling than is demanded by their dependent economic situation."  The present ineffectiveness of the Negro schools is a reflection of the type of educational preparation which the social and economic setting appears to demand.

AN ANALYSIS OF THE FINANCIAL BASIS OF PUBLIC SCHOOL
EDUCATION IN ALABAMA, 1900-1930

In addition to social and economic factors influencing the education of Negroes at public expense in Alabama is the important consideration that the Negro schools are a portion of a dual educational system maintained for a minority group which is without political power but must receive what educational funds are expended upon its children from the same general tax sources as those open to white children.  The Negro schools, accordingly, become competitors with the white schools for educational money; and no survey of factors influencing public provisions for Negro children could at all be adequate without understanding the conditions surrounding the demands of white children upon the State for tax-supported schools.

## THE ALABAMA STATE TAX SYSTEM

The Alabama Constitutions of 1819, 1861, and 1865 are described by a Brookings Institution Survey as "open," so far as taxation was concerned; "the exercise of the taxing power was discretionary with the legislature except for the provision that 'all lands liable to taxation in this State, shall be taxed in proportion to their value'."[32]   The Constitution of 1868 marked the first step toward restricting, through the Constitution, the taxing power of the legislative branch.[33]   This fact is paradoxical in view of the common belief that the 1868 Constitutional Convention in no wise protected the interests of those persons with large property interests.   In truth, the Constitution of 1868 was dictated by persons who had a wider concept of governmental services to the people than their agrarian predecessors, but who had an even more keenly developed sense of the necessity for protection of business and commercial interests.

The Constitution of 1875, according to Governor O'Neal, was designed: ".   .   .   .   to place constitutional inhibitions on legislative power, to reduce expenditures and make impossible the renewal of that saturnalia of misgovernment and extravagance, which during the Reconstruction had brought the State to the verge of bankruptcy and governmental chaos .   .   .   ."[34]

The result was the limitation of state taxes by the Constitution of 1875 to 7½ mills.   The Constitution of 1901 was enacted at a time when the State had enjoyed a surplus for five preceding years; accordingly, a reduction was made in the Constitutional tax limit from 7½ to 6½ mills.[35]   It has been shown above that the permission accorded counties by the Constitution of 1901, to levy a one-mill tax for schools, was in the nature of a compromise to afford the fiction of lower taxes and greater provision for education.[36]

The thorough-going rate limitations of the 1901 Constitution are described by the Brookings Institution as "crude and inadequate."[37]   The result in Alabama has been the "haphazard development of privilege or license taxes, special assessments, etc."[38]   The Constitutional limitations on taxation in Alabama are held to have "distorted and warped" the development of the entire revenue system of the State.[39]

A survey of the taxing machinery of the State shows that the license and corporation taxes adopted in the intervening years have been a makeshift, while "the framework of the revenue system has been congealed by constitutional restrictions."[40]    The Brookings Survey characterizes the paradox as accentuated by a change in the State from an agricultural to an industrial economy.[41]

The Convict Department was vital in the financial structure of the State until recent years, yielding, of all state revenues, 4.5 per cent in 1900, 19.9 per cent in 1910, and 20.7 per cent in 1920. The abolition of the convict lease system, beginning in 1927, by 1930 had made this source of income insignificant.

TAXATION AND EDUCATION

Educational financing in Alabama rests, according to the Brookings Survey, on (a) constitutional and (b) statutory taxes. In both classes are to be found some taxes which are state applied, and others with only local application.   The constitutional state tax comprises principally a three-mill tax levied *ad valorem* on property.   Poll taxes collected and retained within counties are another constitutional tax.  By Amendment III, adopted in 1916, a three-mill district tax was permitted in districts.[42]

For the State at large the result of the taxing system of Alabama was to place "a disproportionate share of the burden of educational support on the owners of property."[43]   In addition to constitutional levies for taxes, the statutory provisions for providing educational money have in recent years been enlarged to include specific and general allotments of funds.  State funds furnished 28.7 per cent of all educational funds in 1927, and 37.0 per cent in 1930.[44]

In 1931 property taxes amounted to 76.5 per cent of all county revenue from taxation; and, in turn, school taxes within the counties accounted for 44.7 per cent of all county tax revenue.

To make this matter more germane to Negro schools, it is only necessary to point out that the burden of a property tax would rest more heavily on the residents of the almost entirely agricultural, black belt counties where Negroes lived in large numbers, than in industrial areas where there are smaller percentages of Negroes.  With Negroes owning little or no land, and possessing, at the polls, no power, it is easy to understand how effective the slogan "Don't pay taxes to educate Negro children" might be among white farm owners.

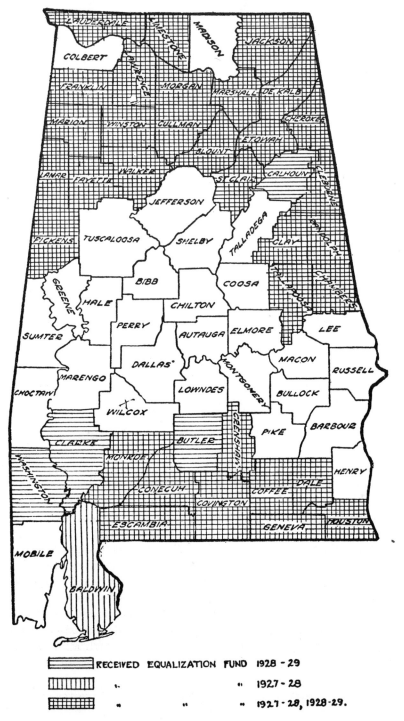

FIGURE 7. EQUALIZATION IN ALABAMA

An analysis of tax revenues for schools in three differing counties—Jefferson, highly industrialized; Jackson, a "white" rural county; and Wilcox, a rural "black belt" county—shows significant changes since 1920 in the source of educational moneys, as well as the great reliance of rural counties upon State funds for educational expenditures. Thirty-seven and sixty-six hundredths per cent of all tax revenues in Jackson County in 1930 was derived from local tax funds; 23.50 per cent in Wilcox County; while 77.44 per cent of tax revenue for schools in Jefferson County was derived from local taxes. State funds accounted for the high total of 59.76 per cent of all tax revenue for schools in Wilcox County, and for 44.37 per cent of the tax revenue for schools in Jackson County, while only 16.61 per cent of this revenue in Jefferson County was derived from State funds.

In 1920 the percentage of aid received from the State, of total school monies, was remarkably similar in all counties; 64.18 per cent for Jackson, 64.14 per cent for Jefferson, and 65.70 per cent for Wilcox. In the ten-year period since 1920 legislation regarding education shifted the support of schools for Jefferson County —and, likewise, for other industrial communities—almost entirely to the community, while maintaining the high percentage of total cost borne by the rural counties.

This significant trend may be explained by the Alabama Equalization Law of 1927 which provided for help to "poor" counties determined by a variety of indices of ability to support schools.[45] Figure 7 indicates the distribution of this supplementary aid in the school year 1928-1930.

There are two classes of counties that do not participate in benefits of the Equalization Fund. The first includes those counties, like Jefferson and Mobile, with industrial and urban centers which might be presumed to yield sufficient taxes to support schools without any equalizing aid. The second class, however, presents a highly paradoxical situation; for it includes the black belt counties where Negroes occur in heavy percentages in the population, while, at the same time, possessing some of the lowest per capitas of assessed valuation in the State. The paradox consists in the fact that the counties which do not receive equalization aid in Alabama are, first, the richest, and, second, the poorest counties in the State.

The explanation of this paradox lies in the *Requirements for*

*Participation in the Equalization Fund;* and in the simple fact that the black belt counties use the general state appropriation received per capita for Negro educables as an equalization fund; a device by which they save themselves from levying local taxes. In other words, even though among the poorest in the State, the black belt counties in general would find it more expensive to qualify for participation in the Equalization Fund through maintaining the minimum standards for Negro schools, than to receive such aid.

To participate in the Equalization Fund in Alabama in 1930, a county must have (a) levied both the one-mill and three-mill county-wide taxes; and, for maximum participation, have also levied the three-mill district tax in all districts in the county. (b) The participating county was required to have maintained, "as nearly as practicable," the same length of term in all schools within the county. (c) A minimum term length of 140 days for elementary and 180 days for high schools was required. (d) The county was required to have expended funds equivalent to a minimum program adopted by the State Board of Education.

The relative valuations of white and Negro teacher units may be gauged from the 1928-1929 program which proposed values of $708 and $354, respectively, for the two racial systems. A teacher unit is defined by the Alabama regulations as including thirty pupils in average daily attendance during the preceding year "in other than one-teacher schools; with one-teacher rural schools, where consolidation is impracticable, being counted as units even though the attendance does not meet the stipulated figures."[46] (e) The participating county was required to have expended an amount for teachers' salaries "at least 75 per cent of the current expenses."[47] (f) It was finally stipulated that counties must meet such other regulations as might be set up by the State Board of Education.

## TYPICAL BUDGETS

The source of funds for Negro schools, theoretically, is the same as that for all other children enrolled in the public schools. An examination of typical budgets indicates the precise nature of the problem of financing Negro schools. Lowndes County, a "black" county, Jackson County, a "white" county, and the cities of Birmingham and Montgomery reflect fairly typical situations.

The assessed valuation of Lowndes County in 1930 was $6,-485,309, giving, with its total of 11,014 black and white children between the ages of 6 and 20, a per capita valuation of $588. Jackson County had in the same year an assessed valuation of almost twice as much, $11,826,064, giving a valuation per capita for the 12,474 Negro and white children in the county of $948. In any scientific system of equalization, the expert would be inclined to regard Lowndes as the "poor" county and Jackson, by comparison, as a relatively "rich" county.

However, we find that the white children of Jackson county enrolled in school in 1929-1930 had total expenditures per capita of only $24.72, while the white children of Lowndes County had total per capita expenditures of $95.93. The per capitas for Negro children in the two counties show a reversed standing, with Jackson County paying $7.79 for each of the Negro children enrolled while Lowndes County paid only $4.76 for each Negro child enrolled.

This apparently paradoxical situation is not difficult to explain. Wealth as shown by assessed valuation is illusory so far as reflecting the true capacity of the two counties to support schools for their *white* children. The Negro children of Lowndes County furnish the explanation for the tremendous total payment made for white children in the county. There were enumerated in 1930 at the time of the biennial school census, 975 white and 10,059 Negro children between the ages of 6 and 20. The State apportionment in that year amounted to $4.86 per child of school age from the state distributive school fund, and, for the 11,014 children of both races, amounted to $53,525 for Lowndes County —$4,739 on account of the 975 white children, and $48,786 on account of the 10,039 Negro scholastics.

The solution of Lowndes County's educational problem is clear. By spending a total of $22,049 of the amount derived from the state apportionment on all schools for Negro children, a residue of $26,737 is left which can be devoted to the education of white children of the county. The expenditure budget of $80,103 for the white children of the county may count this sum as an initial income item. To this may be added the $4,739 received as a state apportionment for white children. A state "bonus" fund for high school attendance adds $3,000, a state illiteracy fund, $164 more. A state erection, repair and equipment fund gives an additional $355. A state county-high-school grant of $4,500 made uniformly to each of the sixty-seven counties of the state is an additional item. An elementary-school attendance fund of $5,466, contributed to in some degree by the attendance of Negro children; an attendance fund based on high-school enrollment and attendance, amounting to $5,205; and state funds for vocational education amounting to $780, with Federal funds in the sum of $480, give a total of $51,246, which in itself would provide a per capita payment for the white children of the county, without the levy of a single local tax, twice as large as the total payments made in Jackson County for white children. Lowndes County levies local taxes in the ratio of only one dollar for school purposes to every $258.00 of assessed valuation, while Jackson County, with a per capita payment for white children almost four times smaller than Lowndes, is forced to raise locally one dollar to every $160.36 of assessed valuation.

In connection with the statement frequently made that Negro schools are not deserving more aid because Negroes pay no taxes, it is interesting to note that in 1930 Lowndes County paid, altogether, $58,730.32 into the State Treasury of Alabama, and received back from the state for pensions and schools alone $60,664.68. Of the property assessed in the county, $1,674,082 represented public utility corporation valuations of property which, comprised principally of holdings of such corporations as the Louisville and Nashville Railroad, the Western Railway of Alabama, and the Alabama Power Company, was probably owned by "foreign" stock and bond holders not even resident in the State. Assuming that all other property in the county was owned by white people resident there, we have a "native tax" of $43,572, in return for which, as pointed out above, $60,664 was returned to the county for schools and pensions alone, without including such additional services financed by the state treasury as highways and courts. Logically, the white school children of Lowndes County might be regarded as having been educated at the expense of outside interests, as it might be claimed that Negro children are educated at the expense of the white people of Lowndes County.

An analysis of these expenditures indicates how new services render almost impossible the prospect of obtaining any equalization of educational expenditures for Negroes in such a black belt county as Lowndes. A per capita of $24.19 was paid in 1930 for the transportation, alone, of white children, compared to a per capita payment of $4.76 for all expenses for the Negro schools; and, in fact, Lowndes County in 1929-1930 spent only slightly less per capita for the transportation of each white child than Jackson County spent for all expenses for the education of its white children. The per capita expenditures for fuel, light, and water for the white high school child was $3.36, 70 per cent of the total per capita expenditures for Negro children.

The situation in Jackson County has been noted by implication. The only fund which it shares to the exclusion of Lowndes County is the Equalization fund, which adds $9,831 to the resources of the county. It is of the greatest significance, historically considered, to note here that each of the state funds, with the exception of the attendance and equalization funds, gave approximately equal payments to the counties, irrespective of burden. In this we may see the power of the politically dominant "black belt" counties until very recent years in placing all state apportionments on a blanket county basis. The equalization fund, enacted in 1927, marks (a) the decline of the black belt as a political factor; and (b) a specifically devised instrument to meet the requirements of white children in the "white" counties by setting up a fund to offset the great advantage of the black counties derived from racial discrimination in the use of other state funds.

The net result of this peculiar system, unique in the respect that it could occur only in Southern states, is that a "poor" county like Lowndes has a per capita payment for white children four times as high as that in Jackson County, which has assessed wealth twice as great. Another peculiar feature is that the equalization law, by an ironic twist, is obliged to "equalize" education in the state by giving money to a county with an assessed valuation of $948 for each educable while the county with an assessed valuation of $588 is levying very low local taxes and refuses the offer of "equalization" because it would cost too much to put it into effect.

Sample budgets for the cities of Birmingham and Montgomery indicate the wide variations in payments for services rendered to Negro and white children in urban centers. In Jackson County, and in Birmingham and Montgomery, more money is spent on Negro children than is received by the unit in state apportionments.

DEVELOPMENT OF PUBLIC SCHOOLS FOR NEGROES—1900-1930

In the face of a grossly inadequate provision for financing public schools for Negroes in the period surveyed it would be a mistake to conclude that no progress has been made. A brief summary of salient facts with reference to the condition of the schools from 1900 to 1930 indicates that the Negro schools have enjoyed steady improvement, although by comparison this progress has been exceeded by what has been done in the development of public schools for white children. The percentage of educables enrolled has increased, during the period, from 55.9 to 76.9 per cent for whites, and from 43.4 to 61 per cent for Negroes.

A further analysis by areas within the State shows that much of the improvement in the enrollment in Negro schools is due to progress made in the urban and industrial centers. The industrial "Mineral Area" showed in 1930 a high percentage of 89.14 Negro educables enrolled, as compared to a low of 53.06 per cent in the Black Belt.

A study of grade distribution shows steady improvement for the schools in this significant index of general efficiency. Here appears the same picture shown by the percentage of educables enrolled, with the industrial and urban centers beginning to approximate a normal distribution, but with the rural, black belt centers showing an abnormally high percentage of children enrolled in the beginning school grades, and little or no high-school enrollment.

In some instances the development of a small sprinkling of the total enrollment in the high-school grades has been accompanied by an even greater accumulation in the lower grades than existed before. In excess of 75 per cent of the total enrollment in the Black Belt (Area VII) is to be found in the first three grades, compared to slightly more than 53 per cent in the Mineral Area (Area III). The only areas showing a normal distribution of the pupils over the grades, consistent with the increased enrollment, were Areas III and X. On the whole, the increased enrollment in the Negro public schools of Alabama from 1920 to 1930 has not been accompanied by a corresponding development of efficiency which might be expected to redistribute, more normally, grade placement throughout the system.

## TERM LENGTH

It is difficult to get an adequate picture of the extension of the school term length in the State. In 1920 an average length of term for rural Negro schools was reported of 87 days, as compared to 113 days reported in 1930; while urban schools reported a term length of 155 in 1920 and 175 in 1930. Individual counties reveal a highly varied picture. Dallas County reported a school term of 100 days in 1900, 76 in 1910, and 95 in 1930. Lowndes had a term of 94 days in 1900, but one of only 89 in 1930.

In general, the length of term in schools provided for Negro rural children in Alabama has been extended from 1900 to 1930 from approximately four and one-half to nearly six months. Urban schools have developed a term almost nine months long. The typical rural school term in the Black Belt, however, was in 1930 less than five full school months, and little progress is noticeable here as compared to thirty years before.

## ILLITERACY

For the State at large, the illiteracy of Negroes over ten years of age has been reduced spectacularly during the past forty years. In 1900, 69.1 per cent of Negroes in Alabama were reported illiterate.[48] By successive decades, this percentage has dropped steadily to 57.4 per cent in 1900, 40.1 per cent in 1910, 31.3 per cent in 1920, and to 26.2 per cent in 1930.[49]

An analysis of the state illiteracy figures by areas shows the decisive character of the social and economic factors basic to this index of educational efficiency.

TABLE X

PERCENTAGE OF NEGRO ILLITERACY—1910-1930—BY AREAS

| Area | 1910 | 1930 |
|:---:|:---:|:---:|
| I | 40.09 | 25.07 |
| II | 42.18 | 28.65 |
| III | 25.74 | 16.75 |
| IV | 35.74 | 24.66 |
| V | 34.67 | 19.91 |
| VI | 53.36 | 26.61 |
| VII | 45.65 | 31.53 |
| VIII | 42.90 | 27.85 |
| IX | 41.75 | 31.75 |
| X | 29.67 | 21.32 |

A close correlation exists, both between the incidence of illiteracy and various indices of economic and social disorganization,
and between the relative rate of reduction of illiteracy and social
and economic factors. The Black Belt reports the highest rate of
Negro illiteracy with the exception of a contiguous rural area.
The industrialized Area III reports the lowest index of illiteracy.

It is clear that the high rates of illiteracy observable here are
directly traceable to the effects of a poor educational system, and
the social and economic defects characteristic of the milieu which
surrounds the Negro population.

## SECONDARY SCHOOLS

In 1930, of 109,216 Negro children of high-school age in Alabama, only 5.8 per cent were in high school, as compared to 29.5
per cent of whites. The development of the public Negro high
school in Alabama is of such recent growth as to demand but
little attention in a historical sense. An extended discussion of
the rural Negro high school will be found in the following section
having to do with the work of philanthropic bodies in public education; for high-school work for rural Negroes in Alabama to 1930
was almost entirely a matter of stimulation from the Slater Fund
and the General Education Board.

The State report for 1911 first reports Negroes as in high-
school grades. The lack of specification regarding the type of
high school described must lead us to place little reliance on these
early figures. In many instances it is probable that figures of public high-school enrollment in the period from 1910-1920 consisted
largely of adventitious grades with work of no real consequence
which had been superimposed on an elementary school by an am-
bitious teacher. In 1912 there were reported in high-school grades
724 Negroes. Of this number 201 were reported from Jefferson
County, with the next largest number from Barbour County[50]  In
1916 the number attending high school was reported as 1,428; and
in 1920 as 1,595. In 1926 the number reported was 3,435, and
in 1930, 6,365.[51] Of the last-named number, 3,128 were reported
from Jefferson County alone.

The low status of high-school education for Negroes in the
State may be judged from the fact that Montgomery, the Capital
City, with a Negro population in excess of 30,000, maintained no
public senior high school for Negroes in 1930. In the same year
50.5 per cent of all Negroes enrolled in the tenth, eleventh, and

twelfth grades of public high schools in the State were to be found in one high school in Birmingham, the Industrial High School. In 1930 there were 22 counties where Negroes were in excess of 12.5 per cent of the population, and in which Negroes of high-school age numbered 38,183, that had no four-year high school accessible. Nine counties with a Negro high school population of 22,705 had no four-year high school. These were black belt counties, in each of which Negroes were in excess of 51 per cent of the total population.[52]

## THE TEACHER

On account of diversified reporting practices in the State Reports, it is impossible to obtain, by counties, an exact description of several highly important facts concerning Negro teachers. The change from certification based on examination to certification based on training makes it difficult to make a comparative estimate.

As to adequacy, the period from 1910 to 1930 shows a gradual adjustment of the teaching staff to something approaching reasonable ratios between the teaching staff and the student enrollment per teacher. By areas, enrollment per teacher ranged from 42.6 to 63.7 in 1910, and from 38.6 to 53.7 in 1936. The Black Belt had the highest ratio of students enrolled per teacher in 1910 and in 1930. The smallest ratios for both years appear in the "white" counties, showing that with a sparsely settled Negro population a small ratio is maintained which is not an index of superior teaching conditions. This fact is reflected in higher costs for educational services in "white" counties as compared to the Black Belt counties.

TABLE XI
ENROLLMENT OF NEGRO CHILDREN PER TEACHER, 1910, 1930

| Area | 1910 | 1930 |
|---|---|---|
| I | 61.3 | 47.8 |
| II | 63.7 | 44.8 |
| III | 57.0 | 48.1 |
| IV | 42.8 | 28.0 |
| V | 64.3 | 50.5 |
| VI | 59.0 | 42.9 |
| VII | 69.0 | 53.7 |
| VIII | 62.5 | 45.2 |
| IX | 56.4 | 46.7 |
| X | 52.2 | 38.6 |

Comparative figures for training over a period of years are wanting.  As the result of an investigation made in 1930-1931, Caliver reports the following data for Alabama teachers:

TABLE XII*

PERCENTAGES OF NEGRO AND WHITE ELEMENTARY TEACHERS OF VARIOUS EDUCATIONAL LEVELS

| 4 Years of High School or Less | | 6 Weeks to 2 Years of College | |
|---|---|---|---|
| Negro | White | Negro | White |
| 19.2 | 2.3 | 72.1 | 65.4 |

| 3 to 4 Years of College | | 1 Year or More of Graduate Work | |
|---|---|---|---|
| Negro | White | Negro | White |
| 8.4 | 30.6 | 0.2 | 1.7 |

*Caliver, *Education of Negro Teachers,* p. 12.

McCuistion found comparable results in a survey conducted in 1930.[53] The vast superiority of the industrial, urban Jefferson County to a Black Belt county like Wilcox is striking.  More than half of the Jefferson County teachers have more than two years of normal or college work in advance of high school graduation; al-

TABLE XIII

EXPENDITURES FOR TEACHERS' SALARIES PER CAPITA NEGRO AND WHITE CHILD ENUMERATED IN ALABAMA BY AREAS—1910-1930

| Area | 1910 | | 1930 | |
|---|---|---|---|---|
| | White | Negro | White | Negro |
| I | $4.76 | $1.06 | $14.39 | $4.48 |
| II | 5.80 | 1.08 | 19.65 | 4.14 |
| III | 9.60 | 2.76 | 31.79 | 13.66 |
| IV | 3.31 | 1.13 | 12.94 | 6.33 |
| V | 4.43 | 1.01 | 17.39 | 4.36 |
| VI | 5.03 | 1.06 | 17.12 | 8.38 |
| VII | 14.55 | .80 | 31.99 | 2.73 |
| VIII | 6.56 | .92 | 18.53 | 3.41 |
| IX | 5.63 | .92 | 14.90 | 3.29 |
| X | 9.57 | 1.79 | 22.19 | 9.40 |

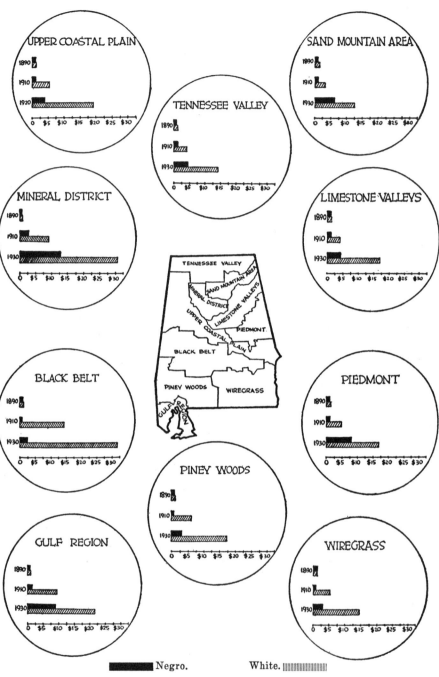

FIGURE 8. EXPENDITURES PER CAPITA SCHOOL CHILD FOR SALARIES OF WHITE AND NEGRO TEACHERS IN ALABAMA, 1890, 1910, 1930

most two-thirds of the Wilcox County teachers have not been graduated from high school.

Salaries of Negro teachers have enjoyed a gradual advance
although they are far from approaching either relatively or absolutely similar advances made in the payment of white teachers.
An analysis of per capita expenditures for each child enumerated
in the years 1910 and 1930 gives an outline of the picture.  A
qualification is that in this period the provision of more teachers
for Negro children results in individual salaries rising more slowly
than the per capita figures might indicate.

CHAPTER XVII

# PHILANTHROPY AND NEGRO EDUCATION

The story of the education of Negroes in Alabama during the last three decades would have little of novelty compared to prior periods, were it not for the influence of certain philanthropic agencies. We briefly survey here the activities of five great educational foundations in the development of public schools for Negroes in the State of Alabama.

## THE PEABODY FUND

Two grants totalling $2,384,000, the first dated February 8, 1867, "for the promotion and encouragement of intellectual, moral or industrial education among the young of the more destitute portions of the Southern and Southwestern States of our Union," constituted the endowment of the George Peabody Fund.[1] The initial donation was accompanied further by a provision that its distribution among this population should be governed ". . . . without other distinction than their needs and the opportunities of usefulness (open) to them."[2] Under the direction of Barnas Sears the Peabody Fund saw as its principal function the development of a public elementary school system in the South by aiding typical centers to develop "free" schools.

The first record of payment to Alabama is found in the *Proceedings* of 1868. The sum of $2,000 was appropriated to Mobile, conditioned on the removal of a tuition fee then charged to pupils in the city schools. The appropriation appears to have been a general one to all schools,[3] and probably included schools for Negroes then in operation in Mobile. Appropriations in the same year to Montgomery, Selma, Talladega, Uniontown, Marion and Tuscaloosa did not include Negroes. In the following year aid was given to Negro schools at Greensboro, Huntsville, Montgomery, and Mobile. Discrimination on the basis of race appeared in the Huntsville and Montgomery grants. In these cities $1,000 was promised for a white school enrolling a minimum of 500 pupils while the enrollment specified for Negroes in each case was 700.[4]

It is uncertain as to whether this policy established a precedent for public school systems in the South.  In a report dated February, 1871, a discriminatory scale of payments was announced as the official policy of the Fund.  A schedule called for paying to white schools enrolling not less than 100 pupils, $300; 150 pupils, $450; 200 pupils, $600; 250 pupils, $800; 300 pupils, $1,000, adding that "at present we pay for colored schools two-thirds of the rates above named."[5]  Dr. Sears justified this discrimination in a letter in which he stated that "it costs less to maintain schools for the colored children than for the white."[6] During successive years Lafayette, Columbiana, Opelika, Selma, Birmingham, Clayton, and Gadsden, were recipients of Peabody funds.

In 1880 the Fund announced a new policy of "concentrating our efforts on normal schools."[7]  No appropriations are listed for public elementary school systems in this year; apparently the Fund did not aid Negro education in the State in any manner.  It was stated that "Alabama has a Normal University of its own for colored teachers, and has six scholarships at Nashville."[8]  The scholarships were $200 grants made to white students to study at the Peabody Teachers' College established in that city.  In 1881 the only Peabody aid reported for the State consisted of six scholarships to the Nashville Normal College.[9]

With the concentration of the Peabody Fund on the Nashville college, assistance to the public education of Negroes in Alabama from 1881 was limited to occasional grants to Tuskegee Institute, to Talladega College, and to the State Normal Schools at Huntsville and Montgomery.  Leavell points out that in the decade from 1883-1892, 86 per cent of Peabody appropriations went toward the stimulation of teacher-training in the Southern States.[10]

In summary, the influence of the Peabody Fund on the public education of Negroes in Alabama was fragmentary.  Appropriations were small and came at a time when larger funds from governmental and religious sources were making a more substantial contribution to the development of a public school system.  In an interim report made to the Trustees of the Fund in 1881 by Mrs. John Hampden Fultz, daughter of Dr. Sears, following the latter's death, there occurs the following significant statement regarding

Montgomery where the Peabody appropriations had formerly been expended principally on a system of schools for white children:

> The people appear too poor to build a proper schoolhouse, and during the past year over one hundred children have been refused admission to the over-crowded building. The New York Missionary Society has erected a handsome brick building exclusively for the colored race, and the white citizens of the city have to endure this painful contrast.[11]

In 1914 the Peabody Fund was dissolved, and $350,000 was turned over to the Slater Fund.[12]

### THE JOHN F. SLATER FUND

In 1882 John F. Slater, of Norwich, Connecticut, gave $1,000,-000 to be used for the education of Negroes; "education in which the instruction of the mind in the common branches of secular learning shall be associated with training in just notions of duty toward God and man, in the light of the Holy Scriptures."[13] From 1882 to 1911 the Slater Trustees authorized appropriations principally to institutions engaged in teacher training. The great majority of these institutions were privately supported.[14] Among the first appropriations of the Fund for the year 1883 were $1,000 to Tuskegee, and $2,000 to the Talladega College.[15] Slater appropriations to Tuskegee increased notably after J. L. M. Curry became Agent for the Fund in 1891. In the year 1897-1898 the State Normal School for Negroes at Montgomery received $3,500 from the Slater Fund, and Tuskegee Institute $8,000.[16] As Curry at this time was also Agent for the Peabody Fund, it is interesting to note that in the same year the Montgomery school received $1,550 and Tuskegee Institute $1,450 from the Peabody Fund.

The early donations of the Slater Fund were made in line with Curry's firm conviction that "Industrial Education" was the solution of the Negro problem. In later years the Slater Fund was notable for an idea as single in its devotion. This newest development of the Slater philanthropy has resulted in what is agreed by many to be one of the most significant recent steps in the education of the Negro.

In 1910 James Hardy Dillard, already serving (since 1908) as President of the Negro Rural School Foundation (Anna T. Jeanes) was made general director of the Slater Fund.[17] In the same year

Dr. Dillard became interested in a school which he hoped might become a rural high school for Negroes, located at Kentwood in Tangipahoa Parish, Louisiana.[18]    The County Training School movement began with the establishment of this school through cooperation between the Slater Fund and the local school authorities.    The initial correspondence shows that Dr. Dillard had in mind from the first the establishment of a "high school"—; the name finally selected for institutions of this sort, "training school," was in some measure a compromise with a desire not to offend the susceptibilities of the persons in the community who might oppose the idea of a high school for Negroes supported by public tax funds.[19]

In Alabama the movement had an interesting background in a parallel development among white persons.    In his report for the biennium, 1904-1906, Superintendent Hill recommended the establishment of county high schools in order that the white youth of the rural areas might have the benefit of a secondary school education.[20]    In 1907 the Legislature established a High School Fund by which, under certain conditions, each county could receive $3,000 from the State to be used in the support of a high school.[21]    At the time there was certainly no notion of providing similar schools for Negroes.    By 1910, 33 Alabama counties had taken advantage of the High School Law, and had established county high schools for whites.[22]

The first County Training School in Alabama was established in Coosa County in 1913.    Negroes donated 100 acres of land and two buildings.[23]    The School's function was expressed as follows by J. L. Sibley, State Agent for Negro schools: "This school will shape its course to meet the needs of the county, offering training in agricultural and vocational lines, and having a department for the preparation of teachers for the rural schools of the State."[24]

The policy of the Slater Fund with reference to these institutions had several fundamental considerations.    It was required (1) that all property used by a county training school should be deeded to the State.    This provision was intended to facilitate the transfer of numerous local Negro high schools supported by innumerable religious sects and local churches, to the State; and to facilitate the assumption, by public authorities, of responsibility for support.    (2) The Slater Fund required an appropriation of not less than $750 for salaries to come from public tax funds.    (3) The teaching was required to extend through the eighth year with the intention expressed of adding at least two years as soon as it became possible. The Fund aimed to lead public authorities to take over support as soon as possible, contemplating a gradual withdrawal of the philanthropy as soon as this aim seemed in process of realization.[25] The growth of the County Training School in Alabama was rapid.

TABLE XIV*

NUMBER OF COUNTY TRAINING SCHOOLS IN ALABAMA AS AIDED BY THE JOHN F. SLATER FUND EACH YEAR FROM 1913-1930

| Year | Number | Year | Number |
|------|--------|------|--------|
| 1913 | 1 | 1922 | 17 |
| 1914 | 1 | 1923 | 20 |
| 1915 | 4 | 1924 | 24 |
| 1916 | 6 | 1925 | 29 |
| 1917 | 7 | 1926 | 33 |
| 1918 | 11 | 1927 | 35 |
| 1919 | 14 | 1928 | 37 |
| 1920 | 14 | 1929 | 38 |
| 1921 | 15 | 1930 | 35 |

*Redcay, *County Training Schools*, p. 40.

The geographical location of these schools follows the distribution of the Negro population, although in several black belt counties in 1930, notably Wilcox, there was no public secondary school for Negroes in the county, with a Negro population aged 15-19 of 2,354. In this county, however, the Snow Hill Institute, now partly maintained by the State, performs many of the functions of such schools elsewhere.[26]

While the originators of the idea had from the first the vision of developing secondary schools for Negroes, the functions of these schools as seen by local and state officials reflects an interesting and highly significant change in public opinion that best justifies the philanthropy and its policies. According to Redcay the first aims of the county training schools were:

1. To supply for the county "a central Negro public training school offering work two or three years in advance of that offered by the common schools."
2. To establish a model Negro school in each county.

3. To improve instruction and achievement.
4. To give industrial and agricultural training.
5. To prepare Negro boys and girls to make a living.
6. To prepare teachers.[27]

In 1916 State Superintendent Feagin stated that these schools were

. . . . designed to give practical training to the Negroes of the county. At present, instruction is offered in agriculture, manual training, cooking, and sewing, with a special course for teachers. . . . If these schools carry out the aims of the county boards of education, they will give the practical training needed by the Negroes of the rural districts.[28]

In this description the county training school was given no secondary school training implications. It was not until 1920 that the possibility of developing these schools as rural high schools for Negroes was accepted by the State Department in its published report. In that year J. S. Lambert, reporting to the State Superintendent as State Agent for Negro schools, wrote as follows: "The ultimate aim is to make (them) four-year high schools, with two years of professional training, but up to the present time very few of them have been able to do work beyond the elementary grades."[29]  In 1930 the State Superintendent, A. F. Harmon, announced a realization of the aim expressed in Lambert's report for 1920.

Measurable advancement was made in the program of secondary education for Negroes during the year in county training schools, in city public schools and in private and denominational schools maintaining high school departments. In their effort to comply with requirements set up by the State Board of Education for standardization and accreditment to institutions of higher learning, faulty standards and equipment were improved in many of the schools.[30]

It is a far cry from the description, in 1916, of the county training school as an institution for "practical training" to that of 1930 when an institution had emerged with the aid of the State which had as one of its principal functions the training of Negro youth for college entrance.

Successive progress reports of the county training schools show how the Slater Board moved increasingly to stimulate local and state authorities to accept responsibility for full support. In 1932 it was reported that while progress was satisfactory in some counties, in others "the work is not gratifying for the reason that the appropriations from the tax funds are too meagre to command sufficient teaching forces to enable the schools to function properly."[31] In that year fifteen county training schools were maintained at a cost of $52,912 for salaries. County appropriations to this total amounted to $22,654; state appropriations, $6,325; Slater Fund appropriations, $5,750; General Education Board appropriations, $9,099; and Smith-Hughes appropriations, $9,084. With 2,801 pupils enrolled in the elementary grades, only 171 were found in high school grades.[32]

By 1926 the number of schools had increased to 29, with an annual salary list of $109,771. Public funds supplied $80,129 of this amount, and the Slater Fund $9,150. Tuition fees were responsible for receipts of $10,347. With an appropriation of $86,-890 for buildings, equipment, and grounds, there was an income of $28,600 from public funds, $8,940 from the General Education Board, $8,300 from the Julius Rosenwald Fund, and $40,150 from private supplement—principally money contributed by Negro patrons to match Rosenwald fund allotments.[33]

The year 1928 marks, perhaps, the most significant forward step in the program of the Slater Board in Alabama to obtain full support for rural Negro high schools. In that year the State Department, through legislation enacted in 1927, provided aid for the Negro county training schools as it had, since 1907, for the county high schools for white students. It will be remembered that prior legislation provided $3,000 available for each county for developing a county high school. In 1928,

For the improvement of teaching conditions, $1,000 was apportioned to each of the 25 county training schools, from the high school fund provided by the recent legislature. This apportionment was made on the express condition that schools receiving such stimulation and support should comply with standards set up by the State Department of Education relative to professional preparation of teachers, school equipment and administrative procedure. The further specification was made that minimum appropriations by county boards of education toward the support of the schools should not fall below the minimum amounts required for the current year.[34]

In 1930 appropriations were made from the High School Education fund to 38 county training schools "to improve the teaching service and to enlarge the high school facilities."[35] The aid provided was limited to a minimum of $500.00 for a school doing no more than Junior High School work, and a maximum of $1,200.00. Senior high school development was stimulated by the State Department by a schedule of aid which granted $200.00 to any senior high school department in a county training school maintaining an average daily attendance of six to ten; $400.00 for an average daily attendance of eleven to fourteen; and $500 for an average of more than fourteen. No school was to receive more than $1,500 for the year.[36]

By 1930-1931 the county training schools had yielded their former function of teacher training almost entirely to the higher schools provided by the State for that purpose.[37]  The State Department of Education, through Superintendent A. F. Harmon, accepted the responsibility of the State to support this work. "From this field of activity, also, philanthropy is gradually retiring.  Fortunately, however, the State is undertaking to compensate for the withdrawal of the Slater Fund and the General Education Board by direct appropriations from the High School Education Fund toward the support of county training schools."[38]

From 1882-1930 the Slater Fund appropriated $705,105 to the cause of the education of Negroes in Alabama.  Of this amount $182,240 is listed as appropriated to public schools, mainly to County Training Schools.[39]

It needs to be remembered that in spite of the great service of this Fund in stimulating secondary education for Negroes in the State there were in 1930 in Alabama nine counties in which Negroes were from 12½ to 25 per cent of the total population with less than four years of high-school work provided by any school; four counties in which Negroes were from 26-50 per cent of the total population with less than four years of high school work provided; and nine counties in which Negroes were more than 51 per cent of the total population with no four-year high school for Negroes.  Altogether, in 1930 there were 38,183 Negroes aged 15-19 living in these counties which had no four-year high school facilities for the race.[40]

### THE ANNA T. JEANES FUND

In his report for 1910 State Superintendent Harry C. Gunnels made a plea for the establishment of a "competent and systematic plan of supervision of rural schools."[41]  Gunnels had in view the condition of the white elementary schools; but all over the South the need for such supervision of Negro schools was even more patent. County Superintendents generally felt no responsibility for the effectiveness of the Negro schools within their areas of control and aside from annual appropriations of small sums paid little or no attention to the Negro schools.

This need was supplied first through the activities of the Negro Rural School Fund (Anna T. Jeanes Foundation) inaugurated in 1907 by a Philadelphia Quaker woman who had previously indicated her interest in the education of Negroes. In 1902 Miss Jeanes gave $10,000 to Hampton Institute and a similar amount to Tuskegee Institute at the solicitation of Principal Hollis B. Frissell of the former school.[42] Some time later she gave $200,000 to the General Education Board for the use of Hampton and Tuskegee. Her first gift specified an interest in the small rural schools in the vicinity of the two normal schools. "Others," she said, "have given to the large schools. If I could, I should like to help the little country schools."[43]

In 1907 Miss Jeanes, after further consultation with Frissell and Booker T. Washington, set aside a fund of $1,000,000 for the "furthering and fostering of 'rudimentary education' in small Negro rural schools." She stipulated that William Howard Taft, Andrew Carnegie, Hollis B. Frissell, Booker T. Washington, and George Foster Peabody be on the trustee board.[44] James Hardy Dillard, then Dean of the Graduate School of Tulane University, was elected President of the Board.[45]

The Fund's interest in supervision came as the result of a project begun in Virginia by Jackson Davis, then Superintendent of the schools of Henrico County. Mr. Davis interested Dr. Dillard in financing supervision for the Negro rural schools in his county in May of 1908.[46] Originally Davis proposed that one teacher should be selected to give demonstrations of good teaching in a centrally located school, spending several days a week in visiting communities and other schools within a radius of a few miles. The extension of this program to the conception of a supervisor for an entire county soon followed.[47] Emphasis was placed on the "industrial teaching" of the early teachers, but with the passing of the years the Jeanes' teachers became the equivalent of supervisors for the Negro school systems. In many instances they exercised the duties of an Assistant Superintendent in charge of Negro schools.

The policy of the Fund was to appropriate money to aid counties to employ such teachers. The first reference to Jeanes' teachers in Alabama in the State Reports occurs in the report of James Sibley, State Supervisor, to the State Superintendent in 1913,[48] although expenditures of the Jeanes Fund began in 1909 in the State.[49] Sibley reported in 1913 that there were 16 Jeanes' teachers employed in 17 counties in Alabama, and that their function was "to act as assistants to the county superintendents, and to stress industrial work."[50] The Jeanes Fund was paying the full salary of these teachers in the majority of cases, for Sibley suggested that the counties should care for the work and make a local payment of from one-half to two-thirds of the necessary salary.[51] In 1915 the number of Jeanes' teachers had increased to 22, serving 19 counties. A "growing feature" noted was the "disposition on the part of the counties to pay a portion of the salaries of those employed."[52]

In all published statements regarding the work of the Jeanes' teachers, emphasis was given to the amount of money which they raised for the benefit of the schools. It is probable that the Jeanes' teachers were occasionally credited with money raised in Rosenwald Building campaigns, in which they generally assisted. The "supplements" raised by the supervisors are a characteristic part of the financing of Negro schools, and such activities constituted one of their major activities. Supplements from patrons go into increasing salaries, frequently by contributions of "kind,"—board, eggs, chickens, and the like—and into extension of terms in many of the short-term counties.

In 1922 it was reported that 24 teachers were employed under the Jeanes plan "to supervise primary instruction in the public schools, to organize industrial classes among pupils, and supervise their instruction in the handicrafts and simple home industries, to form clubs for children and adults without the schools for instruction in home making, and to promote and supervise activities for general community improvement."[53] The exigencies of the World War period from 1917-1918 led to added assistance from the General Education Board for employment of the Jeanes' workers for three months of the year as "Homemakers," emphasizing food conservation and aiding in other emergency war measures.[54] In 1926, 22 teachers were employed, with an average monthly salary of $96.50. With a total salary cost of $21,789, public funds accounted for $9,933, while Jeanes' payments totalled $11,856.[55] In the following year payments from public funds for the first time exceeded the contributions of the Jeanes Fund for salaries, being, respectively, $10,035 and $9,569.[56] With other aid from the Phelps-Stokes Fund and other agencies, the supervisory work in 1928 cost $12,860 to philanthropic sources, and $14,599 to the local taxing bodies.[57]

By 1930-1931 the local authorities had definitely accepted the responsibility for assuming support of this philanthropy and its incorporation in the general system of education for Negroes was assured.  The degree to which this movement had extended may be gauged from an excerpt from the report of State Superintendent A. F. Harmon in 1931:

> The Anna T. Jeanes Foundation is gradually withdrawing its co-operation from this work.  To compensate for the loss of this philanthropic aid, however, increased assistance is being given in many counties from state and county funds.  Last year, 16 supervisors were maintained exclusively at State expense and one wholly by the counties in which she was employed.  The total cost of the service for the year was $45,023, distributed among the several sources as follows: from State funds $20,665; from county funds, $15,168; from Anna T. Jeanes Foundation, $8,730; and from Phelps-Stokes Fund, $460.00.[58]

## THE GENERAL EDUCATION BOARD

Incorporated January 12, 1903, a foundation of John D. Rockefeller, "the method pursued by the General Education Board has been that of cooperation with local effort, and stimulation toward adequate care of existent needs."[59]  No better description is needed of the work undertaken in Alabama by the General Education Board.  No single phase of public or philanthropic effort in the State has been without the aid and guidance of officials supported by the General Education Board.

Specifically the greatest single contribution made by the General Education Board to the education of Negroes in Alabama has come through the State Agents for Negro schools who have occupied positions analogous to assistant state superintendents in charge of the Negro portion of the dual systems; and who have been able to make their offices serve as central clearing houses for practically all of the activities, state as well as philanthropic, intended to benefit Negro schools on a state-wide basis.

In 1910 Jackson Davis was made supervisor for Negro schools in Virginia through a grant from the Peabody Fund. This responsibility was assumed by the General Education Board in 1911.[60] Mr. Davis may be said to have given this office the significance it later enjoyed throughout the South as he must also be credited with originating the idea extended so widely by the Jeanes Fund. In 1911 the General Education Board made possible the employment of N. R. Baker as a Rural School Supervisor for the white schools in Alabama.[61] Reports for 1911 and for 1912 indicate that the supervision of Negro schools was not a function of Mr. Baker.[62] In 1912 the General Education Board appropriated $3,000 for the salary and travelling expenses of a supervisor for Negro Schools. James L. Sibley was appointed under this grant, and began his official duties in March of 1913.[63] Preliminary to actual work in Alabama Sibley spent some time observing the work of Jackson Davis in Virginia.[64] His first report on the work in Alabama is dated November 18, 1913. Successive reports by Sibley and by J. S. Lambert, who followed him in the post, give the first reliable pictures of the condition of the Negro schools to be found in the official literature descriptive of the work of public education in the State.

Sibley's first report acknowledged his debt to the Virginia example of Jackson Davis.[65] The supervision of Negro schools by colored supervisors appeared to him as the greatest need of the times. The Jeanes program, he thought, should be extended to more counties, and more local funds made available in connection with Jeanes payments.[66]

Under the topic of school funds Sibley made a mild suggestion to the effect that county boards might provide more money for the Negro schools. Under the heading, ''An Economic Problem,'' he argued that Negro schools should be improved because they made Negro labor more efficient. Teachers' Institutes were recommended for the improvement of teaching, and one conducted by the Tennessee Coal and Iron Company was cited as a model for others in the State. The establishment of the first County Training School in Coosa County was noted. The work of the School Improvement Leagues in furthering the cause of local school units was lauded. State aid in the building of Negro schools was advocated.[67]

Sibley's report for 1915 shows him helping in forwarding the

Rosenwald building program, and with the expansion of the County Training Schools, fostered by the Slater foundation.[68]   Beginning in 1916, the General Education Board sponsored, through the Jeanes teachers, a program of food conservation by employing the Jeanes teachers to conduct "Home Makers' Clubs" in the summer months.[69]   In 1918 a Negro woman was added to the State Staff for the supervision of the Jeanes Work, and her salary was borne jointly by the General Education Board and by the Jeanes Fund.[70] At the same time the General Education Board was cooperating in the development of the County Training Schools by providing the services of its State Agent and by actual contributions to equipment.[71]   In 1922 another Negro worker was added to the State Staff, supported jointly by the General Education Board and the Rosenwald Fund, to supervise certain aspects of the Negro educational program and to promote the building of Rosenwald schools.[72]

By 1927 the Department of Education included a Division of Negro Education—the result of the stimulation applied by the General Education Board—consisting of a Director, a supervisor, a Negro agent, supported cooperatively by the State and the Rosenwald Fund to promote the building of Negro schools, and a Negro elementary and industrial supervisor maintained wholly by the State.   The last-named person had formerly been employed by the Jeanes and General Education Board philanthropies but by this time had been accepted entirely as an employee of the State.[73] From 1924-1929 the General Education Board expended, in Alabama, $63,000 for state agents, salaries, and travel; $237,000 in aid to the state colleges; $21,500 for equipment of county training schools; and $29,650 for promoting summer schools for Negro teachers.[74]

### THE JULIUS ROSENWALD FUND

The Julius Rosenwald Fund merits a distinctive place in a listing of philanthropic efforts if for no other reason than the vast interest which has attended its operation, and the expenditures involved in the program.   We are interested here in the techniques which were elaborated in connection with this extensive program as well as in the record of construction; for those techniques are most instructive in giving a realistic picture of the problem of educating Negro children in the South.

In 1904 Booker T. Washington succeeded in interesting H. H. Rogers of the Standard Oil Company, who began to make donations to Tuskegee Institute especially for use in connection with an extension program planned by that institution.[75]  The money was spent principally in Macon County for small "model" schools; and from 1905 to 1919 Mr. Rogers, and his family, donated $30,000 for this work.  Under Washington's guidance, the early plans had the principal features of the future Rosenwald building program.  The philanthropy enlisted the support of the Negroes in the local community and appropriations were made on a "matching" basis.[76]  In 1911 Julius Rosenwald visited Tuskegee Institute for the first time and his attention was called to this enterprise by Mr. Washington.  Under the Rogers grants, forty-two school houses had been built in Macon county alone; and other schools had been built in five other nearby counties.

The school houses which were built averaged $1,000 in cost. With their construction went the lengthening of school terms from three and four months to eight and nine months, at an average cost to the people themselves of $3,600 a year.[77]

On June 12, 1912, Booker T. Washington submitted to Rosenwald a "scheme for helping colored schools."[78]  The "scheme" had the following points: (1) The suggestion of an extension to other states, (2) the placement of a general agent in charge, to work through county officials, (3) to start the program first in a few favorable counties, (4) to place responsibility for local aid upon county officials, (5) to insist that the general agent should enlist the support of the local white people for the cause of educating Negroes.[79]  On August 1, 1913, (the date marking Rosenwald's fiftieth birthday) he gave $25,000 to be used in connection with Washington's "scheme."  On June 24, 1913, in line with another suggestion from Booker T. Washington, Rosenwald agreed to give $300 to each of six schools to be constructed on the one-room type. The first school so built was at Loachapoka, Lee County.  The total cost of the building was $942.50, of which amount $150 was raised locally for the site, labor contributed by the Negroes in the amount of $132.50, and $360 in cash donated for the building by white and colored citizens.  The Rosenwald share of this first school was $300.[80]

On June 10, 1914, when the first offer of aid had been absorbed with many applications pending, Mr. Rosenwald agreed to continue his aid to 100 additional buildings with $300 available for each. Fifteen months later ninety-two buildings had been erected. With steadily increasing applications Rosenwald continued to extend the grant of conditional aid. On November 17, 1916, C. J. Calloway, who had charge of the Rosenwald program in his capacity as director of the Extension Department of Tuskegee Institute, wrote to Principal Moton of Tuskegee that 184 school units had qualified for the aid and that there were probably 100 others that were working toward receiving the grant.[81]

With the Rosenwald Building Program assuming these large proportions it was clear that the movement had passed the experimental stage. Accordingly, on October 30, 1917, the "Julius Rosenwald Fund" was incorporated under the laws of the State of Illinois, "for the well-being of mankind."[82]

The next development in the control and organization of the Rosenwald Fund came in 1920. Leavell says,

> As a result of a question which was raised regarding the inferior grade of workmanship and materials that were being used in the construction of some of the Rosenwald schoolhouses, Dr. Fletcher B. Dressler, an authority on schoolhouse buildings and construction, was secured to make a thorough investigation of the Rosenwald school buildings during the fall of 1919. He presented his report in January, 1920. He reported that the new school buildings were better than those which they had superseded; but he found much room for improvement. . . .
> This report marked a crisis in the work of the Rosenwald Fund.[83]

As a result, an independent office of administration was established at Nashville, Tennessee, and S. L. Smith employed as General Agent. In effect this transfer meant a change in administration from the Tuskegee Institute, which, since the death of Booker T. Washington in 1915, had been headed by R. R. Moton.

On January 1, 1928, the Fund was reorganized for a second time, the central offices transferred to Chicago, and a President and staff of officers selected to administer the philanthropy.[84]

ALABAMA BACKGROUND OF ROSENWALD FUND OPERATION

The administrative history of the Rosenwald Fund has an interesting background in prior Alabama educational history. The first gifts of H. H. Rogers to Tuskegee Institute gave valuable stimulation to a school building program for white children. In his report for the Biennium, 1904-1906, W. G. Stevenson, Superintendent of Macon County, stated:

We think the next Legislature should allow the County Board of Education to use any surplus money on hand to assist the patrons in building and furnishing our school houses. The negroes are building quite a number of good houses, and painting them. I don't know where they get this money from, but suppose it to come through the normal colored school at this place. . . . We think the Legislature in its next session should enact a law giving some amount to assist the people to build better and more comfortable school houses, say, 40 per cent of any amount the patrons may give not to exceed $200.[85]

Perhaps as the result of this suggestion the Alabama Legislature in 1907 provided a fund of $67,000, of which $1,000 was at the disposal of each county for the erection or repairing of schoolhouses.[86] School districts were required to raise at least $100, and the State fund was limited to $200 for any one project. A two acre lot was required, and it was provided that the properties must be deeded to the State before the project was eligible for aid.

In 1908 Mr. Stevenson, of Macon County, reported:

I am gratified to say that the country people have shown greater interest in educational matter (sic) than ever before, This is shown by their enthusiastic response to accept the aid given by (the) State for erecting and repairing school houses.[87]

In his report for 1911, State Superintendent Willingham pointed out that many counties were accumulating balances in the Schoolhouse Fund; and the implication is that after building schools for white children to meet the needs of this sparsely settled, minority population, the Black Belt counties no longer took advantage of the Fund for Negroes.[88] In 1912 Willingham stated: "In this connection it is fitting to observe that very little money up to this time has been recommended by the county boards for use in either building or repairing schoolhouses for Negroes."[89] Sibley, State Agent for Negro schools, emphasized this complaint in 1913 in his report to State Superintendent Willingham. The accumulating surpluses in the school house fund of the black belt counties was due, he stated, to the unwillingness of these counties to give Negroes "a fair share of the $1,000 allotted to each county for aid in the erection and repair of rural schoolhouses."[90]

The first Rogers grant, then, may reasonably be taken as a stimulating factor in the development of sentiment for the passage of the Schoolhouse law of 1907, which gave aid only to white schools; and the Rosenwald philanthropy was providing money to do what the counties and local districts would not do for Negro children. In 1916 the State aid fund was doubled and a scale developed for extending aid to schools which in many ways was similar to that later adopted by the Rosenwald Fund. Under the new schedule $300 was appropriated to one-room schools, $450 for two-room schools, $600 for three-room schools, and $1,000 for five-room schools. Before the State aid had been on a 1-1 basis; the new schedule provided that the ratio should be 2-1, with the community providing at least two-thirds of the aid extended.[91] A reciprocal effect is found here between the operation of the Rosenwald Fund for Negroes and the State Aid law for whites; at the time of the new regulations adopted for the white schools, the Rosenwald appropriation was $300 for a one-room school.

### EXTENT OF ROSENWALD BUILDING PROGRAM, 1913-1930

Under Tuskegee administration the Rosenwald building program was largely localized in certain counties contiguous to Macon County where the Institute is located. From available reports it is impossible to separate the precise amount of building done as between 1912-1920, the period of Tuskegee administration, and between 1920-1930, the period of administration from the central office in Nashville; for in numerous cases old buildings were added to through the years, and are reported for both years.[92]

The Rosenwald program was enlarged under the Nashville administration by building larger and more expensive units. The percentage contributed by Negroes, and by the Rosenwald Fund, was much greater during the first period than during the second.

An analysis of building operations in the period from 1920-1930 by geographical areas gives no highly significant results concerning the percentages contributed from various sources. Area X is notable for a small ratio of contributions to total cost

TABLE XV*

SUMMARY OF COMPLETED ROSENWALD BUILDINGS IN ALABAMA
DIVIDED BY PERIODS, 1912-1920 AND 1920-1932

| Contributions | 1912-1920 | | 1920-1932 | |
| --- | --- | --- | --- | --- |
| | Cost | Per Cent | Cost | Per Cent |
| Negroes | $119,556 | 44.33 | $333,400 | 32.84 |
| Whites—Public | 77,883 | 28.90 | 505,401 | 49.77 |
| Rosenwald | 72,200 | 26.77 | 176,620 | 17.39 |
| Total | $269,639 | 100.00 | $1,015,421 | 100.00 |
| Number of Buildings | 194 | | 213 | |

*Table from Leavell, *Philanthropy in Negro Education*, p. 176; and from manuscript report.

derived from Negroes, from whites, and from the Rosenwald Fund, with two-thirds of total costs coming from public sources. This fact suggests how small a sum is necessary for "stimulation" in a favorable situation. The only two Rosenwald buildings in Mobile County showed a total cost of $8,435, with only $1,060 coming from Negroes and the balance from Rosenwald and public funds. One of these two structures alone cost $6,775, of which Negroes contributed only $300, the Rosenwald Fund $1,200, and public funds $5,275.[93]

The geographical location of Rosenwald schools is exposed to so many local variations in attitude and emphasis from the promotional standpoint that there is not too much significance in the fact that there are relatively few Rosenwald schools located in several heavily populated Black Belt counties. In Wilcox County, where only one Rosenwald school was built prior to 1920, and but two in the period from 1920-1930, the explanation is simple. In this county the United Presbyterian Church has for years maintained several missions which are educational centers. More recently the Lutheran Church has maintained from 14 to 17 mission schools in the county. These schools are attractively built and integrated into a system with a superior teaching staff, although not always working in harmony either with local Negroes or with local school authorities.[94]

TABLE XVI*

ROSENWALD SCHOOLS AND SOURCES OF EXPENDITURE IN THE PERIOD
1920-1930 BY ALABAMA AREAS

| Area | Number of Buildings | Total Cost of Buildings, Grounds, and Equipment | Percentage of Cost Contributed by | | | | |
|------|------|------|------|------|------|------|------|
| | | | Negroes | Whites | Public | Rosenwald | Total |
| I | 20 | $ 65,535 | 42.66 | 6.04 | 32.00 | 19.30 | 100.00 |
| II | 37 | 166,634 | 37.68 | 9.89 | 34.13 | 18.30 | 100.00 |
| III | 10 | 70,050 | 39.68 | 11.49 | 34.61 | 14.22 | 100.00 |
| IV | 3 | 10,800 | 41.66 | 4.16 | 32.40 | 21.78 | 100.00 |
| V | 17 | 64,083 | 35.66 | 8.93 | 37.68 | 17.73 | 100.00 |
| VI | 13 | 45,848 | 32.04 | 15.49 | 26.68 | 25.79 | 100.00 |
| VII | 37 | 185,192 | 36.66 | 10.34 | 24.19 | 28.81 | 100.00 |
| VIII | 19 | 82,043 | 34.67 | 20.92 | 25.87 | 18.54 | 100.00 |
| IX | 22 | 88,392 | 32.56 | 4.07 | 45.26 | 18.11 | 100.00 |
| X | 16 | 95,917 | 20.73 | 1.17 | 66.56 | 11.54 | 100.00 |
| Total | 194 | $872,494 | | | | | |

*From manuscript report on Rosenwald Schools in Alabama, loaned by
Mr. S. L. Smith.

The data indicates that these gross figures themselves may
not be wholly reliable as indices of the effort of the groups as
reported in the official figures. For example, a contribution of
$16,150 is ascribed to the Negroes of Jefferson County for the
building of the "Miles Memorial Practice School," out of a total
expenditure of $21,950. The school in question here was attached
to a Negro college, and the donation by "Negroes" was derived
from a Negro church board of education.[95] In the same manner,
"Whites" are credited with the payment of $15,300 toward the
total cost of $24,948 for an eight-room county training school in
Dallas County erected in 1930. It is probable that this large
amount came from some public source, and was credited in the
official reports as proceeding from "whites."[96] The same might
be said of a sum of $15,050 credited to the "whites" of Escambia
County toward the building of a six-room, $22,675 county train-
ing school erected in that county in the school year 1925-1926.

THE TECHNIQUES USED IN THE ROSENWALD BUILDING PROGRAM

The Rosenwald Building Program was organized on the basis of a high-pressure salesmanship campaign. The business of the promoters was that of selling the idea of the education of Negro children to school officials and to white and colored citizens in the communities visited. Under the general direction of S. L. Smith, in charge of the Nashville office, able Negro men with a flair for community organization and crowd persuasion were selected as Rosenwald agents in each of the States. These men were indefatigable in their labors, astute in practical knowledge as to how to deal with Negroes and whites, and gradually worked out a procedure which might be called "sure-fire," as long as any financial resources existed in the communities to which they appealed.

Perhaps the best description of the techniques employed can be found in the actual account of a month's program as reported by M. H. Griffin, Rosenwald Agent in Alabama. Mr. Griffin, at the time of his selection for the post, was a man with a formal education including a two-year normal course. He had been first a coal miner in Walker County, and later a teacher in the rural schools. Finally elevated to the post of principal of the Walker County Training School at Corona, he was the product of a highly practical educational system, considered both formally and informally. His leading preceptor at Huntsville A. and M. Institute, where he attended school, had been William H. Councill, to whom reference has been made in a prior chapter.[97]

We include here excerpts from the report of Mr. Griffin to Mr. S. L. Smith, for the month ending February 28, 1925.[98]

Our main objective this month was to get all of the recently qualified projects contracted out and to get the actual work on the buildings started. To do this we have had to write to contractors, go with them to the jobs, raise extra money to cover extra building expenses, and to fill numerous engagements, which kept us busy and on the go from the first day of the month until the last Sundays included.

1. We had previously set the stage for a big drive at Auburn, where we have been working strenuously to qualify a County Training School. Sunday was a fair day, the crowd was good, and the spirit of the occasion splendid. Promptly at three o'clock the rally got underway, and when the battle was over and the spoils counted it was revealed that we had captured the enemy and had rolled up a net sum of six hundred five dollars and

fifteen cents for the Training School. *I have never seen a squad of soldiers fight with a greater determination.*[99]

2-3.    We spent these dates in the office making our monthly reports, getting out some very important letters to different parties relative to our building activities and holding conferences with Mr. J. S. Lambert, Rural School Supervisor, and other State Officials.

4.    This date was given to Montgomery County at the Levee School, where we have underway a two teacher project. We found a fine people and a determined group to put the project over. *We laid plans and got underway some committees whose duty it will be to work out all details and get the stage set for the financial drive.*[100]

5-6.    We spent these dates with the good people of Fayette County where we have underway a County Training School. We first went to the office of the County Superintendent, where we held a brief conference, got the application blanks for the State and Rosenwald Fund signed, and the deeds for the school site. We brought these papers back with us. After the Conference with the Superintendent we held a meeting with the people and assured them that the project was well underway, and that they would have their school for the next term. I have never seen a happier group of people. It will be remembered that school facilities in Fayette County for our group are very poor.

7.    We spent this date at the Walker County Training School, where a fire recently destroyed the main building. Principal Bullock had arranged temporary quarters and the work of the school was going on unhampered. I found the patrons and friends of the institution very anxious about the future of the school. *We assured them that our interest at this time would not lessen. This gave them heart.*[101]

8.    Again we found ourselves in Talladega County, working at the same old project, "The County Training School." Seemingly this has been one of the hardest projects we have attacked during the four years we have been in the school work. We have had the money (local) on deposit for more than two years, but we have never been able to get the matter of the site settled, as we are consolidating four communities, and each community wants the building located on a different site. We were able to get the people together, injected a little enthusiasm, raised in cash one hundred and fifty dollars, got a *unanimous vote on a site, which had been previously given for this purpose by a fine Christian White woman,*[102] made a definite agreement with the County Superintendent, representing the Talladega County School Board to let the contract for the building. We feel now that the school will be ready for occupancy for the next term of school.

The little one-teacher project at Jenifer, in Talladega County is nearing completion. This has also been a Jonah.

9.  Enroute to Montgomery from Talladega, where we spent a part of the day with the State Normal School in its celebration of Founder's Day.

10-11.  These dates were spent in Tuscaloosa County at the County Training School, and at Samantha where we got underway plans for a two-teacher project. . . .

12.  Enroute to Selma, Alabama, from Tuscaloosa County, where we attended the Farmers' and Teachers' Conference.

13.  We spent this day at Selma University with the farmers and teachers of the county in their annual fair. The exhibits were good and the attendance was very flattering. More than two thousand persons were present during the day and night. There were present experts from the Polytechnic Institute, Auburn, and the great Tuskegee Institute, who instructed the farmers along certain lines, which will prove very helpful to them during this year. We spoke along the lines of improving the educational conditions in the county, which is below par. The conference on a whole was a signal success.

14.  Enroute to Montgomery from Selma. We spent a part of the day in the office reading accumulated mail and answering some very important letters.

16.  In the office holding conferences with state officials and making reports, etc.

17-18.  We gave these dates to Lee County in the interest of the County Training School at Auburn. *We carefully worked out plans for our final drive for local funds to qualify for this project.*[103]

19-20.  We spent these days in Chambers County with the teachers and farmers in their annual fair at the Chambers County Training School, which is the logical community center for the entire county. More than two thousand farmers, teachers, and preachers, white and colored attended this fair. Great streams of local white friends filed through the building viewing the exhibits, and passing favorable comments on the same. The Jeanes Supervisor, Mrs. Mamie Nolan, had every school in the county represented with a creditable exhibit. Several excellent speakers were present and lent words of encouragement to the occasion. These fairs are doing much to build a closer race relation, and to encourage the farmers to do more for the schools. The children are inspired and most assuredly the attendance must be improved.

21.  Enroute to Montgomery from LaFayette.

22.  This was a red letter day for the people of Auburn. *As we stated above this was to be our final effort for qualifying for*

*the County Training School.*[104] The lines were tightly drawn, and the contestants on each side were on the quivive (sic), expecting each moment to go over the top. I have never seen a greater demonstration of real enthusiasm enacted in my life by a humble group of people, working for a real ideal.

*The Mayor of the city, Dr. Yarborough, was present, and he too was worked up to a very high pitch.*[105] When the collection seemed to drag Dr. Yarborough who had given one hundred dollars said, *"if twenty-nine men will join me* we will give five dollars each."[106] This announcement brought the men to their feet, and in a few minutes his suggestion was complied with, and the money on the table. *During this skirmish an old blind colored lady slowly arose and held up a ten dollar bill and said "apply this to the Training School for my children."*[107] As would be expected, the house went wild with enthusiasm, and the old lady was given three rousing cheers by the group. When it seemed that all of the money in the house had been given, and the goal was not reached, we said "Will Auburn Fail," and the crowd roared, no! *Just at this psychological moment brother Moseley, an old veteran more than seventy-five, who had played a conspicuous part in the former rallies, was seen driving at a high rate of speed behind two very skinny horses,*[108] coming towards the building. Some one yelled out "brother Moseley is coming and Auburn cannot fail." He rushed up to the building, dismounted from his carriage, was met by a group of men and carried to the rostrum, and to the amazement ( !) of us all, he laid thirty-five dollars on the table, that he had solicited from friends. At this moment Dr. Yarborough, Mayor, arose and said, *"I will give five hundred dollars from our treasury and five hundred dollas from the white citizens of the city. We are with you, and we shall not stand to see Auburn fail."*[109] Sufficient for me to say that the project was put over in grand style. *We suggested three rousing cheers for our good white friends in Alabama who have stood so loyally by us at each point where we have projected a project, and to Mr. Julius Rosenwald, who is so nobly serving our group.*[110] Enough said.

23. We gave this date to the projects at Davis and Levee in Montgomery County. We are working strenuously to get these two projects over. We feel very much encouraged as one white man gave us two hundred and fifty dollars on the Davis School.

24-25. We spent these dates in Marengo County at the Friendship School, trying to get the building underway. We have the local money, but it has been hard to get the contract out as carpenters are very scarce in this vicinity. We carried a good carpenter with us from Selma, and we now feel that the building will go. We also raised three hundred dollars for this project while we were in the county.

26. We spent this date in Sumpter County, at Livingston, where we have a two-teacher project qualified, trying to get the contract out. We feel that the work on this building will be underway in a few days.

27. We spent this day at the Sumpter County Training School, where we found an excellent organization. We feel that this is one of the best training schools in the state. . . .

28. Enroute to Montgomery from Sumpter county. This has been a very busy and fruitful month for us and for our projects. We have received in every place and in every county visited encouragement from the county superintendent, school boards, local white friends as well as members of our own group.

At present we have twenty-four County Training Schools in operation, and our goal for another year is thirty. We have seven qualified. God bless our efforts.

Respectfully submitted,<br>
M. H. GRIFFIN,<br>
*State Supervisor Teaching-Training and*<br>
*Rosenwald Building Fund Agent for Alabama.*

This report was taken from the dramatic era of the Rosenwald Fund—when the cotton country was in funds, and when each year saw the State of Alabama increase its appropriations for schools. Reports of the State Agents were standardized at a later period: and in 1928 an ominous note appears in the published report of the Division of Negro Education:

Only 53 per cent of the Julius Rosenwald Fund contribution for Negro school buildings for the year was used. This was partly due to advancing standards for school buildings and the high cost of material and labor, but due mainly to economic conditions. In only a few counties are substantial contributions made from local school funds for the building of Negro schools, hence, the difficulty of securing the amount requisite for State and Rosenwald aid.[111]

In 1929-1930 "the building program for colored schools reached the low water mark in Alabama." The commentator was uncertain as to whether this was due to "indifference on the part of Negroes themselves, or to economic conditions beyond their control; . . . indications, however, point to the latter."[112] Negroes "found great difficulty in realizing from private enterprise the amounts requisite to command state and outside aid," and but few counties made contributions from tax funds for this purpose.    Only nine Rosenwald schools were erected or enlarged during the year.[113]    For July, 1931, the Negro State Agent attempted a note of cheer: "We are not at all discouraged with the outlook for the program for the year.    While things are in a state of chaos we think we see signs of light, and that is giving us impetus to go on."[114]

## CHAPTER XVIII

## CONCLUSIONS: NEGRO EDUCATION IN ALABAMA; A STUDY IN COTTON AND STEEL

This study has dealt with educational facilities provided at public expense for the children of Negroes in Alabama. Its concern has been with the social and economic influences which have effected the separate schools in which those children have been formally educated. Separated by custom and law, the two races remain bound together by the inextricable web of the social and economic order of which they are a part. In a study of this kind, therefore, it is as impossible to speak only of schools for Negro children, as though they were an isolated phenomenon that could be excised from the body social for study at any convenient time, as it would be to trace the natural history of an organ of the human body without reference to the larger whole.

The fact of racial difference and the social and economic complex have confirmed the status of the Negro in Alabama as a member of a discrete social caste. To all intents and purposes this socially defined caste at the present time also occupies the status of a discrete economic class, finding employment, in competition with white persons, only on the lowest occupational levels in industry and in agriculture.

The existence of this socio-economic caste, far from being a new phenomenon in Alabama, is a structure older than the State itself. The caste and the concepts surrounding it were brought to the State by migrants to whom the structure, even a hundred years ago, was matter of course. However fruitless the search for "first causes" maybe, the natural history of an institution requires an inquiry into basic forces. Chattel slavery fixed a rigid socio-economic division between the two races. Theoretically, the perfect chattel system would be one in which the number of

287

owners was small enough, and that of chattels large enough, to provide for the complete support of the former by the latter.

In Alabama the number of slaves in proportion to the white population was never large enough to furnish the outlines of the perfect chattel slavery system. Only in one small area of the State—the Black Belt—where the proportion of Negroes to whites was approximately nine to one, were the theoretical conditions of a stable slave system in an agrarian economy met. In the Black Belt, and in fertile valleys elsewhere in the State, a structure of life was developing where all slaves were black, all manual workers were black, while all owners were white, and all entrepreneurs, professional men, managers, and politicians were white.

The vast majority of white people in the State, however, had no slaves, and lived under conditions of life requiring a stratification of the white population down to the occupational strata where lived the blacks, and the blacks only, in the plantation areas. The black slave, deprived of freedom, of mobility, and of education, was yet frequently as fortunate as great masses of white people in the State who had freedom, who possessed without enjoyment the privilege of mobility, who had no better education, food, clothing, or housing, and frequently had not as much. Social classes developed among the white population, and, indeed, even among the blacks; but the imperfect extension of the slave economy throughout the State resulted in a variety of social stratification among the white population unlike anything in either an industrial or agricultural community in the North.

There are two symbols of the century-old development of life in Alabama that reflect the nature, first, of the old pattern, the pattern that has changed but little; and, secondly, of the new pattern, or at least of the more recent pattern of life that shows evidence of change. The one symbol is Cotton, the other, Steel. Cotton brought two races to Alabama; determined, in conformity to the soil, their distribution in the State; and the relationships betwen social and economic classes among white persons. Where black was synonymous with "chattel," and Cotton was the invariable concomitant of both, the fibre is symbolic also of all of the attitudes and convictions developed in the social mind to bulwark the institution—what we might call the folklore, the folkways, the *mores* built into the institution of Negro slavery.

If Cotton made Ante-bellum Alabama, and the slow, hardly-changing *mores* surrounding the relationships of the races and of economic classes within the races, Steel is a symbol of change. Coal, and Iron, and the ultimate Steel, have together formed and dissolved political combinations in the State; dug up and replanted hundreds of thousands of families, white and black; and concentrated populations and wealth in areas that, in 1860, were little more than wilderness. Into the structure built by modern industrialization have been infused the *mores* characteristic of the more primitive cotton economy, especially where the Negro is concerned.

There is one tremendous difference which we cannot now evaluate for its true meaning for the future of a bi-racial culture, or an institution, like the school, in a bi-racial culture. In the ante-bellum agrarian economy based on Cotton and Negro slavery, the labor of Negro slaves was indispensable. Although a slave, he was the foundation of the system and of social and economic life, not only in the cotton producing areas, but in the entire section as well. In an industrial order where social conventions enter frequently to eliminate the Negro as a machine operator, and where his proportion in the general population shows a steady decline, the Negro producer as a Negro is by no means indispensable. What industrialization will mean for the persistence of old racial attitudes in, let us say, the next half-century in Alabama, is by no means clear.

This general summary of the effect of Cotton and Steel in affecting whites and blacks in Alabama lends at least a moiety of illumination to what has happened in the past. The period of political Reconstruction appears as a brief interlude during which external forces sought to obliterate lines of racial caste, and to substitute for the slave economy an economic system which, with the new industry, was to develop along characteristic lines of class differentiation without regard to race. The Humanitarians—the true "Yankee Radicals"—had the vision of a homogenuous social and economic structure with whites and blacks assuming places indiscriminately as laborers, farmers, small entrepreneurs, and capitalists. In such a system competition for a livelihood, for education—for all kinds of preferment—would have been personal, and not racial. The financiers interested in Alabama were certainly less visionary. To them, and to their associates the politicians, this raceless, but socially stratified State, had or lacked appeal in the degree to which it facilitated their own manipulations of government and of industry. Practical minded financiers insisted on Negro participation in politics where a faction found it convenient to have a politically unified white and black lower class; another faction, just as practically minded, objected to the participation of Negroes in politics. At the end there was a lack of insistence on the issue when it no longer served the convenience of the dominant financial factions.

We may conclude, first, that social and economic influences form the basis for the existence of attitudes generated by the existence of a discrete social caste, tending to persist as an economic class; and that the strength of these attitudes are the most powerful forces to be discovered in the study of educational institutions in Alabama. The disfranchisement of Negroes following political reconstruction was a natural consequence of the social and economic definition of the status of the race. Through Negro disfranchisement political parties in Alabama, where they represent economic factions and the economic desires of their members, have accordingly been disproportionately weighted toward the top. Elsewhere, with a homogenuous population, a self-conscious working population might organize its forces to obtain public school legislation; in Alabama a large portion of the lower classes was, after 1875, of practically no moment, an inert mass, so far as legislation was concerned. The influence of the upper social and economic classes of the white population, consequently, was much greater than would have been the case in a racially homogenuous population.

If follows, secondly, that the education of Negroes at public expense in Alabama has depended upon the social and economic utility which this education was thought to have for the class of white persons in control of legislation and finance. Whether this control has been that by slave-owners, humanitarians, planters, financiers, or white farmers and workers, it is obvious that each has wished to provide for Negroes an education designed to meet its own concept of Negro status in the social and economic order.

As the system is competitive where economic advancement is concerned, the limited resources of the state, the peculiar distribution of the white population, and the changing centers of political power by section or by class have placed the distribution of the school fund on a racially competitive basis. It is impossible to say to what degree Negro schools would have been more greatly favored in Alabama if the wealth of the State had, in the past or present, permitted larger expenditures. Certainly urbanization and industrialization have resulted in the provision of better facilities for Negroes than are to be found in rural areas; and in those counties with a small Negro population, schools for Negroes are generally better supported than where a larger population would require a heavier outlay. Whether the crucial difference here is the availability of funds, the degree of temptation to discriminate resulting from the size of the sums involved, or differences in attitudes, is uncertain.

What, then, of future trends? For Negro children involved in the plantation economy, it is reasonably certain that a change in relative provisions for education now made must wait upon fundamental changes in the structure of the economic system that now gives meaning to relations between white and black. And here we may caution ourselves to remember, always, the complexities of the forces which may affect the education of children at public expense. What happens in the next few years in the production of cotton in Brazil, in Russia, in India, in Africa, in China, may be of decisive importance in the education of Negro children in Alabama in the next few decades. A redefinition of Negro status in Alabama agriculture may come as the result of world competition, or as the result of changes in national policy.

Similarly the education of Negroes now living on the fringes of the new industry in Alabama depends upon the future status of that industrial development in relation to domestic and international conditions. Over a long time span, the decreasing proportion of Negroes in the general population may bring their proportion of educables to a level where competition for school funds, like competition for economic preferment, becomes unnoticeable, and so lessens prevailing friction and unwillingness to support Negro schools. The provision of Federal funds to supplement state and local appropriations for schools may, likewise, serve to obviate present competition between whites and blacks for a share of the public school money, a competition in which Negroes are of necessity bound to lose.

These are prospects. What is given is an educational institution directly deriving from the working of a variety of social and economic influences.   The major aspects of that institution solidified several decades ago.   To essay a prophecy of major changes in the immediate future is to anticipate a change in the social and economic order as revolutionary as that catastrophe which, from 1861-1865, destroyed the institution of chattel slavery, and led to the wholly revolutionary acceptance of the principle that Negro children should be educated at public expense.

# BIBLIOGRAPHY

## BOOKS

Alderman, Edwin Anderson and Gordon, Armistead Churchill. *J. L. M. Curry, a Biography.* New York: Macmillan Co., 1911.

*The American Annual Cyclopaedia and Register of Important Events of the Year 1867.* New York: D. Appleton & Co., 1872.

Archer, William. *Through Afro-America.* New York: E. P. Dutton & Co., 1910.

Armes, Ethel. *The Story of Coal and Iron in Alabama.* Birmingham, Alabama: Published under the auspices of the Chamber of Commerce, University Press, Cambridge, Massachusetts, 1910.

Armstrong, Samuel Chapman. *Twenty-two Years' Work of Hampton Institute.* Hampton: Normal School Press, 1893.

Beard, Augustus Field. *A Crusade of Brotherhood, A History of the American Missionary Association.* New York: Pilgrim Press, 1909.

Beard, Charles A. and Mary. *The Rise of American Civilization.* New York: Macmillan Co., 1931.

Berney, Saffold. *Hand-Book of Alabama, A Complete Index to the State, with Map.* Birmingham, Alabama: Roberts & Son, 1892.

Bowers, Claude G. *The Tragic Era, The Revolution After Lincoln.* New York: The Literary Guild, 1929.

Boyd, Minnie Tate. *Alabama in the Fifties.* New York: Columbia University Press, 1932.

Blaine, James G. *Twenty Years of Congress from Lincoln to Garfield.* 2 vols. Norwich: Henry Bill Publishing Co., 1886.

Brawley, Benjamin Griffith. *Doctor Dillard of the Jeanes Fund.* New York: Fleming H. Revell Co., 1930.

Brawley, Benjamin Griffith. *A Social History of the American Negro.* New York: Macmillan Co., 1921.

Brewer, Willis. *Alabama: Her History, Resources, War Record, and Prominent Men.* Montgomery: Barrett & Brown, 1874.

Brown, William Wells. *The Rising Sun; or, The Antecedents and Advancements of the Colored Race.* Boston: A. G. Brown & Co., 1874.

Caliver, Ambrose. *Education of Negro Teachers.* United States Department of the Interior, Harold L. Ickes, Secretary. Office of Education, William John Cooper, Commissioner. Washington: Government Printing Office, 1933.

Caliver, Ambrose. *Secondary Education for Negroes.* Washington: Government Printing Office, 1933.

Carlton, Frank Tracy. *Economic Influences upon Educational Progress in the United States, 1820-1850.* Madison, Wisconsin: Published as Bulletin No. 221 of the University of Wisconsin, 1908.

Carnegie, Andrew. *Autobiography.* New York: Garden City Press, 1933.

Casson, Herbert L. *The Romance of Steel.* New York: A. S. Barnes & Co., 1907.

Child, Lydia Maria. *Letters, with a Biographical Introduction* by John G. Whittier and an appendix by Wendell Phillips. Boston: Houghton Mifflin Co., 1863.

Child, Lydia Maria. *The Freedmen's Book.* Boston: Ticknor & Fields, 1865.

Clark, John B. *Populism in Alabama.* New York: Columbia University Press, 1928.

Clark, Willis G. *History of Education in Alabama, 1702-1889.* Circular of Information No. 3, 1889. Contributions to American Educational History, edited by Herbert Adams. Washington: Government Printing Office, 1889.

Clayton, Victoria V. *White and Black Under the Old Regime.* Milwaukee: Young Churchman Co., 1899.

Clews, Henry. *Fifty Years in Wall Street.* "Twenty-eight Years in Wall Street," Revised and enlarged by a resume of the past twenty years, making a record of Fifty Years in Wall Street. New York: Irving Publishing Co., 1908.

Cotter, Arundel. *United States Steel: A Corporation with a Soul.* Garden City, N. Y.: Doubleday, Page & Co., 1921.

Davis, Horace B. *The Condition of Labor in the American Iron and Steel Industry.* New York: International Publishers, 1933.

Department of Superintendence, National Educational Association, *Eleventh Yearbook. Educational Leadership.* Washington: Department of Superintendence of the National Education Association, 1933.

Donivan, C. E.; Graves, John Temple; Grady, Henry W., et al. *The Possibilities of the Negro in Symposium.* Atlanta: Franklin Printing & Publishing Co., 1904.

Douglass, H. Paul. *Christian Reconstruction in the South.* Boston: Pilgrim Press, 1909.

Drewery, William Sydney. *Slave Insurrections in Virginia.* Washington: Neale Publishing Co., 1900.

Drinker, Frederick E. *Booker T. Washington, The Master Mind of Slavery.* Philadelphia: National Publishing Co., 1915.

DuBois, W. E. Burghardt. *Black Reconstruction.* New York: Harcourt, Brace & Co., 1935.

DuBois, W. E. Burghardt. *The Negro Common School.* Atlanta University Publications, No. 6. Atlanta: Atlanta University Press, 1901.

DuBois, W. E. Burghardt. *The Souls of Black Folk.* Chicago: A. C. McClurg & Co., 1903.

DuBose, John W. *The Mineral Wealth of Alabama and Birmingham.* Illustrated. Birmingham: N. T. Greene & Co., 1886.

Edwards, William James. *Twenty-five Years in the Black Belt.* Boston: Cornhill Co., 1918.

Ferguson, Maxwell. *State Regulation of Railroads in the South.* New York: Published privately by Maxwell Ferguson, 1916.

Fleming, Walter L. *Civil War and Reconstruction in Alabama.* New York: Columbia University Press; Macmillan Co., 1905.

Fleming, Walter L. *Documentary History of Reconstruction,* political, military, social, religious, educational, and industrial, 1865 to the present time. Cleveland, Ohio: A. H. Clark Co., 1906-1907.

Foreman, Clark. *Environmental Factors in Negro Elementary Education.* New York: Published for the Julius Rosenwald Fund by W. W. Norton & Co., 1932.

Gaines, Francis Pendleton. *The Southern Plantation, A Study in the Development and the Accuracy of a Tradition.* New York: Columbia University Press, 1925.

Garrett, William. *Reminiscences of Public Men in Alabama for Thirty Years.* Atlanta: Plantation Publishing Company Press, 1872.

Hamilton, Peter Joseph. *Colonial Mobile,* an historical study, largely from original sources. Boston and New York: Houghton Mifflin Co.; Cambridge: Riverside Press, 1897.

Harrison, W. P. *The Gospel Among Slaves, A Short Account of Missionary Operations Among the African Slaves of the Southern States.* Nashville, Tennessee: Publishing House of the Methodist Episcopal Church, South, 1893.

Hartshorn, William Newton. *An Era of Progress and Promise, 1863-1910.* The religious, moral, and educational development of the American Negro since emancipation. Boston: Massachusetts Priscilla Publishing Co., 1910.

Hawk, Emory Q. *Economic History of the South.* New York: Prentice-Hall, 1934.

Helper, Hinton Rowan. *The Impending Crisis of the South: How to Meet It.* New York: A. B. Burdick, 1860.

Helper, Hinton Rowan. *Nojoque: a Question for a Continent.* New York: George W. Carleton & Co., 1867.

Hensel, William Uhler. *The Christiana Riot and the Treason Trials of 1851:* an historical sketch. Lancaster: New Era Printing Co., 1911.

Herbert, Hilary Abner, *et al. Why the Solid South? or, Reconstruction and its Results.* Baltimore: R. H. Woodard & Co., 1890.

Hood, Bishop J. W., D.D., LL.D. *One Hundred Years of the African Methodist Episcopal Zion Church, or, the Centennial of African Methodism.* New York: A. M. E. Zion Book Concern, 353 Bleecker Street, 1895.

Howard, O. O. *Autobiography.* New York: Baker & Taylor Co., 1907.

Howard, O. O. *First Report of the Commissioner of the Bureau of Refugees, Freedmen, and Abandoned Lands.* Washington: Government Printing Office, 1866.

Jack, Theodore Henley. *Sectionalism and Party Politics in Alabama, 1819-1842.* Menasha, Wisconsin: George Banta Publishing Co., 1919.

Johnson, Charles S. *Shadow of the Plantation.* Chicago: University of Chicago Press, 1934.

Jordan, Lewis G., D.D. *Negro Baptist History, U. S. A., 1750-1930.* Nashville, Tennessee: Sunday School Publishing Board, n.d.

Kelley, William D. *Speeches, Addresses and Letters on Industrial and Financial Questions.* Philadelphia: Henry Cary Baird, 1872.

Kelley, William D. *The Old South and the New. A Series of Letters.* New York: G. P. Putnam's Sons, 1888.

Knight, Edgar W. *Education in the United States.* Boston: Ginn & Co., 1929.

Knight, Edgar W. *Public Education in the South.* Boston: Ginn & Co., 1922.

Leavell, Ullin W. *Philanthropy in Negro Education.* Nashville: George Peabody College for Teachers, 1930.

Mann, Horace. *Slavery: Letters and Speeches.* Boston: B. D. Mussey & Co., 1851.

Martin, Bessie. *Desertion of Alabama Troops from the Confederate Army, A Study in Sectionalism.* New York: Columbia University Press, 1932.

Martin, William Elijius. *Internal Improvements in Alabama.* Johns Hopkins Studies in Historical and Political Science. Baltimore: Johns Hopkins Press, April, 1902.

McCall, Samuel W. *Thaddeus Stevens.* Boston and New York: Houghton Mifflin Co., 1899.

M'Tyeire, H. N. *Duties of Christian Masters,* ed. by Thomas O. Summers, D.D. Nashville: Southern Methodist Publishing House, 1859.

Miller, L. D. *History of Alabama.* Birmingham: Roberts & Sons, 1901 (revised).

Mitchell, Broadus, and George Sinclair. *The Industrial Revolution in the South.* Baltimore, Johns Hopkins University Press, 1930.

Noble, Stuart Grayson. *Forty Years of the Public Schools in Mississippi.* New York: Columbia University Press, 1918.

Nordhoff, Charles. *The Cotton States in the Spring and Summer of 1875.* New York: D. Appleton & Co., 1876.

Nott, J. C., and Gliddon, G. R. *Types of Mankind.* Phiadelphia: Lippincott, Grumby & Co., 1854.

Oberholtzer, Ellis Paxson. *Jay Cooke, Financier of the Civil War.* Philadelphia: George W. Jacobs, 1907.

Owens, Thomas McAdory. *History of Alabama and Dictionary of Alabama Biography.* 4 vols. Chicago: S. J. Clark Publishing Co., 1921.

Phelan, James. *History of Tennessee, the Making of a State.* Boston and New York: Houghton Mifflin Co., 1869.

Phillips, Ulrich B. *Life and Labor in the Old South.* Boston: Little, Brown & Co., 1930.

Pickens, William. *Bursting Bonds, an Autobiography.* New York: Published by the author, 1925.

Pickett, William P. *The Negro Problem—Abraham Lincoln's Solution.* New York: G. P. Putnam's Sons, Knickerbocker Press, 1909.

Pillsbury, Parker. *Acts of the Anti-Slavery Apostles.* Boston: Cupples, Upham & Co., 1884.

Priest, Josiah A. L. *Bible Defense of Slavery; or the Origin, History, and Fortunes of the Negro Race, as deduced from History, Both Sacred and Profane, their natural relations—Moral, Mental, and Physical—to the other races of Mankind, compared and illustrated—their future destiny predicted, etc.* Louisville, Kentucky: J. F. Brennan for Willis A. Bush, 1851.

Proctor, Henry Hugh. *Between Black and White, Autobiographical Sketches.* Boston: Pilgrim Press, 1925.

Redcay, Edward E. *County Training Schools and Public Secondary Education for Negroes in the South.* Washington, D. C.: Published for the John F. Slater Fund by the Monumental Printing Co., 1935.

Riley, B. F. *Alabama As It Is, or, The Immigrants' and Capitalists' Guide Book to Alabama.* Montgomery: W. C. Holt, 1887.

Riley, B. F. *History of the Baptists in the Southern States East of the Mississippi.* Philadelphia: American Baptist Publishing Society, 1898.

Ripley, William Z. *Railroads: Finance and Organization.* New York: Longmans, Green & Co., 1915.

Scott, Emmett J., and Stowe, Lyman B. *Booker T. Washington, Builder of Civilization.* New York: Doubleday, Doran & Co., 1926.

Skaggs, William H. *The Southern Oligarchy.* New York: Devin-Adair Co., 1924.

Simmons, William J., D.D. *Men of Mark: Eminent, Progressive, and Rising.* Cleveland: George M. Rewell & Co., 1887.

Somers, Robert. *The Southern States Since the War, 1870-1871.* London and New York: Macmillan Co., 1871.

Spero, Sterling D., and Harris, Abram. *The Black Worker.* New York: Columbia University Press, 1932.

Stephenson, Gilbert T. *Race Distinctions in American Law.* New York: D. Appleton & Co., 1910.

Stone, Alfred Holt. *Studies in the American Race Problem.* New York: Doubleday, Page & Co., 1908.

Straker, David Augustus. *The New South Investigated.* Detroit: Published by the author, 1906.

Talbot, Edith Armstrong. *Samuel Chapman Armstrong, a biographical study.* New York: Doubleday, Page & Co., 1901.

Tarbell, Ida M. *The Life of Judge Elbert H. Gary, the Story of Steel.* New York: D. Appleton & Co., 1925.

Thompson, Holland. *The New South, A Chronicle of Social and Industrial Revolution.* New Haven: Yale University Press, 1919.

Tremain, Henry Edwin. *Sectionalism Unmasked.* New York: Bonnell, Silver & Co., 1907.

Washington, Booker T. *An Autobiography, the Story of My Life and Work.* Napierville, Illinois: J. L. Nichols & Co., 1901.

Washington, Booker T. *My Larger Education, Being Chapters from My Experiences.* New York: Doubleday, Page & Co., 1911.

Washington, Booker T. *The Future of the American Negro.* Boston: Small, Maynard & Co., 1902.

Washington, Booker T. *Working with the Hands.* New York: Doubleday, Page & Co., 1904.

Washington, Booker T. *Up From Slavery, An Autobiography.* New York: Doubleday, Page & Co., 1901.

Washington, E. Davidson. *Selected Speeches of Booker T. Washington.* Garden City: Doubleday, Doran & Co., Inc., 1932.

Weeks, Stephen B. *The History of Public School Education in Alabama.* U. S. Bureau of Education, 1915, Bulletin No. 12. Washington: Government Printing Office, 1915.

West, Anson. *Methodism in Alabama.* Nashville: Southern Methodist Publishing Co., 1893.

Wickersham, J. P. *History of Education in Pennsylvania.* Lancaster: Publisher for the author, 1886.

Wilson, Henry. *Anti-Slavery Measures in Congress, 1861-1864.* Boston: Walker, Wise & Co., 1864.

Woodburn, James Albert. *The Life of Thaddeus Stevens. A Study in American Political History, especially in the period of the Civil War and Reconstruction.* Indianapolis: Bobbs-Merrill Co., 1903.

Woodson, Carter G. *The History of the Negro Church.* Washington: Associated Publishers, 1921.

Work, Monroe N. *The Negro Yearbook, 1914-1915.* Tuskegee Institute, Alabama: Published by the Negro Year Book Publishing Co., 1914.

Wright, Arthur D. *The Negro Rural School Fund, Inc., 1907-1933.* Washington: Negro Rural School Fund, Inc., 1933.

ARTICLES AND PAMPHLETS

*Anti-Slavery Tracts.* New Series, No. 1. Correspondence between Lydia Maria Child and Gov. Wise, 1860. New York: American Anti-Slavery Society, 1860.

Becker, Joseph A. "Effects of the Boll Weevil upon Cotton Production in the United States," *International Cotton Bulletin,* June, 1924.

Bond, Horace Mann. "Two Racial Islands in Alabama," *American Journal of Sociology,* Vol. XXXVI (January, 1931).

Bromberg, F. G. "Reconstruction in Alabama, A Paper Read Before the Iberville Historical Society," *Mobile Register,* Mobile, 1905.

Coulter, Ellis Merton. *The Cincinnati Southern Railroad and the Struggle for Southern Commerce, 1865-1872.* Reprinted from *A History of Kentucky.* Chicago: American Historical Society, 1922.

Curry, J. L. M. "Limitations of Taxation," *Baptist Quarterly Review.* Cincinnati: Published by J. H. Barnes, 1884.

Division of Research and Information. *Apportionment and Distribution of Alabama's Equalization Fund.* Authorized by the State Board of Education, 1930.

Hollander, A. N. J. Den. "The Tradition of the 'Poor White'," *Culture in the South.* Edited by W. T. Couch. Chapel Hill: University of North Carolina Press, 1934.

Johnson, Charles S. "The Social Philosophy of Booker T. Washington," *Opportunity Magazine,* Vol. VI, No. 4 (April, 1928), pp. 102-06.

Kendrick, Benjamin. "History as a Curative," *Southern Review,* Vol. I, No. 3 (1936), pp. 540-51.

Long, L. E., *et al.* "Costs of Producing Cotton in Fifteen Selected Areas in 1923." Preliminary Report, United States Department of Agriculture, 1925 (mimeographed).

Mabry, G. Woodford. *A Reply to Southern Slanderers: In Re The Nigger Question.* Grove Hill, Alabama: By the author, 1933.

McCuistion, Fred. *The South's Negro Teaching Force.* Nashville: Julius Rosenwald Fund, Southern Office, 1931.

Morgan, John Tyler. *Common School Education.* Speech of the Hon. John T. Morgan of Alabama, in the Senate of the United States, January 30, 1888. Pamphlet issued under frank. Washington: Government Printing Office, 1888.

Mitchell, Broadus. "Growth of Manufacturing in the South," *Industry in the South.* Annals of the American Academy of Political and Social Science, Vol. 153, 1931. Philadelphia: American Academy of Political and Social Science, 1931.

Nott, J. C. "The Mulatto a Hybrid; probable extermination of the two races if the whites and blacks were allowed to intermarry," *American Journal of Medical Science,* June, 1843.

Pope, J. D. "Types of Farming Areas," *Agriculture of Alabama.* Alabama Department of Agriculture and Industries. Montgomery, Alabama, 1930.

Russ, William A., Jr. "Registration and Disfranchisement Under Radical Reconstruction," *Mississippi Valley Historical Review,* Vol. XXI, No. 2, pp. 163-81.

Scroggs, William O. "The New Alabama, 1880-1909," *The South in the Building of the Nation*. 12 vols. Vol. Two. Richmond: Southern Historical Publication Society, 1910.

Smith, Eugene Allen. "The Geological Formations of Alabama in Their Industrial and Agricultural Relations," *The Mineral Wealth of Alabama and Birmingham*. John W. DuBose, editor. Birmingham: N. T. Greene & Co., 1886.

Washington, Booker T. "Industrial Education for the Negro," *The Negro Problem, A Series of Articles by Representative American Negroes of Today*, W. E. B. DuBois, Paul Lawrence Dunbar, Charles W. Chestnutt, *et al.* New York: James Pott & Co., 1903.

Washington, Booker T. "The Negro in Labor Unions," *Atlantic Monthly*, III (June, 1913), 756-67.

Woodson, Carter G. "Free Negro Owners of Slaves in the United States in 1830," *Journal of Negro History*, Vol. IX, January, 1924.

Wooten, E. A. "Cotton in the Texas Plains Area," *United States Department of Agriculture Yearbook, 1926*. Washington: Government Printing Office, 1926.

LEGISLATIVE DOCUMENTS

Aikin, John G. *Digest of the Laws of the State of Alabama to 1843*. Philadelphia: Alexander Tower, 1843.

*Acts and Resolutions, 39th Congress, 2nd Session*. Washington: Government Printing Office, 1867.

*Acts of the Board of Education, 1868*. Bound with the *Acts of the General Assembly, 1868*.

*Acts of the Fifth Biennial Session of the General Assembly of Alabama*. Montgomery: Bates & Lucas, 1856.

*Acts of the Fourth Biennial Session of the General Assembly of Alabama*. Montgomery: Brittan & Blue, 1854.

*Acts of the General Assembly, 1868*. Montgomery: John G. Stokes & Co., 1868.

*Acts of the General Assembly, 1869-1870*. Montgomery: John G. Stokes & Co., 1870.

*Acts of the General Assembly of Alabama, passed at the Session of 1874-1875*. Montgomery: W. W. Screws, 1875.

*Acts of the General Assembly of Alabama, passed at the Session of 1890-1891*. Montgomery: Smith, Allred & Co., 1891.

*Acts of the Session of 1865-1866 of the General Assembly of Alabama*. Montgomery: Reid & Screws, 1866.

*Biographical Directory of the American Congress, 1774-1927*. Sixty-ninth Congress, 2nd Session, House Document No. 783. Washington: Government Printing Office, 1928.

Box, Leroy F. *Laws Relating to the Public School System of Alabama*. Montgomery: Barrett & Brown, 1878.

*The Congressional Globe*. Appendix, 39th Congress, 1st Session. Washington: Government Printing Office, 1866.

*The Debates of the Constitutional Convention of the State of Iowa, 1857*. Davenport: Luse, Lane & Co., 1857.

*Journals and Acts of the Board of Education, and Board of Regents, of the State of Alabama*. Montgomery: W. W. Screws, 1871.

*Journal of the Board of Education, 1873*. Montgomery: Arthur Bingham, 1874.

*Journal of the Constitutional Convention of the State of Alabama, 1875.* Montgomery: W. W. Screws, State Printer, 1875.

*Journal of the House of Representatives of the General Assembly of Alabama, Fourth Biennial Session, November 14, 1863, to February 18, 1854.* Montgomery: Brittan & Blue, 1854.

*Journal of the House, General Assembly of Alabama, 1872-1873.* Montgomery: W. W. Screws, State Printer, 1873.

*Journal of the House of Representatives, 1875-1876.* Montgomery: W. W. Screws & Co., 1876.

*Journal of the House, General Assembly of Alabama, Session from November 13, 1888, to February 28, 1889.* Montgomery: Brown Printing Co., 1889.

*Journal of the House of Representatives of the General Assembly of the State of Alabama, Session of 1890-1891.* Montgomery: Smith, Allred & Co., 1891.

*Journal of the House of Representatives of the State of Alabama, Session of 1907.* Montgomery: Brown Printing Co., 1907.

*Official Journal of the Constitutional Convention of the State of Alabama.* Held in Montgomery, 1867. Montgomery: Barrett & Brown, 1868.

McCauley, Pat. Official Stenographer. *Proceedings of the Constitutional Convention of Alabama of 1901.* Montgomery: Montgomery *Advertiser,* 1901. Published as supplements to the *Advertiser;* later reprinted and issued, unbound. The pages are unnumbered.

Ormond, John J., Bagby, Arthur P., Goldthwaite, George, with head notes and index by Henry C. Semple. *The Code of Alabama.* Montgomery: Brittan & De Wolf, 1852.

Poore, Ben Perley. *Congressional Directory,* 43rd Congress, 1st Session. Washington: Government Printing Office, 1873.

Thorpe, Francis Newton. *The Federal and State Constitution Colonial Charters, and other organic laws of the States, Territories, and Colonies now or heretofore forming the United States of America.* Washington: Government Printing Office, 1909.

Turner, John O. *Special Acts of Public School Laws of the State of Alabama.* Montgomery: Brown Printing Co., 1897.

NEWSPAPERS AND PERIODICALS

*Alabama Journal.* Published at Montgomery, Alabama, 1827.

*American Freedmen.*

*American Missionary.*

Athens *Courier.* Published at Athens, Alabama.

Birmingham *Age-Herald.*

Chicago *Tribune.*

*Clarke County Democrat.* Published at Grove Hill, Alabama.

*Colored Alabamian.* Published at Montgomery, Alabama.

*Commercial and Financial Chronicle,* Vol. XVI, No. 411; Vol. XVI, No. 398; Vol. XVII, No. 442; Vol. XIX, No. 487; Vol. XXI, No. 534; Vol. XXII, Nos. 553, 555.

*Memphis Commercial-Appeal.*

Mobile *Times and Register.*

Montgomery *Advertiser.*

*Nationalist.* Published at Mobile, Alabama.

New York *Tribune.*
New York *Daily Tribune.*
New York *World.*
Sheffield *Standard.*  Published at Sheffield, Alabama.
Tuscumbia *Weekly Dispatch,* 1890.
*Weekly Mail.*  Published at Montgomery, Alabama.

REPORTS

Abercrombie, John W.  *Biennial Report of the Department of Education of the State of Alabama, for the Scholastic Years ending September 30, 1899, 1900.*  Montgomery: A. Roemer, 1900.
Abercrombie, John W.  *Annual Report for the Scholastic Year Ending September 30, 1922.*  Montgomery: Brown Printing Co., n.d. 1922(?)
Ainsworth, Brigadier General Fred C., and Kirkley, Joseph W.  *The War of the Rebellion: Official Records of the Union and Confederate Armies.*  Washington: Government Printing Office, 1900.
Alabama Testimony, *The Joint Select Committee to Inquire into the Condition of Affairs in the Late Insurrectionary States.*  Washington: Government Printing Office, 1872.
Alvord, John Watson.  *Semi-Annual Reports on Schools and Finances of Freedmen.*  First-Tenth Reports.  Washington: Government Printing Office, 1866-1870.
*Annual Meeting of the Alabama Commercial and Industrial Association.*  Held at New Decatur, Alabama, April 18, 19, 1900.  Department of Agriculture, State of Alabama.  Montgomery: Brown Printing Co., 1900.
Armstrong, H. Clay.  *Report of the Superintendent of Education for the year Ending September 30, 1882.*  Montgomery: W. D. Brown & Co., 1882.
Armstrong, H. Clay.  *Report of the Superintendent of Education for the Year Ending September 30, 1884.*  Montgomery: Barrett & Co., 1884.
*A Study of Education in Alabama.*  Bulletin 41, Department of the Interior.  Washington: Government Printing Office, 1919.
Barksdale, Jelks.  *Mineral Production of Alabama for 1927.*  Geological Survey of Alabama, Walter Bryan Jones, State Geologist.  University, Alabama, July, 1929.  Birmingham: Birmingham Printing Co.
Brewer, Willis.  *Report of the Auditor of Alabama for the Year Ending September 30, 1880.*  Montgomery: Allred & Beers, 1881.
Buford, Jefferson.  *Report from the Committee on Education of the Senate of Alabama on a memorial from the American Association for the Advancement of Science in relation to the importance of the State's instituting a Geological Survey, favorable to the bill to provide such a survey.*  January 19, 1850. n.p., n.d.
Bland, S. H.  *Annual Report of the State Auditor of Alabama for the fiscal year ending September 30, 1930.*  Montgomery: Wilson Printing Co.
Brandon, William W.  *Annual Report of the State Auditor of Statistics for the fiscal year ending September 30, 1910.*  Montgomery: Brown Printing Co., State Printers and Binders.

Cloud, N. B.  *Official Report of the Superintendent of Public Instruction on the Troubles in the Mobile Free Public Schools.*  Appended to Report of Superintendent to Governor, dated August 18, 1869; in official papers.

*Chronicles of the Union League of Philadelphia, 1862-1902.*  Philadelphia: Printed for the Union League by William R. Fell, 1902.

Dowell, Spright.  *Annual Report for the Scholastic Year Ending September 30, 1919.*  Montgomery: Brown Printing Co., n.d. 1920(?)

Eaton, John.  "Special Report to the U. S. Commissioner of Education."  *Report of the U. S. Commissioner of Education to the Secretary of the Interior.*  Washington: Government Printing Office, 1871.

*First Biennial Reports of the Inspectors of Convicts.*  Montgomery: Barrett & Co., 1886.

Gunnels, Harry C.  *Annual Report of the Department of Education, for the Scholastic Year Ending September 30, 1909.*  Montgomery: Brown Printing Co., 1909.

Harman, A. F.  *Annual Report for the Scholastic Year Ending June 30, 1931.*  State of Alabama, Department of Education, Montgomery.  Montgomery: Wilson Printing Co., n.d.

Harris, John G.  *Thirty-seventh Annual Report of the Superintendent of Education, September 30, 1891.*  Montgomery: Smith, Allred & Co., 1892.

Harris, John G.  *Thirty-eighth Report of the Superintendent of Education, September 30, 1892.*  Montgomery: Smith, Allred & Co., 1892.

Hill, Isaac W.  *Biennial Report of the Department of Education, for the Scholastic Years ending September 30, 1905, 1906.*  Montgomery: Brown Printing Co., 1907.

Hodgson, J. H.  *Report for the Scholastic Year January 1, 1871, to September 30, 1871.*  Alabama, Superintendent of Education.  Montgomery: W. W. Screws, 1871.

Hogue, Cyrus D.  *Report of the Auditor of Alabama for the year ending September 30, 1890.*  Montgomery: Smith, Allred & Co., 1891.

Hogue, Cyrus D.  *Report of the Auditor of Alabama, 1889-1890.*  Montgomery: Brown Printing Co., 1890.

House Report IV, 39th Congress, 2nd Session, *Affairs of Southern Railroads.*  Washington: Government Printing Office, 1866.

House Report No. 262, 43rd Congress, 2nd Session.  *Affairs in Alabama.*  Washington: Government Printing Office, 1875.

Institute for Government Research of the Brookings Institution, *Report on a Survey of the Organization and Administration of the State and County Governments of Alabama,* submitted to the Governor, B. M. Miller.  5 vols.  I. *Organization and Administration of the State Government of Alabama;* II. *Organization and Administration of the State Government* (Cont.); III. *Financial Administration of the State Government of Alabama;* IV. *Taxation of the State Government of Alabama;* V. *County Government in Alabama.*  Montgomery: Wilson Printing Co., State Printers, 1932.

Lee, H. F.  *Annual Report of the State Auditor of Alabama for the fiscal year ending September 30, 1920.*  Montgomery: Brown Printing Co., 1920.

McKleroy, John M.  *Report of Superintendent of Public Instruction for the State of Alabama, Year Ending 30th September, 1876.*  Montgomery: W. W. Screws, 1876.

Moore, William H. *Report of the Commissioner to Investigate and audit claims against the State of Alabama, on account of the Alabama and Chattanooga Railroad.* Montgomery: Arthur Bingham, State Printer, 1873.

*Ninth Annual Report of the American Missionary Association, 1855.* New York: American Missionary Society, 1855.

Palmer, Solomon. *Thirty-first Annual Report of the Superintendent of Education for the State of Alabama, September 30, 1885.* Montgomery: Barrett & Co., 1885.

Poor, Henry V. *Manual of the Railroads of the United States for 1868-1869: together with an appendix containing a full analysis of the debts of the United States, and of the several states.* New York: N. V. and H. W. Poor, 1869-1870, 1870-1871, 1878-1879.

*Proceedings of the Trustees of the Peabody Education Fund.* Boston: John Wilson & Co., 1875.

*Publications of the John F. Slater Fund,* No. 3: "Education of the Negroes since 1860," Jabez L. M. Curry, by the Trustees, Baltimore, 1894.

Reynolds, R. M. *Report of the Auditor of the State of Alabama, Year Ending September 30, 1871.* Montgomery W. W. Screws, 1871.

*Race Problems of the South; report of the proceedings of the first annual Conference of the Southern Society for the promotion of the study of race conditions and problems in the South.* Richmond: B. F. Johnson Publishing Co., 1900.

*Report of the Joint Committee on Reconstruction,* 39th Congress, 1st Session. Report No. 30. Part III. Washington: Government Printing Office, 1866.

*Report of the United States Commissioner of Education for 1894-1895.* Washington: Government Printing Office, 1895.

Riggs, Joel. *Report of the Comptroller of Public Accounts of the State of Alabama, November 1, 1851, to September 30, 1852.* Montgomery: Brittan & Blue, 1853.

Scott, Emmett Jay. *Negro Migration During the War.* New York: Oxford University Press, 1920.

Smith, Eugene Allen. "Cotton Production in Alabama," *Report on Cotton Culture.* Tenth Census, Vol. V, Part II. Washington: Government Printing Office, 1884.

Southern Commission on the Study of Lynching. *Lynchings and What They Mean.* Atlanta: Published by the Commission. (n.d., *circa* 1932.)

Speed, Joseph H. *Report for the Scholastic Year Ending September 30, 1873.* Montgomery: Arthur Bingham, State Printer, 1874.

Trustees of the John F. Slater Fund. *Documents Relating to the Origin and Work of the Slater Trustees.* Occasional Papers No. 1, 1894. Baltimore: Published by the Fund, 1894.

Tuomey, M. *First Annual Report on the Geology of Alabama.* Tuscaloosa: M. D. J. Slade, 1850.

Turner, John C. *Biennial Report, Superintendent of Education for Alabama, 1896-1897, 1897-1898.* Montgomery: Roemer Printing Co., 1898.

*Twelfth Annual Report of the American Missionary Association, 1858.* New York: American Missionary Association, 1858.

United States
  Census Office, Bureau of the Census:
    *Seventh Census, 1850. Statistical View of the United States.* Washington: A. O. P. Nicholson, Public Printer, 1854.
    *Eighth Census of the United States. 1860.* Population of the United States in 1860. Washington: Government Printing Office, 1864.
    *Ninth Census of the United States, 1870.* Population. Washington: Government Printing Office, 1872.
    *United States Census, 1860. Report on the Productions of Agriculture.* Washington: Government Printing Office, 1883.
    Bureau of the Census, *Negroes in the United States, 1790-1915.* Washington: Government Printing Office, 1918.
    *Population of the United States, 1880.* Washington: Government Printing Office, 1883.
    *Compendium, Eleventh Census, 1890. Population.* Washington: Government Printing Office, 1892.
  Bureau of Mines:
    *Mineral Resources of the United States, 1929.* Washington: Government Printing Office, 1930.
Vance, Rupert B., Ph.D., Edited by. *The Negro Agricultural Worker Under the Federal Rehabilitation Program.* Section 1, Part 1: *The Negro Farmer: Marginal Man in Agricultural Readjustment.* Part 2: *Landlord-Tenant Relations in the South.* Mimeographed at Fisk University, 1935.
White, W. S. *Annual Report of the State Auditor of Alabama for the Fiscal Year Ending September 30, 1900.* Montgomery: A. Roemer, 1900.

UNPUBLISHED MATERIALS

Curry, J. L. M. *Papers, Ms. Collection.* Montgomery: State Department of Archives.
Griffin, M. H. *Series of Monthly Reports on Progress of the Rosenwald Building Program.* Submitted by M. H. Griffin, State Rosenwald Agent, from 1924-1931. Loaned from Southern Rosenwald Offices by S. L. Smith.
Smith, S. L. *Report on Rosenwald Schools Constructed in Alabama.* Loaned from Office of S. L. Smith, Nashville, Tennessee.
Swearingen, Mack Buckley. *The Penetration of the South by Northern Capital during Reconstruction.* Unpublished Master's Thesis, University of Chicago, 1923.

# NOTES

## NOTES FOR CHAPTER I

[1] Eugene Allen Smith, "The Geological Formations of Alabama in their industrial and Agricultural Relations," *The Mineral Wealth of Alabama and Birmingham*, pp. 1-15. John W. Dubose, ed. (Birmingham: N. T. Greene & Co., 1886.)

[2] Minnie Tate Boyd, *Alabama in the Fifties*, p. 25. (New York: The Columbia University Press, 1932.) Theodore Henley Jack, *Sectionalism and Party Politics in Alabama*, 1819-1842, p. 3. (Menasha, Wisconsin: George Banta Publishing Co., 1919.)

[3] L. D. Miller, *History of Alabama*, p. 306. Rev. ed. (Birmingham: Roberts & Sons, 1901.)

[4] Boyd, *op. cit.*, pp. 1-9.

[5] J. D. Pope, "Types of Farming Areas," *Agriculture of Alabama*, pp. 53-65. Alabama Department of Agriculture and Industries. (Montgomery, Alabama, 1930.)

[6] M. Tuomey, *First Biennial Report on the Geology of Alabama*, pp. 29-64. (Tuscaloosa: M. D. J. Slade, 1850.)

[7] Saffold Berney, *Hand-Book of Alabama, A Complete Index to the State, with Map*, p. 472. (Birmingham, Alabama: Roberts & Son, 1892.)

[8] Jefferson Buford, *Report from the Committee on Education of the Senate of Alabama on a memorial from the American Association for the Advancement of Science in relation to the importance of the State's Instituting a Geological Survey, favorable to the bill to provide such a Survey*. Jan. 19, 1850. n.p., n.d.

[9] Ethel Armes, *The Story of Coal and Iron in Alabama*, pp. 370-71. (Birmingham, Alabama: Published under the auspices of the Chamber of Commerce, University Press. Cambridge, Massachusetts, 1910.)

[10] Peter Joseph Hamilton, *Colonial Mobile, an historical study, largely from original sources*, pp. 289, 306, 311, 322. (Boston and New York: Houghton Mifflin Co., The Riverside Press, Cambridge, 1897.)

[11] Portions of these communities are still extant. See Horace Mann Bond, "Two Racial Islands in Alabama," *American Journal of Sociology*, XXXVI (January, 1931), pp. 552-61.

[12] Walter L. Fleming, *Civil War and Reconstruction in Alabama*, p. 5. (New York: The Columbia University Press, Macmillan & Co., Agents, 1905.) Boyd, *Alabama in the Fifties*, p. 18; Thomas McAdory Owens, *History of Alabama and Dictionary of Alabama Biography*, II, pp. 1134-35. In four volumes. (Chicago: S. J. Clark Publishing Co., 1921.)

[13] Fleming, *ibid.*

[14] *Ibid.*, p. 6.

[15] *Ibid.*, pp. 10, 11, 137f., 505.

[16] Jack, *Sectionalism and Party Politics in Alabama*, p. 16.

[17] *Ibid.*, p. 16.

[18] Pope, *Agriculture of Alabama*, pp. 53-65.

[19] Jack, *op. cit.*, p. 17.

[20] *Ibid.*

[21] *Ibid.*, p. 16.

[22] Fleming, *Civil War and Reconstruction*, p. 10.

[23] Jack, *Sectionalism and Party Politics*, p. 85.

[24] *Acts of the Fourth Biennial Session of the General Assembly of Alabama*, p. 14. (Montgomery: Brittan and Blue, 1854.)

[25] *Journal of the House of Representatives of the General Assembly, Fourth Biennial Session, Nov. 14, 1853 to Feb. 18, 1854*, pp. 441-43. (Montgomery: Brittan and Blue, 1854.)

[26] *Ibid.*

[27] *Acts of the Fifth Biennial Session of the General Assembly of Alabama*, pp. 34, 45. (Montgomery: Bates & Lucas, 1856); Edwin Anderson Alderman and Armistead Churchill Gordon, *J. L. M. Curry, A Biography*, p. 106. (New York: Macmillan Co., 1911.) Stephen B. Weeks, *The History of Public School Education in Alabama*, p. 57. U. S. Bureau of Education, Bulletin No. 12, 1915. (Washington: Government Printing Office, 1915.)

[28] Jack, *Sectionalism and Party Politics*, p. 83.

[29] Willis Brewer, *Alabama: Her History, Resources, War Record, and Prominent Men*, p. 64. (Montgomery: Barrett & Brown, 1874.)

[30] Bessie Martin, *Desertion of Alabama Troops from the Confederate Army, A Study in Sectionalism*, Chap. IV. (New York: Columbia University Press, 1932.)

[31] Fleming, *ibid.*, p. 88.

[32] Cf. Pope's classification of agricultural areas, above, pp. 8-10. It is significant that this geographical area should have its physical name corrupted into an epithet for the white people resident there.

[33] *Civil War and Reconstruction*, p. 108.

[34] *Ibid.*

[35] A. N. J. Den Hollender, "The Tradition of the 'Poor White'," in *Culture in the South*, ed. by W. T. Couch, p. 402. (Chapel Hill: The University of North Carolina Press, 1934.)

[36] *Ibid.*, p. 405.

[37] John J. Ormond, Arthur P. Bagby, George Goldthwaite, with head notes and index by Henry C. Semple, *The Code of Alabama*, p. 58. (Montgomery: Brittan & De Wolf, 1852.)

[38] *Ibid.*, p. 89.

[39] *Ibid.*, p. 78.

[40] *Ibid.*, p. 424.

[41] *Ibid.*, p. 377.

[42] *Ibid.*, p. 241.

[43] *Ibid.*

[44] *Ibid.*

[45] *Ibid.*

[46] *Ibid.*, p. 242.

[47] *Ibid.*

[48] *Ibid.*

[49] William Sydney Drewery, *Slave Insurrections in Virginia*, pp. 27 ff. (Washington: Neale Publishing Co., 1900.)

[50] *Ibid.*

[51] Alabama Code, *op. cit.*, p. 390.

[52] Carter G. Woodson, "Free Negro Owners of Slaves in the United States in 1830," *Journal of Negro History*, IX (January, 1924), 44.

[53] *The Eighth Census of the United States, 1860*, p. 8. (Washington: Government Printing Office, 1864.)

[54] *Alabama Code, op. cit.*, p. 590.

[55] *Ibid.*, pp. 242 ff.

[56] Francis Newton Thorpe, *The Federal and State Constitutions, Colonial Charters, and Other Organic Laws of the States, Territories, and Colonies Now or Heretofore Forming the United States of America*, II, pp. 649 f. (Washington: Government Printing Office, 1909.)

[57] W. E. B. DuBois, *The Negro Common School*, p. 18. (Atlanta: Atlanta University Press, 1901.)

[58] *War of the Rebellion Records*, Series IV, Vol. ii, p. 941. (Washington: Government Printing Office, 1900.)

[59] *Ibid.*, Series IV, Vol. I, p. 1088; letter of S. Huggins Cleveland to George W. Randolph, Secretary of War, CSA.

[60] *Ibid.*, Series IV, Vol. II, p. 197.

[61] *Ibid.*

[62] Speech of Hon. J. A. Garfield of Ohio, in Appendix, *Congressional Globe*, 39th Congress, 1st Session, p. 165. (Washington: Government Printing Office, 1866.)

[63] *Alabama Code, op. cit.*

[64] Josiah Priest, A. M., *Bible Defense of Slavery; or the Origin, History, and Fortunes of the Negro Race, as deduced from History, Both Sacred and Profane, their natural relations—Moral, Mental and Physical—to the Other Races of Mankind, compared and illustrated—their future destiny predicted, etc.*, Preface iv. (Louisville, Ky.: J. F. Brennan for Willis A. Bush, 1951.)

[65] Ulrich B. Phillips, *Life and Labor in the Old South*, p. 202. (Boston: Little, Brown & Co., 1930.)

[66] Victoria V. Clayton, *White and Black Under the Old Regime*, pp. 170 ff. (Milwaukee: The Young Churchman Co., 1899.)

[67] Speech of Thomas Heflin, in Alabama Constitutional Convention of 1901, 54th Legislative Day, *Official Proceedings of the Constitutional Convention of the State of Alabama, May 21, 1901, to September 3, 1901.* (Montgomery: Brown Printing Co., 1901.) See also Owens, *History of Alabama*, II, pp. 1251-54.

Mr. Heflin said, *apropos* the Negro of 1901,

''I am not an enemy to the negro. I am a friend to him in his place. My father owned more slaves than any man in Randolph county. I love the old time Southern negro. He was in his place as a slave, and happy and contented as such. . . . I love to think of the old black mammy. . . . We like to think of old Ephraim, sitting around the fire picking his banjo and eating roasted potatoes and 'sich.' We love to go back and bring them back to memory; *but you take the young negro of today.* . . .'' (Italics mine.)

Discounting this eulogy of the ''old negro'' and the distaste for the ''young negro'' as the exaggerated, nostalgic shading of a demogogue, the speech remains as a significant document testifying to the existence of an attitude and belief which had as wide popularity as the speaker.

[68] Hinton Rowan Helper, *The Impending Crisis of the South: How to Meet it*, p. 413. (New York: A. B. Burdick, 1860.)

[69] Hinton Rowan Helper, *Nojoque; A Question for a Continent*, p. v. (New York: George W. Carleton & Co., 1867.)

[70] *Alabama Testimony, The Joint Select Committee to Inquire into the Condition of Affairs in the late insurrectionary States*, p. 492. (Washington: Government Printing Office, 1872.)

[71] *Alabama Testimony, op. cit.*, p. 550.

[72] *Ibid.*, p. 1179.

[73] Charles Nordhoff, *The Cotton States in the Spring and Summer of 1875*, pp. 5-6. (New York: D. Appleton & Co., 1876.)

[74] Hollender, *op. cit.*, p. 417.

## NOTES FOR CHAPTER II

[1] H. N. M'Tyeire, D. D., *Duties of Christian Masters*, ed. by Thomas O. Summers, D. D., p. 156. (Nashville, Tennessee: Southern Methodist Publishing House, 1859.)

[2] *Ibid.*

[3] William Sydney Drewery, *Slave Insurrections in Virginia*, pp. 27, ff. (Washington: Neale Publishing Co., 1900.)

[4] *Ibid.*, p. 91.

[5] John G. Aikin, *Digest of the Laws of the State of Alabama to 1843*, p. 397. (Philadelphia: Alexander Tower, 1833.)

[6] *Ibid.*

[7] Francis Newton Thorpe, *The Federal and State Constitutions, II*, p. 649, f. (Washington: Government Printing Office, 1909.)

[8] John Eaton, "Special Report to the U. S. Commissioner of Education," *Report of the U. S. Commissioner of Education to the Secretary of the Interior*, p. 323. (Washington: Government Printing Office, 1871.)

[9] Willis G. Clark, *History of Education in Alabama, 1702-1889.* Circular of Information No. 3, 1889. Contributions to American Educational History, ed. by Herbert Adams, p. 222. (Washington: Government Printing Office, 1889.)

[10] *Ibid.*

[11] *Eighth Census of the United States. Social Statistics*, p. 8. (Washington: Government Printing Office, 1852.)

[12] House Report No. 262, 43rd Congress, 2nd Session. *Affairs in Alabama*, p. 1110. (Washington: Government Printing Office, 1875.)

[13] *Acts of the Fifth Biennial Session of the General Assembly of Alabama*, p. 50. (Montgomery: Bates and Lucas, State Printers, 1856.)

[14] Ulrich Bonnell Phillips, *Life and Labor in the Old South*, p. 194. (Boston: Little, Brown & Co., 1929.)

[15] Francis Pendleton Gaines, *The Southern Plantation, A Study in the Development and the Accuracy of a Tradition*, p. 235. (New York: Columbia University Press, 1925.)

[16] Bishop J. W. Hood, D. D., L. L. D., *One Hundred Years of the African Methodist Episcopal Zion Church, or, the Centennial of African Methodism*, p. 236. (New York: A. M. E. Zion Book Concern, 1895.)

[17] *Ibid.*

[18] William J. Simmons, D. D., *Men of Mark: Eminent, Progressive and Rising.* (Cleveland: George M. Rewell & Co., 1887.)

[19] *Ibid.*, pp. 1027-30.

[20] *Ibid.*, pp. 390-93.

[21] *Ibid.*, p. 651.

[22] *Ibid.*

[23] *Ibid.*

[24] *Ibid.*, p. 652.

[25] W. E. Burghardt DuBois, *Black Reconstruction*, p. 490. (New York: Harcourt, Brace & Co., 1935.) The interesting statement that Rapier attended Franklin College, a white "Campbellite" ante-bellum college near Nashville, is made by the Honorable J. C. Napier, of Nashville, who (now 93 years old) was a contemporary of Rapier.

[26] Gaines, *The Southern Plantation*, p. 235.

[27] *Life and Labor in the Old South*, p. 276.

[28] *Alabama Journal*, May 25, 1827. (Published at Montgomery.)

[29] *Ibid.*

[30] *Seventh Census of the United States, 1850, Population and Social Statistics*, p. 428. (Washington: Government Printing Office, 1852.)

[31] Owen, *History of Alabama and Dictionary of Alabama Biography, II*, p. 252.

[32] *Clarke County Democrat*, Grove Hill, Alabama, February 11, 1858.

[33] Booker T. Washington, "Industrial Education for the Negro," *The Negro Problem, A Series of Articles by Representative American Negroes of Today*, p. 11. W. E. Burghardt DuBois, Paul Lawrence Dunbar, Charles W. Chestnut, *et al.* (New York: James Pott & Co., 1903.)

[34] *Ibid.*

[35] *Report of the Joint Committee on Reconstruction. Thirty-ninth Congress, First Session, Report No. 30*, Part III, p. 34. (Washington: Government Printing Office, 1866.)

[36] Phillips, *op. cit.*, p. 202.

[37] Lewis G. Jordan, D. D., *Negro Baptist History U. S. A., 1750-1930*, (Nashville, Tennessee: The Sunday School Publishing Board, n. d.)

[38] Carter G. Woodson, *The History of the Negro Church*, p. 118. (Washington: The Associated Publishers, 1921.)

[39] *Civil War and Reconstruction in Alabama*, p. 227.

[40] W. P. Harrison, *The Gospel Among Slaves, A Short account of missionary operations among the African slaves of the Southern states*, pp. 292-300. (Nashville, Tennessee: Publishing House of the Methodist Episcopal Church, South, 1893.)

[41] Fleming, *op. cit.*, p. 226.

[42] Gaines, *The Southern Plantation*, p. 235.

[43] Booker T. Washington, *An Autobiography, The Story of My Life and Work*, p. 137. Atlanta Exposition Speech. (Napierville, Illinois: J. L. Nichols & Co., 1901.)

[44] Fleming, *op. cit.*, p. 227.

[45] John Tyler Morgan, *Common School Education. Speech of the Hon. John T. Morgan of Alabama, in the Senate of the United States*, January 30, 1888. Pamphlet issued under frank. (Washington: Government Printing Office, 1886.)

[46] *Testimony Taken by the Joint Select Committee to Inquire into the condition of affairs in the late insurrectionary States. Alabama I*, p. 406. (Washington: Government Printing Office, 1872.)

NOTES FOR CHAPTER III

[1] *Civil War and Reconstruction in Alabama.* (New York: The Columbia University Press: Macmillan, 1905.)

[2] *In Black Reconstruction.* (New York: Harcourt, Brace and Co., 1935.) W. E. DuBois hints at a re-examination of the nature of the Alabama debt. However, he gives Fleming's figure as *bona-fide* for 1874, and makes no later correction of this as a final figure.

[3] *Congressional Globe*, January 24, 1864.

[4] Fleming, *Civil War and Reconstruction*, p. 378.

[5] *Ibid.*, p. 384.

[6] Victoria M. Clayton, *White and Black Under the Old Regime*, p. 166. The presiding judge was Mrs. Clayton's husband.

[7] *Alabama Testimony* (Ku Klux Investigation), *Joint Select Committee to Inquire into the Condition of Affairs in the Late Insurrectionary States*, p. 226. (Washington: Government Printing Office, 1872.)

[8] *Op. cit.*, p. 166.

[9] *War of the Rebellion Records*, pp. 1041-1042. Series I, Vol. XLIX. (Washington: Government Printing Office, 1900.)

[10] Willis Brewer, *Alabama: Her history, resources, war record, and Prominent men.* (Montgomery: Barrett and Brown, 1874.) p. 64.

[11] Alabama Testimony, *op. cit.*, pp. 876-877.

[12] Fleming, *op. cit.*, p. 403.

[13] *Ibid.*, pp. 394-397.

[14] *Alabama Testimony*, p. 1815.

[15] William A. Russ, Jr., "Registration and Disfranchisement under radical Reconstruction," *The Mississippi Valley Historical Review*, Vol. XXI, No. 2, pp. 163-181.

[16] *The Cotton States in the Spring and Summer of 1875*, p. 10. (New York: D. Appleton and Company, 1876.)

[17] The Northern Humanitarians, and many Negro writers, have been usually in the school of "perfectionism," regarding the Negro ex-slave as a sort of noble savage. Many persons writing from what, for the sake of History, is unfortunately denominated "The Southern Point of View," are tempted to view the question of the Negro from the reverse side of ethico-moral interpretation, regarding the Negro as a preternaturally depraved and vicious animal.

Another confusing interpretation has been that derived from the Plantation Tradition, according to which the rôle of the Negro during Reconstruction (in which period the traditionally simple, trusting, and child-like Negro was somewhat out of character) was attributed to the evil influences of vicious carpetbaggers upon a naturally childish, wholesome nature.

DuBois (*Black Reconstruction*) states that the personal attitude toward racial equality is the decisive factor in the interpretation of Reconstruction. Hinton Helper, an articulate "poor white," took the view (*Nojoque: a question for a Continent*. New York: George W. Carleton, 1867) that Negroes were a sub-human, vicious, and depraved branch of the human family. Fleming certainly had an implicit belief in the inferiority of the Negro. Yet he argued that Reconstruction faults were not original with the Negro, but due to his vicious Northern leadership.

It may not be necessary to add that in this essay, considering, as we do, the nature of "social forces," these varied beliefs regarding the essential equality or inequality of the Negro have a bearing not so much as regards their experimental validation, but rather in so far as they entered, as historical facts, into the behavior of participants in the action of the period.

[18] Fleming, *op. cit.*, p. 515.

[19] *Ibid.*, p. 517.

[20] William Wells Brown, *The Rising Sun: or the antecedents and advancement of the colored race.* (Boston: A. G. Brown & Co., 1874.) See also, *Biographical Dictionary of the American Congress, 1774-1927*, p. 1445. Sixty-ninth Congress, 2nd Session, Ho. Document No. 783. (Washington: Government Printing Office, 1928); see also, Ben. Perley Poore, *Congressional Directory*, p. 5. Forty-third Congress, 1st Session. (Washington: Government Printing Office, 1873.)

[21] *Ibid.*

[22] *Alabama Testimony*, p. 208.

[23] *Ibid.*, p. 445.

[24] *Ibid.*, p. 375.

[25] *Ibid.*, pp. 1016-1022.

[26] *Ibid.*, p. 233.

[27] James A. Woodburn, *The Life of Thaddeus Stevens. A Study in American Political History, especially in the period of the Civil War and Reconstruction.* (Indianapolis: Bobbs-Merrill Co., 1913.)

[28] O. O. Howard, *First Report of the Commissioner of the Bureau of Refugees, Freedmen, and Abandoned Lands*, p. 2. (Washington: Government Printing Office, 1866.)

[29] *Ibid.*

[30] If pursued, this policy would have settled approximately one-tenth of the Negro population on subsistence homesteads; and it is instructive to remember the amount of ridicule heaped upon this notion of the Negroes, especially in view of our current enthusiasm for the reform of farm tenantry in the South.

[31] *Congressional Globe*, May 8, 1866, p. 2459.

[32] *Ibid.*, Jan. 18, 1866, p. 299.

[33] Fleming, *op. cit.*, p. 515.

[34] W. E. B. DuBois, *The Souls of the Black Folk*, p. 22. (Chicago: A. C. McClurg & Co., 1903.)

[35] *Freedmen's Bureau Report*, Oct. 31, 1866. General Grant appointed Colonel John Eaton, later Commissioner of Education for the United States, to be in charge of work among the Freedmen in the Western Department as early as 1862. The work of maintaining these services was considered one of the elements in the work of a Chaplain, and the practice continued after the war. Most of these chaplains were New England educated Humanitarians.

[36] *War of the Rebellion Records*, Series I, Vol. XLIX, Part II, p. 729.

[37] *Op. cit.*, p. 429.

[38] The reader may note in Fleming's comments an astonishing and amusing parallel to middle-class reactions in the South to the New Deal relief program for Negroes. Substitute "WPA" or "AAA" or "PWA" for "Freedmen's Bureau," and one has a typical interview with any contemporary planter, housewife, or employer. During the summer of 1937, this writer

talked to a Negro planter in Louisiana who had more than one hundred tenant families on his ''place'' and whose comments on the ''New Deal'' paraphrased almost word for word Fleming's description of the work of the Bureau in disorganizing labor.

[39] Frank Tracy Carlton, *Economic Influences upon Educational Progress in the United States, 1820-1850*, pp. 41-42. (Madison, Wisconsin: Published as Bulletin No. 221 of the University of Wisconsin, 1908.)

[40] Broadus Mitchell and George Sinclair Mitchell, *The Industrial Revolution in the South*, p. 1. (Baltimore: The Johns Hopkins Press, 1930.)

[41] Horace Mann, *Slavery: Letters and Speeches*, p. 9. (Boston: B. D. Musey & Co., 1851.)

[42] Gilbert T. Stephenson, *Race Distinctions in American Law*, p. 167. (New York: D. Appleton and Co., 1910.)

[43] Claude G. Bowers, *The Tragic Era, the revolution after Lincoln*, p. 77. (New York: The Literary Guild, 1929.) Bowers repeats salacious gossip concerning Stevens' private life.

[44] J. P. Wickersham, *History of Education in Pennsylvania*, pp. 333-338. (Lancaster: Published for the author, 1886.)

[45] Samuel W. McCall, *Thaddeus Stevens*, p. 38. (Boston and New York: Houghton Mifflin Co., 1899.)

[46] William Uhler Hensel, *The Christiana Riot and the Treason Trials of 1851: an historical sketch*. (Lancaster: New Era Printing Co., 1911.)

[47] McCall, *op. cit.*, Chapters X-XVI.

[48] *Ibid.*

[49] *Ibid., passim.*

[50] William Paxson Oberholtzer, *Jay Cooke, Financier of the Civil War*, II, p. 28. (Philadelphia: George W. Jacobs, 1907.)

[51] *Congressional Globe.*

[52] *Ibid.*, March 11, 1868, pp. 1818-1819.

[53] *Ibid.*, March 26, 1868, p. 2141.

[54] *Chronicles of the Union League of Philadelphia, 1862-1902*, pp. 203, 402. (Philadelphia: Printed for the Union League by William Fell, 1902.)

[55] Thomas M. Owens, *History and Dictionary of Alabama Biography*, II, p. 778, (Chicago: S. J. Clark Publishing Co., 1921.)

[56] *Congressional Globe*, May 11, May 14, 1868.

[57] *Ibid.*

## NOTES FOR CHAPTER IV

[1] Charles A. and Mary Beard, *The Rise of American Civilization*, II, p. 105.

[2] *Op. cit.*, p. 180.

[3] Brigadier General Fred C. Ainsworth and Joseph P. Kirkley, *The War of the Rebellion: Official Records of the Union and Confederate Armies*. Series IV, Vol. I, p. 1091. (Washington: Government Printing Office, 1900.)

[4] *Ibid.*, Series III, Vol. IV, pp. 762-774.

[5] United States Census, 1880. *Report on the Productions of Agriculture*, pp. 28-29. (Washington: Government Printing Office, 1883.)

[6] Fleming, *op. cit.*, Chapter XXXIX.

[7] Robert Somers, *The Southern States Since the War, 1870-1871*, p. 115.

[8] *Ibid.*, p. 117.

[9] *Ibid.*, p. 126.

[10] *Affairs of Southern Railroads*, Ho. Rept. IV, 39th Congress, 2nd Session.

[11] Fleming, *op. cit.*, pp. 253-254.

[12] *Ibid.*, p. 255.

[13] *Ku Klux Conspiracy*, I, p. 175.

[14] *Ibid.*

[15] *Alabama Testimony, Ku Klux Conspiracy*, pp. 226-227.

[16] *Ku Klux Conspiracy*, I, p. 170.

[17] *Ku Klux Conspiracy*, I, *Majority Report;* questions during examination of James H. Clanton, pp. 227-240, in *Alabama Testimony*.

[18] *Auditor's Report*, 1871, pp. 33-35.

[19] William Elejius Martin, *Internal Improvements in Alabama*, pp. 66-67. Johns Hopkins Studies in Historical and Political Science. (Baltimore: Johns Hopkins Press, 1902.)

[20] *Ibid.*, p. 68.

[21] E. A. Alderman and A. C. Gordon, *J. L. M. Curry, A Biography*, p. 105. (New York: Macmillan Co., 1911.) This road later merged with the Selma, Rome and Dalton.

[22] *Ibid.*

[23] *Ibid.*, p. 106.

[24] *Ibid.*, p. 107.

[25] Owens, *Biography of Alabama*, IV, p. 1396.

[26] Alderman and Gordon, *op. cit.*, p. 106.

[27] Armes, *op. cit.*, p. 107.

[28] Alderman and Gordon, *op. cit.*, pp. 40-42, 108.

[29] Owens, *op. cit.*, IV, pp. 1572-1573.

[30] Armes, *op. cit.*, p. 107.

[31] George F. Milton, *The Eve of Conflict*, p. 403. (Cambridge: The Riverside Press, Houghton, Mifflin and Co., 1935.)

[32] Ellis Merton Coulter, *The Cincinnati Southern Railroad and the Struggle for Southern Commerce, 1865-1872*, p. 7. Reprinted from *A History of Kentucky*. (Chicago: American Historical Society, 1922.)

[33] Milton, *op. cit.*, p. 374.

[34] *O. R. R.*, Ser. I, Vol. XLIX, Pt. 1, pp. 590, 659, 718; Pt. II, p. 560; Fleming, *Civil War and Reconstruction*, p. 146.

[35] The Patton Government began the convict lease system in 1866 with a lease to James W. Sloss and others. (*First Biennial Report of the Inspectors of Convicts*, containing reprints of special message by Rufus W. Cobb, Governor, dated November 27, 1882. Montgomery: Barrett & Co., 1886.) Patton served as Vice-President of the Alabama and Chattanooga Railroad in 1869-1870 while this road was still partially under the control of the Sloss interests (*Poor's Manual*, 1869-1870, p. 420). The Tennessee and Alabama Central, a Sloss affiliate, held a mortgage on the Alabama and Chattanooga during this period. (Armes, *The Story of Coal and Iron*, p. 216.)

[36] Owens, *Biography of Alabama*, IV, p. 1396.

[37] Fleming, *Civil War and Reconstruction*, pp. 190-195.

[38] "Pig-Iron" Kelley's first visit to Alabama in 1867 was to view the mineral resources of North Alabama and to make speeches for Republican Reconstruction. In Montgomery one of his speeches to Negroes precipitated a race riot. In 1885 he revisited the State, and published a brief book, *The Old South and the New* (New York: G. P. Putnam's Sons, 1888), giving his impressions. Kelley was financially interested in Samuel Noble's iron works at Anniston. His second impressions were bucolically peaceful. He was an adherent of Booker T. Washington and favored the industrial education of Negroes.

[39] Fleming, *op. cit.*, p. 194.

[40] *Affairs of Southern Railroads*, p. 622.

[41] Coulter, *The Cincinnati Southern*, p. 11.

[42] *Affairs of Southern Railroads*, p. 697.

[43] *Affairs of Southern Railroads*, p. 643.

[44] Coulter, *The Cincinnati Southern*, p. 8; Poor's *Manual*, 1870-1871, p. 267.

[45] *Affairs of Southern Railroads*, p. 623.

[46] Armes, *The Story of Coal and Iron*, p. 243.

[47] Morris died March 18, 1891, at Montgomery. The following newspaper account appeared at that time in the Birmingham *Age-Herald:* "He was the richest man in Alabama. . . . He held 660 shares of the 2,000 of the Elyton

Land Company, which in 1874 sold for $17 a share. At his death they were valued at $4,000 a share. He got many shares as the result of a loan to Colonel F. M. Gilmer, who deposited the stock as collateral, and could not repay the loan. He was a private banker.

"He was a calm, and unemotional old man. He was in no sense a developer, as the term is nowadays used. He did not build towns, or railroads, nor factories; but his millions strengthened the confidence of the public."

[48] Armes, *op. cit.*, p. 243.

[49] Herbert L. Casson, *The Romance of Steel*, p. 301. (New York: A. S. Barnes and Co., 1907.)

[50] Casson, *op. cit.*, p. 301.

[51] James Phelan, *History of Tennessee, the Making of a State*, pp. 284-290. (Boston and New York: Houghton Mifflin Co., 1889.)

[52] *Affairs of Southern Railroads*, p. 723.

[53] *Ibid.*

[54] *Ibid.*, p. 722.

[55] Armes, *The Story of Coal and Iron*, pp. 246-247.

[56] George S. Houston, "Message of the Governor, including Report of the Commissioners on the Public Debt," *Journal of the House of Representatives, 1875-1876*, p. 209. (W. W. Screws and Co., 1876.)

[57] Fleming, *op. cit.*, p. 591.

[58] See *Affairs of Southern Railroads*, and *Poor's Manual for the years* indicated for lists of directors and officials.

[59] *Poor's Manual*, 1868-1869, pp. 419-421.

[60] *Ku Klux Conspiracy, Alabama Testimony*, pp. 193-199, 359-361, 1056, 1058, 1411, 1417-1418.

[61] *Poor's Manual*, 1870, 1871, p. 104. In 1866 Patton, as provisional Governor, began the Alabama convict lease system in a contract signed with a Mr. Smith and a Mr. McMillan. Subsequently it was shown that these men were "dummies" for a group which included James W. Sloss and Sam Tate. The convicts were used first for railroad construction, and the highly lucrative, however iniquitous, system of lease to coal mines and foundries followed shortly thereafter. (*First Biennial Report of the Inspectors of Convicts to the Governor, from October 1, 1884-October 1, 1886*, p. 352. (Montgomery: Barrett & Co., 1886.) Incidentally, it is interesting to note that a Captain John O. Bankhead was one of the first official figures in the new convict system. The political as well as economic great-god-father of the present Senator and Congressman was none other than unsung James W. Sloss of North Alabama.

[62] Armes, *The Story of Coal and Iron*, p. 216.

[63] Martin, *Internal Improvements in Alabama*, p. 71.

[64] Fleming, *op. cit.*, p. 593.

[65] George S. Houston, "Message of the Governor," *House Journal, 1875-1876*, pp. 187-217.

[66] *Poor's Manual*, 1878-1879, p. 993.

[67] Armes, *op. cit.*, pp. 243-245.

[68] *Ibid.* This was the nucleus of the Elyton Land Company, which with the development of Birmingham made such immense fortunes for those who were able to maintain their stock.

[69] *Ibid.*, p. 243.

[70] *Ibid.*

[71] Later United States Senator from Alabama.

[72] As the "Bald Eagle of the Mountains," Houston won the battle for "White Supremacy" in 1875, became Governor, and later United States Senator.

[73] Armes, *op. cit.*, p. 245.

[74] *Ibid.*

[75] Coulter, *The Cincinnati Southern*, p. 28.

[76] *Ibid.*, pp. 32-34.

[77] *Ibid.*, p. 44.

[78] *Ibid.*
[79] *Ibid.*, p. 15.
[80] *Ibid.*
[81] Fleming, *op. cit.*, pp. 402-405, 553-568, 514-515.
[82] *Chronicles of the Union League of Philadelphia, 1862-1902*, pp. 3, 401. (Philadelphia: Printed for the Union League by William R. Fell, 1902.)
[83] *Ibid.*, p. 2, 8.
[84] *Ibid.*, p. 393; Fleming, *op. cit.*, p. 553.
[85] Fleming, *op. cit.*, p. 554.
[86] *Ibid.*, p. 556.
[87] *Ibid.*, p. 558.
[88] *Chronicles of the Union League*, p. 235.
[89] *Ibid.*, p. 164.
[90] Fleming, *op. cit.*, p. 555.
[91] *Journal of the Constitutional Convention, 1867, passim.*
[92] Owens, *History and Dictionary of Alabama Biography*, II, p. 778.
[93] *Chronicles of the Union League*, p. 402.
[94] *Congressional Record*, March 11, 1868, pp. 1818-1819; Armes, *op. cit.*, p. 212; William D. Kelley, *Speeches, Addresses and Letters on Industrial and Financial Questions, passim.* (Philadelphia: Henry Cary Baird, 1872.)
[95] *Vide*, p. 33, above.
[96] Fleming, *op. cit.*, p. 509.
[97] Lydia Maria (Frances) Child, *The Freedmen's Book*, p. 263. (Boston: Ticknor and Fields, 1865.) Mrs. Child's text was so extremely radical that even the American Missionary Association refused to circulate it! Their objection, however, was one of religious, not social, orthodoxy. See Lydia Maria Child, *Letters, with a Biographical Introduction*, by John G. Whittier, and an Appendix by Wendell Phillips, p. 201. (Boston: Houghton Mifflin Co., 1883.)
[98] Fleming, *op. cit.*, p. 567.
[99] *Ibid.*, p. 593.
[100] *Ibid.* p. 559.
[101] *Ku Klux Conspiracy, Alabama Testimony*, pp. 7, 8, 35, 88, 170, *et al.* See *Leagues, Loyal*, in index same publication.
[102] Oberholtzer, *op. cit.*, p. 57; Letter of Henry Cooke to his brother, Jay.
[103] *Journal of the House, 1870-1871*, p. 82.
[104] William H. Moore, *Report of the Commissioner to Investigate and audit claims against the State of Alabama, on account of the Alabama and Chattanooga Railroad*, pp. 3-4. (Montgomery: Arthur Bingham, State Printer, 1873.)
[105] *Ku Klux Conspiracy, Alabama Testimony*, p. 226.
[106] *Poor's Manual, 1868*, p. 251.
[107] Owens, *op. cit.*, III, p. 726.
[108] Fleming, *op. cit.*, pp. 508, 512, 625, 630, 638.
[109] Houston, Message of the Governor, *House Journal, 1875-1876*, pp. 187-217.
[110] Fleming, *op. cit.*, p. 508.
[111] Moore, *op. cit.*, p. 3.
[112] *House Journal, 1870-1871*, p. 82.
[113] *Commercial and Financial Chronicle*, May 17, 1873, Vol. XVI, No. 411, p. 659; December 13, 1873, Vol. XVII, No. 442, p. 803.
[114] *Ibid.*, p. 180.
[115] *Commercial and Financial Chronicle*, Vol. XVI, No. 398.
[116] *Ibid.*, Vol. XIX, No. 487, p. 423; Armes, *The Story of Coal and Iron*, p. 252.
[117] Fleming, *op. cit.*, pp. 583ff.
[118] Henry W. Clews, *Fifty Years in Wall Street*, pp. 254ff. (New York: Irving Publishing Co., 1908.)
[119] *Ibid.*, p. 302.

[120] *Ibid.*, p. 254.

[121] *Ibid.*

[122] *Ibid.*, p. 244.

[123] Armes, *op. cit.*, p. 180. (Kelley, *The Old South and the New, passim;* Poor's *Railroad Manual, 1870-1871*, p. 408.)

[124] Fleming, *op. cit.*, p. 793.

[125] *Ibid.*, p. 792. Italics mine.

[126] Italics mine.

[127] Nordhoff, *The Cotton States in 1875*, p. 89.

[128] Clews, *op. cit., passim.*

[129] William Z. Ripley, *Railroads: Finance and Organization*, p. 584. (New York: Longmans, Green & Co., 1915. Fink, it will be remembered, was the guiding hand in the early L. & N. penetration of Alabama, and in formulating the merger between the South and North and the L. & N. that defeated the designs of the Russell Sage, Republican Alabama and Chattanooga).

[130] *Ibid.*

[131] Ripley, *op. cit.*, p. 585.

[132] See *Poor's Railroad Manuals* for given years, *passim.*

[133] *Poor's Railroad Manual, 1876*, p. 476.

[134] *Ibid.*, pp. 476, 484, 671.

[135] *Ibid.*, p. 484.

[136] Owens, *History of Alabama and Dictionary of Alabama Biography*, III, p. 357.

[137] *Ibid.*

[138] *Ibid.;* Armes, *op. cit.*, pp. 17, 147.

[139] Owens, *op. cit.*, III, p. 357.

[140] In *Affairs of Southern Railroads,* or in successive *Poor's Manuals.*

[141] *Ibid.*, p. 384.

[142] *Ibid.*, 1871, p. 393.

[143] *Ibid.*, 1869, p. 104. In *Poor's Manual, 1870-1871*, p. 267, it is noted that the L. & N. leased the M. & O. in 1867 for ten years.

[144] *Ibid.*, 1871, p. 268.

[145] *Ibid.*, 1869, p. 266.

[146] *Ibid.*, 1871, p. 114.

[147] *Ibid.*, 1871, p. 122.

[148] *Ibid.*, 1876, p. 671.

[149] *House Journal, 1875-1876*, p. 192.

[150] *Ibid.*, p. 193.

[151] *Poor's Railroad Manual, 1869-1870*, p. 470.

[152] *House Journal, 1875-1876*, p. 194.

[153] *Ibid.*, p. 195.

[154] *Ibid.*, pp. 195-196.

[155] *Op. cit.*, p. 581.

[156] *House Journal, 1875-1876*, p. 196.

[157] *Poor's Railroad Manual, 1875-1876*, p. 671.

[158] *Ibid., 1868-1869*, p. 266.

[159] *Ibid., 1870-1871*, p. 393.

[160] *House Journal, 1875-1876*, pp. 196-197.

[161] Clews, *Fifty Years in Wall Street, passim.*

[162] Armes, *The Story of Coal and Iron*, p. 180.

[163] *Fifty Years in Wall Street*, p. 255.

[164] *House Journal, 1875-1876*, pp. 197-199; *Ibid.*, 1876-1877, pp. 252-254.

[165] *House Journal, 1875-1876*, p. 199.

[166] *Ibid.*

[167] *Ibid.*

[168] See p. 51, above.

[169] (No author), *The Hill Country of Alabama, U. S. A.; or, the land of rest*, pp. 95-96. (London: Published for the English Committee of Bondholders, 1878.)

[170] *House Journal, 1875-1876,* p. 191.
[171] *Ibid.;* see also *The Hill Country of Alabama,* pp. 95-96.
[172] *House Journal, 1875-1876,* p. 202.
[173] *Ibid.,* 1876-1877, p. 255.
[174] The Brookings Institute, in a recent study of the Alabama financial structure, point out that the reason Alabama had an archaic tax limit for schools was because of a strangle-hold upon state government by planters and industrialists, who had engrafted this limitation in the State Constitution of 1875. See *Taxation of the State Government of Alabama,* p. 47. Vol. 4, pt. 3. (Montgomery: Wilson Printing Co., 1932.)
[175] *Op. cit.,* pp. 585-586.
[176] Edgar W Knight, *Education in the United States,* p. 468. (Boston: Ginn & Co., 1929.)
[177] Ellwood P. Cubberley, *Public Education in the United States,* p. 435. (Cambridge: The Riverside Press, Houghton Mifflin Co., 1924.)
[178] See p. 45, above.
[179] *Commercial and Financial Chronicle,* Vol. XXI, No. 534, September 18, 1875, p. 276.
[180] *Journal of the Constitutional Convention of the State of Alabama of 1875,* pp. 35-36. (Montgomery: W. W. Screws, State Printer, 1875.)
[181] *Commercial and Financial Chronicle,* January 29, 1876, Vol. XXII, No. 553, p. 110.
[182] *Ibid.*
[183] Governor Houston and his successor, Governor Cobb, who, as suggested— above, were closely associated with James W. Sloss, turned the convict system from a liability into a profitable business.
[184] *House Journal, 1876-1877,* pp. 254-256; *Commercial and Financial Chronicle,* February 12, 1876, Vol. XXII, No. 555.
[185] *Ibid.*
[186] *House Journal, 1875-1876,* p. 204.
[187] *Brookings Institution Survey, op. cit.,* p. 245; Weeks, *op. cit., passim.*

## NOTES FOR CHAPTER V

[1] Brewer, *Alabama,* p. 542.
[2] *Ibid.*
[3] *Alabama Testimony, Ku Klux Investigation;* Testimony of Lewis E. Parson, p. 77-101.
[4] Fleming, *Civil War and Reconstruction,* p. 358.
[5] *Ibid.,* p. 359.
[6] *Ibid.,* pp. 360 ff.
[7] Fleming insists (pp. 462, 607) that "The provisional government adopted the ante-bellum public school system and put it in operation" and that "The schools were open to both races, from six to twenty years of age, separate schools being provided for blacks." For evidence pro and con, see Chapter VII.
[8] *Ibid.,* p. 359.
[9] Blaine, *Twenty Years in the Senate,* II, p. 94.
[10] Fleming, *op. cit.,* pp. 394, 397.
[11] *Acts and Resolutions, 39 Congress, 2nd Session,* p. 60. (Washington: Government Printing Office, 1867.)
[12] Fleming, *op. cit.,* p. 475.
[13] *Ibid.*
[14] William A. Russ, Jr., *Registration and Disfranchisement under Radical Reconstruction,* p. 178. *The Mississippi Valley Historical Review,* Vol. XXI, No. 2, pp. 163-81. See also, Benjamin B. Kendrick, "History as a Curative," *The Southern Review,* Vol. I, No. 3 (Winter, 1936), pp. 540-51.

[15] Fleming, *op. cit.*, p. 491.

[16] Russ, *op. cit.*, pp. 165 f.

[17] Fleming, *op. cit.*, p. 491.

[18] Russ, *op. cit.*, p. 168.

[19] *New York World*, November 11, 1867; *The American Annual Cyclopaedia and Register of important events of the year 1867*, p. 30. (New York: D. Appleton & Co., 1872.)

[20] *The Chicago Tribune*, November 8, 1867.

[21] F. G. Bromberg, *Reconstruction in Alabama, a paper read before the Iberville Historical Society*, I, pp. 3f.

[22] Fleming, *Civil War and Reconstruction*, pp. 518-19.

[23] *Ibid.*, p. 517.

[24] *Ibid.*, p. 518.

[25] *Ibid.*, p. 519.

[26] The *New York World*, November 11, 1867.

[27] The *Chicago Tribune*, November 8, 1867.

[28] Fleming, *op. cit.*, p. 517.

[29] *Ibid.*, p. 518.

[30] Owens, *History of Alabama*, Chaps. III, IV.

[31] *op. cit.*, p. 4.

[32] Fleming, *op. cit.*, p. 518; *Journal of the Convention, passim.*

[33] The *Chicago Tribune*, November 15, 1867.

[34] New York *Daily Tribune*, December 7, 1867. Bingham was a Stevens "Green-backer."

[35] *House Report No. 262, 43rd Congress, Second Session*, p. lxx. (Washington: Government Printing Office, 1875.)

[36] Fleming, *op. cit.*, p. 522.

[37] *Ibid.*, p. 531.

[38] *Ibid.*, p. 530.

[39] Owens, *Annals of Alabama*, p. 715.

[40] Brewer, *Alabama*, p. 71; Fleming, *op. cit.*, pp. 546 f.

[41] Fleming, *op. cit.*, p. 547; Brewer, *op. cit.*, pp. 71 f; *Alabama Testimony, Ku Klux Investigation, vide* Testimony of General Clanton. General Clanton felt very bitterly toward Parsons, still a Conservative, who advised the Conservatives in their tactics, through the February election, and then in the Spring turned Republican.

[42] Brewer, *Alabama*, p. 71.

[43] *Ibid.*, p. 508.

[44] Boyd, *Alabama in the Fifties*, pp. 14, 26, 29: *vide* Testimony of N. B. Cloud in *Ho. Rept. 262, 43rd Congress, Second Session*, pp. 288-94.

[45] Fleming, *op. cit.*, p. 738; but Bromberg (*op. cit.*) says there were only twelve Negroes. Some "negroes" on Fleming's list were reported elsewhere, by Fleming, as white. Fleming relied on "anti-radical" newspaper sources to identify the assembly membership.

[46] Both as a paramount political issue, and as a topic for historians, more attention has been given to the work of the Legislature in regards to railroad legislation than to any other aspect of the Reconstruction work. *Vide* Fleming, *op. cit.*, pp. 587-606; *Alabama Testimony, Ku Klux Investigation*, Testimony of Governor R. B. Lindsay, General Clanton, *et al.*

[47] *Official Journal of the Constitutional Convention of the State of Alabama*, p. 61. Held in Montgomery, Alabama. (Montgomery: Barrett & Brown, 1868.)

[48] *Ibid.*, p. 263.

[49] *Ibid.*, pp. 265-69.

[50] *Ibid.*, pp. 63-64.

[51] *Vide Acts of the General Assembly: 1868.* (Montgomery: John G. Stokes & Co., 1868.) *Ibid.*, 1869-1870. (Montgomery: John G. Stokes & Co., 1870.)

[52] Fleming, *op. cit.*, p. 750.

[53] *Ibid.*, p. 748.
[54] *Ibid.*, p. 633.
[55] Owens, *Annals of Alabama*, p. 716.
[56] Fleming, *op. cit.*, pp. 508, 512, 625, 630, 638.
[57] William Garrett, *Reminiscences of public men in Alabama, for thirty years*, pp. 632-45. (Atlanta, Georgia: Plantation Publishing Company's Press, 1872.)
[58] Fleming, *op. cit.*, p. 508.
[59] Owens, *op. cit.*, p. 717; Fleming, *op. cit.*, p. 753.
[60] Fleming, *op. cit.*, p. 753.
[61] *U. S. Census, 1870, Population.*
[62] *Journal of the House, General Assembly of Alabama, 1872-1873*, pp. 16 f. (Montgomery: W. W. Screws, State Printer, 1873.)
[63] Nordhoff, *The Cotton States in 1874-1875*, p. 91.
[64] New York: A. B. Burdick Co., 1860.
[65] New York: George W. Carlton & Co., 1867.
[66] Nordhoff, *op. cit.*, p. 91. Montgomery *Advertiser*, January 14, 1874.
[67] Nordhoff, *op. cit.*, p. 91.
[68] See controversy between *Alabama State Journal*, Montgomery (Republican), April 1, April 8, 1874, and Montgomery *Advertiser* (Democrat), same dates.
[69] Report of Barnas Sears, General Agent, in *Peabody Proceedings*, I, 406.
[70] *Coburn Report*, p. 309.
[71] *Ibid.*, p. 299.
[72] *Ibid.*, p. 144.
[73] Montgomery *Advertiser*, April 9, 1874; the Wilcox County Grange pledged itself (1) not to bail out Negroes charged with theft, (2) not to hire Negroes who were Republican, (3) not to allow Republican Negroes to occupy houses.
[74] See *Coburn Report*, pp. 520 ff.; Fleming, *Civil War and Reconstruction*, p. 778.
[75] *Op. cit.*, pp. 583-84.
[76] *House Report 262, 43rd Congress, Second Session* (Coburn report), p. 857.
[77] *Ibid.* Italics mine.
[78] *Fifty Years in Wall Street*, pp. 254-55.
[79] *Op. cit.*, p. 792. Italics mine.
[80] Fleming, *op. cit.*, p. 772.
[81] *Ibid.*, p. 774; *Coburn Report*, p. 293.
[82] p. 793.
[83] *Journal of the House, 1874*, pp. 26 f.
[84] *Ibid.*, pp. 26-28.
[85] Owens, *Annals of Alabama*, p. 718.
[86] *Ibid.*, p. 719.
[87] *Journal of the Constitutional Convention of 1875*, pp. 170-171. (Montgomery: W. W. Screws, State Printer, 1875.)


NOTES FOR CHAPTER VI


[1] Willis G. Clark, *History of Education in Alabama, 1702-1889*, p. 27. Circular of Information No. 3, 1889. Contributions to American Educational History, ed. by Herbert Adansa. (Washington: Government Printing Office, 1889.)
[2] *Ibid.*, p. 27.
[3] *A Study of Education in Alabama, Bulletin 41*, p. 35. Department of the Interior. (Washington: Government Printing Office, 1919.)
[4] *Ibid.*, p. 35.

[5] Clark, *op. cit.*, pp. 220-22.

[6] John G. Eaton, *Special Report to the U. S. Commissioner of Education, in Annual Report, U. S. Bureau of Education*, p. 323. (Washington: Government Printing Office, 1871.)

[7] Clark, *op. cit.*, p. 222.

[8] There are "Negro creoles" now living in Mobile who claim to have attended the Catholic schools with white children within the last twenty years.

[9] *Eighth Census of the United States, Social Statistics.*

[10] *House Report No. 262, 43rd Congress, Second Session: Affairs in Alabama*, p. 1110. (Washington: Government Printing Office, 1875.)

[11] *Bulletin 41*, p. 36.

[12] *Ibid.*

[13] Stephen B. Weeks, *The History of Public School Education in Alabama*, p. 57. United States Bureau of Education, Bulletin No. 12, 1915. (Washington: Government Printing Office, 1915.)

[14] *Acts of the Fourth Biennial Session of the General Assembly of Alabama*, p. 14. (Montgomery: Brittan & Blue, 1854.)

[15] *Acts of the Fifth Biennial Session of the General Assembly of Alabama*, p. 34. (Montgomery: Bates & Lucas, 1856.)

[16] Weeks, *Public School Education in Alabama*, p. 74.

[17] *Ibid.*, p. 54.

[18] Clark, *op. cit.*, p. 241.

[19] *Ibid.*, p. 84.

[20] Edgar W. Knight, *Public Education in the South*, p. 314. (Boston: Ginn & Co., 1922.)

[21] Fleming, *op. cit.*, p. 462.

[22] *Ibid.*, p. 607.

[23] *Ibid.*, p. 802.

[24] It would have been absurd to do so, with a statute making it a criminal offense to educate Negroes.

[25] Francis Newton Thorpe, *The Federal and State Constitutions, Colonial Charters and Other Organic Laws of the States, Territories, and Colonies now or heretofore forming the United States of America*, I, p. 110. (Washington: Government Printing Office, 1909.)

[26] *Ibid.*, p. 124.

[27] *Acts of the Fifth Biennial Session of the General Assembly*, p. 45.

[28] *Report of Joseph Hodgson, for the Scholastic Year January 1, 1871 to September 30, 1871*, p. 9.

[29] *Ibid.*, p. 10.

[30] *Report of the Joint Committee on Reconstruction*, p. 17, 39th Congress, 1st Session, Report No. 30. (Washington: Government Printing Office, 1866.) The credibility of the witness is not great, from reading his other testimony; however, in this instance Mobley approved of what the Alabama legislator had told him.

[31] *Acts of the Session of 1865-1866 of the General Assembly of Alabama*, p. 128. (Montgomery: Reid & Screws, State Printers, 1866.)

[32] See Chapter VII, above.

[33] *Joint Committee on Reconstruction*, Pt. III, p. 30. Testimony of General Clinton B. Fisk.

[34] *Ibid.*, p. 7. Testimony of Major General Hatch.

[35] *Ibid.*, p. 34.

[36] *Ibid.*, p. 117. Testimony of Gen. Tarbell. Before the War Dr. Nott had written several books and pamphlets proving the physical and mental inferiority of the Negro; J. C. Nott and G. R. Gliddon, *Types of Mankind*. (Philadelphia: Lippincott, Grumbu & Co., 1854); J. C. Nott, "The Mulatto a Hybrid; probable extermination of the two races if the whites and blacks were allowed to inter-marry," *American Journal of Medical Science*, June, 1843, pp. 252-56; *et al.*

[37] Walter Lynwood Fleming, *Documentary History of Reconstruction, political, military, social, religious, educational and industrial*, I, p. 423. (Cleveland: A. H. Clark Co., 1906-1907.)

[38] *Ku Klux Report, Alabama Testimony*, p. 234.

[39] Alderman and Gordon, *J. L. M. Curry, a Biography*, p. 201.

[40] Fleming, *Documentary History of Reconstruction*, II, p. 176. The letter bears all the marks of "inspiration." The editor of the Selma *Times* at this time was a young Kentuckian, Robert McKee, who had been in Alabama only a few months. See Brewer, *Alabama*, pp. 230-31.

[41] Fleming, *Documentary History of Reconstruction*, p. 177.

[42] *Ku Klux Report, Alabama Testimony*, pp. 234 ff.: See appended answer to editorial in Montgomery *Advertiser* of January 27, 1869.

[43] "Pastoral Letter of Bishops," in Fleming, *Documentary History of Reconstruction*, II, p. 250.

[44] *Documentary History*, II, p. 271.

[45] "Reports of the Baptist Home Mission Board, 1866," in Fleming, *Documentary History*, II, p. 248.

[46] *Ibid.*

[47] *Ibid.*

[48] *Ibid.*

[49] Alderman and Gordon, *op. cit.*, p. 201; *Ku Klux Report*, p. 236.

[50] *Ku Klux Report*, p. 236.

[51] Alvord, *Second Semi-Annual Report*, p. 6.

[52] See Chapter VIII, above.

[53] Jabez L. M. Curry, "Education of the Negroes since 1860," *Publications of the John F. Slater Fund*, No. 3. (Baltimore: By the Trustees, 1894.)

[54] See Augustus Field Beard, *A Crusade of Brotherhood, A History of the American Missionary Association*. (New York: Pilgrim Press, 1909.)

[55] William Edward Burghardt DuBois, *The Negro Common School*, p. 22. Atlanta University Publications, No. 6. (Atlanta: Atlanta University Press, 1901.)

[56] *W. O. R. R.*, Series III, Vol. I, p. 1091.

[57] *American Missionary*, Vol. viii, No. 7 (July, 1864), p. 179.

[58] *W. O. R. R.*, III, Vol. I, p. 109.

[59] See Chapter III, above.

[60] John Watson Alvord, *Semi-Annual Report on Schools and Finances of Freedmen*, p. 2. First Report. (Washington: Government Printing Office, 1867.)

[61] *Ibid.*, p. 4.

[62] *Ibid.*

[63] Alvord, *First Semi-Annual Report*, p. 4.

[64] Alvord, *Third Semi-Annual Report*, p. 32.

[65] Alvord, *Second Semi-Annual Report*, p. 2.

[66] Fleming, *Civil War and Reconstruction*, p. 460.

[67] Alvord, Jan. 1, 1866, *First Semi-Annual Report*, p. 4; July 1, 1866, *Second Report*, p. 2; Jan. 1, 1867, *Third Report*, p. 17; June 30, 1867, *Fourth Report*, p. 33; Jan. 1, 1868, *Fifth Report*, pp. 12-13; other data from Summary in *Tenth Report*.

[68] Beard, *op. cit., passim*.

[69] *Ibid.*, pp. 100-101, 103 f.

[70] DuBois, *The Negro Common School*, p. 33.

[71] *Ku Klux Testimony, Alabama;* testimony of the Reverend Lakin, pp. 111-159.

[72] *The American Freedman*, May, 1866.

[73] *Ibid.*, August, 1866, p. 80.

[74] *Ibid.*

[75] *The American Missionary*, April, 1867, p. 75.

[76] *Ibid.*

[77] Alvord, *Sixth Report*, p. 64.

[78] *41st Congress, 2nd Session, Ho. Ex. Doc. No. 121,* pp. 370 f.

[79] Alvord, *Fifth Report,* p. 32.

[80] Fleming, *Civil War and Reconstruction,* pp. 322 ff.

[81] *Ibid.* It is clear that the basic trouble was the objection of the Mobile Board to the action of the State Board by which the A. M. A. was given State funds over the head of the Mobile Board and without control over the A. M. A. schools by the Mobile Commission.

[82] Alvord, *Fourth Report,* p. 4.

[83] Alvord, *First Semi-Annual Report,* p. 4.

[84] Alvord, *Third Semi-Annual Report,* p. 16.

[85] ''Creoles,'' for whom schools were already in vogue, were distinguished then, and still are, from ''colored people'' or Negroes.

[86] *The Mobile Times and Register,* May 3, 1867.

[87] Clark, *History of Education in Alabama,* p. 271.

[68] *Ibid.*

[89] *Ibid.*

[90] *House Report No. 262,* 43rd Congress, 2nd Session, p. 527.

[91] *Proceedings of the Trustees of the Peabody Education Fund,* I, 106. (Boston: John Wilson & Co., 1875.)

[92] Clark, *op. cit.,* p. 272.

[93] The *Acts* establishing a system of schools for Negroes in the District of Columbia in 1864 ''ordered the white school board to pay over to them (i. e., the Negro school board) the Negro *pro rata* of the school monies according to population.'' In 1862 Congress had directed that the Negro *pro rata* of taxes collected from Negroes be used to support Negro schools. See Henry Wilson, *Anti-Slavery Measures in Congress, 1861-1864,* Chp. VIII, ''Education of Colored Youth in the District of Columbia.'' (Boston: Walker, Wise & Co., 1864.)

[94] Fleming, *Civil War and Reconstruction,* pp. 480-481.

[95] *Ibid.,* pp. 322 f. For full account see N. B. Cloud, *Official Report of the Superintendent of Public Instruction on the troubles in the Mobile Free Public Schools.* Appended to Report to Governor, dated August 18, 1869.

[96] *Ibid.*

[97] *Peabody Proceedings, op. cit.,* I, p. 210.


## NOTES FOR CHAPTER VII

[1] *Journal of the Convention of 1867,* p. 10.

[2] Owens, *History of Alabama and Dictionary of Alabama Biography,* II, pp. 845-46.

[3] Fleming, *Civil War and Reconstruction,* p. 518.

[4] *Ibid.,* p. 526.

[5] *Ninth Annual Report of the American Missionary Association,* 1855, p. 47. (New York: American Missionary Society, 1855.)

[6] *Ibid.*

[7] *Twelfth Annual Report of the American Missionary Association,* 1858, p. 41. (New York: American Missionary Association, 1858.)

[8] Skaggs, *The Southern Oligarchy,* p. 94.

[9] John M. McKleroy, *Annual Report, 1867,* p. 123.

[10] Fleming, *op. cit.,* p. 518.

[11] *Ibid.,* p. 519.

[12] *Ibid.,* p. 617. Fleming states here that Finley was ''doorkeeper of the First Board.'' But he was a member of the State legislature that convened on July 13, 1868.

[13] Owens, *op. cit.,* III, p. 248. Fleming, however, says Buckley was ''a hard-shell preacher'' (p. 440), ''known among the 'malignants' as 'the high priest of the nigger bureau' '' (p. 448).

[14] Owens, *op. cit.,* III, p. 248.

[15] *Ibid.*

[16] *Ibid.*, pp. 1285-1286.

[17] In either Garrett's *Reminiscences*, Brewer's *Alabama*, or Owen's *History of Alabama and Dictionary of Biography.*

[18] Fleming, *op. cit.*, pp. 517-18.

[19] *Journal of the Constitutional Convention of 1867*, p. 237.

[20] Francis Newton Thorpe, *Federal and State Constitutions*, II, pp. 1150-1152.

[21] *The Debates of the Constitutional Convention of the State of Iowa, 1857*, p. 79. (Davenport: Luse, Lane & Co., 1857.)

[22] Thorpe, *op. cit.*, II, 1150-52.

[23] *Ibid.*, I, 148-50.

[24] It is clear that the reason this section did not appear in the Alabama article was that the ''Carpetbaggers'' on the Committee could have required a time-limit for residential qualification with but poor grace.

[25] This section was in the majority report of the Iowa Convention of 1857, word for word; but was amended as in Iowa Section 8. The minority report said of this and other sections precisely what the Conservatives in Alabama later said of the Alabama Board: ''Because said Board of Education are clothed with powers, dangerous, as *precedents*, to the liberties of a free and enlightened people'' (*Iowa Debates, op. cit.*, p. 78.)

[26] Note modification of powers as amended, with limitations imposed.

[27] The Iowa General Assembly promptly abolished the Board in 1864, the first session after which this clause became operative. It is probable that the Alabama General Assembly would have done the same before the enactment of the Constitution of 1875, if the same privilege had been theirs.

[28] *Journal of the Constitutional Convention of 1867*, p. 237.

[29] Thorpe, *op. cit.*, II, p. 1153.

[30] Owens, *History of Alabama and Dictionary of Alabama Biography*, Chap. IV.

[31] See p. 90, above.

[32] Fleming, *op. cit.*, p. 522; *Annual Cyclopaedia*, 1867, p. 33.

[33] *Journal of the Convention*, p. 237.

[34] *Ibid.* Carraway's amendment was evidently intended to clarify the stand of Negro members. Similarly, when a resolution to invalidate interracial marriages was presented, Carraway presented an amendment, ''provided, that any white man cohabiting with a colored woman be sentenced to prison for life'' (*Journal of the Convention*, p. 187).

[35] New York, December 6, 1867.

[36] *Op. cit.*, pp. 521, 519.

[37] *Ibid.*, p. 518.

[38] *Journal of the Convention*, p. 242.

[39] November 8, 1867.

[40] Alvord, *Fifth Report*, p. 48.

[41] *Acts of Alabama, 1868*, p. 6.

[42] Fleming, *op. cit.*, p. 609.

[43] Owens, *op. cit.*, IV, pp. 1204-05.

[44] *Ibid.*, III, p. 381.

[45] *The Weekly Mail* (Montgomery), December 15, 1869.

[46] Owens, *op. cit.*, III, p. 395.

[47] Alvord, *Third Report*, p. 16.

[48] N. B. Cloud, *Annual Report to the Governor, 1869.*

[49] *Acts of the Board of Education, 1868*, p. 159. Bound with *Acts of the General Assembly, op. cit.*

[50] *Acts of the Board of Education, 1868*, p. 148.

[51] N. B. Cloud, *op. cit.*, p. 15.

[52] *Acts of the Board of Education, 1868*, p. 148.

[53] J. H. Hodgson, *Report of the Superintendent of Public Instruction, 1871*, p. 12.

[54] See *Reports, op. cit.*

[55] *Reports, 1871, 1872.*

[56] *Reports, 1873, 1874.*

[57] N. B. Cloud, *Report for 1869*, p. 8.

[58] *Ibid.*, p. 9.

[59] *Ibid.*

[60] *Ibid.*

[61] *Ibid.*, p. 10.

[62] J. H. Hodgson, *Report for 1871*, p. 12.

[63] *Ibid.*, p. 41.

[64] *Ibid.*, p. 45.

[65] *Ibid.*, p. 59.

[66] *Report*, dated January 28, 1871. Hodgson was reporting for the fiscal year from October 1, 1869, to September 30, 1870. He had succeeded Cloud on November 25, 1870. The fact that the fiscal year was changed in the midst of Cloud's administration, and that Hodgson gave what report was made for the partial year from January 1, 1870, to September 30, 1870, may explain the utter confusion found in these reports.

[67] *Ibid.*, p. 21.

[68] *Ibid.*, p. 7.

[69] Joseph H. Speed, *Report for the Scholastic Year Ending September 30, 1873*, pp. 4-7.

[70] *Peabody Proceedings*, II, p. 109.

[71] J. H. Hodgson, *Report for 1871*, p. 7.

[72] *Ibid.*, pp. 86-88.

[73] The white teachers would have received $357,787, according to Hodgson's averages; the teachers of Negro schools, $102,207. Counting $39,000 in addition for county superintendents, we have a close approximation to the amount estimated to be apportioned.

[74] Weeks, *op. cit.*, p. 104, quoting from *State Reports of Speed*.

[75] *Ibid.*

[76] *Report for 1871*, p. 86.

[77] *Ibid.*, pp. 86-88.

[78] State Board of Education, *Annual Report, 1930*, pp. 258-59. (Montgomery: State Board of Education, 1930.)

[79] See attached "Teacher's Monthly Report." Others examined in Archives of the State of Alabama. (Montgomery, Alabama.)

[80] J. H. Hodgson, *Report for 1871*, p. viii.

[81] Joseph H. Speed, *Report for 1873*, p. 157.

[82] J. H. Hodgson, *Report for 1871*, p. 52. Special letter from M. H. Yerby, of Hale County.

[83] Weeks, *Public School Education in Alabama*, p. 89.

[84] Fleming, *op. cit.*, p. 624; Barnas Sears, in *Peabody Proceedings*, I, p. 408.

[85] Fleming, *op. cit.*, p. 631.

[86] *Ibid.*, p. 630.

[87] J. H. Hodgson, *op. cit.*, pp. 86-87. Italics mine.

[88] *State Report, 1875*, p. 179.

[89] *Ibid.*, p. 91.

[90] *Journal and Acts of the Board of Education, and Board of Regents, of the State of Alabama*, p. 106. (Montgomery: W. W. Screws, 1871.)

[91] *Ibid.*, p. 115.

[92] *Acts of the Board of Education, 1873*, p. 21. (Montgomery: Arthur Bingham, 1874.)

[93] *Acts of the Board of Education, 1871*, p. 104.

[94] Owens, *History of Alabama*, II, p. 1083.

[95] *Ibid.*; *Peabody Proceedings*, I, p. 310.

[96] *Op. cit.*, p. 54.

[97] J. H. Hodgson, *Report for 1871*, p. 20.

[98] *Ibid.*
[99] *Ibid.*, p. 53.
[100] *Ibid.*, p. 121.
[101] *Acts of the Board of Education, 1871,* pp. 117, 119.
[102] *Ibid.*
[103] *Acts of 1871,* p. 117.
[104] *Ibid.*
[105] *Acts of the Board of Education, 1872,* pp. 14-15.
[106] *Journal of the Board of Education, 1873,* p. 69; *Acts, 1873,* p. 19.
[107] Owens, *Op. cit.,* I, p. 4.
[108] *Acts of the Board of Education, 1873,* p. 122.
[109] *Journal of the Board of Education, 1871,* p. 15.
[110] *Ibid.*, p. 48.
[111] Owens, *op. cit.,* III.
[112] *Journal of the Board of Education, 1871,* p. 55.
[113] *Ibid.*, December 11.
[114] Fleming, *op. cit.,* p. 616.
[115] *Journal of the Board, 1871,* December 13.
[116] *Ibid.*
[117] *Ibid.*
[118] *Ibid.*
[119] *Ibid.*
[120] *Journal of the Board, 1873,* p. 75.
[121] *Ibid.*, p. 16.
[122] *Ibid.*, p. 53.
[123] *Acts of the Board of Education, 1873,* p. 16.
[124] *Journal of the Board of Education, 1873,* p. 69.
[125] *Acts of the Board of Education, 1873,* p. 19; Owens, *op. cit.,* I, p. 4.
[126] *Journal of the Board of Education, 1874,* pp. 48-49.
[127] *Ibid.*
[128] *Ibid.*, p. 49
[129] *Journal of the Board of Education, 1874,* pp. 37, 88.
[130] *Acts of the Board of Education,* p. 53.
[131] John M. McKleroy, *Annual Report, 1875,* pp. 122-23.
[132] *Ibid.*, p. 32.

## NOTES FOR CHAPTER VIII

[1] *Civil War and Reconstruction in Alabama,* p. 627.
[2] *Public Education in the South,* pp. 339, 377 f.
[3] Fleming, *op. cit.,* p. 626.
[4] *Ibid.*, p. 465.
[5] *Race Problems of the South; report of the Proceedings of the first annual Conference of the Southern Society for the promotion of the Study of race conditions and problems in the South,* pp. 105-113. (Richmond: B. F. Johnson Publ. Co., 1900.)
[6] Alderman and Gordon, *J. L. M. Curry, a Biography,* p. 201.
[7] B. F. Riley, *History of the Baptists in the Southern States East of the Mississippi.* (Philadelphia: American Baptist Publishing Society, 1898.)
[8] Fleming, *Civil War and Reconstruction,* pp. 456, 626, 627; Anson West, *Methodism in Alabama.* (Nashville: Southern Methodist Publishing Co., 1893.)
[9] Alvord, *Second Semi-Annual Report,* p. 6.
[10] Alderman and Gordon, *op. cit.,* p. 212.
[11] *Report of the Joint Committee on Reconstruction,* p. 28.
[12] *Report of the Joint Committee on Reconstruction,* 39th Congress, 1st Session, Report No. 30, Pt. III, p. 17. (Washington: Government Printing Office, 1866.)

[13] *Ibid.*

[14] Knight, *Education in the United States.*

[15] *Ku Klux Testimony, Alabama,* p. 238. Italics mine.

[16] *Ibid.*

[17] *Ibid.*

[18] *Ibid.*

[19] *Ibid.,* pp. 431, 450.

[20] *Ibid.,* p. 445.

[21] *Ku Klux Testimony, Alabama,* p. 446.

[22] Victoria V. Clayton, *White and Black under the Old Regime,* p. 166.

[23] *Ibid.,* p. 185.

[24] *Ibid.,* pp. 185-186.

[25] *Ku Klux Testimony, Alabama,* p. 1802.

[26] *Alabama State Report, 1871:* Report for Talladega County by Wm. L. Lewis, Supt., p. 78.

[27] *Alabama State Journal* (Montgomery), May 1, 1869. This was the same Saunders who testified before the Ku Klux Committee that he believed Negroes should be educated even as slaves, as education would make them better slaves.

[28] *The American Missionary,* November, 1865 (Editorial), Vol. IX, No. 11.

[29] *Ibid.* (Editorial), August, 1867, Vol. XI, No. 8.

[30] *Ibid.*

[31] *Ibid.*

[32] Beard, *op. cit.;* see p. 37, above.

[33] *Civil War and Reconstruction,* p. 627.

[34] *Vide Anti-Slavery Tracts.* New Series. No. 1, Correspondence between Lydia Maria Child and Gov. Wise, 1860. (New York: American Anti-Slavery Society, 1860.) Parker Pillsbury, *Acts of the anti-slavery apostles.* (Boston: Cupples, Upham & Co., 1884.)

[35] Lydia Maria (Frances) Child, *The Freedmen's Book,* p. vi. (Boston: Ticknor & Fields, 1865.)

[36] See Chaps. IV and V, above.

[37] Child, *op. cit.,* p. 263.

[38] The *American Missionary,* August, 1878, p. 243.

[39] See p. 113, above.

[40] *Vide Ku Klux Testimony, Alabama,* pp. 1042-43, 1047, 1087, 1114-15, 1117-18 ff.

[41] *Ibid.; Vide* evidence of Peter M. Dox, *re* William Luke; evidence of Ignatius Few, pp. 1080-84.

[42] Clayton, *White and Black under the Old Regime,* p. 170.

[43] Alvord, *Fourth Report,* p. 72.

[44] *Ibid.*

[45] The *Nationalist,* Mobile, Alabama, April 25, 1867.

[46] Alvord, *First Report,* p. 4.

[47] The *American Missionary,* Vol. XI, No. 9 (September, 1867), p. 205.

[48] Alvord, *Sixth Report,* p. 64.

[49] The *Alabama Journal* (Montgomery), June 12, 1869.

## NOTES FOR CHAPTER IX

[1] *War of the Rebellion Records,* Ser. I, Vol. XLIX, Pt. II, p. 728.

[2] David Augustus Straker, *The New South Investigated,* p. 87; (Detroit: By the Author, 1906.)

[3] *Ibid.,* p. 87; Somers, *The Southern States,* pp. 128 f; Nordhoff, *The Cotton States,* p. 21.

[4] *House Report No. 262,* 43rd Congress, 2nd Session, p. 529.

[5] *Op. cit.,* p. 129.

[6] *House Report No. 262, op. cit.,* p. 529.

[7] Straker, *op. cit.,* p. 87.

[8] *The New South, A Chronicle of Social and Industrial Evolution,* p. 64. (New Haven: The Yale University Press, 1919.)

[9] William H. Skaggs, *The Southern Oligarchy,* pp. 234-35.

[10] Mack Buckley Swearingen, "The Penetration of the South by Northern Capital During Reconstruction." Unpublished Master's thesis, University of Chicago, 1923. For description of Southern Banking, see Emory Q. Hawk, *Economic History of the South,* pp. 530-39. (New York: Prentice-Hall, 1934.)

[11] John B. Clark, *Populism in Alabama,* pp. 32-33. (New York: Columbia University Press, 1928.)

[12] Skaggs, *The Southern Oligarchy,* p. 270.

[13] Rupert P. Vance, *Human Factors in Cotton Culture,* pp. 6-10. (Chapel Hill, University of North Carolina Press, 1929.)

[14] Owens, *History of Alabama,* I, p. 584.

[15] Eugene Allen Smith, "*Cotton Production* in Alabama," *Report on Cotton Culture,* p. 62. Tenth Census, Vol. V, Part II.

[16] Smith, *Ibid.;* Somers, *The Southern States,* p. 117; Owens, *History of Alabama,* I, p. 408; Hollender, *Culture in the South,* pp. 424 f.; *Ku Klux Conspiracy, Alabama Testimony,* pp. 159-225.

[17] *Ku Klux Conspiracy, Alabama Testimony,* p. 207.

[18] Hollender, *op. cit.,* pp. 424 f.

[19] Smith, *Report on Cotton Culture,* pp. 62-63.

[20] *Ibid.*

[21] Armes, *The Story of Coal and Iron in Alabama,* pp. 370-71.

[22] Boyd, *Alabama in the Fifties,* p. 25.

[23] Bureau of the Census: *Negroes in the United States, 1790-1915,* p. 59. Bulletin 129. (Washington: Government Printing Office, 1918.)

[24] Owens, *History of Alabama,* I, p. 647.

[25] *Ibid.,* I, p. 283.

[26] Armes, *op. cit.,* p. 158.

[27] See Chapter IV, above.

[28] John W. Dubose, *The Mineral Wealth of Alabama and Birmingham Illustrated,* p. 164. (Birmingham: N. T. Greene & Co., 1886.)

[29] *Ibid.*

[30] *Ibid.,* pp. 75 ff.

[31] B. F. Riley, *Alabama As It Is, or, The Immigrant's and Capitalist's Guide Book to Alabama,* pp. 13, 31. (Montgomery: W. C. Holt, 1887.)

[32] *Ibid.,* p. 62.

[33] *Ibid.,* p. 68.

[34] Owens, *History of Alabama,* I, p. 412.

[35] Broadus and George Sinclair Mitchell, *Industrial Revolution in the South.* (Baltimore: The Johns Hopkins University Press, 1930.)

[36] Tuscumbia *Weekly Dispatch,* February 18, 1890.

[37] *Ibid.,* March 25, 1890. The principal textile area in Alabama, however, developed not in the Tennessee Valley, but along the Georgia-Alabama State line.

[38] Jack, *Sectionalism and Party Politics in Alabama,* Chapter 2.

[39] Clark, *Populism in Alabama,* p. 172.

[40] Henry Edwin Tremain, *Sectionalism Unmasked,* p. 130. (New York: Bonnell, Silver & Co., 1907.)

[41] Clark, *op. cit.,* pp. 101-102.

[42] *Ibid.,* p. 24.

[43] Fleming, *Civil War and Reconstruction,* pp. 782-95.

[44] Armes, *The Story of Coal and Iron in Alabama,* p. 245; Chapter IV, above.

[45] Owens, *History of Alabama,* III, p. 357; Chapter IV, above.

[46] Clark, *op. cit.,* p. 26.

[47] *Ibid.*

[48] Clark, *Populism in Alabama, passim;* Owens, *History of Alabama,* I, pp. 566 ff.

[49] Owens, *History of Alabama,* I, p. 666.

[50] Sterling D. Spero and Abram Harris, *The Black Worker,* p. 42. (New York: The Columbia University Press, 1932.)

[51] Clark, *op. cit.,* p. 89.

[52] *Ibid.,* p. 91.

[53] *Ibid.,* p. 89.

[54] *Ibid.,* p. 63.

[55] The *Montgomery Advertiser,* August 16, 1890.

[56] Clark, *op. cit.,* pp. 156 ff.

[57] *Ibid.,* p. 156.

[58] Tremain, *Sectionalism Unmasked,* p. 70. Tremain quotes J. C. Manning, Populist leader.

[59] Clark, *op. cit.,* p. 180.

[60] *Ibid.,* p. 176.

[61] Joel Riggs, *Report of the Comptroller of Public Accounts of the State of Alabama,* November 1, 1851, to September 30, 1852, p. 187. (Montgomery: Brittan & Blue, 1853.)

[62] *Ibid.,* pp. 64 f.

[63] R. M. Reynolds, *Report of the Auditor of the State of Alabama,* Year ending September 30, 1871, pp. 104 f. (Montgomery: W. W. Screws, 1871.)

[64] *Ibid., passim.*

[65] Willis Brewer, *Report of the Auditor of the State of Alabama* for the year ending September 30, 1880, *passim.* (Montgomery: Allred & Beers, 1881.)

[66] Cyrus D. Hogue, *Report of the Auditor of the State of Alabama* for the year ending September 30, 1890, *passim.* (Montgomery: Smith, Allred & Co., 1891.)

## NOTES FOR CHAPTER X

[1] See Chap. IX, above.

[2] See Chap. VII, above.

[3] John McKleroy, *State Report for 1875,* p. 41.

[4] *Peabody Proceedings,* II, p. 109.

[5] Clark, *Populism in Alabama,* p. 25.

[6] Owens, *History of Alabama,* I, p. 521.

[7] *Ibid.,* p. 564.

[8] Clark, *Populism in Alabama,* p. 67.

[9] *Ibid.,* p. 59; Owens, *op. cit.,* I, p. 667.

[10] *History of Education in Alabama,* p. 122.

[11] John O Turner, *Special Acts of Public School Laws of the State of Alabama,* p. 3. (Montgomery: Brown Printing Co., 1897.)

[12] *Ibid.,* pp. 3-4.

[13] *Ibid.,* pp. 43-47.

[14] *Ibid.,* p. 44.

[15] *Ibid.,* pp. 69-75.

[16] *Ibid.,* pp. 73-74.

[17] Solomon Palmer, *Thirty-Third Annual Report of the Superintendent of Education,* pp. 14-15. (Montgomery: W. D. Brown & Co., 1887.)

[18] *Journal of the House of Representatives of the General Assembly of the State of Alabama,* Session of 1890-1891, p. 33. (Montgomery: Smith, Allred & Co., 1891.)

[19] The Montgomery *Advertiser,* July 1, 1876.

[20] August 12, 1876.

[21] August 16, 1876.

[22] August 15, 1876.

[23] August 10, 1876.

[24] The Montgomery *Advertiser*, August 15, 1876.

[25] *Ibid.*

[26] *Ibid.*, April 29, 1877.

[27] *Acts of the General Assembly of Alabama*, passed at the session of 1874-1875, p. 61. (Montgomery: W. W. Screws, 1875.)

[28] Emmett J. Scott and Lyman B. Stowe, *Booker T. Washington, Builder of Civilization*, p. 3. (New York: Doubleday, Doran & Co., 1926.)

[29] *House Report No. 262*, 43rd Congress, 2nd Session, *Affairs in Alabama*, p. 113.

[30] Scott and Stowe, *op. cit.*, pp. 3-4.

[31] August 12, 1892.

[32] The Montgomery *Advertiser*, December 1-2, 1892.

[33] *Ibid.*, December 2, 1892.

[34] *Ibid.*

[35] *Ibid.*, April 2, 1891.

[36] Spero and Harris, *The Black Worker*, p. 137.

[37] *Ibid.*

[38] The Montgomery *Advertiser*, June 10, 1892.

[39] W. H. Skaggs, *The Southern Oligarchy*, p. 113.

[40] It is significant here that Senator Morgan took for granted that the children would be utilized in making the crop. The tenant system of contracts was based on the tenant's labor force, which included not only the male head of the family and his wife, but also all of the children. The more children that a tenant might have, the more land he could obtain from a landlord. Any schooling which interferes with the work of these children in raising the crop is frequently looked upon, even today, as a betrayal of the terms of the contract, so far as the landlord is concerned.

[41] John Tyler Morgan, *Common School Education*, p. 794. Speech in the Senate of the United States, January 30, 1888. Issued as separate, from *Congressional Record*. (Washington: Government Printing Office, 1888.)

[42] J. L. M. Curry, Speech before General Assembly of Alabama, reported in the Montgomery *Advertiser*, February 2, 1889.

[43] H. Paul Douglass, *Christian Reconstruction in the South*, pp. 122-23. Boston: Pilgrim Press, 1909.

[44] The Montgomery *Advertiser*, February 6, 1885.

[45] *Ibid.*, February 2, 1889.

[46] *Ibid.*, June 28, 1885.

[47] Broadus Mitchell, "Growth of Manufacturing in the South," *Industry in the South*, p. 24. Annals of the American Academy of Political and Social Science, Vol. 153, 1931. (Philadelphia: The American Academy of Political and Social Science, 1931.)

[48] Spero and Harris, *The Black Worker*, p. 354.

[49] *Ibid.*, p. 286.

[50] *Ibid.*, pp. 214-15.

[51] *Ibid.*

[52] *Ibid.*, p. 245.

[53] Owens, *History of Alabama*, II, p. 1308

[54] John W. Dubose, *The Mineral Wealth of Alabama*, p. 109. Italics mine.

[55] *Ibid.*, p. 113.

[56] *Ibid.*, p. 129.

[57] *Ibid.*

[58] Alabama Industrial Board, *Report*, p. 80.

[59] *Alabama Commercial Association, 1900 Meeting*, p. 52 f. Department of Agriculture. (Montgomery: The Brown Printing Co., 1900.)

[60] August 1, 1900.

[61] William Archer, *Through Afro-America*, pp. 128-29. (New York: E. P. Dutton & Co., 1910.)

## NOTES FOR CHAPTER XI

[1] Thorpe, *Federal and State Constitutions,* pp. 176-177.

[2] *Ibid.*

[3] Leroy F. Box, *Laws Relating to the Public School System of Alabama,* p. 23. (Montgomery: Barrett & Brown, 1878.)

[4] Thorpe, *op. cit.,* part XIII, Sec. 1, p. 176.

[5] Box, *op. cit.,* pp. 16-17

[6] *Ibid.,* Italics mine.

[7] *Acts of 1874-1875,* p. 61.

[8] John McKleroy, *Report of the Superintendent of Education,* September 30, 1876, p. 10. (Montgomery: W. W. Screws, 1876.)

[9] Leroy F. Box, *op. cit.,* pp. x-xi

[10] *Ibid.*

[11] Thorpe, *op. cit.,* Sec. 8, p. 177.

[12] *Civil War and Reconstruction,* p. 634.

[13] The Montgomery *Advertiser,* September 2, 1877.

[14] *Ibid.*

[15] *Ibid.*

[16] H. Clay Armstrong, *Report of the Superintendent of Education* for the year ending September 30, 1882, p. 6. (Montgomery: W. D. Brown & Co., 1882.)

[17] Solomon Palmer, *Thirty-Third Annual Report,* p. 15.

[18] John O. Turner, *Special Acts of School Laws,* pp. 69-75.

[19] H. Clay Armstrong, *Report of the Superintendent of Education* for the year ending September 30, 1884, p. 10. (Montgomery: Barrett & Co., 1884.)

[20] Solomon Palmer, *Thirty-First Annual Report of the Superintendent of Education for the State of Alabama,* September 30, 1885, p. 12. (Montgomery: Barrett & Co., 1885.)

[21] *Ibid.,* p. 14.

[22] Solomon Palmer, *Thirty-Third Annual Report,* p. 9.

[23] *Ibid.,* p. 145.

[24] Solomon Palmer, *Thirty-Fourth Annual Report of the Superintendent of Education,* year ending September 30, 1888, p. 9. (Montgomery: W. D. Brown & Co., 1888.)

[25] See Chapter IX, above.

[26] *Ibid.*

[27] July 14, 1888.

[28] July 15, 1888.

[29] July 17, 1888.

[30] *Ibid.*

[31] *Ibid.*

[32] The Athens *Courier,* December 1, 1888.

[33] While 57.1 per cent of Clarke County's population in 1890 was Negro, making it a Black Belt county, the choice of McLeod to present the motion to increase was evidently strategy, motivated by the white counties.

[34] Percentage Negro in 1890, 76.9 per cent.

[35] The Montgomery *Advertiser,* December 4, 1888.

[36] Percentage Negro in 1890, 9.6 per cent. Located in the Southeastern "white belt."

[37] The Montgomery *Advertiser,* December 4, 1888.

[38] Percentage Negro in 1890, 29.9 per cent. Located in the Tennessee Valley.

[39] The Montgomery *Advertiser,* December 4, 1888.

[40] Percentage Negro in 1890, 34.3 per cent. Located in North Central Alabama.

[41] The Montgomery *Advertiser,* December 4, 1888.

[42] Percentage Negro in 1890, 38.3 per cent. Located in the Tennessee Valley.

[43] The Montgomery *Advertiser*, December 4, 1888.

[44] Percentage Negro in 1890, 36.3 per cent. Located in the Mineral District.

[45] The Montgomery *Advertiser*, December 4, 1888.

[46] *Journal of the House, General Assembly of Alabama*, Session from November 13, 1888, to February 28, 1889. (Montgomery: Brown Printing Co., 1889.)

[47] The Montgomery *Advertiser*, December 4, 1888.

[48] *Ibid.*, December 5, 1888; *Journal of the House, op. cit.*

[49] December 4, 1888.

[50] The Montgomery *Advertiser*, December 5, 1888.

[51] The Montgomery *Advertiser*, December 5, 1888. See, especially, speech of Mr. Benners, of Hale County.

[52] Solomon Palmer, *Thirty-Sixth Report of the Superintendent of Education* for the year ending September 30, 1890, pp. 3-5. (Montgomery: Brown Printing Co., 1890.)

[53] Cyrus D. Hogue, *Report of the Auditor of Alabama*, p. iv. (Montgomery: Brown Printing Co., 1890.)

[54] *Thirty-Sixth Report*, p. 8.

[55] *Ibid.*, p. 14.

[56] *Ibid.*, p. 15.

[57] *Ibid.*, p. 15.

[58] *Ibid.*

[59] *Ibid.*

[60] *Ibid.*

[61] The Montgomery *Advertiser*, February 3, 1891.

[62] *Ibid.*

[63] *Ibid.*, February 4, 1891.

[64] *Ibid.*

[65] *Ibid.*

[66] *Ibid.*

[67] See Chapters IV, XV.

[68] The Montgomery *Advertiser*, February 4, 1891.

[69] *Ibid.*, February 6, 1891.

[70] *Ibid.*, February 8, 1891.

[71] *Ibid.*, February 10, 1891.

[72] *Ibid.*

[73] *Ibid.*

[74] *Ibid.*

[75] *Ibid.*

[76] *Ibid.*

[77] Box, *Laws Relating to the Public School System*, p. 23. Italics mine.

[78] *Acts of the General Assembly of Alabama*, passed at the Session of 1890-1891, p. 554. (Montgomery: Allred & Co., 1891.) Italics mine.

[79] John G. Harris, *Thirty-Seventh Annual Report of the Superintendent of Education*, September 30, 1891. pp. 195-96.

[80] *Ibid.*, p. 196.

[81] Harris, *Thirty-Seventh Report*, p. 190. Italics mine.

[82] Harris, *Thirty-Eighth Report of the Superintendent of Education*, September 30, 1892. (Montgomery: Smith, Allred & Co., 1892.)

[83] Harris, *Thirty-Seventh Report*, p. 44. Italics mine.

[84] Isaac W. Hill, *Biennial Report of the Department of Education of the State of Alabama* for the scholastic years ending September 30, 1905, and 1906, p. 4. (Montgomery: Brown Printing Co., 1907.)

## NOTES FOR CHAPTER XII

[1] Miller, *History of Alabama*, p. 301.

[2] Skaggs, *The Southern Oligarchy*, p. 132.

[3] Pat McGauley, Official Stenographer, *Proceedings of the Constitutional Convention of Alabama of 1901*. Montgomery: The Montgomery *Advertiser*, 1901. Published as supplements to the *Advertiser*; later reprinted and issued, unbound. The pages are unnumbered.

[4] Benjamin Griffith Brawley, *A Social History of the American Negro*. (New York: Macmillan Co., 1921.)

[5] Skaggs, *The Southern Oligarchy*, p. 143.

[6] Gilbert T. Stephenson, *Race Distinctions in American Law*. (New York: D. Appleton & Co., 1910.)

[7] Southern Commission on the Study of Lynching, *Lynchings and What They Mean*, p. 73. Atlanta: Published by the Commission (n. d., *circa* 1932.)

[8] Owens, *History of Alabama*, II, p. 917.

[9] The Montgomery *Advertiser; passim;* the Sheffield *Standard;* June 22, 1901, April 28, 1894, *passim.*

[10] *Proceedings of the Convention*, 4th day.

[11] *Ibid.*, 12th day.

[12] *Civil War and Reconstruction*, pp. 800-801.

[13] Scroggs, "The New Alabama," *The South in the Building of the Nation*, p. 322.

[14] *The Southern Oligarchy*, p. 131.

[15] *Proceedings*, 79th day, speech of Mr. Freeman.

[16] *Ibid.*, 74th day.

[17] *Ibid.*, 81st day.

[18] *Ibid.*, 74th and 79th days, for typical speeches.

[19] *Ibid.*, 74th day.

[20] *Ibid.*, 7th day.

[21] *Ibid.*

[22] *Ibid.*

[23] *Ibid.*, 14th day.

[24] *Ibid.*, 43rd day.

[25] *Ibid.*

[26] *Ibid.*, 52nd day.

[27] *Proceedings*, 7th day.

[28] *Ibid.*, 53rd day.

[29] *Ibid.*

[30] *Ibid.*

[31] *Ibid.*

[32] *Ibid.*, 52nd day.

[33] *Ibid.*, 54th day.

[34] *Ibid.*, 52nd day.

[35] *Ibid.*

[36] Miller, *History of Alabama*, p. 301.

[37] *Proceedings*, 54th day.

[38] *Ibid.*, 53rd day.

[39] *Ibid.*

[40] *Ibid.*, 54th day.

[41] This speech is notable because it contains in brief compass many of the stereotypes characteristic of the new definition of the Negro status. Oates (Proceedings, 53rd day) had referred to the fact that Negroes were a valuable labor force in the Black Belt. He had given, as an example, the fact that all of the Negro linemen employed by telegraph companies in Montgomery were Negroes. Heflin's obvious disgust at the spectacle of the Negro in such a position reflects the force of economic competition between white and black laborers which, probably, was basic in the changed opinion referred to by Oates, and constantly exploited by Heflin. In other words, Heflin was exploiting this economic jealousy for political purposes; and, in so doing, he was intensifying it. In this lay the difference between the Populists and the Democratic insurgents. The Populists had a real program of basic economic reform; the insurgents turned economic dissatisfaction into racial antipathy,

and used the end result for their own peculiar purposes. On the other hand, the ''Oligarchy'' regarded the Negro as a basic economic asset. Holtzclaw's petition (*Proceedings*, 43rd day) was an ingenuous recognition of this fact, and an appeal to the agricultural and industrial ''Oligarchy'' intended to emphasize the Negro's willingness to be exploited by the employers if they were favored, in such exploitation, over their economic rivals, the poorer whites. This tacit willingness to co-operate with the employers, to the disadvantage of white workmen, must have increased the antipathy of white workmen generally to Negroes and to Negro leaders.

[42] *Proceedings*, 54th day. This is a good document in illustrating the manner in which men like Heflin attained political power by turning the Populistic discontent against the basic economic structure into antipathy toward Negroes. The Negroes in the meantime allied themselves with the employing classes (at least, Negro leaders attempted such an alliance). To some degree this procedure accentuated the hatred which the white working people might have felt for the Negroes. It was much like the pattern of slavery repeating itself; the poorer white people, with no slaves, hating the institution of chattel slavery, hating the white people and the Negroes identifying themselves, so far as was possible, with the dominant economic interests that promised to afford some protection and patronage, while exploiting Negro labor for its own selfish purposes, and to the detriment of white labor.

[43] *Proceedings*, 39th day. Cunningham was an employee of the Pratt Mines, one of the Sloss enterprises (Inspectors of Convicts, *First Biennial Report to the Governor*, pp. 240-49. Montgomery: Barrett & Co., 1885.) He was also physician to the Alabama Shipbuilding Company, which had been financed partially by the Louisville and Nashville Railroad in 1899 at the instance of J. P. Morgan and O. H. P. Belmont (Armes, *The Story of Coal and Iron*, pp. 430, 465). In 1906 Cunningham was the unsuccessful candidate for Governor against Braxton Bragg Comer (Owens, *op. cit.*, III, pp. 444-45). Comer, who inaugurated a violent ''anti-railroad'' campaign which was partially defeated by ex-Governor Jones's injunctions (Scroggs, ''The New Alabama,'' *The South in the Building of the Nation*, p. 324), as Federal Judge, had himself been a convict lessor (Inspectors of Convicts, *First Biennial Report*, p. 79) in the days when the ''native'' capitalists—Sloss, De Bardeleben, and others—were controlling the political machinery of the State.

[44] *Proceedings*, 39th day.
[45] *Ibid.*, 35th day.
[46] *Ibid.*, 35th day.
[47] *Ibid.*
[48] *Ibid.*
[49] *Ibid.*
[50] *Ibid.*
[51] In his autobiography, *Up From Slavery*, Washington states that his only knowledge of his father was that he was a white man (p. 3).
[52] *Proceedings*, 74th day.
[53] *Ibid.*, 79th day.
[54] *Ibid.*

## NOTES FOR CHAPTER XIII

[1] *Proceedings*, 32nd day.
[2] *Ibid.*, 2nd day. This argument was popular with all factions.
[3] It is impossible to escape the conviction that the majority of the delegates believed that disfranchisement of Negroes would be a much more difficult task than it actually proved to be. Coupled with this was an exaggerated notion as to the degree to which Negroes were then sharing in the educational facilities of the State. As the *State Reports* had discontinued the printing of expenditures by race in 1891, it is probable that while the delegates from the white counties knew that discrimination was being practiced in the ap-

portionment of the school fund, they had no idea of the extremity to which the apportionment had proceeded in the Black Belt counties. The length to which the debates and plans went in seeking a way to discriminate, together with the acquiescence of the white counties in proposed plans *to make discrimination possible*, makes it obvious that this was so. Else, the white counties would certainly have been less agreeable in the proposed plans for distributing the school fund.

[4] *Proceedings*, 2nd day.

[5] *Ibid.*

[6] *Ibid.*, 32nd day. The income from Corporation and license taxes was growing rapidly, but no one anticipated that these sources of revenue would, in the future, outweigh in importance the property taxes as the principal dependence of the State in seeking new revenue.

[7] *Proceedings*, 32nd day.

[8] *Ibid.*

[9] This proposal meant that voters should be counted by the value of the property owned by the voter: i.e., a voter with $10,000 worth of property would have his vote count for ten times as much as the man worth $1,000.

[10] *Proceedings*, 35th day.

[11] Like the State, almost every county had its ''Black Belt'' and ''White Belt.'' The census figures report the population of minor civil districts, smaller than the county unit, by race only for the 1870 and 1930 census. These reports show the concentration of Negroes within counties on the fertile lowlands, with the whites principally located on the uplands, as characteristic of the State at large.

[12] *Proceedings*, 35th day, 72nd day.

[13] Stuart Grayson Noble, *Forty Years of the Public Schools in Mississippi.* (New York: Columbia University Press, 1918.)

[14] *Ibid.*, 8th day.

[15] *Proceedings*, 8th day, for Ordinance by Mr. Samford; 10th day, for Ordinance by Mr. Bethune, of Bullock County; 11th day, for Ordinance by Mr. Jones, of Wilcox County.

[16] *Proceedings*, 8th day.

[17] *Ibid.*

[18] *Ibid.*, 37th day.

[19] *Ibid.*

[20] *Ibid.*

[21] In the Brookings Institution study (*Taxation of the State Government of Alabama*, p. 78. Montgomery: Wilson Printing Co., 1932) the income for the State from ad valorem taxes is estimated at $7,633,000. As corporation property amounted to approximately one-fourth of this payment, the application of Mr. Ashcraft's proposal would probably in practice (if faithfully adhered to) have given to Negro schools from state, county, and district taxes, from this one source alone, more money than was spent on the public education of the Negro in 1930. Total expenditures in that year were $2,165,000, with Negroes representing 38.5 per cent of the population of the State.

[22] *Proceedings*, 37th day.

[23] *Ibid.*

[24] *Proceedings, op. cit.*, 43rd day.

[25] *Ibid.*

[26] *Ibid.*

[27] *Ibid.* Italics mine, referring to changes from old Constitution.

[28] *Ibid.*

[29] *Ibid.*

[30] *Ibid.*

[31] *Proceedings*, 43rd day.

[32] *Ibid.*

[33] The Minority was arguing that the general apportionment should be open to both races, the local tax according to the taxes paid.

[84] Probably a weak argument to show that the intention of the section was not discriminatory.

[35] The Minority report here introduced the stereotype of ''rape'' as a stratagem to gain additional flavor for their appeal.

[36] *Proceedings*, 43rd day.

[37] The Minority arguments from court decisions were quite *naive*, as the lawyers on the Majority side of the Committee easily showed.

[38] *Proceedings*, 43rd day.

[39] *Ibid.*, 71st day.

[40] See pp. 239 ff., above.

[41] *Proceedings*, 71st day.

[42] *Ibid.*, 72nd day.

[43] *Ibid.*

[44] *Ibid.*

[45] *Ibid.*, 8th day.

[46] *Ibid.*, 72nd day.

[47] In subsequent debate Mr. Ashcraft said that the ''1/4'' was a misprint, and that all he asked for was 1 mill. This shows the general carelessness with which the Minority Report was attended.

[48] *Proceedings*, 72nd day.

[49] *Ibid.*

[50] *Ibid.*

[51] *Ibid.*

[52] *Ibid.*

[53] *Ibid.*

[54] *Ibid.*

[55] *Ibid.*

[56] *Ibid.*

[57] *Ibid.*

[58] *Ibid.*

[59] *Ibid.*

[60] *Ibid.*

[61] *Ibid.* Because of the wealth of shibboleths and stereotypes in which Mr. Heflin's speeches abound, they are, precisely for that reason, all the more valuable documents for our purpose. It is interesting to observe that a denial of Negro ability to learn and progress was, at the same time, coupled with a fear that he *was* learning and advancing.

[62] *Proceedings*, 72nd day.

[63] *Ibid.*

[64] *Ibid.* The appeal of Jones to the ''nobler'' impulses of the dominant white men was a typical class argument for the education of Negroes, used by J. L. M. Curry, Booker T. Washington, W. H. Councill, and other white and Negro advocates. So was that of Heflin, the difference being in the economic classes among whites to which the two groups appealed.

[65] *Proceedings*, 72nd day.

[66] *Ibid.* Striking here is the similarity of this argument for the education of Negroes, given in 1901, in spirit and terminology to that given in 1865-1868 in Alabama by Clanton, Curry, and others.

[67] Edgar W. Knight, *Education in the United States*, pp. 474 ff. (Boston: Ginn & Company, 1929.)

[68] John W. Abercrombie, *Annual Report for the Scholastic Year Ending September 30, 1922*, p. 85. (Montgomery: Brown Printing Company, n. d. (1922?).

### Summary B

1. IF ALABAMA IS TO GIVE HER *WHITE* CHILDREN EDUCATIONAL OPPORTUNITIES EQUAL TO THE AVERAGE MAINTAINED THROUGHOUT THE UNITED STATES IN 1930

[69] Spright Dowell, *Annual Report for the Scholastic Year ending September 30, 1919*, p. 1741. (Montgomery: Brown Printing Company, n.d.) (1920?.)

[70] The Brookings Institution, Institute for Governmental Research, *Taxation of the State Government of Alabama*, p. 47. Report on a Survey submitted to Governor B. M. Miller. In Five Volumes. Volume 4, Part 3. (Montgomery: Wilson Printing Company, n.d.) (1932.?)

[71] *Ibid.*, p. 44.

[72] *Ibid.*, p. 52.

[73] Fleming, *Civil War and Reconstruction*, Appendix 11; Levinson, *Race, Class and Party in America*, pp. 44, 110, Appendix.

[74] Levinson, *op. cit.*, Appendix.

[75] *Ibid.*, p. 110. "Even the suspicion of friendliness towards Negroes, involving no 'use' of their votes, could be turned against a candidate. This was most amusingly demonstrated in Birmingham. In 1925, the two chief contenders for the city's highest office were J. M. Jones and W. J. Adams. The campaign was warmly fought, and towards election day, Adams' headquarters charged the Jones people with 'spreading various malicious and ridiculous reports over the city in an undercover appeal to prejudice.' Among them was the charge that if Adams was elected he would appoint fifty Negro policemen. Adams was defeated. Four years later the same two men contested for the same office. This time the Adams people got in first with the 'nigger lover' charge. Jones, it was claimed had during his term of office actually appointed four Negro policemen. He was 'forcing social equality' by establishing one man street cars, on which both races must use the same door. But alas! Adams was defeated again. He was a Roman Catholic."

## NOTES FOR CHAPTER XIV

[1] Booker T. Washington, *Up From Slavery, An Autobiography*, p. 1. (New York: Doubleday, Page and Company, 1901.)

[2] *Ibid.*

[3] *Ibid.*, pp. 45-47.

[4] *Ibid.*, pp. 73, 87, 94.

[5] *Ibid.*, p. 107; Emmett J. Scott and Lyman B. Stowe, *Booker T. Washington, Builder of Civilization*, p. 1. (New York: Doubleday, Doran and Co., 1926.)

[6] *Ibid.*, p. 111.

[7] Edith Armstrong Talbot, *Samuel Chapman Armstrong, a biographical study*, passim. (New York: Doubleday, Page and Company, 1901.)

[8] Samuel Chapman Armstrong, *Twenty Two Years' Work of Hampton Institute*, p. 1. (Hampton: Normal School Press, 1893.)

[9] *Ibid.*, p. 2.

[10] Armstrong, *op. cit.*, p. 2.

[11] *Op. cit.*, p. 107.

[12] In *Up From Slavery*, p. 259, Washington says of Emmett J. Scott, ". . . . my faithful secretary, who handles the bulk of my correspondence and keeps me in daily touch with the life of the school, and who also keeps me informed of whatever takes place in the South that concerns the race. I owe more to his tact, wisdom and hard work than I can describe."

[13] Scott and Stowe, *op. cit.*, p. 1.

[14] John O. Turner, *Special Acts of Public Schools Laws of the State of Alabama*. (Montgomery: The Brown Printing Co., 1897.)

[15] *Up From Slavery*, p. 119.

[16] Department of Superintendence, National Education Association, Eleventh Yearbook. *Educational Leadership*, Insert bet. pp. 270-271. (Washington: Department of Superintendence of the National Education Association, 1933.)

[17] Edwin Anderson Alderman and Armistead Churchill Gordon, *J. L. M. Curry, A Biography*, p. 3. (New York: The Macmillan Company, 1911.)

[18] *Ibid.*, pp. 26-27.

[19] *Ibid.*, p. 26.

[20] *Ibid.*, pp. 29-30.

[21] *Ibid.*, p. 59.

[22] *Ibid.*, p. 61.

[23] *Ibid.*, p. 66.

[24] *Ibid.*, p. 74.

[25] *Ibid.*, p. 75.

[26] *Ibid.*, p. 82.

[27] *Ibid.*, p. 76.

[28] *Ibid.*

[29] *Ibid.*, p. 106.

[30] *Ibid.*, pp. 105, 108. This was the Sloss Railroad, which, with George Houston, Sloss, and Pryor as directing agents, consolidated with the Louisville and Nashville R. R. in 1868, and played so prominent a part in Reconstruction politics.

[31] *Ibid.*, p. 151.

[32] *Ibid.*, p. 201.

[33] *Ibid.*, pp. 153-193.

[34] *Ibid.*, p. 249.

[35] Washington, *Up from Slavery*, p. 193.

[36] Alderman and Gordon, *op. cit.*, p. 456.

[37] Washington, *Up From Slavery*, p. 193.

[38] Booker T. Washington, *My Larger Education, Being Chapters from My Experiences*, pp. 57-38. (New York: Doubleday, Page and Company, 1911.) *Up from Slavery*, pp. 194-195, 247, 305.

[39] *Proceedings of the Trustees of the Peabody Education Fund*, III, pp. 136, 162; IV, p. 268. (Boston: John Wilson and Co., 1875.)

[40] *My Larger Education*, p. 58. This testimony is not to be found in any other published literature on Curry. Both he and his biographers emphasize the fact that he was, from the very end of the Civil War, heartily in favor of the education of Negroes. Alderman and Gordon, *J. L. M. Curry*, state: "Curry was, from the moment of the fall of the Confederacy, occupied in mind and heart with the probable future of their people. On May 15, 1866, he had a conference at Marion . . . . with reference to the education of the freedmen of the town." (p. 301.) "Curry first appeared as a friend of negro education in the summer of 1865 (sic), when he presided over a mass meeting in Marion which made provision for negro schools." (p. 424.) In the same volume, Curry is quoted as saying, "it may be pardonable vanity to record the fact that in Marion, Alabama, in 1866, aided by Gov. Moore and Messrs. McIntosh and Raymond, the pastors of the Baptist and Presbyterian churches, a meeting was called which passed resolutions, prepared and introduced by myself, favoring the education of the colored people *by the white people of the South*." (p. 334; italics mine.)

Washington could have been mistaken; or he might have left out part of the story; or Curry may not have told all of the story to him. If Washington was accurate in reporting this conversation, Curry's qualification that his early efforts favored "the education of the colored people *by the white people of the South*" becomes intelligible, as does his reference to the changed attitude experienced after visiting several Negro schools. For the only Negro schools in Marion at that period (1866) were supported by "Northerners," i.e., the American Missionary Association and the Freedmen's Bureau. It would also confirm the opinion of Buckley, that the support of the movement to educate Negroes in Alabama just after the Civil War, on the part of the Southern whites, was prompted by "an appeal to sectional and sectarian prejudice, lest (the work being inevitable) the influence which must come from it be realized by others." (*Third semi-annual Report, Schools for Freedmen*, p. 16.)

[41] Alderman and Gordon, *op. cit.*, pp. 456-457.
[42] *Ibid.*
[43] J. L. M. Curry, "Limitations of Taxation," *The Baptist Quarterly Review*, issues of April, May, June; pp. 155-166. (Cincinnati: Published by J. H. Barnes, 1884.)
[44] *Ibid.*, p. 158.
[45] *Ibid.*, p. 159. In the Brookings Institution *Survey of Taxation in Alabama* (Vol. 4, Part 3, pp. 42-56, Montgomery: The Wilson Printing Co., 1932), identical sentiments are quoted from certain Alabama men of public life. The *Survey* editors make this comment: "It is a sad commentary on representative government if the claim is justified that the representatives of the people are arbitrary in their enactments and cannot be trusted to translate into law the will of the majority. It is doubtful, however, that this sentiment rests wholly upon such a questionable base. It is more likely that it runs much deeper and involves a distrust of democracy itself." *Ibid.*, pp. 41-42.
[46] J. L. M. Curry, "Limitations on Taxation," p. 165.
[47] *Ibid.*
[48] *Ibid.*, p. 159.
[49] *Peabody Proceedings*, III, p. 268.
[50] Alderman and Gordon, *op. cit.*, p. 426.
[51] *Ibid.*
[52] *Ibid.*
[53] Alderman and Gordon, *op. cit.*, p. 336.
[54] *Address before General Assembly of Alabama*, reported in the Montgomery *Advertiser*, February 2, 1889.
[55] *Address* before Montgomery Conference on Race Problems, p. 108.
[56] *Address* before General Assembly, reported in the Montgomery *Advertiser*, December 23, 1900.
[57] *Address* before General Assembly, reported in the Montgomery *Advertiser*, February 2, 1889.
[58] *Ibid.*
[59] *Ibid.*
[60] *Report of the United States Commissioner of Education for 1894-1895*, p. 1277.
[61] Stephen B. Weeks, *Public School Education in Alabama*, p. 129. (U. S. Bureau of Education, 1915, Bulletin No. 12.) (Washington: Government Printing Office, 1915.)
[62] *Report of the U. S. Commissioner of Education, 1884-1895*, p. 1277.
[63] Weeks, *op. cit.*, p. 130.
[64] William J. Simmons, *Men of Mark*, pp. 390-393. (Cleveland: George M. Revell and Co., 1887.)
[65] John Temple Graves, "The Problem of the Races," in C. E. Donivan, John Temple Graves, Henry W. Grady, et al., *The Possibilities of the Negro in Symposium*, p. 17. (Atlanta: The Franklin Printing and Publishing Company, 1904.)
[66] *Coburn Report*, p. 1234. Councill wrote a letter to the Committee, September 24, 1874, stating that he had been "the regular Republican nominee for the legislature for Madison county," and that he would have been elected had it not been for the intimidation of Negro republicans at the polls.
[67] *Up From Slavery*, pp. 92-93. Washington campaigned for the city of Charleston in an election to determine the seat of government in West Virginia. He said that he was urged to make politics his life's work, but he declined. "Even then I had a strong feeling that what our people most needed was to get a foundation in education, industry, and poverty, and for this I felt that they could better afford to strive than for political preferment."
[68] *Finding a Way Out, an Autobiography*, pp. 10-14, recounts how Moton achieved some prominence as a speaker in Virginia, and was urged to run for the state legislature. He was quite willing to do so, but he was not yet

twenty-one years of age, and his mother refused to sign a certificate to the effect that he was.

[69] Simmons, *op. cit.*, p. 391.

[70] Montgomery *Advertiser*, February 4-13, 1891.

[71] *Ibid.*; William Newton Hartshorn. *An Era of Progress*, p. 356. (Boston: Massachusetts Priscilla Publishing Co., 1910.)

[72] Montgomery *Advertiser*, December 4-11, 1896, January 20-29, 1897.

[73] Cf. Montgomery *Advertiser*, Nov. 29, 1896, letter to the Editor from the Negro Baptist Convention, describing resolutions passed by that organization to take the fund from the Huntsville School and "locate it more centrally."

[74] The Sheffield *Standard* (Sheffield, Alabama), July 21, 1900.

[75] Quoted in Alfred Holt Stone, *Studies in the American Race Problems.* (New York: Doubleday, Page and Company, 1908.)

[76] John W. Abercrombie, *Biennial Report of the Department of Education of the State of Alabama*, p. 17. For the Scholastic Years ending September 30, 1899, 1900. (Montgomery: A. Roemer, 1900.)

[77] *Ibid.*, p. 64.

[78] *My Larger Education*, pp. 21-50.

[79] *Ibid.*, p. 23.

[80] *Ibid.*

[81] Charles S. Johnson, "The Social Philosophy of Booker T. Washington," *Opportunity Magazine*, 2:102-6. (April, 1928.)

[82] *Ibid.*, p. 102.

[83] *Ibid.*, p. 103.

[84] Johnson, *op. cit.*, p. 102; Graves, *op. cit.*, p. 17.

[85] The New York *Tribune*, August 23, 1895.

[86] *Ibid.*

[87] *Ibid.*

[88] *Ibid.*

[89] The Montgomery *Advertiser*, August 1, 1895.

[90] The Chicago *Tribune*, August 4-8, 1895. At a Negro protest meeting in Chicago, a Negro lawyer, James Walters, provoked the wrath of those present by declaring that the fault was not that of the Italians, but of the mine owners. He was obliged to escape through a plate glass window.

[91] *Up from Slavery*, p. 205.

[92] *Ibid.*, p. 211.

[93] *Ibid.*, p. 223.

[94] *Ibid.*, p. 221.

[95] *Ibid.*

[96] *Up From Slavery*, p. 218.

[97] *Ibid.*, p. 220.

[98] *Ibid.*, p. 221.

[99] *Ibid.*

[100] *Ibid.*

[101] *Ibid.*, p. 220.

[102] *Ibid.*

[103] *Ibid.*

[104] *Ibid.*, p. 226.

[105] *Ibid.*, p. 227.

[106] Owens, *History of Alabama*, IV, pp. 1522-1523.

[107] John B. Clark, *Populism in Alabama.* (New York: Columbia University Press, 1928.)

[108] Scott and Stowe, *Booker T. Washington*, p. 49.

[109] *Ibid.*, pp. 50-51.

[110] The Memphis *Commercial-Appeal*, October 17, 1901; Scott and Stowe, *op. cit.*, p. 54.

[111] William D. Scroggs, "The New Alabama, 1880-1909," *The South in the Building of the Nation*, Vol. II, p. 326. (Richmond: The Southern Historical Publication Society, 1910); Maxwell Ferguson, *State Regulation of*

*Railroads in the South*, pp. 446-448. (New York: Published privately by Maxwell Ferguson, 1916.)

[112] *Ibid.*

[113] *Ibid.*

[114] *Journal of the House of Representatives of the State of Alabama*, Session of 1907, pp. 254, 316, 2954. (Montgomery: Brown Printing Company, 1907.)

[115] William P. Pickett, *The Negro Problem—Abraham Lincoln's Solution*, p. 222. (New York: G. P. Putnam's Sons, The Knickerbocker Press, 1909.)

[116] *Ibid.*, p. 224.

[117] *Ibid.*

[118] Scott and Stowe, *op. cit.*, p. 312.

[119] *Ibid.*

[120] *Ibid.*, p. 313.

[121] *Ibid.*

[122] *Ibid.*, p. 250.

[123] *Ibid.*, p. 257. "*Up From Slavery* has brought more money to Tuskegee than all the other books, articles, speeches, and circulars written by Mr. Washington himself and the many others who have written or spoken about him and his work."

[124] Washington, *Up From Slavery*, p. 257.

[125] *Ibid.*, p. 182.

[126] *Ibid.*

[127] *Ibid.*, p. 245.

[128] Andrew Carnegie, *Autobiography*. (New York: Garden City Press, p. 266.)

[129] *Ibid.*

[130] Scott and Stowe, *op. cit.*, p. 258.

[131] Washington, *My Larger Education*, p. 71.

[132] Scott and Stowe, *op. cit.*, p. 257.

[133] Washington, *My Larger Education*, p. 71.

[134] Scott and Stowe, *Booker T. Washington*, p. 79.

[135] *Ibid.*, 257; *The Colored Alabamian* (Montgomery), July 10, 1909. In his speech at Suffolk, Washington said, "the late Mr. H. H. Rogers asked me to make a trip over his new road, with the idea of seeing and finding out what the condition of the colored people is and of reporting to him what might be done to further improve their condition, as well as to further promote friendly relations between the black people and the white people." The official publicity department of Tuskegee Institute issued this statement, with the release of the speech: "The late Mr. Rogers' request was that Dr. Washington should speak to the colored people along the line of his new railway, emphasizing industry, thrift, and morality; urging education along practical lines, encouraging them to increase in usefulness, and, as far as possible, to cement friendly relations between the races."

[136] Scott and Stowe, *op. cit.*, p. 257.

[137] *The Colored Alabamian* (Montgomery), July 10, 1909.

[138] Washington, *Up From Slavery*, pp. 188-189; Frederick E. Drinker, *Booker T. Washington, the Master Mind of a Child of Slavery*. (Philadelphia: National Publishing Company, 1915.)

[139] *Ibid.*

[140] Scott and Stowe, *op. cit.*, p. 80; Washington, *Up From Slavery*, p. 216.

[141] Washington, *Up From Slavery*, p. 195; *My Larger Education*, p. 77.

[142] Scott and Stowe, *op. cit.*, p. 220.

[143] *Ibid.*, p. 79.

[144] Washington, *My Larger Education*, p. 54.

[145] *Ibid.*, pp. 61-62, 57-68.

[146] *Ibid.*, pp. 59-60.

[147] *My Larger Education*, pp. 59-60.

[148] *Ibid.*, pp. 71-74.

[149] *Ibid.*, p. 77.

[150] *Ibid.*, pp. 73-74. This description reads, strangely enough, as though Washington had his tongue in his cheek.

[151] Spero and Harris, *The Black Worker*, p. 129. (New York: The Columbia University Sterling Press, 1932.)

[152] *Ibid.*

[153] Booker T. Washington, "The Negro in Labor Unions," *The Atlantic Monthly*, Vol. III, pp. 756-757. (June, 1913.)

[154] *Ibid.*, pp. 756-757. Washington was widely criticized by labor leaders for his failure to espouse the cause of union labor. While attempting no defense, Washington pointed out, in this article, that labor unions generally discriminated against Negro workers.

[155] J. L. M. Curry, "Report of the General Agent to the Trustees," pp. 229-230. *Proceedings of the Trustees of the Peabody Education Fund*, 1881-1887. Vol. III. (Cambridge: John Wilson and Sons, 1888.)

[156] Alderman and Gordon, *op. cit.*, p. 268.

[157] *Ibid.*, p. 325.

[158] *Up From Slavery*, pp. 42-63; Armstrong, *Twenty-Two Years' Work at Hampton Institute*, pp. 10-33.

[159] *Ibid.*

[160] *Ibid.*, p. 66.

[161] *Up From Slavery*, p. 53.

[162] *Ibid.*, p. 138.

[163] Booker T. Washington, "Report for Tuskegee Normal School," p. 23, in H. Clay Armstrong, *Report of the Superintendent of Education of Alabama for the year Ending September 30, 1882.* (Montgomery: W. D. Brown and Company, 1883.)

[164] E. Davidson Washington, ed., *Selected Speeches of Booker T. Washington.* "The Educational Outlook in the South," pp. 1-11. (Garden City: Doubleday, Doran and Company, Inc., 1932.)

[165] J. L. M. Curry, "Report of the General Agent, October, 1882," in *Proceedings of the Peabody Education Fund*, III.

[166] Washington, *Selected Speeches of Booker T. Washington*, p. 4.

[167] Washington, *Up From Slavery*, pp. 120-121.

[168] Washington, *Selected Speeches*, p. 4.

[169] *Ibid.*, p. 6.

[170] Washington, *Up From Slavery*, p. 126.

[171] *Ibid.*, p. 52.

[172] Washington, *My Larger Education*, p. 142; *Up From Slavery*, p. 155; *Selected Speeches*, p. 66.

[173] *Up From Slavery*, pp. 87-91.

[174] William Pickens, *Bursting Bonds, an autobiography.* (New York: Published by the Author, 1923.) Pickens attended Talladega College, and later studied at Yale, where he was elected Class Orator on his graduation. His struggles for an education were much like those of Washington. Henry Hugh Proctor, *Between Black and White, Autobiographical Sketches.* (Boston: The Pilgrim Press, 1925.) Proctor attended Fisk University, and entered the Congregational ministry in the South. Like Pickens, he was an ignorant, raw, country boy when he entered Fisk University; his experiences were much like those of Washington at Hampton.

In the J. L. M. Curry *Papers, Ms. Collection*, File 7, Alabama State Department of Archives, at Montgomery, there is a *ms.* report by Wallace Buttrick of a visit to Montgomery and Tuskegee, in May, 1902. Buttrick said "We attended for a half hour or more the commencement exercises of the Negro normal school, of which Mr. Paterson is the principal. There I visited the industrial departments, with which I was not at all favorably impressed. With the exception of the sewing department they do not seem to have any possible relation to educational work, the various superintendents of industries being nothing more than tradesmen of a rather indifferent sort, I should say.

"Later we went to Miss White's school, and I was most agreeably surprised to find that, pedagogically considered, this is the best school I visited at the South, always excepting, of course, Hampton, Spellman, and Tuskegee. The sewing department is carefully graded and serves the double purpose of training the mind and hand. From simplest stitches to the best kind of plain dress making these girls receive splendid training. In the cooking department and in the department where they are trained for domestic service and to a certain limited extent for nurses, the work is excellent.

". . . . I can only say that the contrast between this school and the normal school mentioned above reflected great credit on Miss White's school. Of course, I am aware that from the social point of view Miss White has been open to criticism, exciting the suspicion and dislike of white people. She is an intense person, calculated, I should judge, to go alone rather than in cooperation with any one else; but as I have said, pedagogically considered here is the best school I saw in the South on this trip.''

Miss White was a New England woman who remained at Montgomery until 1928, when, blind and infirm, she was obliged to close her school. However excellent her school, her persistence in ''social equality'' won for her, as Buttrick states, the general disfavor of the white community. The school was conducted for girls from the Negro population of Montgomery; while a small tuition was charged, it was not socially discriminatory.

[175] *Up From Slavery*, pp. 174-176.
[176] *The American Missionary*, December, 1880, p. 402.
[177] Drinker, *Booker T. Washington*, pp. 138-140.
[178] *The American Missionary*, August, 1881.
[179] *Ibid.*, July, 1920.
[180] *Selected Speeches*, p. 7.
[181] *Peabody Proceedings*, III, pp. 229-230.
[182] The Alabama Female Conference College, a Methodist school for white girls at Tuskegee. Washington probably wanted to get money for it to bolster good will.
[183] See *Twenty-Five Years in the Black Belt*. Edwards, a Tuskegee graduate, established a school, with the patronage of Washington, at Snow Hill, in Wilcox County.
[184] *J. L. M. Curry, Manuscript Collection*, File 7. Seen in the Department of Archives of Alabama, Montgomery, Alabama.
[185] Booker T. Washington to John O. Turner, *Report (ms.)*, February 20, 1896. In Curry Collection, File 7.
[186] *Ibid.*
[187] Scott and Stowe, *op. cit.*, p. 44.
[188] No testimony to Washington's personality is more eloquent than the utter devotion to, and belief in him, characteristic of the great masses of Negroes.
[189] James H. Dillard, in the ''Introduction'' to *Selected Speeches of Booker T. Washington*, says, ''I have sometimes thought that Dr. Washington was at his best in the Farmers' Conference held annually at Tuskegee. In these meetings he showed a simplicity, directness, and candidness that were altogether refreshing. At times there might be an interchange of wit and repartee between him and some humble farmer who ventured to dissent from some opinion.''
[190] Washington, *The Future of the American Negro*, pp. 121-122.
[191] *Ibid.*, p. 122.
[192] The Montgomery *Advertiser*, January 22, 1897.
[193] *The Colored Alabamian* (Montgomery), Dec. 17, 1910, Dec. 7, 1912.
[194] Washington, *Up From Slavery*, pp. 116.
[195] Washington, *My Larger Education*, p. 305.
[196] *Ibid.*
[197] *Ibid.*, p. 308.
[198] Scott and Stowe, *op. cit.*, p. 176.

[199] B. B. Comer, ''Quadrennial Message of the Governor of Alabama to the Legislature,'' *Journal of the House of Representatives of the State of Alabama, Session of 1907*, pp. 31-32. (Montgomery: Brown Printing Company, 1907.)

[200] *Ms.* Letter, Booker T. Washington to John O. Turner, in Curry Collection, File 7.

[201] *Shadow of the Plantation.* (Chicago: University of Chicago Press, 1934.)

[202] *Ibid.*, pp. 143-145.

[203] *Ibid.*, p. 143.

[204] Robert E. Park, ''Introduction,'' *Shadow of the Plantation.*

[205] *Shadow of the Plantation*, p. 144.

[206] *Ibid.*

[207] *Ibid.*, p. 145.

[208] *Ibid. passim.*

[209] *State Reports for given years, passim.*

[210] *Ibid.*

[211] *Ibid.*

[212] *Ibid.*

[213] *Ibid.*

[214] A. F. Harman, *Annual Report for the Scholastic Year Ending June 30, 1931, State of Alabama*, p. 397, Department of Education, Montgomery. (Montgomery: The Wilson Printing Co., n.d.—probably 1932.)

[215] *Ibid.*, pp. 362-363.

[216] *Ibid.*, p. 347.

[217] Isaac W. Hill, *Biennial Report of the Department of Education*, p. 81. *For the Scholastic Years Ending September 30, 1905, September 30, 1906.* (Montgomery: The Brown Printing Company, 1907.)

[218] Weeks, *Public School Education in Alabama*, pp. 172-173.

[219] Harry C. Gunnels, *Annual Report of the Department of Education. For the Scholastic Year Ending September 30, 1909*, p. 66. (Montgomery: The Brown Printing Company, 1909.)

## NOTES FOR CHAPTER XV

[1] Joseph A. Becker, ''Effects of the Boll Weevil upon Cotton Production in the United States,'' *International Cotton Bulletin*, June, 1924, pp. 519-24.

[2] *Ibid.*; Rupert B. Vance, ''The Negro Agricultural Worker'' (see Occupations); E. O. Wooten, ''Cotton in the Texas Plains Area,'' *U. S. D. A. Yearbook, 1926*, pp. 271-74. Washington: Government Printing Office, 1926.)

[3] *Ibid.*

[4] ''Costs of Producing Cotton in Fifteen Selected Areas in 1923.'' Preliminary Report, U. S. D. A., July, 1925 (mimeographed). Average price, spot cotton, New Orleans, 1923: 30c a pound.

[5] Vance, ''The Negro Agricultural Worker,'' p. v.

[6] Grist, *Agriculture of Alabama*, p. 63.

[7] *Ibid.*

[8] *Vide* Booker T. Washington, *Working with the Hands*, pp. 135-50. (New York: Doubleday, Page & Co., 1904.)

[9] Monroe N. Work, *Negro Year Book, 1914-1915*, p. 294. (Tuskegee Institute, Alabama: Published by the Negro Year Book Publishing Co., 1914.)

[10] Vance, ''The Negro Agricultural Worker,'' p. viii.

[11] *Ibid.*, p. 178.

[12] *The Shadow of the Plantation*, pp. 208-09. (Chicago: University of Chicago Press, 1934.)

[13] Owens, *History of Alabama*, II, p. 1308.

[14] The *Montgomery Advertiser*, January 8, 1900.

[15] *Report, 1900*, p. 80.

[16] Casson, *The Romance of Steel*, pp. 306-08.

[17] An entirely different story is told by a critic of the United States Steel Corporation, whose account differs widely from Miss Tarbell's eulogistic report. "The companies used convict labor as long as they could. Through a misunderstanding the Tennessee Coal and Iron Company (subsidiary of U. S. Steel) did not get its quota of convicts on lease in 1911. President George Gordon Crawford of the T. C. I. protested vigorously to the chairman of the State Board of Convict Inspectors, on the ground that if the company could not use convicts it would have to build houses for free labor." (See Horace B. Davis, *The Condition of Labor in the Iron and Steel Industry*, p. 147. (New York: The International Publishers, 1933.)

[18] Ida N. Tarbell, *The Life of Judge Elbert H. Gary, the Story of Steel*, p. 310. (New York: D. Appleton & Co., 1925.)

[19] Spero and Harris, *The Black Worker*, p. 213.

[20] *Ibid.*

[21] Davis, *Labor and Steel*, p. 147.

[22] Spero and Harris, *The Black Worker*, p. 354.

[23] *Ibid.*, pp. 247-49.

[24] *Ibid.*, p. 214.

[25] *Ibid.*

[26] *Ibid.*, p. 208.

[27] *Ibid.*, p. 247.

[28] *Ibid.*, p. 247, 286, 354.

[29] *Ibid.*, p. 247.

[30] Spero and Harris, *op. cit.*, pp. 286, 334.

[31] The *Montgomery Advertiser*, January 10, 1874; January 17, 1874; May 5, 1874; January 6, 1877; January 19, 1877; January 1, 1889.

[32] Emmett Jay Scott, *Negro Migration*, p. 63.

[33] The *Montgomery Advertiser*, September 27, 1916.

[34] Scott, *op. cit.*, p. 64.

[35] *Ibid.*, p. 63.

[36] *Ibid.*, p. 81. There is a footnote regarding the "helpful suggestions" that were made from Tuskegee: "to encourage the farmer to plant peanuts, soy beans, velvet beans and cotton as cash crops; to create a cash market for such crops named above as at present have no cash market; to encourage tenants to grow fall and winter gardens and to plant at least five acres of oats to the plow, seed being furnished when necessary; . . . ." The other suggestions, like the foregoing, were intended to introduce agricultural reforms to modify the share-cropping system of cotton culture.

[37] *Ibid.*

[38] *Ibid.*, p. 82. Interestingly enough, Tuskegee Institute was also aiding in the migration by supplying skilled workers from its graduates and students to Northern plants requesting such labor. "At brief intervals Tuskegee sent up four, then five, then eight, and then six men, most of whom had had training in machinery and molding. The total number of Tuskegee boys was 32." (Scott, *Negro Migration*, p. 107.)

[39] December 12, 1916.

[40] October 7, 1916.

## NOTES FOR CHAPTER XVI

[1] Chapter X, above.

[2] Tarbell, *The Life of Albert H. Gary*, p. 310.

[3] *Ibid.*

[4] *Ibid.*

[5] Davis, *Labor and Steel*, p. 170.

[6] Cotter, *United States Steel: A Corporation with a Soul*, p. 171.

[7] *Ibid.*, p. 176.

[8] *Ibid.*

[9] *Ibid.*
[10] *Ibid.*, p. 177.
[11] *Ibid.*
[12] Cotter, *op. cit.*, p. 177.
[13] Quoted in Tarbell, *op. cit.*, p. 313.
[14] Tarbell, *Ibid.*, p. 311; Cotter, *op. cit.*, p. 171.
[15] Italics mine.
[16] Tarbell, *op. cit.*, p. 313.
[17] Davis, *Labor and Steel*, p. 146.
[18] *Ibid.*, p. 147.
[19] *Ibid.*, pp. 147-48.
[20] On application to the office of the Assistant Superintendent, in Birmingham, in 1930. these data were said not to be available.
[21] Clark Foreman, *Environmental Factors in Negro Elementary Education.* (New York: Published for the Julius Rosenwald Fund, Chicago, by W. W. Norton & Co., 1932.)
[22] Cotter, *op. cit.*, p. 177.
[23] Cited in the *New York Times*, October 26, 1921.
[24] *Ibid.*
[25] *Ibid.*
[26] *Ibid.*
[27] G. Woodford Mabry, *A Reply to Southern Slanderers: In Re the Nigger Question.* (Grove Hill, Alabama: By the Author, 1933.)
[28] *Ibid.*
[29] *Ibid.*
[30] *The Shadow of the Plantation*, p. 129.
[31] *Ibid.*, p. 143.
[32] *Taxation of the State Government of Alabama*, p. 37. Report on a survey submitted to Governor B. M. Miller, Vol. 4. Part 3, prepared by the Institute for Government Research of the Brookings Institution, Washington, D. C., 1932. (Montgomery: The Wilson Printing Company, 1932.)
[33] *Ibid.*, p. 38.
[34] *Ibid.*, p. 39.
[35] *Ibid.*, pp. 39-40.
[36] See Chapter XIII, above.
[37] Brookings Institution Survey, *op. cit.*, p. 45.
[38] *Ibid.*, p. 47.
[39] *Ibid.*
[40] *Ibid.*, p. 59.
[41] *Ibid.*
[42] *Brookings Survey*, Vol. I, Part I, p. 266.
[43] *Ibid.*, p. 276.
[44] *Ibid.*, p. 264.
[45] Department of Education, *Equalization in Alabama* (pamphlet). (Montgomery: State Department of Education, 1929.)
[46] *Apportionment and Distribution of Alabama's Equalization Fund*, p. 4.
[47] *Ibid.*, p. 7.
[48] *Negro Population in the United States, 1790-1915*, p. 415.
[49] *Fifteenth Census Reports on Population, Illiteracy*, p. 1231.
[50] *Annual Report, 1911*, pp. 35-40.
[51] *Annual Reports, passim.* Although Alabama adopted officially the 6-3-3-plan in 1920, figures given here are for enrollment in the last four grades. Few of the Alabama "Junior High Schools" or "High Schools" for Negroes have separated buildings. See Edward E. Redcay, *County Training School and Public Secondary Education for Negroes in the South*, pp. 67-68. (Published for the Slater Fund; Washington, D. C.: The Monumental Printing Co., 1935.)
[52] Caliver, *Secondary Education for Negroes*, p. 28.
[53] Fred McCuistion, *The South's Negro Teaching Force.* (Julius Rosenwald Fund, Southern Office: Nashville, Tennessee, 1931.)

## NOTES FOR CHAPTER XVII

[1] Leavell, *Philanthropy in Negro Education*, pp. 59-60; *Peabody Proceedings*, I, pp. 1-7.

[2] *Ibid.*

[3] *Ibid.*, p. 211.

[4] *Ibid.*

[5] Leavell, *op. cit.*, p. 86.

[6] *Ibid.*

[7] *Peabody Proceedings*, p. 261.

[8] *Ibid.*, p. 262.

[9] *Ibid.*, p. 352.

[10] *Ibid.*, p. 93.

[11] *Ibid.*, p. 352.

[12] Leavell, *op. cit.*, p. 93.

[13] Trustees of the John F. Slater Fund, *Documents relating to the Origin and Work of the Slater Trustees*, Occasional Papers No. 1, 1894, pp. 9-10.

[14] Leavell, *op. cit.*, pp. 62-66.

[15] *Ibid.*, p. 64.

[16] John O. Turner, *Biennial Report, Superintendent of Education for Alabama, 1896-1897*, p. 190. (Montgomery: Roemer Printing Company, 1898.) It is significant that in the report of the total receipts of the Negro state supported institutions the Superintendent was careful to append a statement as follows: "persons examining this report should be careful to distinguish between the amounts paid by the State and those derived from Peabody, Slater, Morrill, Donations and other sources, and in speaking of these schools, not to make the statement that many do, that the State paid it all. These schools have other resources that will appear in another table." And in the report for Tuskegee Institute for the same year (p. 182) it appears that Booker T. Washington is shielding his income behind the respectable cloak of the Peabody Fund by saying "From the Peabody and other donations we have received $95,906.81" when his total Peabody income was only $1,550.

[17] Benjamin Brawley, *Doctor Dillard of the Jeanes Fund*, pp. 56-58, 73-75. (New York: Fleming H. Revell Co., 1930.)

[18] Edward R. Redcay, *County Training Schools and Public Secondary Education for Negroes in the South*, pp. 24-30.

[19] *Ibid.*, pp. 25-29.

[20] Isaac W. Hill, *Biennial Report, 1904-1906 Superintendent of Education for Alabama*, p. 10. (Montgomery: Brown Printing Co., 1907.)

[21] *Bulletin 41*, p. 236.

[22] *Annual Report*, 1910, p. 10.

[23] H. J. Willingham, *Annual Report*, 1913, p. 50.

[24] *Ibid.*

[25] Redcay, *County Training Schools*, p. 31.

[26] Edwards, *Twenty-five Years in the Black Belt*.

[27] Redcay, *op. cit.*, p. 35.

[28] Wm. F. Feagin, *Annual Report*, 1916, p. 77.

[29] John W. Abercrombie, *Annual Report*, 1920, p. 31.

[30] *Annual Report*, 1930, p. 83.

[31] Abercrombie, *Annual Report*, 1922, p. 54.

[32] *Ibid.*

[33] *Ibid.*, 1926, p. 48.

[34] R. E. Tidwell, *Annual Report*, 1926, p. 71.

[35] A. F. Harman, *Annual Report*, 1930, p. 83.

[36] *Ibid.*

[37] *Ibid.*, 1931, p. 81.

[38] *Ibid.*, p. 81.

[39] Caliver, *Secondary Education for Negroes*, p. 28.

[40] *Ibid.*

[41] *Ibid.*

[42] Arthur D. Wright, *The Negro Rural School Fund, Inc.*, 1907-1933, p. 8. (Washington: The Negro Rural School Fund, Inc., 1933.)

[43] Brawley, *op. cit.*, p. 57.

[44] Wright, *op. cit.*, p. 9.

[45] *Ibid.*, p. 32.

[46] *Ibid.*, pp. 12-17.

[47] Brawley, *op. cit.*, pp. 59-64.

[48] *Ibid.*, pp. 45-46.

[49] Wright, *op. cit.*, p. 171.

[50] Willingham, *Annual Report*, 1913, pp. 45-46. Report of J. L. Sibley.

[51] *Ibid.*

[52] Wm. F. Feagin, *Annual Report*, 1915, p. 52. Report of J. L. Sibley.

[53] Abercrombie, *op. cit.*, 1922, p. 53.

[54] Spright Dowell, *Annual Report*, 1919, p. 120. Report of J. S. Lambert.

[55] Abercrombie, *op. cit.*, 1926, p. 48.

[56] R. E. Tidwell, *Annual Report*, 1927, p. 81.

[57] *Ibid.*, p. 74.

[58] Harman, *op. cit.*, 1931, p. 78.

[59] Leavell, *Philanthropy in Negro Education*, p. 66.

[60] *Ibid.*, pp. 100-101.

[61] Willingham, *op. cit.*, 1911, p. 16.

[62] *Ibid.*, also 1912, p. 28.

[63] *Ibid.*, 1913, p. 32.

[64] *Ibid.*, p. 44.

[65] *Ibid.*

[66] *Ibid.*

[67] *Ibid.*

[68] Feagin, *op. cit.*, 1915, p. 53.

[69] *Ibid.*, 1916, p. 70.

[70] Dowell, *op. cit.*, 1918, p. 97.

[71] *Annual Reports, passim.*

[72] Abercrombie, *op. cit.*, 1926, p. 50.

[73] Tidwell, *op. cit.*, 1927, p. 82.

[74] Leavell, *op. cit.*, p. 180.

[75] Washington, *My Larger Education*, p 133.

[76] Leavell, *op. cit.*, p. 77.

[77] *Ibid.*, p. 111.

[78] *Ibid.*, p. 77.

[79] *Ibid.*

[80] *Ibid.*, p. 110.

[81] *Ibid.*, p. 111.

[82] *Ibid.*, p. 112.

[83] *Ibid.*, p. 113.

[84] *Ibid.*, p. 79.

[85] Isaac W. Hill, *Biennial Report*, 1904-1906, p. 81.

[86] Weeks, *Public School Education in Alabama*, pp. 172-74.

[87] Harry C. Gunnells, *Biennial Report*, 1906-1908, p. 83.

[88] Willingham, *op. cit.*, 1911, pp. 11-15; Weeks, *op. cit.*, p. 173.

[89] *Annual Report*, 1912, p. 20

[90] Willingham, *op. cit.*, 1913, p. 50.

[91] Feagin, *op. cit.*, 1916, p. 16.

[92] Various published reports are available. A manuscript report, showing basic data for each Rosenwald school built in Alabama from 1913 to and including 1930, does not so differentiate by exact amounts for additions after the period 1912-1920. This manuscript was kindly loaned for inspection by the author from the office of Mr. S. L. Smith, Director of the Nashville Office of the Fund.

[93] Manuscript Report on Alabama Rosenwald Schools.

[94] Noted by author on survey for Rosenwald Fund, 1930.

[95] From manuscript report.

[96] *Ibid.*

[97] Biographical account as given in interviews.

[98] From Manuscript reports of M. H. Griffin to Mr. S. L. Smith, loaned to author.

[99] This military terminology represents actual organization used in "rallies" for raising money for Rosenwald schools.

[100] Each Rosenwald money-raising program was definitely planned far in advance.

[101] The pontifical spirit of this passage was not without justification. The name of Rosenwald carried such prestige among rural Negroes as to make the agent one of the most important persons who might appear in any Negro community.

[102] The fact that the donor was "a fine Christian white woman" was hardly an incentive to debate. Who could cast a negative vote against her?

[103] Note how much care was spent in preliminary planning; with this, the second of visits to Auburn in this month, preparatory to the third and final "drive."

[104] *Ibid.*

[105] Note technique of having leading white citizens on hand to give approval to project.

[106] This particular rally, as with others, had each feature as carefully staged in advance as any theatrical production.

[107] Note appositeness of this feature of rally.

[108] The dramatic appearance of "brother Moseley" was also pre-arranged.

[109] Note another pre-arranged touch lent by the Mayor to the crowd enthusiasm, when it was apparently waning.

[110] These meetings, from reports, are seen to have been highly conventionalized, yet peculiarly spontaneous. This account may serve to emphasize the rôle of the Rosenwald Fund in making a contribution to attitudes perhaps more valuable than the buildings actually constructed. The projects furnished an opportunity for whole communities of whites and Negroes to come together and to work with genuine enthusiasm and with rare good fun, for the ideal of educating Negro children.

[111] Tidwell, *op. cit.*, 1928, p. 75.

[112] Harman, *op. cit.*, 1930, p. 87.

[113] *Ibid.*

[114] *Manuscript Report*, M. H. Griffin to S. L. Smith.

# INDEX*

Abercrombie, John W., 218, 301, 338, 345, 346

Adams, Lewis, founder of Tuskegee Institute, 139-40, 197, 215

*Advertiser,* The Montgomery, 138, 140, 143, 146, 152, 230, 234, 235

Agricultural Areas of Alabama, 2ff.

Agricultural resettlement, proposed, 310 (*n.* 30)

Agriculture, reorganization of, after War, 120-5; and population changes, 128; Tuskegee Institute and, 220-1; changes in, 1900-1930, 226ff.; educational objectives as defined by, 245-6

Aikin, John G., 299, 301, 307

Ainsworth, Brigadier-General Fred C., 301, 311

Alabama and Chattanooga R. R., as guiding genius of Republicans, 46; seized by State, 51; *also,* 38, 43, 46, 50, 58, 126, 312 (*n.* 35), 315 (*n.* 129)

Alabama and Tennessee River R. R., 38

Alabama Power Company, 253

Alabama State Teachers College, 87, 107-10, 205

Alderman, Edwin Anderson, 293, 312, 320, 324, 336, 337, 340

Alvord, John Watson, 301, 320, 321, 324

American Baptist Home Mission Society, 82

American Missionary Association, 82-4, 95, 105-6, 118, 216, 314 (*n.* 97)

Amos, Negro trusty, aid acknowledged, xii

Apportionment of School Fund, equality of during Reconstruction, 101-5, 148; method changed in 1890, 155-9; effect of act of 1891 on, 159-63; discrimination in, Macon county, 222-4; 246ff.

Apprenticeship proposed for freedmen, 77-8, 112-3

Archer, William, 293, 328

Areas of Alabama, 1-3

Armes, Ethel, 293, 305, 312, 315, 326

Armstrong, H. Clay, 301, 329

Armstrong, Samuel Chapman, 195-6, 217, 293, 335

Atlanta University, 216

Attitudes, see racial attitudes

Atwood, W. Q., 16

Bagby, Arthur P., 300, 306

Baker, R. R., 273

Baldwin, William H., 213, 222

Bankhead, John O., 313 (*n.* 61)

Baptists advocate education of Negroes, 80

Barksdale, Jelks, 301

Beard, Augustus Field, 293, 320, 325

Beard, Charles A. and Mary, 293, 311

Becker, Joseph A., 298, 342

Belmont, August, 42

Berney, Saffold, 293, 305

Bethea, T. B., 55

Bingham, Arthur, 323

Birmingham, origin of, 45, 51, 126, 312-13 (*n.* 47, 68)

Birmingham, site causes capitalist's quarrel, 46; Negro labor in, 145; Industry and Schools in, 146; United States Steel in, 232; recent politics in, 335 (*n.* 75)

Black Belt, as area, 1-2; and early school controversy, 6; Negro Democrats in, 70; opposes ante-bellum equalization, 74; opposes ante-bellum public schools, 75; economic decadence of, 122ff., 132-33; Negroes voted in, 128; Democrats control State, 129-31; Negro Democrats as tool of, 140-1; attempts change in apportionment basis, 149; vote on education appropriation, 154; vast educational discriminations in, 161f.; affect of political dominance on white schools, 163; "Oligarchy" controls, 166; politics of in 1901, 170-1; stand on local taxation, 187; decline of cotton production in, 227; Negro population decreases in, 236; wealth decreases in, 238; educational objectives in, 246; typical educational budget in a county of, 251-8; educational progress in, 1900-1930, 255; Rosenwald Fund in, 279-80; *also,* 60, 181, 222, 226

*\*n.* preceding numeral denotes footnote citation.

background of, 195-6; J. L. M. Curry and, 199, 336 (n. 40); William H. Councill and, 203-5; begins career as politician, 204, 337 (n. 67); builds Tuskegee Institute around race problem, 205-8; master of racial psychology, 205-8; Atlanta Exposition Speech of, 206-8; and social classes among whites, 207-14; responsible for Federal judicial appointment, 209; educational discipline of, 216; summary of educational influence of, 217-20; Wallace Buttrick on, 218; as man of the folk, 219; influence on economic system, 220-1; and "great man" theory of education, 224; and Rosenwald Fund, 275-7; William D. "Pig-Iron" Kelley a friend of, 312 (n. 38); parentage of, 332 (n. 51); and H. H. Rogers, 339 (n. 135); also, 16, 18, 20, 140, 189, 228, 243, 270, 297, 299, 308, 309, 335, 336, 339, 342, 346

Washington, E. Davidson, 297

Watterson, Henry, 213

Wayland Seminary, attended by Booker T. Washington, 216

Wealth, changes in centralization of, 132ff., 231 (chart), 132-4; industrialization and, 234; redistribution of, 1890-1930, 238; equalization not based on, 252-8

Weatherford, W. D., aid acknowledged, xii

Weeks, Stephen B., 75, 137, 297, 319, 323, 337, 342, 346

West, Anson, 297

Western Railway of Alabama, 54, 253

White children and Negro schools, 135ff.; Negro competition for tax money with schools for, 179ff.; enrollment increase of, 136; racial discrimination affects schools for, 251-8; expenditure by area for schools for, 261; influence of Rosenwald Fund on schools for, 277

"White Supremacy," defended by George Houston, 53

White, W. S., 304

Whiting, John, 45

Wickersham, J. P., 297, 311

Wilcox county, expenditures in, 1876-1930, 162

Willingham, H. J., 345, 346

Wills Valley R. R., 43

Wilson, Henry, 297, 321

Wiregrass Area, 236

Woodburn, James Albert, 297, 310

Woodson, Carter G., 297, 299, 306, 308

Wooten, E. A., 299

Work, Monroe N., 297, 342

Wright, Arthur D., 298, 346

Yordy, Benjamin, 87

# *Atheneum Paperbacks*

# Atheneum Paperbacks

## HISTORY

## HISTORY—ASIA

## THE NEW YORK TIMES BYLINE BOOKS

# Atheneum Paperbacks

# *Atheneum Paperbacks*

# *Atheneum Paperbacks*

# *Atheneum Paperbacks*

## THE WORLDS OF NATURE AND MAN

## LITERATURE AND THE ARTS